Twilight Teams

Jeffrey Saint John Stuart

Published by
SARK PUBLISHING
128 Spring Street
Gaithersburg, MD 20877

ISBN 0-9672235-0-4

Library of Congress Catalog Card Number: 99-93264

Cover photo of Ebbets Field in Brooklyn is from the Corbis/Bettman Archive, New York, New York

To order additional copies, please contact
SARK PUBLISHING
128 Spring Street
Gaithersburg, MD 20877
(301) 869-3882

PRINTED AND BOUND IN THE UNITED STATES OF AMERICA BY
MAVERICK PUBLICATIONS, INC. • P.O. BOX 5007 • BEND, OREGON 97708

TABLE OF CONTENTS

THANKS

"UNLESS someone like you cares a whole awful lot,
nothing is going to get better. It's not."

from *The Lorax* by Dr. Seuss

To those who passed before:

To my father, Leander, a bacteriologist with an honorary PHD, who transferred his love of baseball to me.

To my mother, Christine, an English major, for her belief in me. She didn't care much for baseball but would be delighted that I have written a book.

To my sister Carol, a painter and the real artist in the family, for giving me the courage to test my own creative talents.

To Clay Everett, a former co-worker who loved the Dodgers.

To Bill Sullivan, former owner of the Boston Patriots of the National Football League and Public Relations director for the 1952 Braves, for his input, encouragement, and for vouching for the accuracy of my chapter on the 1952 Boston Braves.

To those still with us:

For emotional support:

To my brothers Monty, Christopher, and Jamie, and my sisters Ann and Lynn.

To Greg Norris, a co-worker, friend, and baseball fan whose knowledge of the game, admittedly, far exceeds my own, for his humor and his daily inspirations.

To Glenn Serra, Public Relations Director for the Atlanta Braves. He put me in contact with people connected with the Boston Braves who could, and did, help me. That put the whole project in motion.

To Mike Keough and Bob Brady of the Boston Braves Historical Society. They gave me a lift early on in the process.

For painstaking edits of individual chapters:

To Ed Walton of Fairfield, Connecticut, a Red Sox fan, bird dog scout, member of the Boston Braves Historical Society, and author of *The Rookies* and *This Date in Boston Red Sox History.*

To Will Anderson of Bath, Maine, a former New York Giant fan and author of *Was Baseball Really Invented in Maine.*

To Don Wescott of Gaithersburg, Maryland, a Dodgers' fan and volleyball teammate.

To Richard Murphy of Gaithersburg, Maryland, also a volleyball cohort.

To David Gough of Alexandria, Virginia , a former Senators' fan and author of *They've Stolen Our Team,* a book about the 1960 Washington Senators.

And

To Norman Kurland, editor of *The Flatbush Faithful* for printing excerpts of my manuscript in his newsletter.

And special thanks to Peggy Ketteman at Maverick Publications for her editing, art selections, insight, patience and hard work.

Finally

To former Seattle Mariners pitcher, Salome Barojas, who I never met, for curious personal reasons. Maybe only Greg Norris will completely understand.

in Transition
(1953 - 1971)

And the sun
No longer shone
In the same afternoons
In the same cities.

Beyond the Great Mississippi
By Jordan A. Dutch
October 1973

C onstancy. For fifty years, a period of time longer than the cold war, the face of Major League Baseball was etched in stone. From 1903 to 1953 baseball was the unchallenged national pastime, and the franchised structure of the Major Leagues was as sacred as the game itself. The American and National Leagues had eight teams each. Just ten cities had Major

League franchises. Boston, St. Louis, Philadelphia, and Chicago each had one American League and one National League team. New York had two National League franchises, and one American League team. Single teams in Cleveland, Detroit, and Washington rounded out the American League circuit. There were single National League franchises in Cincinnati and Pittsburgh. There were no Major League teams west of the Mississippi River. Within each league, each team hosted four home series against the other seven teams. There were doubleheaders practically every Sunday. Monday and Thursday were the usual travel days.

In the two formative decades prior to 1900 many cities hosted a professional baseball team for a short time. Various professional leagues formed, merged, and sometimes disbanded. Many teams folded. Some relocated.

But by 1900 the situation had begun to stabilize. In 1903 the more established National League, the senior circuit, reluctantly accepted the existence of the fledgling American League. The two competing leagues came to a working agreement. Each league maintained a separate identity. There would be no regular season inter league games scheduled. The relocation of the American League Baltimore franchise to New York completed the formation of the junior circuit. The structure of Major League Baseball was set.

There were no immediate challenges to this basic structure. Most of the major population centers in 1903 fell within the drawing area of these sixteen major league franchises. Annual attendance averaged 300,000 paying customers per club. A supportive minor league network already reached throughout much of the remainder of the country.

The limits of radio signal coverage, and the time constraints of train travel, served to protect the tranquility.

Local owners, sportsmen with a some sense of community involvement, built and maintained their own ballparks. For the most part they took their modest profit or loss pretty much in stride. Players, however, were property. Under the reserve clause of each player's contract they were bound exclusively to a single team.

Though the game was somewhat insulated from change, it wasn't entirely immune to outside influence. It was changing. By 1908 baseball was already becoming a big business, attracting investors, speculators, and competitors as well as fans. Annual attendance figures now averaged 450,000 paid admissions per club. There was money to be made in this enterprise.

THE FEDERAL LEAGUE

Not surprisingly, a challenge to the Major League structure soon arose. In 1913 James Gilmore, a wealthy businessmen with a primary interest in coal mining, convinced several other substantial investors to financially back the formation of a third major league, the Federal League. The federal league had been a mid-western based league.

The well financed new league built new ballparks in Indianapolis, Chicago, Baltimore, Buffalo, Brooklyn, Kansas City, Pittsburgh, and St. Louis. Chicago Cubs' star shortstop Joe Tinker was the first established player to jump to the new league, joining the new Chicago Whales. Many other very good players in other cities followed suit. The FL did not honor the reserve clause.

Indianapolis won the first Federal League championship in 1914. Chicago took top honors in 1915. Faced with mediocre attendance, and impending U.S. involvement in the first world war, the fledgling league lasted just two full seasons. Team owners filed an antitrust suit against the existing major leagues in 1914. The league owners settled out of court, closing operations.

But the settlement was generous. The frightened Major league franchise owners assumed liability for all outstanding Federal League player contracts. Federal League owners were permitted to purchase the established clubs in Chicago and St. Louis. The remaining financiers received sizeable cash settlements.

WORRIES ABOUT EXPANSION

The Federal League threat was gone. But more cities wanted baseball teams. However, both American and National League owners wanted to avoid expansion. They also wanted to maintain restrictive player contracts. If the number of teams was allowed to mushroom, the owners believed that the overall quality of play would be diluted. If players were allowed to move about freely from club to club, the more talented players would gravitate to the wealthier, and more aggressive franchises. The competitive balance of the two leagues would be impaired.

Expansion would also complicate scheduling, and travel. Within the compact existing structure, it was possible to coordinate schedules so that two clubs from one city could share travel arrangements and expenses. In St. Louis and New York, the American and National League teams shared the same ballpark. The existing structure was convenient for now.

THE "BLACK SOX" SCANDAL

Holding the lid on expansion was one problem. Maintaining the integrity of the game was another. With fan interest at record levels in 1919 the game had also attracted the interest of the professional gamblers. A crisis of confidence occurred. Seven Chicago White Sox players conspired to "fix" the 1919 World Series in return for one hundred thousand dollars from gambling interests. The "Chicago Seven" threw the Series, losing to the National League champion Cincinnati Reds, a heavy underdog, five games to three. The incident became known as the "Black Sox" scandal. The public was justifiably outraged.

Federal Judge Kennesaw Mountain Landis, who had successfully negotiated the settlement with the Federal League, was installed as commissioner for life in 1921. He was granted sweeping authority to deal as he saw fit with any events "detrimental" to the game. Public confidence was restored. Baseball prospered throughout the twenties, surviving even the early years of the depression.

THE THIRTIES—ECONOMIC DECLINE

By the early thirties, however, there was a dramatic decline in attendance. St. Louis, and other two team cities, were particularly hard hit. In 1933, the St. Louis National League Cardinals were in such financial difficulty that the team requested league permission to move to Detroit. Permission was denied. The American League Tigers, claiming territorial rights, blocked the move. Baseball's economic difficulties continued into the 1940's,

In 1941, the American League Browns sought approval to shift the franchise to Los Angeles after reaching a tentative accord with the minor league Pacific Coast team there. The negotiations were interrupted by American entry into the second World War. The first franchise shift of the modern era would have to wait.

THE WAR YEARS

With the Japanese attack on Pearl Harbor, Baseball's immediate concern became survival. Stars like Ted Williams, Joe DiMaggio, Hank Greenberg, Bob Feller, as well as journeymen players like Elmer Valo, Hugh Mulcahy, Joe Marty, and Sibby Sisti were among hundreds of players inducted into military service.

THE MEXICAN LEAGUE

When the war ended, economic prosperity resumed. But new Commissioner Happy Chandler had to confront another challenge to the Major Leagues. When the Mexican League began pirating major league players during the spring training season of 1946, Chandler quickly imposed a five year ban on players that jumped to the Mexican League. Still, the lure of money still proved irresistible to some.

New York Giant outfielder Danny Gardella, and St. Louis Cardinals' pitchers Max Lanier and Fred Martin, jumped to the Mexican League and faced the five year ban imposed by Commissioner Chandler. The Mexican League, which had no reserve clause in its contracts, folded in 1949. The three players filed suit in Federal Court, challenging Baseball's reserve clause. But they lost.

Cardinal's owner Fred Saigh was instrumental in settling this challenge to the reserve clause out of court. This was important because the owners feared they would lose any direct legal challenge to the reserve clause.

THE POST WAR YEARS—EXPANSION

With baseball's cherished "monopoly" temporarily preserved, Commissioner Chandler was free to turn his attention to the issue of expansion.

In 1946 the Pacific Coast League petitioned the Commissioner to elevate the entire league to Major League status. There were exhaustive meetings. The cities involved were extensively examined. The potential drawing power in each city was discussed. Founded in 1903, The Pacific Coast League was the oldest, and most established of the minor leagues. It consisted of six teams: the Portland Beavers, Oakland Oaks, Sacramento Solons, Hollywood Stars, Los Angeles Angels, and San Francisco Seals. Joe DiMaggio, and Ted Williams were among it's most prestigious alumni.

Based on the results of these evaluations the Pacific Coast League itself determined that only Los Angeles, and San Francisco had genuine big league potential. It ceased efforts to become a third major league.

But change was coming. Expansion was unavoidable. Airplane travel was now the preferred mode of transportation, allowing baseball to extend it's reach. Television was in its infancy, but was already a factor to be taken into consideration.

FRANCHISE SHIFTS

Major League executives considering the problems attendant with expansion determined that a reasonable course of action would be to move one team out of cities with two teams. Initial attention would be given to those cities where one franchise was in particular financial difficulty, and the drawing area wasn't sufficient to support two teams.

This approach would satisfy the desire of new cities with growing populations to acquire Major League franchises. They would not tamper with the functional structure of the existing leagues, and would not remove Major League Baseball, entirely, from cities that already had franchises. The single, remaining, team in each city would have exclusive television rights. Moreover, the plan avoided the problems attendant with stocking new franchises. The player talent pool was not diluted.

The National League, using these guidelines, approved the transfer of the Boston Braves to Milwaukee, Wisconsin in March, 1953. The American League quickly followed suit, permitting the transfer of the St. Louis Browns to Baltimore at the start of the 1954 season, and the Philadelphia Athletics to transfer to Kansas City at the close of that season. These moves left the American League Red Sox in Boston, the National League Cardinals in St. Louis, and the Phillies in Philadelphia.

The lack of competition from local race tracks in Milwaukee, and Kansas City, was a consideration in approving these franchise shifts. Racing was growing extremely popular in the Philadelphia and Boston metropolitan areas. Local tracks in the New York area regularly out drew the Dodgers, Giants, and Yankees combined. The effect of such competition in smaller areas was obvious. With Ohio and Kentucky race tracks so close to Cincinnati, there was talk of shifting the Reds as well. There was top notch racing at Pimlico in Baltimore. Baltimore, however, had a larger population base than Kansas City, or Milwaukee.

By 1955 the Major Leagues had thus expanded from ten cities to thirteen, retaining the original two eight team league structure. They hadn't entirely abandoned any city.

These initial franchise moves weren't entirely unexpected. The Braves, Browns, and Athletics had all been struggling financially. There wasn't any strong organized opposition to any of these moves. Although, over a fifty year period, the teams involved had become rooted in, and part of, their respective communities. There were still stunned and disillusioned fans.

SHOCK WAVES FROM MILWAUKEE

For the 1953 season 2,000,000 paying customers visited Milwaukee's County Stadium to watch the National League Braves. That startling fact did not go unnoticed. In August 1957, shock waves hit the baseball world. Horace Stoneham announced he was moving the New York Giants to San Francisco. In October 1957. Walter O'Malley followed suit, making public his intention to relocate the popular Brooklyn Dodgers to Los Angeles. The Dodgers played seven "home" games, at Roosevelt Stadium in Jersey City in both the 1956 and 1957 seasons. Allowing the Dodgers or the Giants, however, to relocate to the West Coast seemed incredible, not only to legions of New York fans, but to fans in other cities. The moves received far more national attention than the previous franchise shifts. So much baseball legend was connected to Ebbets Field, and the Polo Grounds. The motivation of the owners came into serious public question.

The Dodgers drew one million fans in 1957, finishing in third place. The Giants drew 650,000, finishing sixth. The first place American League Yankees drew 1,500,000 fans during the 1957 season. Neither the Giants nor the Dodgers was really struggling financially. Ebbets Field and the Polo Grounds, however, were aged facilities. The surrounding areas were in decay. Moreover, there was a glut of televised baseball in the New York area.

The astonishing success of the relocated Boston Braves in Milwaukee in 1957 marked the end of an age of innocence in the history of American sports. Perini's success had sparked a gold rush. Owners of other baseball teams, and franchises in the emerging National Football League, the National Basketball Association, and the National Hockey League, took notice. With the promise of untapped financial bonanzas awaiting in new cities, the delicate balance between game, and business, tilted sharply toward the business side. Exempted from antitrust legislation largely because of their roots to the community, it was clear that the same owners who invoked the reserve clause to deny players the right to move about freely for financial gain wouldn't deny themselves the opportunity to move about freely to seek the most lucrative deal available.

The relocation of the Braves, Browns, Athletics, Giants, and Dodgers had not diluted the product. Baseball still had just sixteen teams, but the number of cities with major league baseball had grown from ten to fifteen.

PRESSURE TO RETURN TO NEW YORK

The intensely negative public response to the National League abandonment of New York didn't go unheeded. With the encouragement of Mayor Robert Wagner, New York businessman Bill Shea, and the influential Branch Rickey, helped put together financial backing for a third major league. Shea was a business man with no baseball background. Rickey, however, had a long and distinguished baseball history, spanning fifty years. He been the president and general manager of the Dodgers, general manager of the Cardinals and Pirates, field manager of both the St. Louis Browns and Cardinals, a major league scout, and a big league catcher with the Cincinnati Reds, St. Louis Browns, and New York Yankees. The Cardinals won six National League pennants and four World Championships during his tenure as GM. The Dodgers won two pennants. He was the man who brought Jackie Robinson to Brooklyn. His background and prestige gave the effort to form another league strong credibility. Although the proposed "Continental" league never materialized, the efforts of Rickey and Shea did force the eventual return of a National League Franchise to New York.

EXPANSION

Further expansion of the Major Leagues couldn't be accomplished by moving one team out of a two team area. The only two team city left was Chicago. Both the Cubs and White Sox, however, were well supported. In 1961 the American League expanded to ten teams adding a new franchise in Los Angeles, and a new expansion team in Washington. Ironically, The new Los Angeles Angels, the first true expansion team in more than half a century, made Los Angeles a new two franchise city. The existing Washington Senators relocated to Minneapolis-St. Paul, becoming the Minnesota Twins.

The original Washington Senators, a charter member of the American League, had played in the Nation's Capital in for seventy-five years. The placement of a new franchise in Washington pacified Congressional critics, forestalling attempts to remove baseball's exemption from anti trust legislation.

The two new teams drafted players from the existing American League clubs in order to stock their own rosters. For the first time, the existing talent pool had been diluted.

The National League followed suit, holding their own expansion drafts to stock new franchises in New York, and Houston for their debut in the 1962 season. National League baseball returned to New

York after a five year absence. There were now twenty Major League baseball teams operating in seventeen cities.

That twin ten team league structure was maintained until 1969. But jet travel, and the growth of the television industry, made the game more accessible. Growing urban areas built new municipal stadiums. They offered attractive rental and concession packages to attract existing, or expansion, franchises. The temptation was great.

In 1966, after thirteen seasons in Milwaukee the Braves' franchise once again relocated. This time Atlanta was the recipient of a Major League franchise. The Braves had done remarkably well in Milwaukee for eight seasons. After purchasing the Braves from Lou Perini in 1962, the new owners proved remarkably intolerant of mediocre attendance figures in the seasons that followed. They readily accepted the lucrative enticements offered by Atlanta, including a substantially larger television contract than the Braves had in Milwaukee. Never establishing a loyal fan base in thirteen seasons in Kansas City, the Athletics moved to Oakland in 1968.

There were still other cities hungry for baseball. The Major Leagues expanded again in 1969. Kansas City returned to the American League after an absence of just two years. Seattle became the fourth member of the original Pacific Coast League to be awarded a Major League franchise, The "Pilots", however, quickly fell victim to the economic difficulties facing the city of Seattle. The franchise moved to Milwaukee in 1970. Milwaukee thus returned to the Major Leagues, after an absence of only four years.

The National League awarded franchises to San Diego, and Montreal. The Montreal "Expos" thus became the first Major League team located outside the continental United States. San Diego became the fifth team located on the West Coast.

There were now twenty-four major league teams located in twenty one cities. Twin twelve team leagues now constituted the basic structure of the Major Leagues.

THE LAST FRANCHISE SHIFT

At the end of 1971, the American League voted to abandon the Nation's Capital, allowing the expansion of the Washington Senators to transfer to Dallas. The franchise was renamed the Texas "Rangers."

Washington was the last original major league franchise city to lose its baseball team. Along with the Boston Braves, St. Louis Browns, Philadelphia Athletics, New York Giants, and Brooklyn

Dodgers, they had played Major League baseball in the same city for more than fifty years. They were part of the baseball constant for fifty years. Their legacy remains a part of the history of the city they left behind. There are fans in all these cities who still feel abandoned. This book is dedicated to them.

The following chapters feature a brief chronology of each franchise prior to relocation, focusing on World Series appearances, Hall of Famers, and significant team and individual contributions. The final season of each team is summarized. The final game is highlighted. The events leading up to and surrounding the eventual relocation are examined.

THE 1952
BOSTON BRAVES

Yesterday's Almost Gone

... What so proudly we hailed at the twilights'
last gleaming,,,,
O'er the land of the free, and the home of
the BRAVE

In the struggle for the hearts and minds of Boston's baseball fans, the National League Braves were clear losers to the American League Red Sox. In 1952, the Braves were starting their seventy-seventh season. They had a longer tenure in Boston than their American League counterparts, the Red Sox. In 1901 Ban Johnson placed an American League team in Boston to challenge the existing National League Braves. He largely succeeded. The Braves never out drew the Red Sox in the fifty years that both competed in the hub city.

In 1948, their second pennant winning season since 1900, the Braves drew a record 1,455,439 fans. But the Red Sox also drew a record 1,558,798. They finished second to Cleveland in the American League only after losing the first playoff game in Major League history. In 1952 Braves' attendance dwindled to 281,278. The ball club tumbled to seventh place in the standings.

Major League club owners were considering expanding into new territories in the spring of 1953. It wasn't surprising that they focused most of their attention on the Braves, and the American League Browns.

BRAVES FIELD, BOSTON

Bounded by Commonwealth Avenue, Gaffney Street, Babcock Street, and the Boston and Albany Railroad tracks. Home of the Boston Braves from August 18, 1915 to September 21, 1952. (Photo from The National Baseball Library and Archive Collection, Cooperstown, New York and Boston University.)

1952 BOSTON BRAVES

Front row—Gordon, Dittmer, Logan, Thorpe, Keeley, coach; Grimm, manager; Cooney, coach; Chipman, Sisti. **Middle row**—Daniels, Surkont, Cole, Jester, Spahn, Torgeson, Cusick. **Back row**—Johnson, Burris, Mathews, Wilson, Burdette, Jethroe, Jones, Cooper. (Photo from The Sporting News Collection, St. Louis, Missouri.)

		Games at position	Bats	Avg.	
C	Walker Cooper	89	R	.235	
1B	Earl Torgeson	105	L	.230	
2B	Jack Dittmer	90	L	.193	
SS	Johnny Logan	117	R	.283	
3B	Eddie Mathews	142	L	.242	**25 HR 115 Strikeouts***
LF	Sid Gordon	142	R	**.289**	**25 HR**
CF	Sam Jethroe	151	SW	.232	**28 Stolen bases**
OF	Jack Daniels	87	L	.187	
RF	Bob Thorpe	72	R	.260	
2B	Sibby Sisti	33	R	.212	
1B	George Crowe	55	L	.258	
C	Paul Burris	50	R	.220	
SS	Jack Cusick	28	R	.167	
C	Ebba St. Claire	34	SW	.213	
2B	Roy Hartsfield	29	R	.262	
OF	Pete Whisenant	14	R	.192	
OF	Willard Marshall	16	L	.227	
2B	Bill Reed	14	L	.250	
IF	Buzz Clarkson	14	R	.200	
IF	Billy Klaus	7	L	.000	

PITCHERS

L	Warren Spahn	40 W **14**	L 19	2.98 ERA	**183 Strikeouts***
R	Max Surkont	31 W 12	L 13	3.77 ERA	
R	Jim Wilson	33 W 12	L 14	4.23 ERA	
R	Vern Bickford	26 W 7	L 12	3.74 ERA	
R	Ernie Johnson	29 W 6	L 3	4.11 ERA	
R	Virgil Jester	19 W 3	L 5	3.33 ERA	
R	Dick Donovan	7 W 0	L 2	5.54 ERA	
R	Gene Conley	4 W 0	L 3	7.82 ERA	
L	Dick Hoover	2 W 0	L 0	7.71 ERA	
R	Bert Theil	4 W 1	L 1	7.71 ERA	

RELIEF PITCHERS

R	Lew Burdette	45 W 6	L 11	3.61 ERA	**7 Saves**
R	Sheldon Jones	39 W 1	L 4	4.76 ERA	1 Save
L	Bob Chipman	29 W 1	L 1	2.81 ERA	0 Saves
R	Dave Cole	22 W 1	L 1	4.03 ERA	0 Saves

MANAGERS

	Tommy Holmes	W 13	L 22
	Charlie Grimm	W 51	L 67

Bold Type—led club
* Led league

The transfer of either club would fall within the proposed relocation guideline of transferring one team out of two team cities. In 1952 the Browns nearly doubled the Braves yearly attendance, drawing 518,796. But they had drawn less than 300,000 fans for three consecutive prior seasons. Controversial owner Bill Veeck was actively campaigning for permission to move the St. Louis franchise to Milwaukee.

Braves' owner, Lou Perini, wasn't as open about his desire to move. At the end of the 1952 season, Perini told reporters that he planned to keep the ball club in Boston. "But I'm not going to be stubborn about it," he said. "We are going to pick up a check representing the greatest financial loss in the history of baseball." He speculated that Los Angeles, Oakland, San Francisco, and Hollywood merited consideration if a move became necessary. He also mentioned Houston and Milwaukee.

He insisted there were few, if any, parallels between Veeck's situation in St. Louis and his own in Boston. The owner of the debt ridden Browns acknowledged financial difficulty. Perini claimed, "I don't owe anyone a dime." However, he wasn't making a dime either.

Veeck unintentionally set in motion the chain of events that ended with the Braves' transfer to Milwaukee. In early March of 1953 Clifford Randall of the Greater Milwaukee Stadium Committee offered the Braves half a million dollars in compensation for moving the Braves' primary farm, the Milwaukee Brewers, to Toledo. That would clear the way for the Browns to move to Milwaukee. Braves' Vice President Joseph Cairnes refused the offer. "We wouldn't stand in the way of Milwaukee getting into the Major Leagues," said Cairnes. "But before we give up the franchise we want a Triple A franchise with the same potential." "Talk of putting a major league team in Milwaukee has placed us in a bad position," said Perini. "We have to protect our own investment in the Brewers," he said. He proposed that the owners delay the transfer of any club before the end of the season. It was Perini's own team that eventually made a move.

Ironically, the Brewers won consecutive American Association championships from 1943 to 1945 under the ownership of the colorful Veeck, a brash promoter. Veeck's Brewers led the League in attendance. Because the loss of the Milwaukee franchise would considerably weaken the league, the Dodgers, owners of the team in St. Paul, the Giants, owners of the Minneapolis Millers, and the Cardinals, owners of the team in Columbus, all opposed the move.

IT'S OFFICIAL—BRAVES MOVE TO MILWAUKEE

But when the Braves lost to the New York Yankees in an exhibition game at their spring training headquarters in Bradenton, Florida on March seventeenth, it turned out to be their last game as a representative of the city of Boston.

The next day, at the Yankees' spring training facility at St. Petersburg, outfielder Sid Gordon homered with a man on in the first. Rookie Bob Buhl pitched five no hit innings. The Boston Braves led, two to nothing. Before New York came to bat in the sixth inning at Al Lang Field, word was passed to the Braves' bench, and to the 2957 fans that the National League had approved the transfer of Boston franchise to Milwaukee. The Yankees then scored five times off new pitcher Dick Donovan in the inning. The Milwaukee Braves lost, five to three, and became the first ball club to abandon a city in fifty years. Pitcher Warren Spahn and infielder Sibby Sisti were not with the team that afternoon. They were in a TV Station in Tampa, filming a promotion for the "Boston" Braves. The news came so suddenly that when the players posed for a team photo for the front page of the "Milwaukee Sentinel" there were not enough caps with an "M" on them. Several players wore caps with the more familiar "B" on them.

Just two days before, the American League President Will Harridge refused Veeck permission to move the Browns. "The numerous problems involved precluded a transfer of the franchise by reason of the short period of time before the opening of the nineteen fifty-three season," said American League President, Will Harridge. "In view of the improved attendance of the Browns in nineteen fifty-two, and the urgent request from the numerous St. Louis fans for retention of the club in St. Louis, the league looks forward to increased support of the St. Louis fans."

The Thursday, March nineteenth edition of the *Boston Daily Record* had a black mourning band around its page one headline, "It's Official— Braves Go to Milwaukee." Directly below the headline was a picture of Manager Charlie Grimm, and the Braves' bench, as they received word. The grounds keepers were already busy preparing Braves Field, host to major league baseball for thirty-seven years, for a new season that would never come. The Braves were gone. The 1953 All-Star Game, scheduled for Braves Field in Boston, was transferred to Cincinnati.

"We had planned to go next year," said Perini. "I had hoped to leave Boston with a better club. The move this year was the result of great pressure applied by the Milwaukee citizens to get major league ball this year. We had it in mind so, we decided to go this year." He claimed that television had influenced his decision, because it made Boston a one team city. He also cited the obvious lack of fan support. A poorly organized last minute attempt by local businessmen to keep the team in Boston had predictably failed.

Boston Mayor John Hynes called the move "a body blow to Boston." I do not believe Milwaukee can or will be able to support the Braves as well as Boston did." Massachusetts Governor Christian Herter was described as very disappointed. Two past Chamber of Commerce presidents were in Florida for talks with Perini when the move was announced. They wired back, "Long live Yawkey and the Red Sox."

Hotel Manager, Everett Kerr, estimated the annual loss in revenue to Boston to be $1,250,000. At the Warren Spahn Diner across the street from Braves Field, Joel Greenberg, Spahn's partner in the enterprise, remarked, "We knew it might happen. But we were surprised it happened so fast. It would have been nicer to have Warren here. But he will consider spending his winters here if business is good."

Officials at Braves Field reported that "several hundred" telephone calls had been received. National League President Warren Giles deplored the lateness of the move. The season was set to open in less than a month. 1,274,216 tickets for the Boston Braves had been printed. They were burned in a bonfire built in the stadium outfield near the Jury Box. A bus poster commemorating the event was captioned "Former Braves Tickets Go Up In Smoke."

The timing caused a quick revision in the already published 1953 National League schedule. The Pirates, becoming an "eastern team", inherited the original schedule planned for the Braves. The Braves, now a "western" team, took over the Pirates' schedule.

Pittsburgh general manager and former Dodger president, Branch Rickey, feigned outrage. "Judas priest," he said. "No wonder Perini wanted to get out of Boston." The Pirates' first fifteen games were now against the pennant contending Dodgers, Giants, and Phillies.

Shirley Povich, Washington Post Sports Columnist, noted:

> The Boston teams, both the Braves, and the Red Sox, always were the most covered clubs in the majors. In Boston, in Florida, and on the road, the Braves always had in tow three waves of baseball journalist. In Boston, the archaic custom of letting the ball teams pick up the check for the traveling writers persists an as many as three reporters often covered the club for the same newspaper. They were on the cuff, feeding off the bounty of Lou Perini, Braves' owner. Perhaps a factor in Perini's switch to Milwaukee was his realization that he no longer would have to feed, house, and

transport the Boston baseball reporting battalions. Out in Milwaukee, he has to underwrite the expenses of only two baseball writers. One of them has ulcers, and isn't much for the feed bag.

THE HISTORY

From 1876 to 1882, Boston's National League team was called the Red Caps, Reds or Red Stockings. They were known as the Beaneaters from 1883 until 1906. In 1907 and 1908, they played as the Doves. From 1909 to 1911, they were billed as the Rustlers. The name Braves took hold in 1912. It was abandoned briefly. From 1936 to 1940, the club played as the Boston Bees before the name Braves resurfaced. Boston's long history in the National League was certainly not glorious. Although, prior to 1900 they won eight pennants.

In 1887 the board of directors gave executive control of the ball club to Arthur Soden, William Conant, and James Billings. Known as the "Triumvirs", these three men guided the franchise for thirty years. They were very influential in the development of the Major Leagues.

First baseman Deacon White lead the league in slugging percentage in 1877, batting .387. Outfielder Jim O'Rourke batted .362, and shortstop Harry Wright played steady defense to lead Boston to their first league title. Wright was also the manager. Pitcher Tommy Bond won forty games. The team finished first again in 1878. Bond posted his second straight forty win season. The significant defection of Wright, and O'Rourke, to the Providence Grays in 1879, led to the institution of the reserve clause in the National League. Boston President Soden insisted on the measure. The Grays won first place honors. Though Bond won forty-three games, Boston finished second, five games behind Providence.

Bond developed arm trouble in 1880, winning a mere twenty-six games. The club slipped to sixth place. Under new manager John Morrill, they rebounded quickly, claiming their third pennant in 1883. Morrill, a first baseman, second baseman Jack Burdock, third baseman Ezra Sutton, and outfielder Joe Hornung all batted over .300. Jim Whitney won thirty-seven games. Charlie Buffington won twenty-four. The same two pitchers, victimized by a lack of offense, lost fifty-nine games in 1885. Boston finished fifth.

PREMIER BRAVE: "KING" KELLY

Prior to the start of the 1887 season, Boston acquired the mustachioed Mike "King" Kelly from the Chicago Cubs for the truly extravagant sum of $10,000. Known for his ability to execute the hit and run and his flamboyant slides, Kelly was a gambler, and a heavy drinker, off the field. He was, however, the games' first superstar, and certainly the most popular player in the history of Boston's National League franchise. In his first year he stole eighty-four bases. He batted .394. For another $10,000 dollars, the Braves purchased pitcher John Clarkson from the Cubs in 1888, positioning themselves for the most successful decade in their history.

In 1889, Boston finished second, one game behind the New York Giants. John Clarkson won forty-nine games. First Baseman Dan Brouthers batted .373, and Old Hoss Radborn posted his third twenty win season for the Beaneaters. Radborn had previously won fifty-nine games with Providence in 1884. With Kelly too hung over to play, the Braves lost the final game of the season to Cleveland.

In 1890, Kelly, and several other Beaneater stars, jumped to a new Players League team in Boston. The League was formed in opposition to Soden's favored reserve clause. Brouthers batted .330, and Radborne won twenty-seven games to lead the new Boston Reds to the league championship. Former Beaneater left fielder, Harry Richardson, batted .326. Kelly was the Reds' player manager. Meanwhile, the depleted Braves finished fifth in the National League.

The Players League died after one season. The Reds joined the American Association in 1891. The Triumvirs rebuilt the Braves quickly under the guidance of new Manager Frank Selee. Third baseman Bill Nash, and second baseman Joe Quinn returned to the Braves, who finished first in the National League again in 1891. Charlie "Kid" Nichols won thirty games. Shortstop Herman Long hit .287. Meanwhile Kelly's Reds finished first in the American Association. Brouthers won the league batting title with a .350 average, and a .516 slugging average. Hall of Fame outfielder Hugh Duffy batted .336. Charles Buffington won twenty-nine games.

In 1892, the American Association merged with the rival National League, forming one "National" league with twelve teams. The Beaneaters won the first half title in a split season format. Former Reds star Duffy led the team with a .302 batting average during the regular season. Nichols won thirty-five games. Jack Stivetts also won thirty-five. The Braves (102-48) became the first major league team to win 100 or more games in a season. They met the Cleveland Spiders, second half champions, for an intra-league World Series. In the opening game Stivetts pitched all eleven innings for Boston. Cy Young, who led the league with thirty-six wins, pitched all eleven for the Spiders. The duel between two Hall of Famers was called because of darkness, ending in a scoreless tie. Boston won the next five games to win the Series. Nichols finished his career in 1906 with 361 career victories. Duffy batted .378 in 1893, and .438 in 1894. He finished his career in 1906 with a .330 average.

Though there was no post season title series in 1893, Boston finished first again. Outfielder Tommy McCarthy batted .363. Duffy batted .378. Nichols won thirty-four games.

Boston won the National League title again in 1897. Outfielder Chick Stahl batted .359 during the regular season. Third baseman Jimmy Collins batted .346. Outfielder Billy Hamilton batted .344. Duffy batted .341. Nichols lead the league with thirty-one wins. Hamilton batted .367 in 1898, leading the Beaneaters to their last pennant. Nichols won thirty-one games, Ted Lewis won twenty-six games, and Vic Willis won twenty-five. The Braves lost an intra-league post season series to runner-up Baltimore. The Orioles claimed the "Temple Cup", donated as a prize by noted Pittsburgh sportsman William C. Temple. Braves' pitching allowed fifty-four Oriole runs in the five game series.

Willis, a right hander, was the last Boston Braves' player inducted into the Hall of Fame, selected by the Veterans Committee in 1995, eighty-five years after his career ended. He hurled 388 complete games in a career that extended from 1898 to 1910. He set the National League record of forty-five complete games in a single season in 1902, posting twenty-seven victories for a team finished in last place.

Manager Frank Selee, who managed the Braves from 1890 through 1905, was inducted into the Hall of Fame on July 25, 1999, 90 years after his death at 49 years of age. The Braves captured five pennants during his tenure.

The great Cy Young finished out his career with the 1911 Braves, winning four and losing five. His five hundredth and seventh and last victory came in a Braves' uniform.

Former New York Giant shortstop John Montgomery Ward, now a lawyer, and New York millionaire James Gaffney purchased the team in 1912, following the death of previous owner William Russell. They renamed the team "Braves", redesigned the uniforms, and refurbished the South End Grounds ballpark. The team, however, finished last in 1912 before rebounding to a fifth place finish in 1913 under new manager George Stallings.

The 1914 "Miracle Braves" won the pennant in their last season at the South End Grounds ballpark. Ex Cubs' great Johnny Evers, part of the fabled "Tinkers to Evers to Chance" double play combination in Chicago, anchored a solid infield along with shortstop Rabbit Maranville. Both are in the Hall of Fame. Right handed pitchers Bill James, and Don Rudolph won fifty-three games between them. Lefty

Tyler won sixteen. The Braves, in last place in mid-July, stormed past the fading New York Giants to win the National League pennant by ten and one-half games. The magic carried over for second year manager Stallings. In the World Series the Braves steam rolled Connie Mack's favored Philadelphia Athletics in four games.

THE BALLPARK

Because of the limited seating capacity of the South End Grounds, the 1914 Series was played at the newly built Fenway Park, home of the Red Sox, which had opened in 1912. In 1916 the Braves returned the favor, allowing the hometown Red Sox, winners of the American League Pennant, to play their World Series games at their own, newly built Braves Field.

Braves Field sometimes referred to as the "Wigwam" officially opened on August eighteenth, 1915. The attendance of 42,000 was the largest crowd ever to witness a major league game to that date. It was referred to as the "Beehive" for the five seasons that the club was known as the Bees. Sometimes, it was simply called "National League Park." Bounded by Commonwealth Avenue, Gaffney Street, and Babcock Street near the Charles River, it was home to the Boston National League franchise for thirty-seven years.

Constructed by new club owner James Gaffney, it was one of the first steel and concrete facilities. Occasionally, fluke home runs would bounce through the openings in the scoreboard located on ground level in left field. There was no second deck although a covered grandstand seated 18,000. The upstairs offices, and the clubhouse, were accessed by a stairway on the third base side. Bleachers along each foul line seated 10,000 each. A small bleacher section in right field accommodated 2000 more. Because that section attracted only twelve paying customers one day it became known afterward as the "jury box." Former Braves' fan Beth Hickock, now of Bennington, Vermont, recalls the park organist would play a funeral dirge after Braves' losses.

In 1915, and again in 1916 the Braves, returning the Red Sox hospitality of two years before, allowed the American League pennant winners to play their World Series games at their new park which had a larger seating capacity than Fenway. The Sox defeated the Philadelphia Phillies in 1915 and the Brooklyn Dodgers in 1916 winning both series in five games. The year of 1916 was Gaffney's last as owner of the Braves. He sold the team at a considerable profit to a group of businessmen including the bankers who financed the building of Braves

Field. Ex-Harvard football coach Percy Haughton assumed the club presidency. Manager Stallings did not get along well with the new ownership but he guided the team to a third place finish after finishing second in 1915. The club sunk to sixth in 1917, however.

In 1918 New York businessman George Washington Grant purchased the Boston team. His remained in New York. A close friend of Giant's manager John McGraw, Grant had a box seat at the Polo Grounds. His brief absentee ownership was marked by charges that he was maneuvered by the Giants. The team finished seventh in 1918 and rebounded to sixth in 1919.

In 1920 Braves Field was the site of twenty-six inning contest between Boston and the Brooklyn Dodgers. Joe Oeschger of the Braves pitched sixteen scoreless innings. The game was called because of darkness. It ended tied at one to one.

The highlight of Grant's ownership was a fourth place finish in 1921. Outfielder Billy Southworth, acquired from the Pirates in an unpopular trade for shortstop and local hero Maranville, batted .308. The club fell back into the National League cellar in 1922. They would not finish as high as fourth again until 1933.

In 1923 Judge Emil Fuchs, a deputy attorney general of New York State, purchased the last place Braves from Grant, hiring legendary New York Giant pitcher Christy Mathewson as club President. Fuchs, relatively free of New York influence, moved to Boston.

Mathewson, one of the first five inductees into the Hall of Fame served as Braves' President from 1923 to 1925. But the team finished last in two of the three seasons.

Hall of Fame first baseman George Sisler, a former Browns' hero, and Hall of Fame second baseman Rogers Hornsby, a former Cardinal great, spent twelve seasons playing in the same infield at Sportsman's Park in St. Louis. They were teammates on the 1928 Braves' squad. Thirty-two year-old Hornsby won the batting title with a .387 average. Thirty-five year-old Sisler batted .340. The team finished seventh. Hornsby was traded to the Chicago Cubs in 1929. In 1930, Braves' outfielder Wally Berger, one of a number of players acquired in the Hornsby deal, set a rookie record with thirty-eight home runs. He batted in 119 runs while batting .310.

The Red Sox imposed upon the hospitality of the Braves from 1929-1932, playing all Sunday afternoon games at Braves Field because of Fenway's closeness to a church.

Fuchs himself replaced Rodgers Hornsby as manager at the start of the 1929 season. Despite his ignorance of the games' finer points, the club played well for the first month of the season. But legal matters required his return to New York. The team finished last.

Fuchs tenure as owner of the Braves peaked with respectable back to back fourth place finishes in 1933 and 1934. But a last place finish in 1935 was the low ebb in franchise history. The team won only thirty-eight games. Fuchs signed Babe Ruth for the 1935 season as a part time player and "assistant" manager along with a somewhat vague promise that Ruth would be manager eventually. Ending his career with Boston, Ruth hit only six home runs, with just twelve RBIs, and compiled a meager .181 average. However, he hit a home run off Giant ace Carl Hubbell in his first at bat for the Braves. And he bid a spectacular farewell, in June 1935, with home runs in his final three major league at bats at Forbes Field in Pittsburgh. The last, number 714, was the first ever hit completely out of Forbes Field. The managerial promise was never fulfilled, however, and Ruth remained bitter in retirement.

Former Pittsburgh infielder Bill McKechnie managed the Braves from 1930 to 1937. The team finished no higher than fourth place. Fellow Hall of Famer Casey Stengel managed the Braves from 1938 to 1944. The Braves finished no higher than fifth during his tenure. Right hander Bill Posedel, however, won fifteen games for the 1939 Braves. He won twelve in 1940. Second baseman Carvel "Bama" Rowell, from Citronelle, Alabama, batted .305 in 1940. After long careers in Pittsburgh, Hall of Famers Paul and Lloyd Waner, "Big Poison" and "Little Poison",played in Boston's outfield in 1941. Both were well past their prime. But Lloyd hit .412 in nineteen games. Paul hit only .279 in ninety-five games. Infielder John Dudra hit .360.

After ten seasons with the Cincinnati Reds, Hall of Fame catcher Ernie Lombardi joined the Braves in 1942, claiming the National League batting title with a .330 average. The club finished seventh. There was rebuilding to do.

Perini, and fellow construction business partners, Guido Rugo, and C.J. "Joe" Maney, bought out other stockholders in 1944. The trio, referred to as "The Three Little Steam Shovels" by the local press, installed lights at Braves Field, expanded the farm system, and instigated numerous trades. Perini hired Billy Southworth, who had guided the Cardinals to three pennants, as manager. All this effort culminated in the 1948 Pennant.

Outfielder Tommy Holmes, established a number of franchise records in 1945, batting .352 with twenty-eight home runs, forty-seven doubles. He hit in thirty-seven straight games, and drove in 177 runs.

The original Braves Field was 402 feet down each foul line, and 550 feet to deep center. It isn't surprising that there were no home runs hit there until 1917, five years after the park opened. The "Little Shovels" renovated the park in 1946, reducing the distance to the left field fence to 337 feet down the line. The distance to the right field fence was shortened to just 319 feet. It was still 390 feet to the deepest part of center field. That was 160 feet shorter than the original distance.

The refurbishing of the park was not quite completed by opening day, 1946. The new coat of green paint on the seats was still wet. Thousands of fans found their clothes stained with green blotches. There were several thousand dollars in damage claims. With the gracious permission of amused Red Sox owner, Tom Yawkey, the Braves played the next few home games at Fenway Park, allowing the paint at Braves Field to dry thoroughly.

On April fifteenth, 1947, The Braves were the visitors at Ebbets Field when Jackie Robinson played his first major league game. In that season Braves' third baseman Bob Elliott took home National League Most Valuable Player honors in the first of his five seasons in Boston. He batted .317 with twenty-two home runs while driving in 113 runs.

SPAHN AND SAIN AND PRAY FOR RAIN

A popular slogan during the 1948 championship season was "Spahn and Sain, and pray for rain," a reference to a pitching staff that wasn't particularly deep. Spahn and Sain combined for an impressive thirty-nine victories that year. But Manager Tommy Holmes observed that overlooked right handers Vern Bickford and Bill Voiselle, actually filled out the four man starting rotation quite adequately. Voiselle was thirteen and thirteen. He had thirty-seven starts, and a 3.63 ERA. That compared with thirty-six starts, and a 3.71 ERA, for Spahn. And Bickford won eleven games with a 3.27 ERA.

A corollary to the Spahn and Sain refrain, applied to "Milwaukee" Braves in 1957 and 1958, was "Spahn and Burdette and two days of wet." The duo combined for eighty victories over the two seasons, leading Milwaukee to the National League pennant both years. Spahn won twenty-two games in 1958. Burdette won twenty. Bob Rush was a distant third in wins with ten.

In 1948 Boston's last national league pennant winners beat the legendary Bob Feller twice in the World Series. But Cleveland won in six games. One hundred television sets were placed on the Boston Common for the October classic, and 50,000 Boston fans gathered there to watch. Fans numbering 120,000 watched the three games in person at Braves Field. The 1948 season attendance figure was 1,455,439.

Following a player rebellion against the tyrannical Southworth after the 1949 season the keystone of the 1948 champions, second baseman Eddie Stanky, and shortstop Alvin Dark were traded to New York for outfielders Sid Gordon and Willard Marshall, shortstop Buddy Kerr, and pitcher Sam Webb. Sain, a twenty game winner in 1950 was traded to the Yankees in 1951.

Catcher Phil Masi was dealt to Pittsburgh in 1949. Bob Elliott, home run leader of the Braves in 1948, was traded to the Giants just prior to the start of the 1952 season. Veteran first baseman Earl Torgeson was the only reminder of the 1948 infield on the 1952 squad.

Tommy Holmes, who had replaced Billy Southworth as manager at the mid point of the 1951 season, was the only remaining member of the 1948 outfield. Jeff Heath retired in 1949. Left handed pitcher Mike McCormick was traded to the Dodgers for Pete Reiser.

THE FINAL SEASON

In April 1952 fans were looking forward to the season with the hope that comes every spring. Few were thinking that this would be the Braves' last season in Boston. There had been no franchise shifts for fifty years. The Braves' resourceful Public Relations director, Bill Sullivan, future owner of the New England Patriots of the National Football League, had reason for optimism. Thirty-one-year-old left hander Spahn, was a future member of the Hall of Fame. He had won twenty games in each of the three previous seasons, and in four of the past five. Right handers Max Surkont and Jim Wilson combined for nineteen victories in 1951. The mound staff should have looked even stronger. Promising left handers Chet Nichols and Johnny Antonelli were both in military service. So was catcher Del Crandall. Nichols, as a rookie in 1951, had an eleven and eight record with an impressive 2.88 era. Antonelli was the Braves' top draft pick in 1948.

Offensively Torgeson, catcher Walker Cooper, and outfielders Sid Gordon and Sam Jethroe, were expected to hit with some power. Cooper hit .300 and homered eighteen times in 1951. In 1950, Jethroe, a five time Negro League all-star, hit eighteen home runs, stole thirty-five bases, a league high, and was named the Rookie of the Year. Mathews, a highly touted twenty-one-year-old third baseman, was expected to be a candidate for the Rookie of the Year honors in 1952.

Thirty-year-old rookie Bill Reed started the season at second base. He had been the American Association's All-Star second baseman in 1951 batting .311 for the Milwaukee Brewers. And light hitting Jack Cusick, acquired from the Cubs in the off season opened the year at shortstop, although twenty-five-year-old rookie Johnny Logan made a strong bid to start at the position with an impressive spring training performance.

The daily radio voices of the fifty-two Braves were Jim Britt, and Tom Hussey. Television was in its infancy. The TV announcer for the few games televised locally in the immediate Boston area was Bump Hadley. A pitcher with the New York Yankees in 1937, Hadley beaned Detroit Tigers' Hall of Fame catcher Mickey Cochrane. The pitch ended Cochrane's career.

APRIL

Spahn drew the starting assignment for the home opener on Tuesday, April fifteenth, against the Brooklyn Dodgers. Only 4649 saw Massachusetts Governor Paul A. Dever throw the ceremonial first pitch. On a chilly, overcast afternoon, Jethroe homered in the third inning, scoring the first run of the season. After the Dodgers scored three runs in the top of the fifth, Torgeson opened the bottom half of the inning with a double. He scored the final run of the game on a single by Gordon. Brooklyn southpaw Preacher Roe retired the last thirteen hitters he faced. The Dodgers won, three to two.

On Wednesday, the Dodgers chased starter Max Surkont with four runs in the top of the first inning. Boston's Walker Cooper doubled with the bases loaded in the bottom of the inning. But the Dodgers scored five more in the third inning. The visitors won, fourteen to eight. There were twenty Dodger hits, and seven errors by the Braves. On Thursday night the Dodgers won again, eight to two. Rookie outfielder Pete Whisenant spoiled Johnny Schmitz's shutout bid with a bases loaded single in the sixth inning. Returning from military service, Whisenant was regarded as a top prospect in the Braves' organization, batting .312, hitting twenty four home runs and driving in 119 runs with the Braves' double-A farm team in Denver in 1950.

In the Phillies home opener on Friday, April eighteenth at Shibe Park, Boston trailed, two to nothing, when Torgeson walked to start the top of the ninth. Gordon and reserve outfielder Willard Marshall then homered back-to-back on consecutive pitches to give the Braves their first victory of the year, three to two. Starter Jim Wilson allowed just three Philadelphia hits.

On Saturday Jethroe hit a two-run homer in the sixth inning. But Boston fell behind, seven to four, before tying the game on a three-run homer by Mathews in the eighth. For the second straight game, the Braves staged a winning rally in the ninth inning. Pinch hitter Jack Daniels singled to open the inning. Reed sacrificed him to second. Singles by Jethroe and Torgeson followed, giving the Braves their second straight win, a nine to seven victory over Philadelphia.

On April twentieth, the Braves split their first Sunday doubleheader of the season, losing the opener to the Phillies, four to three, in ten innings, and winning, two to one, behind strong pitching by Dave Cole. In the eighth inning of the second game, Jethroe singled to right, scoring pinch runner Sibbi Sisti with the winning run.

The three wins in four games at Philadelphia improved the Braves' record to three wins and four losses. It was the Braves' high water mark in their final season in Boston.

At Ebbets Field in Brooklyn on Tuesday, April twenty-second, the Dodgers swept a doubleheader, winning the opener, two to one, and the second game, three to one.

WILHELM HOMERS FOR THE GIANTS

On Wednesday night, the Braves lost again at the Polo Grounds, nine to five. The game was notable, however, because, in the fourth inning, rookie relief pitcher Hoyt Wilhelm of the Giants hit a home run in his first major league at bat, against rookie left hander Dick Hoover. The Hall of Fame knuckle ball specialist recorded 142 more wins in a distinguished twenty year career. But he never hit another home run.

On Thursday night, Mathews doubled with the bases loaded in the top of the tenth, giving the Braves a six to three win over the Giants in the final game of the road trip. Former Braves' hero Bob Elliott had two hits. In the fifth inning, Giant Manager Leo Durocher protested that Spahn had quick pitched Willie Mays. "A pitch delivered before the batter is reasonably set in the batter's box is fully as dangerous as the so-called bean ball," said Durocher. "I just want protection from such trickery for my batters." Umpire Art Gore ejected Durocher. Catcher Cooper fell into the Giants dugout while chasing a four pop. He was sidelined for ten days.

When the Braves returned to Boston, three of four scheduled games with Philadelphia were rained out. Only 1893 fans watched Philadelphia ace Robin Roberts shutout the Braves, eight to nothing, on Saturday, April twenty-sixth. Game time temperature was forty-two degrees.

The Braves finished up the month at Pittsburgh's Forbes Field. On Tuesday, April twenty-ninth, Holmes benched the slumping Marshall, and started Bob Thorpe in right field. Thorpe responded with three hits, leading the Braves to a five to one win. Spahn picked up his first win of the year pitching all nine innings. He also contributed two hits, and a run batted in. On the final day of the month, Boston lost eleven to five. It was Dave Cole's final appearance. He was sent back to the minors after the game. The Braves lost all seven home games in April. They were a respectable five and two on the road. They were in seventh place, six games behind the first place Dodgers.

MAY

Boston began the month of May at Crosley Field in Cincinnati. The Thursday afternoon game time temperature was an unusually warm eighty-nine degrees. Errors by Jethroe, Torgeson, and Mathews led to two unearned runs. The Reds won, seven to six. Jim Wilson won his first game of the year on Friday night, out dueling the Reds' Ken Raffensburger, two to one. He also drove in both Boston runs with a second inning single. Cincinnati won the Series, two games to one with an eight to one victory on Saturday, May third. Three Boston errors contributed to a five run Boston rally in the fifth inning.

On May fourth in St. Louis the Cardinals won the opener of a Sunday doubleheader, four to three. Jethroe doubled to open the ninth, but did not score. He tripled to open the second game, however, and scored on a double by Mathews. Surkont won his first game of the year, five to one.

The road trip ended in Chicago. On Tuesday, May sixth, Johnny Klippstein shut out the Braves on two hits, two to nothing. The Wednesday night game was called because of cold weather. On Thursday night Marshall's bases clearing triple in the fourth highlighted a four run rally. Trailing six to four, the Cubs loaded the bases with two out in the ninth inning. Burdette came in to get the final out.

Returning to Braves Field on Saturday May tenth, Boston lost a four to two decision to the Giants. New York won for the tenth time in eleven games. Mathews homered in the fourth to tie the game at two all. Elliott, making his first appearance in Boston since donning a New York uniform, singled and scored in a two-run Giants' rally in the seventh inning. A Sunday afternoon doubleheader with the Giants was rained out.

Play resumed on Tuesday, May thirteenth. In the first night game of the year in Boston, Bickford scattered nine hits, defeating Pittsburgh, three to one. Mathews homer in the fifth was the only extra base blow among six Boston hits.

THE SMALLEST HOME CROWD

Winning consecutive games for the first time during the season, the Braves defeated Pittsburgh again on Thursday night, May fourteenth. The game was tied, three to three, after nine innings. Gus Bell of the Pirates homered in the top of the tenth. George Crowe led off the bottom of the inning with his first major league homer to tie the game. With one out, Daniels walked. Later in the inning Pirates' shortstop George Strickland bobbled Whisenant's grounder, allowing Daniels to score the game winner. Boston won four to three. There were only 1105 fans at Braves Field. It was the smallest home crowd of the year.

In a by now all too familiar occurrence, the opener of a three game series with St. Louis was postponed because of cold, threatening weather. On Friday, May sixteenth, the Braves won their third in a row, defeating the Cardinals, eight to three, behind the seven hit pitching of Spahn. On Saturday, however, the modest winning streak ended. The Cardinals survived a three-run seventh inning rally, winning five to four.

More bad weather forced cancellation of a Sunday double header against Cincinnati. The first two games of a scheduled three game series against the Cubs were also postponed. When play resumed on Thursday night, May twenty second, Chicago won the first game of a doubleheader, three to nothing.

In the second game, Spahn hurled the first shutout of the season by a Boston pitcher, winning five to nothing. Jethroe hit his fourth homer of the year. Thorpe hit his first major league homer. The Braves finished the abbreviated home stand with four wins and three losses. They were averaging less than 4200 paid admissions per game. Bad weather had forced the postponement of ten home games, including three doubleheaders. Several other games were played in cold and dreary conditions. Boston closed the month on the road with series at New York, Philadelphia, and Brooklyn.

In the opener at the Polo Grounds on Friday, May twenty third, Sal Maglie won his eighth straight for the Giants, five to three. Jethroe walked to open the game, went to third on a single by Mathews. He scored on an infield out. The Braves didn't score again until light hitting Ebba St Claire homered in the ninth following a double by Crowe.

Surkont retired the first nine batters he faced. But shortstop Alvin Dark keyed a five run New York fourth inning with a two-run homer.

The Giants turned back the Braves again on Saturday, five to four. Gordon opened the ninth inning with a homer into the upper left field stands off Hoyt Wilhelm. Thorpe singled home another run, cutting the Giant lead to a run. But for the second straight game, Torgeson grounded into a game ending double play.

A Sunday doubleheader in New York, and the opener of a three game series in Philadelphia were rained out.

In the opener of a doubleheader on Tuesday night, May twenty-seventh, Spahn pitched all twelve innings, defeating the Phillies, four to two. Philadelphia's Robin Roberts lasted just eight innings failing to complete a game for the first time during the 1953 season. Jethroe homered in the sixth. Singles by Daniels, Sisti, and Hartsfield produced the winning runs in the top of the twelfth. The second game went ten innings before the Phillies won, five to four.

The Dodgers closed out the month extending their complete mastery over the Braves. On Thursday, May twenty-ninth, at Ebbets Field Jackie Robinson broke a three to three tie with a two-run homer in the fifth. The Dodgers won, seven to three. In the first game of a Memorial Day doubleheader, Gordon homered twice to give the Braves a three to one lead. Hodges homered with two on in the eighth to give the Dodgers a five to three lead. Mathews doubled and scored in the ninth. But Brooklyn won again, five to four. The Dodgers breezed to an eleven to two win in the second game.

The Braves were mired in seventh place ahead of only the hapless Pirates. The first two months of the season had been disastrous. Poor fielding, and an inability to hit left handed pitching were contributing factors. The club lost six of the first seven times they faced southpaws.

Management was making long range moves to strengthen the club. They purchased the contract of eighteen year-old outfielder Henry Aaron from the Indianapolis Clowns of the Negro League, assigning him to the Eau Clair Bears minor league franchise.

Also looking for more immediate results, Perini fired the amiable Holmes who referred to his players as teammates. He replaced him with Charlie Grimm. "That's baseball," said a teary Holmes. "It's no disgrace to be replaced by Charlie Grimm."

Grimm appointed Walker Cooper team captain. He installed Logan, a fan favorite, as the starting shortstop. Feeling he had taken over a "pretty fair ball club", Grimm was optimistic. Preparing to open a three game series in Cincinnati, he told reporters "I'll try to win, and win quickly." He took over a seventh place club that was thirteen games in back of the first place New York Giants.

JUNE

Raffensberger of the Reds, another left hander, beat Vern Bickford of the Braves in a pitching duel, one to nothing, in the opener of a Sunday doubleheader on June first, spoiling Jolly Cholly's debut. But the Braves won the second game, nine to four, supporting Spahn's fifth straight win, with eighteen hits. Jethroe had four hits. Mathews had three, including his eighth home run of the season. On Monday Max Surkont struck out eleven, beating the Reds, four to one. in the rubber game of the series. Crowe hit his seventh homer of the year.

On Tuesday night in St. Louis, Wilson stretched the winning streak to three games, beating the Cardinals, three to two. Crowe blasted his eighth homer of the year over the right field pavilion in the eighth inning.

On Wednesday June fourth, St. Louis right hander Cloyd Boyer shut out Boston, six to nothing. But on Thursday, Spahn won his fifth straight, beating the Cardinals in the rubber game, eight to three. Gordon's three-run homer keyed a seven run Braves' rally in the first inning. It was the Braves' fourth victory in five games under new management.

On Friday, June sixth at Wrigley Field, the Cubs routed the Braves, seven to two. Mathews homered in the ninth inning. Chicago won easily again on Saturday, nine to three. Cooper pulled a hamstring sliding into third base. He was lost to the club for three weeks. Only light hitting Paul Burris, and Ebba St. Claire were available as back up catchers.

The Sunday June eighth doubleheader at Chicago drew 38,514, the largest crowd to see a Braves' game all season. The Cubs scored four times in the first inning of the opener. Johnny Logan tripled with the bases loaded in the second cutting the Cubs lead to four to three. The Cubs scored three more in the third. Gordon homered in the fifth to close out the scoring. Chicago won, seven to five. A grand slam by Jethroe, and an unexpected three-run homer by light hitting Sisti, provided all the Boston scoring in the second game, powering a seven to six Boston victory. Right hander Ernie Johnson won in his first major league starting assignment.

The Braves moved on to Pittsburgh's Forbes Field on Monday, June ninth. Wilson pitched all nine innings, winning three to two. Fortunately for Boston, Ralph Kiner's blast into the left field screen in the sixth was ruled foul. Pirates' manager Billy Meyer was ejected for arguing correctly that no part of that screen was in foul territory.

The Pirates rallied for five first inning runs on Tuesday night, winning seven to five. Surkont allowed just five hits on Wednesday night, but lost five to nothing. A solo homer by Ralph Kiner in the third, and a three-run blast by Gus Bell backed Murray Dickson's shutout pitching for the Pirates.

The Braves romped to an eleven to two win over Pittsburgh in the final game of the long twenty-one game road trip on Thursday. Burdette relieved Johnson with no one out in the second inning. He allowed just one hit over the final eight innings. Battery mate Paul Burris, substituting for the injured Cooper, had four hits including a three-run homer in the fourth inning, and a bases loaded double in the fifth.

Friday the thirteenth of June was unlucky for the Braves. Seven and seven under Grimm, they finally returned to Boston to begin the longest home stand of the season. Chicago's Bob Rush allowed just three hits, shutting out Boston, five to nothing. Spahn pitched all fifteen innings on Saturday, struck out eighteen batters, and hit a sixth inning home run. But a two out triple by Cubs' center fielder Hal Jeffcoat in the fifteenth inning drove in the two runs, giving Chicago a three to one victory.

But more strong pitching on Sunday led Boston to their first double-header sweep of the season. There was a surprisingly large home crowd of 9100. In the opener Wilson allowed just seven hits. Jethroe singled to open the game, stole second, and scored on a wild throw by second baseman Eddie Miksis. Mathews homered in the sixth to account for the only earned Boston run. The Braves beat the Cubs, four to one. Surkont, struck out nine and yielded only two scratch singles in the second game. He shut out Chicago, two to nothing. No Cubs' batter reached second base. A pair of Logan singles drove in runs in the second and fourth innings.

In the first game of a doubleheader on Tuesday night, June seventeenth, Bickford gave Boston another strong pitching performance, defeating the Reds, five to one. The win extended the Braves' winning streak to three games. Logan doubled home two runs in the sixth inning. The second game was rained out and rescheduled as part of a doubleheader on Wednesday night. The Reds won the first game on Wednesday night, June eighteenth, seven to six, ending the brief winning spree. Rookie Virgil Jester took the loss in his first major league start. Although Spahn struck out eleven batters in the second game, he suffered his third straight loss. Cincinnati won, three to one, sweeping the doubleheader. But Spahn did take over the league lead in strikeouts. He had seventy-nine. Chicago's Bob Rush had seventy.

St. Louis starter Gerry Staley was seeking his tenth victory on Friday, June twentieth. But Boston scored a season high ten runs in the sixth inning, defeating the Cardinals, twelve to seven. Returning to the Braves' lineup, Cooper had three hits and four RBIs. Called upon in a rare relief appearance, Spahn halted a seven run St Louis outburst in the top of the seventh. He then homered in the eighth. The Cardinals, however, swept the remaining three games of the series, outscoring Boston, cumulatively, twenty-three to four.

Boston managed to find some offense of its own, defeating the Pirates, nine to three, on Monday, June twenty-third. Mathews twelfth homer of the year put him one ahead of Gordon in the National League home run race.

TRIPLE PLAY EXECUTED AGAINST THE BRAVES

On Tuesday night Pittsburgh turned a triple play in the third inning. But Boston won again, four to three. With Jethroe on second, and Thorpe on first, Torgeson line to Pirates' shortstop Dick Groat, who tagged second for the force on Jethroe. Groat threw to first for the third out. Wilson, the winning pitcher, singled to open the ninth. He later scored the winning run on a single by Crowe. Boston won again on Thursday night, five to three. Gordon hit his twelfth homer to draw even with Mathews.

The three victories over the Pirates marked the second series sweep of the year. It was the third time during the season that the club posted three consecutive victories. Grimm closed out his first home stand with seven victories and six defeats.

Opening another road trip at Ebbets Field, Cooper hit a three-run homer off Johnny Schmitz in the first inning on Friday night, June twenty seventh. But the Dodgers scored four runs in the bottom of the inning, coasting to an eight to three victory. Johnson walked in two runs. Brooklyn had twelve hits.

On Saturday Spahn lost his fifth straight, four to two. It was his ninth straight loss at Ebbets Field over several seasons. With two on and two out in the sixth, Mathews doubled off the left field screen to given Boston a two to one lead. The score was tied two to two in the bottom of the ninth when Hodges lined a two-run homer off Spahn, deep into the left field stands.

FORMER MANAGER HOLMES SINGLES
TO DEFEAT BRAVES

Boston came close again on Sunday afternoon. But the Dodgers prevailed again, six to five. Sisti, Gordon, and Cooper all homered in the third inning, giving Boston a four to three lead. After the Dodgers scored two in the bottom of the sixth, Gordon homered again to tie the score in the top of the seventh. In the home seventh, recently fired Braves' manager Tommy Holmes, newly acquired by the Dodgers, pinch hit for Dodger starter, Clyde King, and lined a single to center, scoring George "Shotgun" Shuba with the winning run. "I'm happy I made the hit," Tommy said, "but I assure you there was nothing personal in it. I just wanted to help out the club I'm playing for now."

The series sweep extended the Brooklyn winning streak over Boston to eleven games. Exploiting the Braves' weakness against left handers, the Dodgers had started southpaws in all eleven games. Chris Van Cuyk started four times. Preacher Roe and Johnny Schmitz started three games apiece. Ken Lehman had one start. While Brooklyn pitching held the Braves in check, the Dodgers' team batting average against the Braves was a whopping .339.

The Braves returned home on the final day of June for a Monday night doubleheader with New York. Leo Durocher, serving a four game suspension, watched his team win both games from a perch on the roof of Braves Field. Sal Maglie won his eleventh game for the Giants in the opener, defeating the Braves, eight to seven. Larry Jansen shut out the Braves in the second game, four to nothing. The Braves closed the month with five straight defeats. They remained in seventh place, twenty games out.

JULY

The visiting Giants extended the Boston losing streak to six on Tuesday, July first, winning again six to three. Bobby Thomson hit his third homer of the series. Mathews homered, tripled, and scored twice, accounting for all the Boston scoring.

TORGESON VS YVARS—THE FIGHT

After Torgeson singled in the bottom of the first, the Giant catcher, Sal Yvars, picked up the bat where Torgeson had dropped it. He pounded the bat on the plate. The inning ended without incident. But as the Braves left the field in the middle of the second inning, Torgeson charged into the Giants' first base dugout. He threw a left hook at the surprised Yvars, who was bending down fastening his shin guards. A bench emptying brawl ensued. Torgeson and Bickford were ejected by Umpire Larry Goetz. Still in exile, Giant manager Durocher could only watch from an inauspicious seat in far away center field.

Torgeson, fined one hundred dollars by National League President Warren Giles, explained:

> I didn't think anything of it, until as we exchanged sides Whitey Lockman (Giants' first baseman) said to me — I think Yvars broke your bat. That had me pretty mad. When the Giant inning ended I ran to the bat rack. Sure enough my bat was split. I took off my glasses, and went after Yvars!

This incident may have motivated the Braves temporarily. Spahn broke his personal five game losing streak, beating New York, two to one, on Wednesday July second, tossing a brilliant five hitter. The Giants broke a scoreless deadlock in the seventh inning, when Torgeson, playing left field, dropped Alvin Dark's fly ball for a two base error. Dark later scored on a sacrifice fly. But Jack Dittmer homered into the right field bullpen with Logan on first in the bottom of the inning to provide the margin of victory. Philadelphia's Curt Simmons then held the Braves to four hits on Thursday, winning two to nothing.

The Braves swept both ends of the fourth of July doubleheader, winning two to one in eleven innings, and then three to two in a regulation nine innings. Mathews hit his fourteenth home run in the eleventh inning of the first game. With the score tied two to two in the eighth inning of the second game, Phillies' shortstop Granny Hamner booted a ground ball off the bat of Cooper. The speedy Jethroe raced home from second base with the winning run.

LARGEST HOME CROWD,
A DODGER RIGHT HANDER, AND A SMALL DOG

For a change of pace the Dodgers threw Carl Erskine, a right hander, at Boston on Saturday, July fifth. Erskine defeated the Braves anyway, five to three, striking out nine. The crowd of 13,405 was the largest of the season at Braves Field. Jethroe led off the Boston first with a home run. But the Dodgers already had a three to nothing lead. The game was delayed in the second inning when a small dog scampered on to the field making friends with right field Umpire Augie Guglielmo. Furillo and Snider finally escorted the mutt off the field.

Brooklyn won their thirteenth straight over the Braves on Sunday, eight to two. Hodges three-run homer off Spahn in the fourth gave Ben

Wade, the second straight right handed Dodger starter against the Braves, a commanding five to nothing lead. Wade hit two home runs. He had three RBIs.

THE ALL-STAR BREAK

Spahn was Boston's lone representative in the 1952 All-Star Game. It was the fifth time he had been selected to represent the National League. He didn't make an appearance in the game. The Nationals won the first rain shortened midsummer classic ever at Shibe Park in Philadelphia, three to two. Jackie Robinson of the Dodgers, and Hank Sauer of the Cubs homered. Bob Rush of the Cubs was the winning pitcher. The game was called after five innings.

Following the all-star break the Braves played their best baseball of the season. Resuming regular season play on the road at Cincinnati on Thursday, July tenth, they lost, five to three. Errors by infielders Sisti, Torgeson, and Dittmer led to two unearned off Braves' starter Wilson in the seventh inning. It was Boston's tenth loss in thirteen games.

THE LONGEST WINNING STREAK

But Spahn pitched a six to one victory over Pittsburgh on Friday night, July eleventh. He also contributed two of the sixteen Boston hits. Logan and Torgeson had three hits each. On Saturday Boston scored four runs in the sixth inning. Pitcher Bickford, Logan, Torgeson and Cooper hit consecutive singles, producing two runs. Mathews doubled home two more. The Braves won, five to two.

In the opener of a Sunday July thirteenth doubleheader, Surkont pitched a six hitter, shutting out the Pirates until the ninth. He registered his first victory in three weeks, four to two. In the second game, three rookies played key roles. Virgil Jester yielded seven hits, recording his first major league victory, two to one. Daniels tripled and scored the tying run on Jethroe's single in the top of the sixth inning. And second baseman Dittmer tripled and scored the winning run in the eighth. The victory was Boston's seventh straight over Pittsburgh.

Boston's longest winning streak of the year crested at five games in Chicago on Tuesday, July fifteenth. The Braves routed the Cubs, ten to three. Cooper hit a two-run homer in the fourth inning. Two singles, five walks, and two errors by Chicago shortstop Roy Smalley lead to six more Boston runs in the fifth.

On Wednesday night, Chicago beat Boston, three to two, in thirteen innings. The struggling Cubs, losers in twenty-one of their past thirty games, broke their own five game losing streak. Chicago first baseman, and Manager, Phil Cavaretta smashed a run scoring single with one out in the final inning. Bickford shut out Chicago, one to nothing, in the final game of the series on Thursday night. He also singled in the seventh inning to drive in the only run of the game.

On Friday, July eighteenth, in St. Louis Gordon hit his fourteenth home run. But a grand slam by Cardinal third baseman Billy Johnson lifted St. Louis to a seven to two win. On Saturday, Wilson hurled a five hitter. Dittmer drove in five runs with a homer, double in a single. The Braves won their only game of the series, six to two. Mathews hit his fifteenth home run in the series finale on Sunday. However, the Cardinals pounded out fourteen hits off Spahn, winning the rubber game, eight to four. Despite the loss, the seven and four road trip was the Braves most successful one of the year.

Back home at Braves Field on Tuesday, July twenty-second, Boston defeated visiting Chicago, six to four. Sisti hit a two-run double in the fifth, and singled home the go-ahead run an inning later. The Cubs won the second game, six to two. On Thursday July twenty fourth, the Braves won, three to one. Wilson picked up his tenth victory. Mathews hit his sixteenth home run. Gordon hit his fifteenth. The attendance was only 1691. The Braves, now twenty-six and twenty-nine under Grimm, had clearly improved on the field. However, they were still struggling badly at the gate.

On Friday, July twenty-fifth, the Pirates broke a six game losing streak, beating the Braves for the first time since early June, three to two. Mathews injured his right knee sliding into third base. He was forced out of the line-up for four days. Gordon hit a two-run homer for Boston on Saturday, tying Mathews for the club lead. But Pittsburgh won again, six to four.

In the opener of Sunday doubleheader on July twenty-seventh, Bickford won his fifth straight, defeating the Pirates, five to two. Daniels hit his first major league home run, sparking a three-run outburst in the fifth inning. The second game was suspended because of darkness with the score tied at three all in the eleventh. It was scheduled to be completed on September twelfth.

It took the surging Cardinals, fresh from a four game sweep of the Dodgers at Ebbets Field, thirteen innings to trip Boston, six to five, on Tuesday night. Sisti batted in two runs for the Braves. But with the bases loaded, and two out, in the thirteenth, he bobbled a slow roller down the third base line, allowing the winning run to score.

Spahn defeated the Cardinals, two to one, on Wednesday night. Mathews celebrated his return to the lineup with his seventeenth homer, a tremendous blast over the center field wall with Logan on board in the fourth. Musial's fourteenth homer in the sixth accounted for the only run off Spahn.

Jethroe hit his ninth homer on Thursday, July thirty-first. But Boston lost, eight to three, to the Cardinals. Twelve of thirteen Braves' hits were singles. They left thirteen runners on base. The team finished July with fourteen wins and thirteen losses. It was their only winning month of the season. They had climbed into fifth place, ahead of Chicago and Pittsburgh. They were twenty-three games back of first place Brooklyn.

AUGUST

August did not begin well. On the first of the month Surkont battled Raffensberger of the Reds for eight scoreless innings at Braves field. But he threw two wild pitches in the ninth, allowing two unearned runs to score.

The Reds won again on Saturday, eight to three. In the opener of a doubleheader on Sunday, Spahn won seven to four. Right hander Bubba Church shut out Boston, four to nothing, in the second game. The split left Boston tied with the Reds for fifth place.

Then after two days of rain, Boston could not turn to Spahn again, or to long gone Johnny Sain. Philadelphia swept both ends of a doubleheader on Thursday, August seventh. Vern Bickford was the hard luck loser in the opener. Roberts won his seventeenth for the Phillies in the opener, two to one. Cooper's single second inning single was the only Boston hit until Crowe doubled in the eighth. Torgeson followed with a single driving in the only Boston run. Bickford was the hard luck loser. In the second game, Gordon hit his seventeenth homer matching Mathews total again. Philadelphia won easily, ten to two.

BRAVES SWEEP DEFENDING CHAMPS

Boston finished the home stand with an impressive sweep of the defending National League Champion Giants. Surkont and Spahn shut out New York, back-to-back, by identical two to nothing scores. On Friday night, August eighth, Surkont was honored by his hometown of Pawtucket, Rhode Island. He needed only one hour and forty-four minutes to complete a four hit shutout. Jethroe opened the game with a single. He legged it to second when New York left fielder Jim Rhodes momentarily bobbled the ball, and went to third on an infield out. He scored on the first of three singles by ex Giant Thorpe. Spahn struck out ten batters on Saturday. Gordon singled in the second, and scored the Braves first run on an infield hit by Sisti. Logan began the sixth inning with a double, and scored on Thorpe's single to right.

After still another rain out, the Braves out slugged the fading Giants in the opener of a doubleheader on Monday, winning eleven to ten. Gordon hit a three-run homer in the second inning. Torgeson hit a two-run homer in a three- run third. After New York scored four times in the top of the eighth to take a ten to seven lead, Dittmer hit a two-run homer in the bottom of the inning, bringing Boston within a run. Mathews followed with a walk. Jethroe tripled him home with the tying run. Then Thorpe, continuing his hot hitting against his former team, lined a single off the pitcher's glove, driving in the go-ahead run. Grimm called his ace, Spahn, in a relief role. The left hander retired the side in order in the top of the ninth.

In the second game, the Braves scored two runs in the first. They were never headed. Burdette was the winner, four to two. Jethroe hit his tenth homer in the fifth inning. He had two of just four Boston hits, scoring three of the four Braves' runs. Although Thorpe was held hitless, he drove in a run in the first inning with a sacrifice fly.

None of the games with the Giants drew more than 5000 fans. The Braves closed the longest home stand of the year with nine victories and ten defeats.

The Braves began their last extended road trip in Philadelphia on Wednesday, August thirteenth. Bickford fractured the middle finger of his pitching hand, attempting to field a smash off the bat of Phillies' third baseman Willie Jones in the fourth inning of the first game of a doubleheader. However, he pitched six complete innings before leaving, giving up only two runs. But Philadelphia's Karl Drews hurled his fifth shutout of the season, winning three to nothing, ending the Braves' winning streak at four games. Jethroe homered twice, doubled, walked twice, stole a base, and drove in four runs in the second game. Mathews hit his eighteenth home run, pulling even with Gordon. Boston won, nine to three. Philadelphia won the Thursday afternoon getaway game, five to three. Jethroe had three more hits.

In New York on Friday, August fifteenth, the Braves played their fifth doubleheader in two weeks. In the opener Boston defeated the Giants for the fifth straight time, four to three. Having personally defeated Boston twelve straight times, New York starter Larry Jansen retired the first twenty-two batters he faced. But Gordon singled with one out in the eighth to end the no-hit bid. He later scored on a single by Daniels. Leading two to one, the Giants fumbled away the game in the ninth inning, allowing three unearned Boston runs. After Logan singled, third baseman Hank Thompson booted Torgeson's bunt. Cooper forced Logan at third. Gordon walked. Then, with the bases loaded, first baseman Whitey Lockman made a diving grab of Mathews smash down the right field line. But Jansen bobbled the throw to first for an error. Torgeson scored to tie the game. Daniels singled off first baseman Lockman's glove to drive in the go-ahead run. A sacrifice fly by Dittmer scored the final Boston run. New York won the second game, three to one.

MORE DOUBLEHEADERS—DUROCHER PROTEST

After Saturday's game was rained out, the two clubs played their second doubleheader of the series. It was the third in seven days for the Giants and Braves. It was Boston's fourth doubleheader of the week. Gordon doubled in the second inning of the first game. He hit a three-run homer in the fifth, leading Boston to a seven to three win. Durocher was ejected in the ninth inning after rubbing the gloss off a ball before handing it to reliever Hal Gregg. After a lengthy argument, Durocher charged third base Umpire Augie Donatelli. He was restrained by Boston manager Grimm who had come out of the dugout to find out what was going on. In the sixth inning home plate Umpire Lee Ballanfant ruled a sliding Bobby Thomson out on a play at third. That call set the stage for the ninth inning confrontation. The second game was called after eight innings because of darkness. The Giants won, four to two.

On Tuesday, August nineteenth in St. Louis, the Cardinals won, seven to five. On Wednesday night, Cardinal lefty Harvey Haddix won, nine to two, in his major league debut. Torgeson homered. He had three of the five Braves' hits.

SPAHN HOLDS ON TO NL STRIKE OUT LEAD

On Thursday night, in a battle for the National League strikeout lead, the Cardinals' Wilmer "Vinegar Bend" Mizell struck out nine. Spahn failed to strikeout a batter. But his season total of 138 was still nineteen ahead of Mizell's total. Gordon hit his twentieth home run in the first inning. But the Cardinals won their seventh straight, three to two.

The Braves were more respectable for the remainder of the road trip. After sweeping two from the Cubs in Chicago, The Braves lost the first game of a doubleheader in Pittsburgh on Sunday, August twenty-fourth, four to three. Pittsburgh third baseman Sonny Senerchia hit his first major league home run in the bottom of the ninth. Rookie Ron Necciai, who won in his major league debut, beaned Daniels in the third. The Braves' outfielder left the game on a stretcher. X-rays proved negative. The Braves took advantage of six Pirates errors in the second game, winning five to three in ten innings.

On Tuesday, August twenty-sixth at Crosley Field, Spahn shut out the Reds, two to nothing. The Braves moved past Cincinnati in the standings, into sixth place. Gordon hit his twenty first home run. The Braves won again on Wednesday night, twelve to seven in ten innings. Mathews hit his nineteenth home run. But in the Braves' final appearance in Cincinnati on Thursday night, the Reds won, five to four, in eleven innings. Cooper's two-run single in the ninth tied the score. But shortstop Roy McMillan singled home the game winner for the Reds in the eleventh.

The Braves returned to Boston to play three consecutive doubleheaders without an off day. Philadelphia swept a doubleheader on Saturday, August thirtieth, four to two and eight to six. Virgil Jester pitched a four hit, one to nothing, shutout in the opening game on Sunday, August thirty-first. He also singled home the only run of the game in the bottom of the ninth inning. But Philadelphia's Jim Konstanty bettered Jester's effort in the second game, pitching a three hit shutout, and doubling home the only two runs of the game in the top of the ninth. The Phillies won, two to nothing. It was the Braves' ninth doubleheader of the month. They were in seventh place again, twenty-nine games out of first.

SEPTEMBER

On September first, the New York Giants played their last two games ever at Braves Field. The Giants won the first game, three to one. But Jethroe reached on a bunt single to start the second game, and scored on Logan's double. Gordon then singled home Logan. That was all the Braves needed. Johnson held the Giants, winning five to one.

Thankfully for the Braves, there was only a single game scheduled for September third, even if it was against the Dodgers. Gordon and Mathews hit back-to-back home runs in the second inning, and Boston added three more runs in the third. Unaccustomed to trailing the

Braves, Brooklyn scored five runs in the top of the fourth to tie the game. Jackie Robinson reached when Dittmer bobbled his grounder to second to open the eighth. He ended up on third, and scored a Snider's sacrifice bunt, giving Brooklyn the lead. But Gordon and Mathews singled to start the Braves' half of the ninth inning. Daniels' sacrifice bunt moved the runners up. Dittmer was walked intentionally, and pinch hitter Spahn struck out. With two out, Jethroe swung at a three and one pitch that looked high, and hit a harmless fly to Furillo in short right field, ending the game. Brooklyn won again, six to five.

GRIMM–ACE

"I gave Sam the take sign on that pitch," said an angry Grimm. "The ball was even with his eyes. If he had taken it, the tying run would have been forced in. Even a little leaguer wouldn't pull one like that."

BRAVES FINALLY BEAT THE DODGERS

After thirteen consecutive losses, Boston finally beat the Dodgers on Thursday, September fourth, six to five. But it took eleven innings. Surkont's pitched his tenth complete game of the season. The Braves scored an unearned run in the first inning, but the Dodgers moved ahead three to won with two runs in the top of the third inning. Gordon's two-run single tied the game in the bottom of the third. The Braves took the lead again with two runs in the sixth.

But Reese singled home two Dodger runs in the seventh to tie the score again. With one out in the eleventh, Logan was hit by a pitch. Campanella was ejected by Umpire Frank Secory for protesting that the ball hat hit Logan's bat. Torgeson's singled, and Cooper hit a sacrifice fly, moving Logan to third. Gordon then singled to center to give the Braves the over due victory. It was only the third loss of the year for Dodger starter Joe Black, National League Rookie of the Year.

Amazingly, the Braves made it two straight over the Dodgers, winning again on Friday, three to one. Wilson allowed just six hits. He singled to open the third inning, and scored the first run of the game. Wilson singled again to open the seventh inning but was forced out at second when Jethroe hit an infield grounder. Jethroe then stole second base. He later scored on a sacrifice fly by Logan. Less than 3000 fans watched the final game of the series. Nevertheless, the long awaited victories over the Dodgers were immensely satisfying to the players.

LONGEST NL GAME OF THE YEAR

On Saturday afternoon, September sixth, the Braves played their third doubleheader against the Phillies in eight days. Philadelphia won the first game, seven to six, in seventeen innings. The three hour and fifty minute contest was the longest of the year in the National League. It ended when Del Ennis homered to lead off the bottom of the seventeenth. Roberts pitched all seventeen innings, despite giving up eighteen hits. Bob Chipman pitched brilliantly in seven innings of relief. He allowed just one hit. Mathews hit his twenty-first homer with two on in the top of the eighth to give the Braves a six to two lead. But the Phillies scored four times in the bottom of the inning. The second game was mercifully suspended at midnight in compliance with the Pennsylvania curfew law with the Braves leading, three to one.

When play resumed on Sunday afternoon Burdette protected that lead for the final one and two-thirds innings, sealing the Boston victory. He pitched all nine innings of the regularly scheduled game as well, but lost, two to one. It was the Braves' final appearance at Shibe Park in Philadelphia.

On September ninth, Boston returned to Braves Field for the last time. In the first game of a series opening doubleheader Spahn shut out the Reds, one to nothing. Consecutive singles by Jethroe, Logan, and Torgeson with two out in the fifth accounted for the only run of the game. In the second game Ted Kluzewski's two-run double in the tenth defeated the Braves, six to five. Gordon hit his twenty-third homer.

SIXTEEN TO NOTHING

On Friday, September twelfth, Ralph Kiner's thirty-fifth and thirty-sixth home runs of the year powered the Pirates to an eight to one victory over in the first game of another doubleheader. But the Braves routed the Pirates, sixteen to nothing, in the second game collecting fifteen hits. The sixteen runs, and fifteen hits, were both season highs.

Backed by a six run outburst in the first inning Spahn shut out the Pirates on Saturday, eight to nothing. He recorded thirteen strikeouts upping his league-leading total to 170. Gordon hit his twenty-fourth homer, three more than Mathews.

LAST HOME VICTORY—SHORTEST NL GAME

But Mathews hit his twenty second homer in the bottom of the ninth inning on Sunday, September fourteenth. Surkont shut out Chicago, one to nothing in the first game of a doubleheader. It was the second time during the year that Spahn and Surkont hurled back-to-back shutouts. Though witnessed by just 3482 fans, it was the last home victory for the Boston Braves. It was also the shortest game of the season in the National League, lasting just one hour and twenty-five minutes. With just a week in between the Braves thus participated in both the longest and shortest games of the season in the National League. From the All-Star break until their final home victory, the Braves played .500 baseball, posting thirty-three wins and thirty-three defeats. Braves' pitching had not given up a run in thirty-seven and one-third innings.

THE LONGEST LOSING STREAK

However, Boston dropped the second game of the doubleheader against Chicago, three to two in ten innings. Gordon hit his twenty-fifth and final home run of the season. But the loss triggered a ten game losing streak, the Braves' longest of year. There were five home and six road games left on the schedule. The Braves, however, could manage only one more victory.

On Tuesday night, September sixteenth the Cardinals subdued Boston twice, eight to six, and five to one. Then, the final home season ended as it began, with a series sweep, by the Dodgers, in the cold and rain. Brooklyn won the rain shortened opener of a doubleheader on September nineteenth, four to two. Boston`s only two hits came in the fourth inning. Mathews singled and Cooper followed with a home run to tie the game. The Dodgers scored two runs in the top of the eighth, taking a four to two lead. With two out in the bottom of the inning, Jethroe swung at a two and one pitch from Joe Black. He grounded out. The Umpires were forced to halt play. Had the game been called before Jethroe's ground out, the Dodgers' runs in the top of the inning wouldn't have counted.

SPAHN PICKS OFF REESE

All 6038 fans saw Spahn's determined bid for his fifteenth win on Saturday afternoon. He pitched all ten innings but the Dodgers won, one to nothing. He walked shortstop Pee Wee Reese to open the game, then picked him off first base. It was the first time all season that anyone had caught the "Little Colonel". Jackie Robinson's fourth hit of the game in the tenth inning drove in the only run of the game. It was Robinson's five hundredth career RBI.

THE END

8822 watched the final game at Braves Field on Sunday, September twenty-first, 1952. But many of those were pulling for the Dodgers. After Logan singled in the fourth inning, Mathews doubled into the right field corner. Furillo over threw the cut off man. Both runners scored. Those were the last two runs ever scored by the Braves in Boston. Logan's second hit, a single in the sixth inning, was the final Boston hit. But Brooklyn scored six times with two out in the eighth inning. When Joe Black retired Logan, Mathews, and Cooper in order in the ninth, Brooklyn had an eight to two victory. The Braves' business in Boston was complete.

The Braves finished the season with a six game New York road swing. Boston lost the opener of a doubleheader at the Polo Grounds on Wednesday, September twenty-fourth, eleven to eight. The Giants battered Spahn in the second game, handing him his nineteenth and final defeat of the season, eight to two. On Thursday night, in the Braves' last appearance at the Polo Grounds, the Giants won again, three to two.

The final series against he League Champion-elect Dodgers in Brooklyn was mostly ceremonial for Brooklyn. Before the game on Friday, September twenty-sixth, there was a big contingent of photographers, and writers, around the home team dugout. But sportscaster Dizzy Dean went to the Boston dugout. He congratulated manager Grimm. "You've done a great job," he said. "But I don't see any camera group around here." "I'll tell ya, Diz," said Grimm, "we had all our pictures taken at spring training." Only 1440 saw the Dodgers win, eight to four.

BRAVES' LAST WIN

The Braves finally stopped their longest losing streak at ten games on Saturday, September twenty-seventh, defeating the Dodgers for their final victory ever, eleven to three. Mathews provided Boston fans with one final season highlight blasting three home runs to tie Gordon for the team home run lead. 4903 fans at Ebbets Field gave the future Hall of Famer a standing ovation when he came to bat for the last time. But he struck out.

On September twenty-eighth, the Braves finished their seventy seventh, and final, campaign as Boston's National League representatives. Johnson was the starter for the Braves. The game ended tied at five, called after twelve innings because of darkness. Boston scored three times in second on singles by Burris, Daniels, and Dittmer. A two out double by Mathews in the top of the ninth inning scored Logan with the final Boston run ever. That tied the game. Burdette, however, walked third baseman Bobby Morgan to open the final inning. Morgan advanced to second on a sacrifice. There were two out. Tommy Holmes, appropriately, was the final batter ever against his former team. He bounced back to Burdette, who caught Morgan in a run down, for the final out. Then the umpires decided it was too dark to play anymore. Torgeson, who along with Spahn led the team in length of service, had three hits, and scored a run.

The Braves finished in seventh place, thirty-two games back, twenty-two games ahead of last place Pittsburgh. But there were, significant individual accomplishments during the 1952 season. On offense, Mathews and Gordon finished the year among the league leaders in home runs. Gordon led the team with a .289 batting average. The speedy Jethroe led the team again in stolen bases with twenty-eight, although bothered by a leg injury, and illness, for much of the season.

Spahn, a seven-year veteran, led the Majors for the third straight year with a career high 183 strikeouts. Despite suffering through his first losing season, he had fourteen wins and five shutouts. Surkont and Wilson were both twelve games winners.

Amazingly, the Braves played in eighteen extra inning games. They won seven. And, mostly due to bad weather, they played twenty-seven doubleheaders, sweeping four, splitting sixteen, and losing seven.

At season's end Perini lamented losses of more than one million dollars in the last two years of his tenure in Boston. But he, and his brothers, were eagerly buying out the remaining "Little Shovels", and other shareholders. He had no intention of selling the franchise, though he didn't intend to stay in Boston. Of the six franchises to abandon their city of origin after more than half a century, the Braves had the highest attendance five years prior to their departure. They also had the lowest attendance in their last year in the city. The decline was the most precipitous.

Braves Field, now Nickerson Field most recently served as the football arena for Boston University. But only the right field pavilion remains from the original park. And BU recently canceled its football program. The scoreboard, originally constructed in 1948 by the C.I. Brink Company at a cost of $70,000, was moved to Municipal Stadium in Kansas City as part of stadium upgrade done there to attract a major league team.

The transfer of the franchise marked Major League Baseball's entrance into the complex age of television, rapidly improving mass communication, and improving public transportation.

In itself, the transfer of the struggling franchise had little impact on the game. But the Braves' subsequent financial success in Milwaukee had huge repercussions. It perhaps marked the loss of innocence. Certainly, big league baseball was now undeniably big business as well. *To quote historian* Arthur M. Schlesinger, "pro baseball died the day the braves moved out of Boston."

THE 1952 BOSTON BRAVES

DAY	DATE	OPPONENT	RESULT	SCORE	PITCHER	ATTENDANCE	RECORD
TUES	04/15/52	BROOKLYN	L	3-2	WARREN SPAHN (0-1)	4694	0-1
WED	04/16/52	BROOKLYN	L	14-8	MAX SURKONT (0-1)	5646	0-2
THUR	04/17/52	BROOKLYN	L	8-2	GENE CONLEY (0-1)	4042	0-3
FRI	04/18/52	AT PHILADELPHIA	W	3-2	LEW BURDETTE (1-0)	15911	1-3
SAT	04/19/52	AT PHILADELPHIA	W	9-7	BERT THIEL (1-0)	9466	2-3
SUN	04/20/52	AT PHILADELPHIA	L	4-3(10)	LEW BURDETTE (1-1)	26011	2-4
SUN	04/20/52	AT PHILADELPHIA	W	2-1	DAVE COLE (1-0)	26011	3-4
TUES	04/22/52	AT BROOKLYN	L	2-1	BERT THIEL (1-1)	25002	3-5
TUES	04/22/52	AT BROOKLYN	L	3-1	JIM WILSON (0-1)	25002	3-6
WED	04/23/52	AT NEW YORK	L	9-5	GENE CONLEY (0-2)	4611	3-7
THUR	04/24/52	AT NEW YORK	W	6-3(10)	LEW BURDETTE (2-1)	4733	4-7
FRI	04/25/52	PHILADELPHIA	RAIN				
SAT	04/26/52	PHILADELPHIA	L	8-0	VERN BICKFORD (0-1)	1893	4-8
SUN	04/27/52	PHILADELPHIA	RAIN				
TUES	04/29/52	AT PITTSBURGH	W	5-1	WARREN SPAHN (1-1)	10008	5-8
WED	04/30/52	AT PITTSBURGH	L	11-5	DAVE COLE (1-1)	2861	5-9
THUR	05/01/52	AT CINCINNATI	L	7-6	VERN BICKFORD (0-2)	2497	5-10
FRI	05/02/52	AT CINCINNATI	W	2-1	JIM WILSON (1-1)	11050	6-10
SAT	05/03/52	AT CINCINNATI	L	8-1	GENE CONLEY (0-3)	3682	6-11
SUN	05/04/52	AT ST LOUIS	L	4-3	WARREN SPAHN (1-2)	19141	6-12
SUN	05/04/52	AT ST LOUIS	W	5-1	MAX SURKONT (1-1)	19141	7-12
TUES	05/06/52	AT CHICAGO	L	2-0	VERN BICKFORD (0-3)	5490	7-13
WED	05/07/52	AT CHICAGO	COLD				
THUR	05/08/52	AT CHICAGO	W	6-4	JIM WILSON (2-1)	2048	8-13
SAT	05/10/52	NEW YORK	L	4-2	WARREN SPAHN (1-3)	5946	8-14
SUN	05/11/52	NEW YORK	RAIN				
TUES	05/13/52	PITTSBURGH	W	3-1	VERN BICKFORD (1-3)	2831	9-14
WED	05/14/52	PITTSBURGH	W	4-3(10)	MAX SURKONT (2-1)	1105	10-14
THUR	05/15/52	ST LOUIS	COLD				
FRI	05/16/52	ST LOUIS	W	8-3	WARREN SPAHN (2-3)	7498	11-14
SAT	05/17/52	ST LOUIS	L	5-4	JIM WILSON (2-2)	5468	11-15
SUN	05/18/52	CINCINNATI	RAIN				
TUES	05/20/52	CHICAGO	RAIN				
WED	05/21/52	CHICAGO	RAIN				
THUR	05/22/52	CHICAGO	L	3-0	VERN BICKFORD (1-4)	2544	11-16
THUR	05/22/52	CHICAGO	W	5-0	WARREN SPAHN (3-3))	2544	12-16
FRI	05/23/52	AT NEW YORK	L	5-3	MAX SURKONT (2-2)	24812	12-17
SAT	05/24/52	AT NEW YORK	L	5-4	JIM WILSON (2-3)	13387	12-18
SUN	05/25/52	AT NEW YORK	RAIN				
MON	05/26/52	AT PHILADELPHIA	RAIN				
TUES	05/27/52	AT PHILADELPHIA	W	4-2(12)	WARREN SPAHN (4-3)	27225	13-18
TUES	05/27/52	AT PHILADELPHIA	L	5-4(10)	SHELDON JONES (0-1)	27225	13-19
THUR	05/29/52	AT BROOKLYN	L	7-3	MAX SURKONT (2-3)	5008	13-20
FRI	05/30/52	AT BROOKLYN	L	5-4	JIM WILSON (2-4)	30703	13-21
FRI	05/30/52	AT BROOKLYN	L	11-2	DICK DONOVAN (0-1)	30703	13-22
SAT	05/31/52	NO GAME		HOLMES	FIRED-GRIMM HIRED MNGR		
SUN	06/01/52	AT CINCINNATI	L	1-0	VERN BICKFORD (1-5)	10614	13-23
SUN	06/01/52	AT CINCINNATI	W	9-4	WARREN SPAHN (5-3)	10614	14-23
MON	06/02/52	AT CINCINNATI	W	4-1	MAX SURKONT (3-3)	4919	15-23
TUES	06/03/52	AT ST LOUIS	W	3-2	JIM WILSON (3-4)	6677	16-23
WED	06/04/52	AT ST LOUIS	L	6-0	DICK DONOVAN (0-2)	6732	16-24
THUR	06/05/52	AT ST LOUIS	W	8-3	WARREN SPAHN (6-3)	4974	17-24
FRI	06/06/52	AT CHICAGO	L	7-2	VERN BICKFORD(1-6)	7572	17-25
SAT	06/07/52	AT CHICAGO	L	9-3	MAX SURKONT (3-4)	18131	17-26
SUN	06/08/52	AT CHICAGO	L	7-5	JIM WILSON (3-5)	38514	17-27
SUN	06/08/52	AT CHICAGO	W	7-6	ERNIE JOHNSON (1-0)	38514	18-27
MON	06/09/52	AT PITTSBURGH	W	3-2	JIM WILSON (4-5)	6973	19-27
TUES	06/10/52	AT PITTSBURGH	L	7-5	WARREN SPAHN (6-4)	10934	19-28

TWILIGHT TEAMS

DAY	DATE	OPPONENT	RESULT	SCORE	PITCHER	ATTENDANCE	RECORD
WED	06/11/52	AT PITTSBURGH	L	5-0	MAX SURKONT (3-5)	9415	19-29
THUR	06/12/52	AT PITTSBURGH	W	11-2	LEW BURDETTE (3-1)	3223	20-29
FRI	06/13/52	CHICAGO	L	5-0	VERN BICKFORD (1-7)	4976	20-30
SAT	06/14/52	CHICAGO	L	3-1	WARREN SPAHN (6-5)	3053	20-31
SUN	06/15/52	CHICAGO	W	4-1	JIM WILSON (5-5)	9100	21-31
SUN	06/15/52	CHICAGO	W	2-0	MAX SURKONT (4-5)	9100	22-31
TUES	06/17/52	CINCINNATI	W	5-1	VERN BICKFORD (2-7)	6455	23-31
TUES	06/17/52	CINCINNATI	RAIN				
WED	06/18/52	CINCINNATI	L	7-6	VIRGIL JESTER (0-1)	6197	23-32
WED	06/18/52	CINCINNATI	L	3-1	WARREN SPAHN (6-6)	6197	23-33
THUR	06/19/52	CINCINNATI	L	7-4	SHELDON JONES (0-2)	2198	23-34
FRI	06/20/52	ST LOUIS	W	12-7	JIM WILSON (6-5)	6458	24-34
SAT	06/21/52	ST LOUIS	L	9-0	MAX SURKONT (4-6)	3479	24-35
SUN	06/22/52	ST LOUIS	L	7-2	LEW BURDETTE (3-2)	10026	24-36
SUN	06/22/52	ST LOUIS	L	7-2	WARREN SPAHN (6-7)	10026	24-37
MON	06/23/52	PITTSBURGH	W	9-3	ERNIE JOHNSON (2-0)	2654	25-37
TUES	06/24/52	PITTSBURGH	W	4-3	JIM WILSON (7-5)	3736	26-37
WED	06/25/52	PITTSBURGH	W	5-2	MAX SURKONT (5-6)	1414	27-37
FRI	06/27/52	AT BROOKLYN	L	8-3	VERN BICKFORD (2-8)	16619	27-38
SAT	06/28/52	AT BROOKLYN	L	4-2	WARREN SPAHN (6-8)	17862	27-39
SUN	06/29/52	AT BROOKLYN	L	6-5	LEW BURDETTE (3-3)	16630	27-40
MON	06/30/52	NEW YORK	L	8-7	MAX SURKONT (5-7)	9010	27-41
MON	06/30/52	NEW YORK	L	4-0	VERN BICKFORD (2-9)	9010	27-42
TUES	07/01/52	NEW YORK	L	6-3	SHELDON JONES (0-3)	5442	27-43
WED	07/02/52	NEW YORK	W	2-1	WARREN SPAHN (7-8)	1923	28-43
THUR	07/03/52	PHILADELPHIA	L	2-0	JIM WILSON (7-6)	1232	28-44
FRI	07/04/52	PHILADELPHIA	W	2-1(11)	LEW BURDETTE (4-3)	7610	29-44
FRI	07/04/52	PHILADELPHIA	W	3-2	VERN BICKFORD (3-9)	7610	30-44
SAT	07/05/52	BROOKLYN	L	5-3	ERNIE JOHNSON (2-1)	13405	30-45
SUN	07/06/52	BROOKLYN	L	8-2	WARREN SPAHN (7-9)	7218	30-46
TUES	07/08/52	ALL-STAR GAME AT PHILADELPHIA					
THUR	07/10/52	AT CINCINNATI	L	5-3	JIM WILSON (7-7)	9530	30-47
FRI	07/11/52	AT CINCINNATI	W	6-1	WARREN SPAHN (8-9)	1771	31-47
SAT	07/12/52	AT PITTSBURGH	W	5-2	VERN BICKFORD (4-9)	4999	32-47
SUN	07/13/52	AT PITTSBURGH	W	4-2	MAX SURKONT (6-7)	12373	33-47
SUN	07/13/52	AT PITTSBURGH	W	2-1	VIRGIL JESTER (1-1)	12373	34-47
TUES	07/15/52	AT CHICAGO	W	10-3	JIM WILSON (8-7)	6694	35-47
WED	07/16/52	AT CHICAGO	L	3-2(13)	LEW BURDETTE (4-4)	6899	35-48
THUR	07/17/52	AT CHICAGO	W	1-0	VERN BICKFORD (5-9)	5963	36-48
FRI	07/18/52	AT ST LOUIS	L	7-2	MAX SURKONT (6-8)	8535	36-49
SAT	07/19/52	AT ST LOUIS	W	6-2	JIM WILSON (9-7)	12833	37-49
SUN	07/20/52	AT ST LOUIS	L	8-4	WARREN SPAHN (8-10)	12363	37-50
TUES	07/22/52	CHICAGO	W	6-4	VERN BICKFORD (6-9)	5280	38-50
WED	07/23/52	CHICAGO	L	6-2	MAX SURKONT (6-9)	4308	38-51
THUR	07/24/52	CHICAGO	W	3-1	JIM WILSON (10-7)	1691	39-51
FRI	07/25/52	PITTSBURGH	L	3-2	WARREN SPAHN (8-11)	4126	39-52
THUR	07/26/52	PITTSBURGH	L	6-4	VIRGIL JESTER (1-2)	2006	39-53
SUN	07/27/52	PITTSBURGH	W	5-2	VERN BICKFORD (7-9)	3719	40-53
SUN	07/27/52	PITTSBURGH	SUSP	3-3 DARK		3719	
TUES	07/29/52	ST LOUIS	L	6-5(13)	LEW BURDETTE (4-5)	6360	40-54
WED	07/30/52	ST LOUIS	W	2-1	WARREN SPAHN (9-11)	5514	41-54
THUR	07/31/52	ST LOUIS	L	8-3	VERN BICKFORD (7-10)	2543	41-55
FRI	08/01/52	CINCINNATI	L	2-0	MAX SURKONT (6-10)	4081	41-56
SAT	08/02/52	CINCINNATI	L	8-3	JIM WILSON (10-8)	1567	41-57
SUN	08/03/52	CINCINNATI	W	7-4	WARREN SPAHN (10-11)	6091	42-57
SUN	08/03/52	CINCINNATI	L	4-0	VIRGIL JESTER (1-3)	6091	42-58
TUES	08/05/52	PHILADELPHIA	RAIN				
WED	08/06/52	PHILADELPHIA	RAIN				

THE 1952 BOSTON BRAVES

DAY	DATE	OPPONENT	RESULT	SCORE	PITCHER	ATTENDANCE	RECORD
FRI	08/08/52	NEW YORK	W	2-0	MAX SURKONT (7-10)	4151	43-60
SAT	08/09/52	NEW YORK	W	2-0	WARREN SPAHN (11-11)	3553	44-60
SUN	08/10/52	NEW YORK	RAIN				
MON	08/11/52	NEW YORK	W	11-10	BOB CHIPMAN (1-0)	3463	45-60
MON	08/11/52	NEW YORK	W	4-2	LEW BURDETTE (5-5)	3463	46-60
TUES	08/12/52	AT PHILADELPHIA	RAIN				
WED	08/13/52	AT PHILADELPHIA	L	3-0	VERN BICKFORD (7-12)	11280	46-61
WED	08/13/52	AT PHILADELPHIA	W	9-3	MAX SURKONT (8-10)	11280	47-61
THUR	08/14/52	AT PHILADELPHIA	L	5-3	WARREN SPAHN (11-12)	3391	47-62
FRI	08/15/52	AT NEW YORK	W	4-3	ERNIE JOHNSON (3-1)	13969	48-62
FRI	08/15/52	AT NEW YORK	L	3-1	LEW BURDETTE (5-6)	13969	48-63
SAT	08/16/52	AT NEW YORK	RAIN				
SUN	08/17/52	AT NEW YORK	W	7-3	MAX SURKONT (9-10)	22918	49-63
SUN	08/17/52	AT NEW YORK	L	4-2	WARREN SPAHN (11-13)	22918	49-64
TUES	08/19/52	AT ST LOUIS	L	7-5	JIM WILSON (10-10)	10403	49-65
WED	08/20/52	AT ST LOUIS	L	9-2(7)	LEW BURDETTE (5-7)	8779	49-66
THUR	08/21/52	AT ST LOUIS	L	3-2	WARREN SPAHN (11-14)	7826	49-67
FRI	08/22/52	AT CHICAGO	W	4-3	MAX SURKONT (10-10)	7883	50-67
SAT	08/23/52	AT CHICAGO	W	2-1	JIM WILSON (11-10)	13702	51-67
SUN	08/24/52	AT PITTSBURGH	L	4-3	VIRGIL JESTER (1-4)	12349	51-68
SUN	08/24/52	AT PITTSBURGH	W	(5-3)10	LEW BURDETTE (6-7)	12349	52-68
TUES	08/26/52	AT CINCINNATI	W	2-0	WARREN SPAHN (12-14)	4779	53-68
WED	08/27/52	AT CINCINNATI	W	12-7(10)	SHELDON JONES (1-3)	6066	54-68
THUR	08/28/52	AT CINCINNATI	L	5-4(11)	SHELDON JONES (1-4)	2346	54-69
SAT	08/30/52	PHILADELPHIA	L	4-2	LEW BURDETTE (6-8)	5277	54-70
SAT	08/30/52	PHILADELPHIA	L	8-6	WARREN SPAHN (12-15)	5277	54-71
SUN	08/31/52	PHILADELPHIA	W	1-0	VIRGIL JESTER (2-4)	6920	55-71
SUN	08/31/52	PHILADELPHIA	L	4-0	MAX SURKONT (10-11)	6920	55-72
MON	09/01/52	NEW YORK	L	3-1	JIM WILSON (11-11)	7253	55-73
MON	09/01/52	NEW YORK	W	5-1	ERNIE JOHNSON (4-1)	7253	56-73
WED	09/03/52	BROOKLYN	L	6-5	WARREN SPAHN (12-16)	6756	56-74
THUR	09/04/52	BROOKLYN	W	6-5(11)	MAX SURKONT (11-11)	6280	57-74
FRI	09/05/52	BROOKLYN	W	3-1	JIM WILSON (12-11)	2749	58-74
SAT	09/06/52	AT PHILADELPHIA	L	7-6(17)	BOB CHIPMAN (1-1)	12474	58-75
SAT	09/06/52	AT PHILADELPHIA	SUSP	3-1 DARK	7TH INNING	12474	
SUN	09/07/52	AT PHILADELPHIA	W	3-1	ERNIE JOHNSON (5-1)	6011	59-75
SUN	09/07/52	AT PHILADELPHIA	L	2-1	LEW BURDETTE (6-9)	6011	59-76
TUES	09/09/52	CINCINNATI	W	1-0	WARREN SPAHN (13-16)	3175	60-76
TUES	09/09/52	CINCINNATI	L	2-0	MAX SURKONT (11-12)	3175	60-77
WED	09/10/52	CINCINNATI	L	6-5(10)	LEW BURDETTE (6-10)	2147	60-78
FRI	09/12/52	PITTSBURGH	L	8-1	VIRGIL JESTER (2-5)	2608	60-79
FRI	09/12/52	PITTSBURGH	W	16-0	ERNIE JOHNSON (6-1)	2608	61-79
SAT	09/13/52	PITTSBURGH	W	8-0	WARREN SPAHN (14-16	1957	62-79
SUN	09/14/52	CHICAGO	W	1-0	MAX SURKONT (12-12)	3482	63-79
SUN	09/14/52	CHICAGO	L	3-2(10)	JIM WILSON (12-12)	3482	63-80
TUES	09/16/52	ST LOUIS	L	8-6	WARREN SPAHN (14-17)	5240	63-81
TUES	09/16/52	ST LOUIS	L	5-1	ERNIE JOHNSON (6-2)	5240	63-82
FRI	09/19/52	BROOKLYN	L	4-2(8)	MAX SURKONT (12-13)	2306	63-83
FRI	09/19/52	BROOKLYN	RAIN				
SAT	09/20/52	BROOKLYN	L	1-0(10)	WARREN SPAHN (14-18)	6038	63-84
SUN	09/21/52	BROOKLYN	L	8-2	JIM WILSON (12-13)	8822	63-85
TUES	09/23/52	AT NEW YORK	RAIN				
WED	09/24/52	AT NEW YORK	L	11-8	ERNIE JOHNSON (6-3)	3018	63-86
WED	09/24/52	AT NEW YORK	L	8-2	WARREN SPAHN (14-19)	3018	63-87
THUR	09/25/52	AT NEW YORK	L	3-2	LEW BURDETTE (6-11)	1269	63-88
FRI	09/26/52	AT BROOKLYN	L	8-4	JIM WILSON (12-14)	1440	63-89
SAT	09/27/52	AT BROOKLYN	W	11-3	VIRGIL JESTER (3-5)	4903	64-89
SUN	09/28/52	AT BROOKLYN	TIE	5-5(12)	JOHNSON-SPAHN-BURDETTE	9453	64-89

THE 1953 ST. LOUIS BROWNS

First in shoes. First in booze.
Last in the American League.

Send in the Clowns

Onward and upward, St. Louis Browns!
We who are faithful will never let you down.
You will arise to play another game.
And once again recapture your old fame.

Onward and upward, St. Louis Browns!
We, your fans, will never wear a frown.
And when we shout "Are you downhearted?
No, we're Brownhearted!" We really mean it.

So onward and upward, St. Louis Browns!
Oh, how we love you, St. Louis Browns!
We really do, St. Louis Browns.

The St. Louis Browns March
By Wall Heim

At the same time the Braves were preparing to open their first season in Milwaukee, the St. Louis Browns were opening their final one in St. Louis. Owner Bill Veeck was negotiating to move his own team to Milwaukee but was preempted

SPORTSMAN'S PARK, ST LOUIS

Bounded by Dodier Street, Grand Boulevard, Sullivan Avenue and Spring Avenue. Home of both the American League Browns and the National League Cardinals from April 23, 1902 until September 27, 1953 when the Browns moved to Baltimore. The Cardinals remained the sole tenants until May 8, 1966. (Photo from The National Baseball Library and Archive Collection, Cooperstown, New York.)

1953 ST. LOUIS BROWNS

Front row—*Dyck, Young, Hunter, Courtney, Veeck, president; Marion, manager; Scheffing, coach, Crandall, coach; Breechen, Kokos.* **Middle row**—*Spackman, assistant trainer; Edwards, Sievers, Cain, Pillette, Lenhardt, Kryhoski, Moss, Durney, traveling secretary; Bauman, trainer.* **Back row**—*Paige, Larsen, Kretlow, Blyzka, Wertz, Littlefield, Stuart, Turley, Groth, Stephens. Batboys Fischman and Kruger seated in front.* (Photo from The Sporting News Collection, St. Louis, Missouri.)

		Games at position	Bats	Avg.	
C	Clint Courtney	103	L	.251	
1B	Dick Kryhoski	88	L	.278	16 HR
2B	Bobby Young	148	L	.255	
SS	Billy Hunter	152	R	.219	
3B	Vern Stephens	46	R	.321	
3B	Bob Elliott	45	R	.250	
RF	Vic Wertz	121	L	.268	**19 HR 70 RBI**
CF	Johny Groth	141	R	.253	10 HR **5 Stolen Bases**
LF	Dick Kokos	83	L	.241	13 HR
OF/3B	Jim Dyck	55/51	R	.213	
OF/3B	Don Lenhardt	77/6	R	.317	10 HR
1B	Roy Sievers	76	R	.270	8 HR
C	Les Moss	71	R	.276	
OF	Hank Edwards	21	R	.198	
IF	Neil Berry	57	R	.283	
3B	Bob Elliott	48	R	.250	
IF	Willie Miranda	17	R	.167	
PH	Dixie Upright	9	L	.250	
3B	Johnny Lipon	7	R	.222	
C	Babe Martin	4	R	.000	
1B	Ed Mickelson	7	R	.133	
OF	Jim Pisoni	3	R	.083	
3B	Mary Marion	3	R	.000	
1B	Frank Kellert	2	R	.000	

PITCHERS

R	Don Larsen	38 W 7	L 12	4.16 ERA	
L	Dick Littlefield	36 W 7	L 12	5.08 ERA	
R	Duane Pillette	30 W 7	L 13	4.48 ERA	
R	Virgil Trucks	16 W 5	L 4	3.07 ERA	
L	Harry Brecheen	26 W 5	L13	3.07 ERA	
L	Bob Cain	32 W 4	L 10	6.23 ERA	
R	Bobo Holloman	22 W 3	L 7	5.23 ERA	
R	Mike Blyzka	33 W 2	L 6	6.39 ERA	
R	Bob Turley	10 W 2	L 6	3.28 ERA	
R	Lou Kretlow	22 W 1	L 5	5.11 ERA	
L	Max Lanier	10 W 0	L 1	7.25 ERA	
R	Hal White	10 W 0	L 0	2.61 ERA	
R	Bob Habenicht	1 W 0	L 0	5.40 ERA	

RELIEF PITCHERS

R	Marlin Stuart	60 W 8	L 2	3.94 ERA	7 Saves
R	Satchel Paige	57 W 3	L 9	3.53 ERA	**11 Saves**

MANAGER

Marty Marion		W 54 L 100

Bold Type—led club
* Led league

by the Braves. At a meeting in Tampa, Florida on March sixteenth, 1953, the American League refused to approve his second option, the transfer of the Browns to Baltimore by a vote of six to two. Only the owners of the Cleveland Indians and Chicago White Sox supported the move.

Veeck said cheerfully, "One thing I've found out is that there are a lot of Browns' fans in St. Louis. Now, if they'll come out to see us play we can do some good." He did not want to sell the ball club but told reporters, "I know that none of the other owners would be unhappy if I did sell," he said. His asking price was $2,400,000, but there were no significant offers from local businessmen.

Prior to the season Veeck had battled with fellow owners, refusing to sign the league's radio and television agreement. He wanted to force teams who televised home games to share the TV revenue with the visiting teams. He had the support of four other owners on the issue. The motion received a favorable, five to three, vote. But it required a three-quarter majority to pass. The New York Yankees, Boston Red Sox, and Cleveland Indians were in open opposition. In reprisal, each refused to schedule home night games against the Browns. Veeck reluctantly relented, signing the League broadcasting agreement. "We figured to lose out, anyway, he confessed, "like we've lost on everything else. They knocked my brains out. But though I'm bloody, I'm still unbowed."

THE HISTORY

Things weren't always this tough for the Browns. A long time ago, from 1885 through 1888, the original Browns won four consecutive American Association championships, and participated in four World Series. This was before the National League Cardinals even existed.

A key figure in this early success was owner Chris Von der Ahe. The bulbous nosed German immigrant, the first owner of the Browns, was a colorful predecessor to the final owner, Veeck. At least Veeck's equal as a promoter, Von der Ahe's primary interest was in luring fans to the stadium, his pleasure resort in the St. Louis suburbs. He referred to his players as "my poys" and to himself as "the smartest feller in baseball." In strictly baseball related matters, he relied on Alfred H. Spink, sportswriter and founder of *The Sporting News,* to make the decisions.

The 1885 post season series with Cap Anson's National League Chicago White Sox ended in a tie. Each team won three games. Anson batted .423 for the Sox, hitting safely in every game. But first baseman, and manager of the Browns, Charlie Comiskey, forfeited the second game in a dispute over an umpires ruling. The Browns committed forty-three errors in the series. Chicago was charged with fifty-nine. There were twenty-seven errors in the final game alone. The Browns won, thirteen to four. Only four of the seventeen total runs scored were earned.

When the same two teams met in the 1886 series, the Browns dropped two of the first three games in Chicago. They swept the final three in St. Louis. With Browns' center fielder Chris Welch on third in the tenth inning of the final game, White Sox catcher King Kelly called for a pitch out. But he bobbled the pitch. Welch successfully stole home. The play was dubbed the "fifteen thousand dollar slide." The winning team took home that much more than the losers.

The 1887 post season was a barnstorming World Series played in ten different cities. The Detroit Wolverines, led by Dan Brouthers, Deacon White, Hardy Richardson, and Jack Rowe, won ten of fifteen games. Second baseman Arlie Latham stole a dozen bases for the Browns, hit .333, and was the pivot man as the Browns turned a rare triple play in the post season.

In their last post season appearance as members of the American Association in 1888, the depleted Browns lost to the National League New York Giants, six games to four. The Giants led by shortstop John Montgomery Ward clinched the Series in eight games.

The Browns, along with several other American Association franchises merged with the National League after the 1891 season. Von der Ahe lacked sophistication. His penchant for promoting his team with side show features, carnival rides, and souvenir give away items, was way ahead of its time. It alienated fellow owners. He sold the few talented players he did have for cash, eventually selling the franchise itself, for cash, in 1899. The new owners renamed the team the Cardinals. They adorned their players in new uniforms, with the now familiar red piping, and bright red stockings.

Ironically, fifty years before Bill Veeck wanted to move the St. Louis Browns to Milwaukee, American League President Ban Johnson moved the Milwaukee Brewers to St Louis. Reclaiming the name Browns for the new franchise in 1902, new owner Ralph Orthwein quickly signed several of the Cardinals' best players, including shortstop Bobby Wallace who hit .322 with the Cardinals in 1901.

From 1903 to 1925 the Browns out drew their National League counterparts fifteen times. Outfielder George Stone batted .358 for the 1906 Browns. But the team finished fifth. Robert Hedges purchased the Browns in 1905. He added a second deck to Sportsman's Park in 1908, increasing the seating capacity to 20,000.

PREMIER BROWN: "GORGEOUS GEORGE" SISLER

Branch Rickey managed the Browns in 1914 and 1915. The club finished no higher than fifth place. Rickey had coached George Sisler at the University of Michigan. He played a major role in bringing Sisler to St. Louis, winning a contract dispute with the Pittsburgh Pirates over rights to the first baseman.

"Gorgeous George" Sisler, a Hall of Famer and the most significant player in the history of the St. Louis Browns, won the American League batting title in 1920, hitting .407. That was better than the Cardinals' first baseman, Rogers Hornsby, who hit .370 to win the National League batting title. Sisler finished with a career average of .340, playing with the Browns from 1915 until 1927.

Outfielder William "Baby Doll" Jacobson batted .355 in 1920. He batted .352 in 1921.

Perhaps one of the most underrated players in baseball history, outfielder Ken Williams hit 185 home runs from 1918 through 1927 and batted over .300 for seven straight years. He became baseball's first 30-30 player in 1922, hitting 39 homes runs and stealing 37 bases. He led the American League in home runs that year. Babe Ruth finished second with 35.

Outfielder Johnny Tobin hit over .300 for five consecutive seasons from 1918 to 1922. He batted .352 in 1920. Right hander Urban Shocker won twenty or more games in four consecutive seasons from 1920 to 1923. He led the Browns to a third place season in 1921, topping out with a twenty-seven and twelve mark. A second place finish in 1922 attracted a franchise record 713,0000 fans for the season. Jacobson hit .317. Shocker won twenty-four games. Sisler hit .420 to Hornsby's .401. Williams hit .332. He led the American League with thirty-nine home runs. Tobin hit .317. The club won a franchise record ninety-three games but finished one game behind the New York Yankees. The Browns led the league in hitting with a team batting average of .313.

Philip Ball, former owner of the Federal League St. Louis Terrapins, bought the Browns in 1915. He moved Rickey into the front office, making him general manager. Rickey, with five more years to go on his contract with the Browns, was unhappy with the move and jumped teams, becoming Vice President of the Cardinals.

Babe Ruth hit nine home runs against the Browns on his way towards a total of sixty in 1927. The Browns finished seventh. But St. Louis surged to third place in 1928. Left handed pitcher "General" Alvin Crowder won a team record twenty-one games.

The perpetually underfinanced, debt ridden, mediocre Browns had to sell several farm teams. Although the Browns signed Hall of Famers Heine Manush, and Goose Goslin, they couldn't afford to keep them. Catcher Rick Ferrell and pitcher Alvin Crowder also escaped the fold. The club finished dead last, drawing less than 100,000 fans, three times in the 1930s. The Browns had to pay half the salary of the ushers, and half the stadium maintenance cost, even though the more popular Cardinals benefitted more from their services. Owner Ball died in 1933. His last act was to hire Cardinal great Rogers Hornsby for his first tour of duty as manager of the Browns.Hornsby guided the Browns from 1934 to 1937. But the club finished no better than sixth place.

Donald Barnes, president of the American Investment Company of Illinois and Bill De Witt purchased the Browns from the Ball heirs in 1936. The club, however, showed little improvement toward the end of the decade although there were significant individual accomplishments. Third baseman Harlond Clift hit .302 in 1936, and .306 in 1937. The Browns avoided the American League cellar, finishing seventh under new manager, Charles "Gabby" Street in 1938. First baseman George McQinn batted .324. But the club fell back into last under manager Fred Haney in 1939.

The Browns' first night game in 1940 drew 24,827, the largest home crowd in twelve years. Cleveland won that night, three to two. The Browns finished sixth. Joe DiMaggio hit safely twenty-two times in twelve games against the Browns on his way to his fifty-six game hitting streak in 1941. The Browns again finished sixth.

The Browns play had improved marginally. But they still faced severe financial obstacles. In December, 1941, owner Donald Barnes nearly completed a deal to transfer the club to Los Angeles. The deal had tentative support from American League owners. The National League Chicago Cubs, parent club of the Pacific Coast League's Los Angeles Stars, had territorial rights to the California city. But Phil Wrigley, president of the Cubs, agreed to allow the move, and to allow the Browns to play in his minor league ballpark there. Sam Breadon, owner of the National League Cardinals, agreed to help subsidize the move. It was in his interest to have only one team in St. Louis. Official ratification of the deal, a formality, was scheduled for December eighth. Unfortunately, the Japanese bombed Pearl Harbor the day before the meeting. The move was tabled, in part because of war time travel restrictions.

But in 1942 the Browns got a badly needed influx of money from St. Louis businessman Richard Muckerman, who assumed the title of club vice president. Under the management of Luke Sewell, the club ascended to third place.

During the second world war, many established stars were in military service. The resulting parity among Major League clubs provided some unexpected results. Minus several key players the Browns slipped to sixth in 1943. Although the 1944 Browns won their first nine games, less than 900 saw their ninth victory at Sportsman's Park. Nonetheless, they rocketed past three other teams in September to win an exciting American League Pennant, out drawing the Cardinals, 508,644 to 461,968. The hitting and defense of shortstop Vern Stephens, and the right handed pitching of Nels Potter, Jack Kramer, and Sig Jakucki led the Browns to their first, and only, American League Pennant. The Cardinals were also pennant winners. St. Louis hosted a Trolley Series. The World Series was played entirely in one park. Although the underdog Browns won two of the first three games, the National League champions rallied for three straight wins to capture the title. The Browns pitching staff posted a 1.49 era against the Cardinals. But the team batted only .183.

The Browns contended again in 1945, finishing third. With the Major League rosters still depleted by the war effort. Pete Gray, a one armed center fielder, earned the opportunity to play for the Browns. At the age of six, he fell off the running board of a vegetable delivery truck. His right arm was caught in the spokes. Naturally right handed, he had to become a left hander.

Gray won the Southern Association Most Valuable Player Award in 1944, batting .333, while stealing sixty-eight bases for the Memphis Chicks. Defensively, the speedy Gray covered a lot of ground. Like modern pitcher Jim Abbott, he caught the ball in his gloved hand, removed the glove with the stump of his right arm, grabbed the ball quickly, and threw. Opposing base runners often took extra bases. Gray hit only .218. However, he struck out only eleven times, and his speed often forced other teams into committing infield errors.

In 1947, Hank Thompson and Willard Brown became the first black players ever to play for the Browns. However, they saw only limited action. The team finished last under manager Muddy Ruel. They rose to sixth in 1948 but fell back to seventh in 1949 despite the presence of the

American League Rookie of the Year, Roy Sievers, who hit sixteen homers, drove in ninety-one runs. He batted .306.

Between 1947 and 1951, the Browns sold or traded many players for cash. More than twenty player transactions and the sale of the Browns' Toledo farm team brought in money. When lawyer Fred Saigh bought the Cardinals in 1947, Browns' owner Bill De Witt, who gained control of the franchise in 1949, unsuccessfully tried to evict his National League counterparts from Sportsman's Park, claiming the sale technically violated the terms of the lease. But Bill De Witt and his brother Charlie, who had both once been vendors at Sportsman's Park, lacked the survival instincts of Washington's Clark Griffith and Philadelphia's Connie Mack. The De Witts gave up the struggle and sold to Veeck.

BILL VEECK

The colorful, innovative Veeck purchased the Browns prior to the 1951 season. He had a successful track record. The Braves' Triple-A farm team in Milwaukee won three consecutive league titles from 1943 to 1945 under Veeck, setting minor league attendance records. As owner of the Cleveland Indians from 1946 to 1949, he daringly signed Larry Doby, and Satchel Paige, the first every day negro players in the American league. In the lower profile market of Cleveland, Veeck and Doby were the American League equivalent of Brooklyn's Branch Rickey and Jackie Robinson in the National League. Veeck also traded popular pitcher Allie Reynolds to the Yankees for second baseman Joe Gordon. In 1948 the Indians won the American League pennant, setting a major league attendance record of 2,620,627.

He staged many innovative promotions. Some were bizarre. There were regular fireworks nights. Two baseball oriented clowns, Max Patkin and Jackie Price, both former minor league players, performed regularly. Patkin, a long nosed, rubbery faced, double jointed comic in a baseball suit, became a featured entertainer, later taking his act to almost every major, and minor league park in the country. Price would hang, by his knees, from a portable trapeze in the batters box ,with a bat, and hit a pitched ball. Veeck also featured midgets racing kiddie cars around the outfield warning track, a flag pole sitter, livestock giveaways. Female fans were not ignored. During the war years, he gave away hard to get nylon stockings to lady fans. And he once gave away Princess Aloha Orchids to the first 20,000 women to come through the turnstiles.

After being eliminated from the pennant race in 1949, Veeck staged a mock funeral, burying the 1948 American League pennant in a shallow grave beneath the flag pole in center field. Veeck, himself, drove the hearse. Indians players joined in the procession. The Indians finished third but still drew more than two million fans.

In his first season in St. Louis, Veeck's antics were reminiscent of Von der Ahe. He celebrated the fiftieth anniversary of the American League and the birthday of Falstaff Brewery with a special promotion at Sportsman's Park. The paid attendance of 18,000 was the largest crowd to see the Browns at home in four years. He presented every body with a slice of birthday cake, a box of ice cream, and a can of "midget beer" as they entered the park. But the real highlight of the afternoon came when a real midget, Eddie Gaedel, popped out of a seven foot birthday cake between games of a doubleheader. Dressed in a Browns' uniform, Gaedel came to bat in the first inning of the second game and walked on four pitches, not even bothering to crouch.

Five days later Veeck held a Grandstand Managers' Day. Everyone who submitted a lineup to the *St. Louis Globe Democrat* newspaper was mailed a ticket, entitling him or her to sit behind the dugout. There were more than 4000 ballots issued.

Participants were given large two sided signs with YES printed in green on one side and NO printed in red on the other. As the regular manager, Zack Taylor, in civilian clothes reclined in a rocking chair beside the dugout and smoked a pipe. Brown's assistant Bob Fishel, standing at the rail behind the dugout, would flash signs covering every conceivable situation such as INFIELD BACK?, SHALL WE WARM UP THE PITCHER? If the majority voted yes the strategy was implemented.

It worked. The Browns defeated the A's, five to three, to end a four game losing streak. Philadelphia manager Jimmy Dykes, protesting that the tabulation of votes delayed the game, played along with the gag, scowling and kicking the dirt. A's owner Connie Mack, seated in the Grandstand Managers section, enjoyed himself immensely.

Right hander Ned Garver won twenty games for the 1951 Browns, becoming the only man to post twenty wins for a club that lost 100 games. The Browns finished eighth and Garver was traded to Detroit.

In Veeck's second season, 1952, the Browns doubled their 1951 attendance figure, drawing 518,000 fans despite a seventh place finish. That was higher than their attendance total in their pennant winning season of 1944. The National League Cardinals who shared Sportsman's

Park drew 913,113, finishing third. It was the first season that the Cardinals had failed to draw a million customers since the end of World War II. With Veeck as a land lord the Cardinals' half of the stadium went unpainted and Cardinal management was denied access to the press room and private boxes. And Veeck believed he could force Fred Saigh, the financially struggling owner of the Cardinals, out of St. Louis. He usurped Cardinal tradition by hiring Hornsby as manager, Harry Brecheen as pitching coach, and Dizzy Dean as a broadcaster. He put as many ex-Cardinals as possible on the active player roster and defiantly challenged the Cardinals to a post season exhibition game. Saigh, who had the phrase "The Cardinals, a dignified St. Louis Institution" printed on the bottom of all Cardinal score cards, refused.

When Saigh was convicted of income tax evasion in 1952, he was fined $15,000 and sentenced to fifteen months at the Federal Penitentiary in Terre Haute, Indiana. Ironically, he tried to sell the team to a Wisconsin group that intended to move the team to Milwaukee. For a time it appeared that Veeck had succeeded in his battle with the Cardinals. But the National League vetoed the deal, pressuring Saigh to sell to a local buyer, Anheuser-Busch, for substantially less than the Wisconsin group offered. If the deal had gone through it would have violated the general expansion guidelines of moving the weaker team out of a two team city. The Cardinals were clearly the better gate attraction. Veeck, so close to succeeding, had lost. He couldn't compete against the unlimited resources of the wealthy beer magnates. Having laid out money for young ball players in anticipation of the move to Milwaukee or Baltimore, Veeck was deeply in debt and had no credit line. He sold Sportsman's Park, an immediate source of revenue, to the new owners of the Cardinals. Veeck netted $800,000 from the ballpark sale. He also sold his Arizona Ranch. But his financial problems were far from over.

Like Von der Ahe long before him, Veeck's eccentricities irritated many of his fellow owners. And he further alienated himself after the 1952 season, advocating that minor leaguers become free agents after one season, and that television revenues be shared with the visiting club. Receiving little support for either proposal, he refused to allow Browns' road games to be televised by the home team. In retaliation, his fellow American League owners eliminated lucrative night games from the St. Louis schedule.

THE BALLPARK

Sportsman's Park, home to the Cardinals and Browns, was located at the corner of Grand Boulevard and Dodier Street. Its most prominent feature was the Anheuser-Busch eagle sign that sat alone above a large mechanical scoreboard and beyond the bleacher section in left field. Encased within a giant letter "A," an eagle electronically flapped its wings to celebrate Cardinal and Browns' home runs. The eccentric Veeck himself lived in an apartment under the stands and allowed a goat to graze on the outfield grass during non game hours.

After several seasons training at Burbank, California, the Browns held their 1953 spring camp at San Bernadino. However, arrangements had been made to transfer their training facility to Yuma, Arizona in 1954.

THE FINAL SEASON

Play by play radio coverage of all the 1953 Browns' games was carried on KXOK AM. The longtime voice of the Browns, former player Buddy Blattner, was teamed with Dizzy Dean in the broadcast booth. WTVI TV, channel fifty-four, televised a limited number of Browns' games.

APRIL

The lame duck Browns had no future in St. Louis but they opened the 1953 season under manager Marty Marion with a flair. Going into the new season, Veeck had added two young right handed hurlers: twenty-two-year-old Bob Turley and twenty-three-year-old Don Larsen, a rookie. But operating under the lights at Sportsman's Park on Tuesday, April fourteenth, it was veteran right hander Virgil Trucks who shut out the visiting Detroit Tigers, ten to nothing. Acquired from the Tigers in an off season deal, the thirty-four year-old Trucks limited his former teammates to just four hits. Slugging first baseman Vic Wertz, hard hitting outfielder Johnny Groth, acquired from the Tigers in the off season, and Roy Sievers were expected to lead the St. Louis offense. Wertz batted .346 for St. Louis in 1952, hitting seventeen home runs. Groth, who batted .306 for Detroit in 1950, was coming off a .284 season. Sievers had been injured in 1952, appearing in just 11 games. But he batted .306 for the Browns in 1949, winning rookie of the year honors. Veteran outfielder Bob Elliott had also been obtained from the Giants to help the offense. But on opening night, Catcher Les Moss, in his ninth season with the Browns, led the attack with three hits. St. Louis scored four times in the first, touching former Brown, Ned Garver, for five hits.

At Comiskey Park in Chicago on Thursday, April sixteenth, southpaw Billy Pierce hurled a one-hit shutout at the Browns, winning, one to nothing. Second baseman Bobby Young's double to right in the seventh inning was the only Browns' hit. Thirty-eight year old Harry "The Cat" Brecheen, a Cardinal for eleven seasons, yielded only two hits in his American League debut, but took the loss. Game time temperature was a cool forty degrees.

On Friday, April seventeenth, the Browns won the second game in Chicago, six to four. Only 972 braved the gloomy thirty-six degree weather. First baseman Vic Wertz homered to put the Browns ahead in the fifth inning. A two-run double by catcher Les Moss highlighted a five run Browns' rally in the seventh that sealed the victory.

With the Browns trailing, seven to four, Wertz hit a three-run homer with two outs in ninth inning of the first game of a doubleheader at Detroit on Saturday, April eighteenth, sending the game into extra innings. In the top of the eleventh inning, Dyck and Wertz singled. Bob Elliot then hit a routine fly ball. But Detroit outfielders, Jim Delsing and Bob Nieman, collided trying to make the catch. The ball fell safely, as Dyck and Wertz raced home. Ex teammate Bob Nieman, who led the Browns with eighteen homers in 1952, homered to open the bottom of the eleventh for Detroit. Trucks, summoned from the bullpen, came on to retire the side and preserve an eight to seven win.

With the scored tied at two all in the second came, pinch hitter Hank Edwards doubled to open the Browns half of the eighth inning. Neil Berry came in to pinch run for Edwards, moving to third on a pinch hit single by Dick Kokos. He scored on a passed ball, giving starting pitcher Duane Pillette, a ten game winner in 1952, his first victory of the year.

FIRST PLACE FOR THE LAST TIME

In a single game on Sunday afternoon, the Browns completed the sweep, defeating the Tigers in eleven innings again, six to three. Relief pitcher Marlin Stuart opened the eleventh with a 400 foot double to center. Young singled him home. Elliott singled home two more runs. The win improved the Browns' early season record to five and one. It placed them in first place in the American League standings for the final time ever.

In Cleveland on Tuesday, April Twenty-first, the Indians snapped the Browns' four game winning streak, winning four to three. Still the Browns completed their first road trip of the year with four wins and only a single defeat.

The Browns began their longest home stand of the year on Friday, April twenty-fourth. Gene Bearden of the White Sox, a former Brown, shut out his former teammates, three to nothing, allowing just three hits. Another former Brown, Tommy Byrne, shut out the Browns for six innings on Saturday. Although Dick Kryhoski hit a grand slam home run in the bottom of the seventh, the White Sox held on to win, six to four.

Elliott, a former member of the now defunct Boston Braves, homered, tripled, and drove in four runs in the opener of a double-header on Sunday April twenty sixth. The Browns defeated Chicago southpaw Billy Pierce, seven to two. In the second game Mike Blyzka, making his major league debut, held Chicago at bay for eight innings but lost, three to nothing.

THE GAME—THE BRAWL

The most dramatic game in the Browns' final season occurred on Tuesday evening, April twenty-eighth. The largest home crowd of the home stand, 13,463, saw the Yankees defeat St. Louis, seven to six.

Yankees' center fielder Mickey Mantle hit a tremendous 484 foot homer with two men on in the third inning. When Mantle doubled and scored a run in the fourth, New York led five to nothing. But Yankees' right hander Vic Raschi could not hold the lead. Wertz hit a bases loaded double with two out in the bottom of the fifth, driving in three runs. After Berra singled home another Yankee run in the top of the sixth inning, the Browns rallied for three more runs in the bottom of the inning, tying the game, six to six. With the bases loaded and one out in the bottom of the ninth, Allie Reynolds struck out pinch hitters Roy Sievers and Elliott to send the game into extra innings.

With one out in the Yankee tenth Gil McDougald doubled. Brecheen then intentionally walked outfielder Joe Collins to get to the pitcher Reynolds, who bounced back to the mound. Brecheen threw to Billy Hunter for the force out on Collins at second base. Seeing McDougald round third, Hunter threw the ball to Clint Courtney. But McDougald barreled into the Browns' catcher, who dropped the ball. The Yankees led seven to six.

The stage was set for the home tenth. An angry Courtney led off the inning with a drive off the wall in right. He tried to stretch the hit into a double. Right fielder Hank Bauer threw quickly to second, but Courtney slid high into Shortstop Rizzuto, spiking him in two places. Courtney was ruled out. But the entire New York infield, including second baseman Billy Martin, converged on Courtney. The Brown's bench emptied. A melee ensued, delaying the game for seventeen minutes. With fans hurling bottles from the stands, Umpire Bill Summers threatened to forfeit the game. After two appeals over the Public Address system by manager Marion order was finally restored. Reynolds was able to record the final two outs.

American League President Will Harridge fined Courtney two hundred fifty dollars. He told reporters, "Courtney violated all the rules of sportsmanship by going extremely high into Rizzuto at second base." Harridge fined Martin, and Billy Hunter one hundred fifty dollars each. He assessed McDougall, Reynolds, and Collins one hundred dollars each.

The final game of the Yankee series was rained out. On Thursday night, Virgil Trucks defeated the Washington Senators, three to one. A three-run homer by Elliott in the bottom of the seventh accounted for all the Browns' scoring. The Browns finished April with seven wins and six losses. It was their only winning month of the season. Two of the eight home games were rained out altogether. Several others were played in bad weather. The Browns were averaging just 7,500 per game. Veeck blamed the indiscriminate use of television, as well as the bad weather, for the low attendance. On the final day of the month, Sportsman's Park was officially renamed Busch Stadium by the new owners, Anheuser-Busch. The Browns were in fifth place, three and one-half games out of first.

MAY

On Friday, May first Washington defeated St. Louis, six to five. Wertz and Kryhoski homered. The Senators won again on Saturday, five to four. A three-run homer by Elliott raised his league-leading RBI total to seventeen. A 442 foot blast in the seventh inning by Wertz cleared the right field stands, hitting a car parked on Greer Avenue.

Boston won their sixth straight in the opener of a doubleheader on Sunday, May third, pounding the Browns fourteen to five. Kryhowski homered twice for St. Louis. But the Browns posted their first victory of the month in the nightcap, six to five. A sacrifice fly by Sievers in the eighth inning scored the winning run. The attendance of 13,463 matched that of the game with the Yankees five days before.

Virgil Trucks defeated Philadelphia on Tuesday night, two to one. Trucks hit his fifth homer of the year with Edwards on board in the sixth inning.

BOBO HOLLOMAN'S NO HITTER

On October fifteenth, 1892, Charlie "Bumpus" Jones became the first pitcher in baseball history to hurl a no-hitter in his Major League debut, defeating the Pittsburgh Pirates, seven to one, in a National League contest in Cincinnati on the last day of the season. On Wednesday night, May sixth, 1953, Browns' rookie right hander Bobo Holloman became only the second pitcher to accomplish this feat. Holloman shut out the American League A's, six to nothing, in Philadelphia. Jones finished his major league career with only two victories. Holloman finished his career with just three wins. But on this magical night, he faced just thirty-one batters, striking out three, walking five, and misplaying a one hopper back to the mound for the only error of the game. Displaying an outstanding sinker, the right hander induced a number of ground outs.

Joe Astroth's sharply hit grounder in the eighth inning was the only real threat to the no-hitter. But shortstop Hunter, ranging far to his left, fielded it cleanly, throwing to first in time. Holloman tired in the ninth, walking the first two men he faced. But he induced Dave Philley's to ground into a double play. And after Loren Babe walked, Eddie Robinson flied to Wertz in right to end the game.

Afterward Holloman told reporters:

> I realized I was going for a no-hitter when I found I was charged with an error on that hopper of Zernial's. But I wouldn't have had it but for that play by Billy Hunter in the eighth. That was the greatest play I've ever seen. I was nervous, but just in the ninth, that was the toughest one. This is the biggest thrill of my life.

Holloman also drove in three runs with two singles, and a sacrifice fly. His victory gave the Browns, ten and nine, a winning record for the final time.

Owner Veeck himself announced over the Public Address system in the middle of the game that fans who had braved the chilly rainy night that rain checks for the game would be honored at any other game on the Browns' home schedule. They thus became the first, and only, crowd ever to see a major league no hitter for nothing. But only a select 2742 witnessed the event.

It was the first nine-inning no hitter by a Brown's pitcher since Bob Groom defeated the Chicago White Sox at Sportsman's Park, two to nothing in 1917. That game, thirty-six years earlier, was also played on May sixth.

Scheduled to start against the Yankees in a rained out game on April twenty-ninth, Holloman was the losing pitcher in a relief appearance against the Washington Senators on May first. Manager Marion wasn't impressed with Holloman in spring training:

> He was too fat. He couldn't run around the field with out folding up. After pitching in Puerto Rico, he ate himself out of shape. Then when he started pitching, he came up with a sore arm. Coach Scheffing told me he had a good fast ball but he sure didn't show it to me until he put it on display against the A's. That boy sure believes in himself. He doesn't mind telling you about it.

The Browns finished out the home stand with three weekend losses to powerful Cleveland. But the Indians had to rally for four runs in the ninth to overtake the Browns, seven to four in the Friday night series opener. A squeeze bunt by Jim Dyck scored Brecheen to put St. Louis ahead four to three in the bottom of the eighth. After retiring the first two batters in the top of the ninth, Brecheen walked the next two batters. He then yielded a double and a home run.

The Browns and Indians battled into the tenth inning on Saturday, May ninth. Kokos singled off starter Mike Garcia in the top of the ninth. He scored the tying run on a single by Young. But the Indians collected three singles off Brown starter Bob Cain in the top of the tenth, winning three to two.

Trucks held the Indians scoreless for seven innings on Sunday, May tenth. The Browns led three to nothing through seven innings. But the Indians slugged four home runs, including a grand slam by Ray Boone in the last two innings. The twelve to three win gave the Indians sole possession of first place, two percentage points ahead of the Yankees.

Holloman was ineffective in his second start on Tuesday, May twelfth, at Philadelphia in the opener of a thirteen game road trip. He walked the first three batters, developing a blister on the middle finger of his right hand. He left the game after just one and one-third innings.

Meanwhile, the Browns pounded out twelve hits off Philadelphia ace Bobby Shantz in five and two-thirds innings.

On Wednesday night Philadelphia's Alex Kellner out dueled Pillette for a two to one victory. Satchel Paige, took the loss in relief. After the game forty-four year old veteran-pitcher Bobo Newsome of the A's insisted Paige wasn't as old as he claimed. "I've been around long enough. I've reached the age when I can say that no one pitching today was pitching in 1917," he said.

Dick Littlefield lost the series opener at Washington on Thursday, May fourteenth, two to one. But Trucks mastered Washington, four to nothing, on Friday night, picking up his fourth victory. Kryhoski homered over the right field wall at Griffith Stadium in the first inning. But Washington's Bob Porterfield shut out the Browns on Saturday afternoon, six to nothing. After Young booted a double play grounder in the first inning, the Senators batted ten men, scoring five runs.

41 PLAYERS USED IN NEW YORK REMATCH

In New York on Sunday, May seventeenth, 42,596 fans, the largest crowd to see the Browns all year awaited the rematch following the April mayhem between the Yankees and Browns at St. Louis. The Yankees again triumphed in ten innings, six to five. Courtney and Martin, again, figured prominently in the outcome.

Catcher Les Moss drove in three runs. Bob Elliott knocked in another, giving the Browns a four to nothing lead after six innings. Mize singled home two New York runs in the seventh. Still Brown's starter Don Larsen took a four to two lead into the bottom of the ninth inning. But with two out pinch hitter Ralph Houk reached on an infield hit. Martin singled. Irv Noren then tripled home both runners, sending the game into extra innings.

Moss's fourth hit of the game opened the St. Louis tenth. Kryhoski's bunt moved him to second. Courtney singled home the go-ahead run. Then Gene Woodling singled to open the Yankee tenth. After fouling off two bunt attempts, Rizzuto doubled to right. Pillette relieved Blyzka. He intentionally walked Lopat, filling the bases. After Houk popped out, Martin singled home the tying and winning runs. The game lasted three and one-half hours. Yankee manager Stengel tied an American League record, using twenty three players. Marion used eighteen players from the Browns' roster. The total of forty-one players used by both managers set a new major league mark The old record was forty set by the Pirates and Braves in 1940 in a twelve inning game. The second game of the scheduled doubleheader was called because of darkness after three and one-half scoreless innings.

On Tuesday, May nineteenth, the emotionally, and physically, drained Browns continued their season at Fenway Park. In the top of the eighth inning, Lenhardt, a former Red Sox, homered over the 400 foot marker in center to tie the game. But Boston shortstop Milt Bolling's two out single off of Paige in the bottom of the inning scored center fielder Tom Umphlett, giving the Red Sox a four to three win.

On Wednesday. May twentieth, the Browns played their second marathon contest in four days. The game lasted fourteen innings. It took three hours and six minutes to complete. Boston won, three to two. In the third inning, Trucks bobbled a ground ball hit back to the mound. He overthrew first base, allowing two unearned runs to score. Larsen came on in relief in the seventh. He allowed only four hits in seven and two-third innings of relief. With two out in the Bottom of the fourteenth inning, however, Boston's Del Wilbur slammed a three and one pitch into the screen above the green left field wall. It was his third pinch homer of the year.

The Indians cut down the Browns, five to one on Saturday, May twenty-third. On Sunday wildness again plagued Holloman in the opener of a doubleheader. He walked five men in two and one-third innings. Cleveland won another five to one decision. Al Rosen hit a three-run homer in the third off former teammate Paige. But Paige was charged with only one earned run in four and two-thirds innings.

In the second game, St. Louis rallied for three runs in the ninth, but fell short, losing, nine to eight. The Browns scored three times in the top of the ninth. With the tying run on second base, Lenhardt struck out to end the game. The Browns scored three runs in the second inning and two more in the fourth, chasing Mike Garcia. In the bottom of the fourth, Boone hit his second grand slam of the year against the Browns.

When the the Browns returned to St. Louis on Monday, May twenty-fifth, Marion used twenty three players against the White Sox, tying the major league record set by Stengel's Yankees against the Browns just a week earlier. But The Sox dealt Brecheen his sixth straight loss, seven to five. Bobby Young doubled twice, and walked, scoring three runs. Lenhardt singled the tying run home in the sixth. A sacrifice fly by Berry in the seventh gave the Browns a five to four lead. The White Sox, however, scored twice in the eighth, reclaiming the lead, and added another run in the ninth. On Tuesday night Chicago dealt the Browns their ninth straight loss, eight to two. Former teammate Tommy Byrne defeated the Browns for the second time.

THE LONGEST WINNING STREAK

But St. Louis broke their long losing streak on Wednesday night, May twenty-seventh, against visiting Cleveland. The Indians were an unlikely opponent for the Brown's to begin their longest winning streak of the year against. Holloman's first home appearance since his no-hit masterpiece attracted only 3954 fans. That, however, was 1500 more than watched his remarkable debut three weeks earlier. The right hander scattered nine hits, and walked only four, leading the Browns to their first victory over the Indians in nine tries. The Browns won, five to one. Cleveland, uncharacteristically, committed three errors. Two of the St.Louis runs were unearned.

The Browns swept the brief series, winning again, seven to five, on Thursday night. Cleveland Starter Hoskins walked the first three batters in the bottom of the fifth. Then he yielded a grand slam homer to Elliott. With the Browns leading six to two, the Indians scored single runs in sixth, seventh and eighth innings. But Paige shut the door, holding his former team scoreless in the ninth.

On Friday, Brecheen, pitching in relief, posted his first American League victory. After suffering six defeats, he held the Detroit Tigers scoreless in the final two innings of an eleven inning contest at Briggs Stadium. The Browns won, eleven to five. Thirty-seven year-old Elliott's double in the eleventh inning was his two thousandth career hit. It ignited a six run rally.

On Memorial Day, the surging Browns extended their winning streak to five games, sweeping a doubleheader from the Tigers, five to four, and thirteen to one. In the first game the thirty-four year-old Trucks, who pitched for Detroit for twelve seasons, earned his fifth victory of the year.

Groth homered in both games. Moss and Wertz knocked in three runs each in the nightcap. The Browns defeated Detroit for the seventh straight time. Bob Cain, who led the Browns' starters with a twelve and ten mark in 1952, won his first game of the year. The Browns collected twenty-eight hits in the doubleheader.

Chicago defeated St. Louis, seven to four, in the opener of a Sunday doubleheader at Comiskey Park on the final day of May. Holloman walked two, giving up four hits in just two and one-third innings, ending the winning streak he had begun four days earlier in Cleveland. The Browns got thirteen hits, but left eleven men on base.

Billy Hunter had four hits in the second game and seven hits on the day, boosting his average to .295. The Browns won the nightcap, seven to four. Winning six of the final seven games of the month, the Browns recorded eleven victories in May, losing eighteen. They had sunk to seventh place. They were eleven games back of the league-leading New York Yankees.

JUNE

When the club returned to St. Louis on Tuesday, June second, Satchel Paige picked up his first victory of the year in his nineteenth relief appearance, defeating Washington five to three. Paige, who matched Bob Cain with a team best twelve and ten mark in 1952, retired all ten men he faced. Kryhoski hit a two-run single in the first. He homered again in the eighth inning, providing an insurance run. This was the Browns' seventh victory in eight games. It was their only win, however, of the fifteen game home stand.

THE LONGEST LOSING STREAK

The longest losing streak of the year in the American League started innocently enough. On Wednesday night, June third, the Browns were competitive in a three to two loss in extra innings to Washington. The Browns tied the game with a run in the bottom of the ninth. Paige pitched the tenth, striking out the first two men he faced. But Senators' third baseman Ed Yost then singled, stole second, and scored the game winner on a single by Wayne Terwilliger. The Senators, however, mauled St. Louis, ten to one, on Thursday night, collecting fifteen hits.

On Friday, June fifth, the Yankees returned to St. Louis for the first time since April twenty-eighth. Johnny Sain shut out the Browns, five to nothing. Remembering the free for all fight during the Yankees last visit, the fans booed Martin each time he came to bat. The volatile Yankee second baseman emphatically denied he was a troublemaker:

> I never started a fight in my life, and I never spiked a player—not even by accident. I play the game hard but cleanly. That's the only way to play it. I admire any man who plays it that way. That goes for Courtney. He hustles all the time. However, if someone deliberately goes out of his way to hurt me or one of my teammates, that's a different story. I'll be there trying to protect myself, and my teammates, just as any player would.

On Saturday afternoon a two-run homer by Kokos in the fifth inning tied the defending American League champs at two to two. But

Martin singled in one of three Yankee runs off Mike Blyzka in the decisive sixth inning. The Yanks won again, six to two.

LARGEST HOME CROWD

On Sunday, June seventh, the largest home crowd of the Browns' final season, 19,795 fans, crowded Busch Stadium. The Yankees easily extended their winning streak to eleven games, claiming both ends of a doubleheader, nine to two, and seven to two. Dyck hit two solo homers in the first game. The second put the Browns ahead, two to one in the bottom of the fifth inning. But a pinch hit grand slam home run by Berra in the seventh helped the Yankees pull away. Groth led off the second game with a homer, and Trucks held a two-run lead through six innings. In the seventh inning, however, the Yankees erupted for seven runs.

On Tuesday evening, June ninth, the Red Sox began their second visit to St. Louis tripping the Browns, six to five, in sweltering ninety-four degree heat. Boston carried a six to two lead into the bottom of the eighth. But a three-run homer by Elliott, his fifth round tripper, closed the gap to a single run.

BOSTON'S PIERSALL GOES SIX FOR SIX

Red Sox center fielder, Jim Piersall, tied a major league record in the first game of a doubleheader on Tuesday, June tenth, with six hits in six trips to the plate. The Red Sox won, eleven to two. Piersall went hitless in five trips in the second game. The Browns scored two runs in the first inning. The Red Sox won, however, three to two. Boston's Willard Nixon had a perfect game going for five and two-third innings on Thursday night. Mound opponent, Virgil Trucks, doubled with two out in the bottom of the sixth, breaking up the no-hitter. The Sox, however, pushed the St. Louis losing streak to eleven games, winning seven to nothing.

St. Louis opened up the final series of the home stand on Friday, June twelfth with a five to three loss to the Athletics, and lost again on Saturday, eight to three. When Philadelphia swept both games on Sunday, June fourteenth, four to one, and three to one, the Browns tied a thirteen-year-old club record of fourteen consecutive losses. All fourteen losses in the 1940 streak came on the road. A struggling veteran, who broke in with the 1940 Cardinals, Breechen saw his personal record drop to one and eight in the second game.

Prior to open, a sixteen game road trip, the Browns traded Trucks, the only winning pitcher in the starting rotation, and third baseman

Elliott, their most reliable hitter, to Chicago for right handed Pitcher Lou Kretlow, catcher Darrell Johnson, and cash. The trade provided more financial relief for the franchise than help on the field. It left reliever Marlin Stuart (3-0) as the only Brown's pitcher with a winning record.

LONGEST AL WINNING AND LOSING STREAKS OF THE YEAR END

At Yankee Stadium on Tuesday, June sixteenth, New York hosted the Browns, trying to extend an eighteen game winning steak. Browns' manager Marion inserted himself into the lineup at third base, but was hitless in five trips. The Browns, however, defeated the Yankees, three to one, ending both the longest winning and losing streak of the 1953 season. The Browns kept constant pressure on Yankees' starter Whitey Ford. Groth singled home a run in the first. And Wertz hit a two-run homer in the top of the fifth. There was some excitement for New York fans in the bottom of the fifth. 30,632 watched New York first baseman Johnny Mize drive a run scoring single to right. It was the two thousandth career hit for the forty year-old slugger who received a lengthy ovation. Play was halted momentarily. The forty-year-old slugger received the ball as a keepsake. But that was the Yankees' only scoring. Pillette allowed just five hits in seven and one-third innings. Satchel Paige struck out Mantle to open the Yankee ninth, then retired Yogi Berra on an easy grounder to Hunter at short. Woodling then singled. But when Gil McDougall followed with an infield pop up, third baseman Marion called off the other infielders and squeezed the ball tightly, sealing the satisfying victory. It was his final appearance as a player.

A degree of normalcy returned the next night. The Yankees started another winning streak, winning five to three. The Browns began another losing streak. Again plagued by a lack of control, Holloman walked five batters in four innings. He walked in a run in the first inning. Martin had three hits, driving in two runs. The Yankees then swept a Thursday night doubleheader. Unbeaten Eddie Lopat shut out the Browns, five to nothing in the opener. Martin homered to break a scoreless deadlock in the sixth inning of the second game. New York's Jim McDonald shut out the Browns in the second game, three to nothing.

The Browns were in free fall. At Fenway Park on Friday, June nineteenth Roy Sievers, hit his first homer of the year in the first inning. It was the Browns first run in three games. But the Red Sox won, four to one. On Saturday afternoon temperatures on the field reached an unbearable 120 degrees. Two of the more than 10,000 fans suffered heat stroke. They had to be rushed to the hospital. The Red Sox won again, four to two. Left hander Mel Parnell held St. Louis to just three hits over the final eight innings. He won his own game with a two-run single in the fourth inning.

The Browns lost for the twentieth time in twenty-one games on Sunday as the Red Sox won the first game of a doubleheader, three to one. But Holloman salvaged the final game in Boston, hurling a two-hit shutout in the nightcap. The Browns won, two to nothing. It was Holloman's third, and last, major league victory. In the fourth inning, Wertz reached on an infield hit. Kryhoski followed with his eighth homer of the year.

Tommy Byrne had already defeated his former teammates twice, as a member of the White Sox. He lost, however, in his first start against the Browns as a Washington Senator. The Browns defeated Washington on Tuesday, June twenty third, four to three. Washington led, one to nothing, after five innings. But the Browns collected eleven hits, scoring a run in the sixth inning, and two more in the seventh. A Sievers home run in the eighth proved to be crucial insurance. The Senators rallied for two runs in the bottom of the ninth. Sievers delivered again with a three-run homer in the eighth inning on Wednesday night. Kokos blasted a two-run homer with two out in the ninth to complete a come from behind victory, seven to six. The Browns completed their fourth series sweep of the year on Thursday night. Brecheen posted his second consecutive win, defeating the Senators, three to one. It was the Browns' fourth straight win.

In Philadelphia on Friday, June twenty sixth, Sievers singled home two runs in the top of seventh to put the Browns on top, five to two. After Philadelphia scored two in the bottom of the inning, Paige in relief of Holloman, retired the side. He pitched a scoreless bottom of the eighth, and retired the first two batters in the ninth. However, the A's then loaded the bases, and Gus Zernial smashed a game winning double. The A's won, six to five.

On Saturday, Duane Pillette hit his first major league homer. He also pitched St. Louis to a six to one victory over the Athletics. Larsen won the opener of a doubleheader on Sunday, June twenty-eighth, four to one. Courtney homered, singled twice, driving in three runs. In the nightcap, A's pitcher Carl Scheib won his own game with an RBI single in the ninth inning. Philadelphia won, two to one.

The Browns won on the final day of the month in Chicago, four to two. 35,825 fans turned out to greet the White Sox, returning home after seven straight victories on the road. But the lowly Browns hammered ten hits off Billy Pierce. The win was the Browns' seventh in nine games, marking their best stretch on the season. It evened their record on the long road trip at eight and eight. The club, however, had only nine wins for the month against twenty-two defeats. They were still in seventh place, twenty-two games behind the league leaders.

JULY

Chicago pounded St. Louis, thirteen to four, at Comiskey Park on the first day of July. The White Sox followed the Browns back to St. Louis for a fourth of July doubleheader. They crushed the Browns again, twice, thirteen to nothing, and, four to two. Former St. Louis teammate, Bob Elliott, had three hits in the nightcap for Chicago.

The Brown's frustration mounted. The Tigers, unable to beat the Browns in seven previous attempts, swept a doubleheader in St. Louis on Sunday, July fifth. In the third inning of the first game, Tigers' catcher Johnny Bucha tried to score on a sacrifice fly. He was tagged out by Courtney for the third out. When he came up swinging, Courtney counter punched, with the ball in his right hand. Both benches emptied. Walt Dropo punched Larsen. Courtney was ejected. Bucha had four hits on the afternoon. Larsen's homer in the third was the only extra base hit among fifteen hits for the Browns who lost, ten to seven.

In the second game, Holloman wilted in one hundred degree heat. He lost again, seven to one. Completing a three game sweep, the Tigers won again, eight to seven, on Monday night. Detroit moved within four percentage points of the seventh place Browns. Ray Boone's eighth homer of the year in the eleventh spoiled five strong innings of relief work by Paige.

On Tuesday, July seventh, the Browns set a major league mark, losing their twentieth straight game at home, six to three. Groth tied the game against the visiting Indians with a three-run homer in the seventh inning. Five errors in the last two innings gave the Indians three unearned runs, ruining a decent performance by Holloman, in his final big league start.

Former White Sox Lou Kretlow, in his first start for the Browns, defeated Cleveland six to three on Wednesday, ending the most recent losing streak at seven games and the home losing streak at twenty. It was the Browns first win at home since June second. Courtney's fifth inning homer was the only one of thirteen Browns' hits for extra bases. Cleveland's Bob Lemon overpowered the Browns, nine to one, in the series finale on Thursday night.

THE HOME RUN SURGE

The Browns were not considered a power hitting team. Through early July, Wertz led the team with ten homers. Kryhoski had nine. But when Jimmy Dyck, Roy Sievers, Don Lenhardt, and Cling Courtney all homered in an eight to four St. Louis win at Tiger Stadium on Friday, July tenth, it marked just the beginning of an astonishing, record setting, home run spree.

Kokos blasted two round trippers on Saturday. Young and Kryhoski added one each. St. Louis beat Detroit again, seven to two. Then Wertz and Lenhardt homered in the first of a pair of games on Sunday afternoon. Paige walked in the winning run in the ninth. Detroit won, eight to seven. Holloman allowed just one run on six hits run in five innings of relief. He was sent to the Brown's farm team in Toronto after the game and never returned to the majors.

The long ball blitz continued in the second game. Wertz and Groth hit round trippers in the second game, pushing the total to twelve homers in four games. The Browns won, three to two, spoiling Ralph Branca's American League pitching debut.

THE ALL-STAR BREAK

Billy Hunter, a rookie, and Satchel Paige, the veteran, represented the Browns in the 1953 All-Star game in Cincinnati on July fourteenth. Warren Spahn of the Milwaukee Braves was the winning pitcher. Hunter entered the game as a pinch runner in the seventh. Paige, in his first appearance in the mid season classic, yielded the final two runs in the eighth inning as the National League won, five to one. Named to the All-Star Team for the second straight year, Paige told reporters:

> It's a mighty big honor. I appreciate it plenty. There were only three things I ever wanted. A long time back I always wanted to pitch in the big leagues. I got to do that. After I came to Cleveland I wanted to pitch in a World Series. In 1948, I got to do that, too. That left only one more thing I wanted—to play on an All-Star team. Now this is the second time I got to do that.

When intra-league play resumed the Browns' homer barrage resumed also. This time against the first place Yankees were the victims. In the first game of a doubleheader at Busch Stadium on Thursday, July sixteenth, New York scored two runs in the top of the first inning. Courtney, Kryhoski, and Dyck, all former Yankees, slammed consecutive blast off Johnny Sain in the bottom half of the inning, tying a major league record for consecutive first inning home runs. In the third inning, Young and Wertz homered. The Browns won eight to six.

The five game total of seventeen home runs tied another major league mark set by the 1940 Yankees. The Browns shared that record with the Yankees until August 1963 when the Minnesota Twins hit nineteen in five games. The best of the Browns' final season in St. Louis was over.

In the second game, the Browns failed to homer off Whitey Ford and the Yankees. However, a walk, combined with a pair of errors by Rizzuto at short, led to three St. Louis runs in the first. Old nemesis Martin, however, singled home a New York run in the second. He tripled home the go-ahead run in a three-run Yankee fourth. New York won, seven to three.

TRIPLE PLAY EXECUTED AGAINST THE BROWNS

With their lead over the second place White Sox reduced to just four games, the Yankees defeated the Browns, six to four on Friday, July seventeenth, executing four double plays, and their second triple play of the season. After Wertz and Lenhardt each walked opening the second inning, Courtney hit a sharp liner to center. Irv Noren, subbing for the injured Mantle, grabbed the liner off his shoe tops as he fell. He fired a strike to Shortstop Rizzuto for the force at second. The relay to Don Bollweg at first was in time to beat the diving Lenhardt. On Saturday afternoon, the Yanks blasted the Browns again, thirteen to two.

SPECULATION ON MOVING THE BROWNS

Though publicly Veeck was saying the Browns weren't for sale, much of the news coverage immediately following the All-Star Break, speculated on the eventual transfer of the franchise.

With the Browns awash in a sea of red ink, there was talk of moving the club to Baltimore soon. Club owners in both leagues had just agreed to prohibit any franchise switches until after October first. But there was speculation that the struggling Philadelphia A's franchise was considering moving to Baltimore soon, preempting the Browns. Toronto, Montreal, Dallas, Denver, Minneapolis, Houston, and Kansas City were all queued up seeking major league franchises. None of these cities, however, was prepared for a mid-season move. Most did not have an acceptable ballpark in which to host major league baseball.

Having counted on a move to Baltimore, Veeck seemingly had run out of stimulating gimmicks in St. Louis. With no illusions, he told New York Times' Columnist Arthur Daley that he actually had three teams, one the field, one going, and one coming:

> Let's look at this thing frankly. George Weiss and Branch Rickey are the shrewdest operators in the business. They are smarter and wealthier than I am. I can't operate the way they do. I consider myself a junk dealer. So I trade five men to get one player. Then I buy back players I've already traded away to fill my positions. Eventually I can be more choosy and selective. But not for a while.

Judging by the Browns' last place standing, it hardly seemed worth the effort. But there was some young talent and the Browns' had half a season in St. Louis left in which to evaluate it.

A GHOST HIT

Brecheen won for the first time in a month in the first game of a doubleheader on Sunday, July nineteenth, defeating Washington, five to four. Sievers put the Browns on top, hitting a two-run homer in the first inning. Dyck's single to left in the seventh inning appeared to score Kokos from third base, and Sievers from second base. On an appeal play, however, the umpire ruled Sievers out for failing to touch third base. That was the third out. Only Kokos run counted. The official scorer ruled that Dyck's "ghost" hit didn't count. It did drive in the winning run, however. After Washington rallied for three runs in the eighth inning, Paige took over, holding the visitors scoreless the rest of the way. Sievers hit another two-run homer in the first inning of the second game. Dyck homered in the third. But the Senators won easily, thirteen to four.

Philadelphia pounded the Browns on Wednesday, July twenty-second, eleven to one. The A's won again on Thursday night. The Browns lost their second fourteen inning game of the season, seven to four. Trailing four to nothing in the bottom of the sixth, the Browns rallied for three runs. Then Kokos doubled home the tying run in the bottom of the seventh. Although Paige hurled six scoreless innings in relief, the A's Eddie Robinson hit a decisive two-run double in the fourteenth.

Boston shut out the Browns in both games of a doubleheader on Friday night, eight to nothing, and six to nothing. The Browns' had not scored a run in twenty-five innings. They scored six times on Saturday, but Boston won anyway, seven to six. Kryhoski hit a bases loaded double in a four run third inning. Kokos homered in the sixth. Boston rallied for two runs in the top of the ninth. The Red Sox won again in the first game of a doubleheader on Sunday, July twenty-sixth, seven to five. Dyck hit two home runs, collecting three RBIs. However, he also committed three errors. The Brown's defeated the departing Red Sox, eight to five in the second game, scoring five times in the first inning. Boston tied the game in the fifth. But Dyck hit his third homer of the day with two men on in the eighth inning to give the Browns the win. The Browns closed out the home stand with their seventh win against eighteen losses. They closed out the month of July with four road losses in Philadelphia, and New York. Through the end of July the Browns had only sixteen home victories against forty-six losses. The Browns' twelve victories in August were the most in any single month during their final season. The ball club was in last place, thirty-four games out.

AUGUST

At Yankee Stadium on Saturday, August first, Lenhardt's three-run homer in the eighth inning gave Brecheen a three to two victory. It also evened the series at one game each. It was Brecheen's third straight win. It was only the third Browns' win over the Yankees in sixteen attempts. The Yankees routed St. Louis, eleven to three, on Sunday. Rookie catcher Gus Triandos doubled home a run for the Browns in his major league debut.

BROWNS BEAT WILLIAMS AND THE RED SOX IN TEN INNINGS

After Browns dropped the first two games of a series in Boston, they posted an eight to seven victory in ten innings in the series finale at Fenway Park on Thursday, August sixth. It was one of the few highlights of the entire second half of the season. In the top of the ninth, former Red Sox Vern Stephens hit a three-run homer, giving the Browns a seven to four lead. The Red Sox rallied to tie the game in the bottom half of the inning, and still had runners on first and third with only one out.

Ted Williams then made a dramatic appearance as a pinch hitter. It was his first at bat after fifteen months of military service in Korea. Responding to a standing ovation, he pulled reliever Stuart's first pitch far into the right field stands, though a few feet outside the foul pole.

He then popped-up harmlessly. Bob Young homered off the right field foul pole in the tenth to give the Browns the win.

On Friday August seventh, Washington blasted St. Louis, twelve to nothing at Griffith Stadium. Pillette and Paige held the Senators to just five hits in the first game of a doubleheader on Sunday, sharing a three to nothing shutout. Washington claimed the second game, twelve to three.

BOONE'S FOURTH SLAM—THIRD AGAINST BROWNS

St. Louis began their only winning home stand of the season on Tuesday, August eleventh, splitting a doubleheader with the Detroit Tigers. In the first game, Lenhardt hit a three-run homer in the home eighth, giving the Browns a five to two victory. The Tigers won the second game, nine to three. On Wednesday night Ray Boone hit his third grand slam of the season off St. Louis pitching, his first as a Tiger. Overall it was his fourth Grand Slam of the Year. Detroit won again, seven to three.

THE SMALLEST HOME CROWD

On Thursday afternoon in St. Louis Kretlow earned the Browns a series split, battling the Tigers' Ned Garver for ten scoreless innings before being removed for a pinch hitter. Stuart completed the shutout, retiring all three batters he faced in the top of the eleventh. Wertz doubled home the games only run in the bottom half of the inning to give St. Louis a one to nothing win. A paid crowd of only 980 was in attendance, the smallest attendance of the season.

BROWNS SWEEP INDIANS

On Friday evening, August fourteenth, Cleveland prevailed, eight to seven. Indians' first baseman Luke Easter hit two home runs. On Sunday, August sixteenth, the Browns closed out the home stand with their most impressive effort of the year, sweeping their only home doubleheader of the season against the third place Indians. In the opener the Browns rallied for six runs in the third inning. Kryhoski's run scoring single in the bottom of the sixth produced a seven to six win.

Littlefield, who left the first game after yielding four runs in the fourth inning, was the winning pitcher in the second game. St. Louis won, seven to five. Wertz hit his thirteenth homer of the year in the fourth inning, scoring the first run of the game. Kryhoski's hit a solo homer in the sixth inning to close out the Browns' scoring. It was Kryhoski's twelfth homer of the year, surpassing his 1952 total of eleven.

On Tuesday night, August eighteenth, at Comiskey Park in Chicago the Browns began a road trip by dropping both ends of a another well played doubleheader before a crowd of 32,638. In the first game, Kretlow lost to Trucks, the man he had been traded for in June, three to two, though he allowed just four hits in six innings. In the nightcap Paige, in a rare start, held the second place White Sox scoreless through the first four innings. A home run in the ninth inning by Wertz accounted for the only St. Louis run. Chicago won, two to one.

BROWNS END PIERCE'S SCORELESS STREAK

On Wednesday night, consecutive sixth inning doubles by Sievers and Lenhardt shattered Chicago starter Billy Pierce's streak of forty consecutive scoreless innings. The Browns won the game in the tenth, four to three, when Moss tripled home a run and scored on a squeeze bunt by Wertz. Rookie Bob Turley struck out the side in the tenth, earning his first major league victory. When Johnny Groth was hit on the left temple by a fast ball from Pierce in the sixth, he fell to the ground unconscious. He left the field on a stretcher and was taken to the hospital. X-rays showed that he had suffered a concussion. He was sidelined until August thirtieth.

In Cleveland on Friday, August twenty-first, St. Louis played their third doubleheader in six days. Again the Browns played hard. Al Rosen, driving for the American League Triple Crown, hit two home runs in the first game, and another in the nightcap. Kryhoski hit his thirteenth homer, and Wertz his fifteenth, in the opener. Rosen's second homer came with two on in the seventh. It broke open a close game. The Indians won seven to three. His third homer of the day came with a man on in the fourth inning of the second game. That was the only scoring off Brecheen before he yielded a run scoring double with two men out in the twelfth. Cleveland won again, three to two.

Garcia won his fifteenth game for the Indians on Saturday afternoon, four to one. The game cost the Browns the services of Wertz who fouled a ball off his instep in the fourth inning.

ROSEN CLAIMS TRIPLE CROWN LEAD

The Indians swept another doubleheader on Sunday afternoon, three to one, and nine to nothing. Rosen claimed the lead in all triple crown categories with three hits in the doubleheader, including his thirty-third homer. Stephens bruised his knee sliding into second in the opener. He joined regulars Wertz, and Groth on the injured list. Wertz and Groth were listed as day to day.

A FINAL WINNING STREAK

On Thursday, August twenty-seventh, the Browns began their final extended home stand. In the first game of a Twilight doubleheader, Wertz celebrated his return to the line up by hitting his sixteenth and seventeenth home runs. His second, with a man on in the bottom of the ninth gave St. Louis a five to four win. Zernial hit his thirty-fourth for Philadelphia, keeping pace with Rosen. Sievers, pinch hitting for Courtney, walked with the bases loaded in the eighth inning of the second game, forcing in the deciding run. Dyck then hit a sacrifice to give St. Louis a three to one win. Stuart (8-2), allowed one hit in two innings of relief. It was the sixtieth and final appearance of the year for Stuart, establishing a club record. Although all his efforts were in relief, he finished the season with the second highest winning percentage in the American League.

Pillette completed the sweep with an eight to three victory on Friday night. Kryhoski banged out a home run, a triple, and a double, driving in four runs. Zernial's hit his thirty-fifth for the A's.

The Browns pushed their final winning streak of any length to four games as Larsen's two-hitter halted Washington, three to nothing, in the opener of a doubleheader on Sunday, August thirtieth. It was their sixth straight home victory. Wayne Terwilliger's single in the eighth broke up Larsen's no hit bid. Lenhardt had three hits, driving in two St. Louis runs. Washington snapped the streak in the second game winning nine to three.

The Browns hit three home runs on the final day of August. But Washington won again, four to three. Solo homers by Lenhardt and Sievers gave the Browns a two to nothing lead. Pitcher Turley homered to tie the game in the seventh. The last place Browns were forty-one games back of New York. They were two games behind seventh place Philadelphia.

SEPTEMBER

When the Yankees visited Busch Stadium for the final time on Wednesday, September second, Allie Reynolds stopped St. Louis, nine to one, yielding only an unearned run in the eighth.

TRIPLE PLAY EXECUTED BY THE BROWNS

The game featured a triple play by the Browns. Mantle singled and Berra reached on an error, opening the fourth inning. Then Gene Woodling lined to Young who tossed to Hunter, covering second, for the force on Berra. Hunter's relay to Kryhoski nipped Mantle for the third out, answering the triple play executed by the Yankees, against the Browns, on July seventeenth in St. Louis. There were only four triple plays made during the 1953 season. The Yankees were involved in three. On Thursday night, New York won in their final regular season appearance ever in St. Louis, eight to five. A three-run homer by Groth in the second inning was wasted.

BIGGEST INNING OF THE YEAR

In the bottom of the fifth inning against the Tigers on Friday, September fourth, the Browns pushed across ten runs in the bottom of the fifth inning. They coasted to a fourteen to six win. A grand slam by Wertz, his eighteenth home run of the year, was the key blow in the biggest inning of the year for St. Louis. Starting pitcher Larsen also homered in the huge fifth.

MEANWHILE IN BALTIMORE

That afternoon in downtown Baltimore, James C. Anderson, President of the City Department of Parks and Recreation, announced that he had reached a tentative agreement with general manager Rudy Schaeffer of the Browns, to bring the franchise to Baltimore. Written agreements concerning the rent on the Baltimore's Memorial Stadium, and revenue from parking and concessions had been initialed. Approval from American League owners was expected.

LAST VICTORY IN ST. LOUIS

With just 1,960 fans in attendance, the lame duck franchise defeated the Tigers again on Saturday afternoon, one to nothing. A twelfth inning homer by Kokos into the right field pavilion gave the Browns their last victory ever in St. Louis. Turley out dueled Ralph Branca.

In a five to two loss to the Tigers on Sunday, Sievers fractured a small bone in his left hand while making a tag in the third inning. He was lost to the Browns for the remainder of the season. Despite the loss, the Browns finished their most successful home stand on the year with six victories and five defeats.

On Monday, September seventh St. Louis began a final road trip. The Indians swept a doubleheader, three to nothing, and ten to seven. In the opener the Indians Bob Lemon gained his nineteenth victory. Groth, who had homered in the fourth, singled home two Browns' runs in the top of the seventh inning to tie the game. The Indians, however, scored three in the bottom half of the seventh. Rosen hit his thirty-ninth home run in the nightcap.

In their final trip to Washington's Griffith Stadium on Wednesday night the Browns earned a split in a doubleheader. Larsen pitched his second shutout in three games, winning two to nothing, in the opener. The Senators captured the final game, two to one, in twelve innings. Kryhoski tripled home the only Browns' run in the top of the ninth. St. Louis had fourteen hits, leaving twelve runners on base.

PILLETTE IS BRILLIANT

Beginning their final visit to Fenway Park in Boston on Friday night, September eleventh, the Browns defeated the Red Sox, two to nothing, behind a brilliant three hitter by Pillette. On Saturday afternoon the Red Sox won, seven to six. in twelve innings. Hunter singled home the tying run in the eighth to send the game into extra innings. Wertz hit his nineteenth, and final, homer of the year.

Larsen won his fourth straight in the opener of a doubleheader in Philadelphia on Sunday, five to two. Bob Trice, a twenty-five year-old rookie Negro right hander, lost in his major league debut. In the second game A's right hander Harry Byrd ended a personal nine game losing streak, shutting out St. Louis, two to nothing. Despite a strong effort, Brecheen lost in the final start of his career. He had only two losing seasons in thirteen years in the majors, winning 133 games and losing 92.

The Yankees had already clinched the American League Pennant. Crown Prince Aki Hito of Japan watched the Browns and Yankees split a meaningless doubleheader in New York on Wednesday night, September sixteenth. Pillette won his second straight, defeating the New York in the opener five to three. Hunter and Lenhardt singled home runs in the sixth. Paige drove in the final run of the game with a single in the ninth. Turley lost the nightcap, three to two, though he allowed only four hits.

LARSEN BEATS THE YANKEES

Larsen won his fifth in a row in the Brown's final appearance at Yankee Stadium on Thursday night, seven to one. Again there were only four Yankee hits. The Yankees lost five times to the Browns in 1953, four times in Yankee Stadium.

THE FUTURE OF THE BROWNS

The media continued to speculate over the future of the Browns. Union Oil reportedly wanted to buy the franchise, and move it to Los Angeles. Bill Veeck visited that city in Mid August, as a representative of Union Oil.

Manager Marion preferred Baltimore. He hoped the matter would be resolved quickly. "I know we'll be able to improve ourselves the moment this is cleared up," he said. "There were a lot of changes that could have been made this season—only our hands were tied because everything was so unsettled."

TRUCKS WINS HIS TWENTIETH

In the second game of a doubleheader on Sunday afternoon, September twentieth, Virgil Trucks, who won five early season games with St. Louis, defeated his former team for the second time, five to two, becoming the first White Sox pitcher in twelve seasons to post twenty victories in a season. Kokos and Kryhoski both homered in the first off Trucks. The right hander yielded only three more hits. First baseman Ferris Fain collected his one thousandth career hit for Chicago. In the opener Chicago starter Bob Keegan pitched his second straight shutout, winning four to nothing.

THE LAST OF SATCHEL PAIGE

The Browns' seven to three victory in Detroit on Tuesday, September twenty-second was their last as a representative of the city of St. Louis. It was also the last victory in the storied career of Satchel Paige. Celebrating his forty-sixth birthday, Paige pitched seven innings. He allowed just four hits. Larsen pitched the final two innings in relief. Groth's three-run homer in the ninth was the key hit of the contest.

Browns' operating losses for the year totaled more than $400,000. Stockholders had already authorized the move of the franchise, and Veeck had tentative agreements with representatives of city of Baltimore. Still, the final decision still rested with the American League.

On September twenty-fourth, the proposed transfer to Baltimore received a set back. Walter White, executive secretary of the National Association for the Advancement of Colored People, wired American League President Will Harridge:

> Because of the city's rigid pattern of segregation, including the exclusion of Negroes from hotels and restaurants, the National Association for the Advancement of Colored People urges the American League not to approve the transfer of the franchise of the St. Louis baseball team to the City of Baltimore.

The move of the Browns to Baltimore was not quite locked into place. There was continuing animosity between Veeck and other American League club owners. The *New York Times* quoted an unidentified major league baseball executive who indicated that other owners preferred Toronto or Montreal over Baltimore. The source further speculated:

> There are at least three clubs who definitely will vote against moving the Browns to Baltimore. Clark Griffith of Washington, and the Macks of Philadelphia, don't want Veeck in between them, under any circumstances. Don't expect the Yankees to vote for Baltimore either. They've been trying to peddle Kansas City to Veeck, who wants no part of it.

The Senators' Griffith opposed any move farther west than St. Louis. "I don't want any changes that will increase our travel difficulties," he said, suggesting Minneapolis as an acceptable location. He pointed out that the New York Giants' Triple A farm team in Minneapolis led the American Association in attendance.

THE END

Before the final night game at Sportsman's Park on Friday, September twenty fifth, some fans hung Bill Veeck in effigy. But there were only 2068 in attendance. And the Browns lost, seven to two. On Saturday afternoon, Rookie center fielder Jim Pisoni homered in the second inning. Hunter hit the final homer of the year for the Browns in the eighth. The White Sox won again, however, six to three.

It all ended for the Browns at Busch Stadium on Sunday, September twenty-seventh. 3174 fans watched Chicago's Billy Pierce post his eighteenth victory, beating Pillette, two to one, in eleven innings. Minnie Minoso's eleventh inning double drove in the winning run. Both starting pitchers completed all eleven innings. The Browns scored their final run ever in the third inning on a double by Johnny Groth, and a single by Ed Mickelson. Former Brown, Jim Rivera tied the game in the eighth inning, homering deep into the leftfield stands. Groth had three hits for the Browns. Lenhardt had two hits, finishing the season with a team best .317 batting mark. The last Brown ever to bat in St. Louis, Jimmy Dyck, popped out to second baseman Nellie Fox, ending the game. The home team ran out of new baseballs and had to complete the game with a recycled ball with a deep gash.

The New York Yankees won the 1953 American League Pennant. Al Rosen won the most American League's Most Valuable Player Award, hitting forty-three home runs, and driving in 145 runs. Washington's Mickey Vernon, edged Rosen .337 to .336. for the batting title, preventing the Cleveland shortstop from winning the Triple Crown. The Browns finished in last place forty-six an one-half games out of first, and seven games back of the seventh place Athletics.

Prior to World Series, American League club owners met in New York to discuss the fate of the Browns. After a ten hour conference on September twenty-ninth, the balloting to ratify the transfer of the franchise to Baltimore was deadlocked at four. Six votes were required for approval. The Yankees, Red Sox, Athletic, and Indians, who had supported the move at a preseason meeting in Tampa, Florida, voted no.

Yankee co-owner Del Webb, who originally favored moving the Browns to Los Angeles, told reporters:

> Baltimore offered a hell of a good deal. What I objected to was that with so many clubs in one area, Baltimore would probably kill the other two cities (Washington and Philadelphia). We have one bad city right now, in Philadelphia. We might have would up with three. Maybe it would have been better to put Baltimore in, and move the other two clubs out.

Philadelphia and Washington voted in support of the move, positioning themselves to gain support for future moves. In fact, owners from both leagues were jockeying for position in a race for expansion to the West Coast. The Pacific Coast League itself had aspirations to elevate itself to the status of a third major league. However, Washington Senators' owner Clark Griffith ridiculed the idea:

> It would be suicide for them to try to become major league. They don't have the players. The best thing for the league would be for Los Angeles to become majors, and the rest of the clubs to form an A or B league.

Both leagues wanted a package deal, including both Los Angeles and San Francisco, in order to simplify scheduling and transportation problems. Some owners, however, felt that neither city had an adequate ballpark in which to stage Major League Baseball. Phil Wrigley, chewing gum magnate, and owner of the National League Chicago Cubs, owned the Pacific Coast League team in Los Angeles, and the small ballpark there, also called "Wrigley Field."

The Baltimore syndicate headed by Clarence W. Miles originally intended to purchase half of Veeck's seventy-nine percent controlling interest in the Browns, allowing Veeck to continue as general manager. Perceiving that the Veeck's continuing presence was a primary obstacle to completing the deal, Miles raised the additional money to buy the Browns outright. On Tuesday, September thirtieth, American League owners approved the sale of the Browns. Baltimore was returning to the American League for the first time since 1903. The original Baltimore franchise had transferred to New York to become the Highlanders, who eventually became the Yankees. At the same meeting the owners passed a resolution that provided for expansion to a ten team league if, and when, it became practical to bring Los Angeles and San Francisco into the Major Leagues.

Despite their suspect won-lost record, the St. Louis Browns franchise left a large legacy. Many of the promotions and giveaways that are now standard at Major League Ballparks were first introduced by the Browns. The carnival atmosphere evident daily throughout the minor leagues today reflects the spirit of Von der Ahe and Veeck, who understood that an afternoon at the Ballpark was supposed to be fun.

THE LAST OF SPORTSMAN'S PARK

The final game in Sportsman's Park-Busch Stadium was a National League contest played on May 8, 1966. St. Louis Cardinals defeated San Francisco Giants, ten to five. Home plate was dug up. It was flown by helicopter to the new Busch Memorial Stadium, where it was installed by Stan Musial.

Demolition of the old park that had served the Browns and Cardinals continuously for seventy-eight seasons began immediately. Cardinals' owner Busch donated the land to a local boy's club. The ball diamond is still there.

THE 1953 ST. LOUIS BROWNS

DAY	DATE	OPPONENT	RESULT	SCORE	PITCHER	ATTENDANCE	RECORD
TUES	04/14/53	DETROIT	W	10-0	VIRGIL TRUCKS (1-0)	11804	1-0
WED	04/15/53	DETROIT	RAIN				
THUR	04/16/53	AT CHICAGO	L	1-0	HARRY BREECHEN (0-1)	11354	1-1
FRI	04/17/53	AT CHICAGO	W	6-4	DICK LITTLEFIELD (1-0)	972	2-1
SAT	04/18/53	AT DETROIT	W	8-7(11)	MARLIN STUART (1-0)	16093	3-1
SAT	04/18/53	AT DETROIT	W	3-2	DUANE PILLETTE (1-0)	16093	4-1
SUN	04/19/53	AT DETROIT	W	6-3(11)	MARLIN STUART (2-0)	7041	5-1
TUES	04/21/53	AT CLEVELAND	L	4-3	HARRY BREECHEN (0-2)	1772	5-2
WED	04/22/53	AT CLEVELAND	RAIN				
FRI	04/24/53	CHICAGO	L	3-0	VIRGIL TRUCKS (1-1)	6947	5-3
SAT	04/25/53	CHICAGO	L	6-4	DUANE PILLETTE (1-1)	4546	5-4
SUN	04/26/53	CHICAGO	W	7-2	DICK LITTLEFIELD (2-0)	5122	6-4
SUN	04/26/53	CHICAGO	L	3-0	MIKE BLYZKA (0-1)	5122	6-5
TUES	04/28/53	NEW YORK	L	7-6(10)	HARRY BREECHEN (0-3)	13463	6-6
THUR	04/30/53	WASHINGTON	W	3-1	VIRGIL TRUCKS (2-1)	2888	7-6
FRI	05/01/53	WASHINGTON	L	6-5	BOBO HOLLOMAN (0-1)	5365	7-7
SAT	05/02/53	WASHINGTON	L	5-4	DON LARSEN (0-1)	3342	7-8
SUN	05/03/53	BOSTON	L	14-5	DICK LITTLEFIELD (2-1)	13463	7-9
SUN	05/03/53	BOSTON	W	6-5	MARLIN STUART (3-0)	13463	8-9
MON	05/04/53	BOSTON	RAIN				
TUES	05/05/53	PHILADELPHIA	W	2-1	VIRGIL TRUCKS (3-1)	3315	9-9
WED	05/06/53	PHILADELPHIA	W	6-0	BOBO HOLLOMAN (1-1)	2473	10-9
FRI	05/08/53	CLEVELAND	L	7-4	HARRY BREECHEN (0-4)	9074	10-10
SAT	05/09/53	CLEVELAND	L	3-2(10)	BOB CAIN (0-1)	7961	10-11
SUN	05/10/53	CLEVELAND	L	12-3	VIRGIL TRUCKS (3-2)	8278	10-12
TUES	05/12/53	AT PHILADELPHIA	W	7-3	DON LARSEN (1-1)	7483	11-12
WED	05/13/53	AT PHILADELPHIA	L	2-1	SATCHEL PAIGE (0-1)	3108	11-13
THUR	05/14/53	AT WASHINGTON	L	2-1	DICK LITTLEFIELD (2-2)	7090	11-14
FRI	05/15/53	AT WASHINGTON	W	4-0	VIRGIL TRUCKS (4-2)	3381	12-14
SAT	05/16/53	AT WASHINGTON	L	6-0	HARRY BREECHEN (0-5)	3906	12-15
SUN	05/17/53	AT NEW YORK	L	6-5(10)	MIKE BLYZKA (0-2)	42596	12-16
SUN	05/17/53	AT NEW YORK	DARK				
TUES	05/19/53	AT BOSTON	L	4-3	SATCHEL PAIGE (0-2)	3733	12-17
WED	05/20/53	AT BOSTON	L	4-3(14)	DON LARSEN (1-2)	4121	12-18
FRI	05/22/53	AT CLEVELAND	RAIN				
SAT	05/23/53	AT CLEVELAND	L	5-1	DICK LITTLEFIELD (2-3)	5816	12-19
SUN	05/24/53	AT CLEVELAND	L	5-1	BOBO HOLLOMAN (1-2)	17278	12-20
SUN	05/24/53	AT CLEVELAND	L	9-8	BOB CAIN (0-2)	17278	12-21
MON	05/25/53	CHICAGO	L	7-5	HARRY BREECHEN (0-6)	4114	12-22
TUES	05/26/53	CHICAGO	L	8-2	DUANE PILLETTE (1-2)	3614	12-23
WED	05/27/53	CLEVELAND	W	5-1	BOBO HOLLOMAN (2-2)	3954	13-23
THUR	05/28/53	CLEVELAND	W	7-5	DICK LITTLEFIELD (3-3)	4068	14-23
FRI	05/29/53	AT DETROIT	W	11-5	HARRY BREECHEN (1-6)	3208	15-23
SAT	05/30/53	AT DETROIT	W	5-4	VIRGIL TRUCKS (5-2)	24007	16-23
SAT	05/30/53	AT DETROIT	W	13-1	BOB CAIN (1-2)	24007	17-23
SUN	05/31/53	AT CHICAGO	L	7-4	BOBO HOLLOMAN (2-3)	19448	17-24
SUN	05/31/53	AT CHICAGO	W	7-4	MIKE BLYZKA (1-2)	19448	18-24
TUES	06/02/53	WASHINGTON	W	5-3	SATCHEL PAIGE (1-2)	4785	19-24
WED	06/03/53	WASHINGTON	L	3-2(10)	SATCHEL PAIGE (1-3)	3957	19-25
THUR	06/04/53	WASHINGTON	L	10-1	VIRGIL TRUCKS (5-3)	3524	19-26
FRI	06/05/53	NEW YORK	L	5-0	BOBO HOLLOMAN (2-4)	9361	19-27
SAT	06/06/53	NEW YORK	L	6-2	MIKE BLYZKA (1-3)	6522	19-28
SUN	06/07/53	NEW YORK	L	9-2	DICK LITTLEFIELD (3-4)	19795	19-29
SUN	06/07/53	NEW YORK	L	7-2	HARRY BREECHEN (1-7)	19795	19-30
TUES	06/09/53	BOSTON	L	6-5	DON LARSEN (1-3)	3714	19-31
WED	06/10/53	BOSTON	L	11-2	MAX LAINIER (0-1)	3693	19-32
WED	06/10/53	BOSTON	L	3-2	DUANE PILLETTE (1-3)	3693	19-33
THUR	06/11/53	BOSTON	L	7-0	VIRGIL TRUCKS (5-4)	2558	19-34

TWILIGHT TEAMS

DAY	DATE	OPPONENT	RESULT	SCORE	PITCHER	ATTENDANCE	RECORD
FRI	06/12/53	PHILADELPHIA	L	5-3	MIKE BLYZKA (1-4)	2414	19-35
SAT	06/13/53	PHILADELPHIA	L	8-3	DICK LITTLEFIELD (3-5)	1340	19-36
SUN	06/14/53	PHILADELPHIA	L	4-1	DON LARSEN (1-4)	4542	19-37
SUN	06/14/53	PHILADELPHIA	L	3-1	HARRY BREECHEN (1-8)	4542	19-38
TUES	06/16/53	AT NEW YORK	W	3-1	DUANE PILLETTE (2-3)	30362	20-38
WED	06/17/53	AT NEW YORK	L	5-3	BOBO HOLLOMAN (2-5)	9279	20-39
THUR	06/18/53	AT NEW YORK	L	5-0	DICK LITTLEFIELD (3-6)	15953	20-40
THUR	06/18/53	AT NEW YORK	L	3-0	BOB CAIN (1-3)	15953	20-41
FRI	06/19/53	AT BOSTON	L	4-1	DON LARSEN (1-5)	10567	20-42
SAT	06/20/53	AT BOSTON	L	4-2	MARLIN STUART (3-1)	7203	20-43
SUN	06/21/53	AT BOSTON	L	3-1	DUANE PILLETTE (2-4)	15785	20-44
SUN	06/21/53	AT BOSTON	W	2-0	BOBO HOLLOMAN (3-5)	15785	21-44
TUES	06/23/53	AT WASHINGTON	W	4-3	BOB CAIN (2-3)	4960	22-44
WED	06/24/53	AT WASHINGTON	W	7-6	MIKE BLYZKA (2-4)	4223	23-44
THUR	06/25/53	AT WASHINGTON	W	3-1	HARRY BREECHEN (2-8)	3511	24-44
FRI	06/26/53	AT PHILADELPHIA	L	6-5	SATCHEL PAIGE (1-4)	2608	24-45
SAT	06/27/53	AT PHILADELPHIA	W	6-1	DUANE PILLETTE(3-4)	2126	25-45
SUN	06/28/53	AT PHILADELPHIA	W	4-1	DON LARSEN (2-5)	4517	26-45
SUN	06/28/53	AT PHILADELPHIA	L	2-1	MIKE BLYZKA (2-5)	4517	26-46
TUES	06/30/53	AT CHICAGO	W	4-2	BOB CAIN (3-3)	35825	27-46
WED	07/01/53	AT CHICAGO	L	13-4	DICK LITTLEFIELD (3-7)	4438	27-47
FRI	07/03/53	RAIN					
SAT	07/04/53	CHICAGO	L	13-0	DUANE PILLETTE (3-5)	6312	27-48
SAT	07/04/53	CHICAGO	L	4-2	HARRY BREECHEN (2-9)	6312	27-49
SUN	07/05/53	DETROIT	L	10-7	DON LARSEN (2-6)	5417	27-50
SUN	07/05/53	DETROIT	L	7-1	BOBO HOLLOMAN (3-6)	5417	27-51
MON	07/06/53	DETROIT	L	8-7(11)	SATCHEL PAIGE (1-5)	2184	27-
TUES	07/07/53	CLEVELAND	L	6-3	BOBO HOLLOMAN (3-7)	8805	27-53
WED	07/08/53	CLEVELAND	W	6-3	LOU KRETLOW (1-0)	3265	28-53
THUR	07/09/53	CLEVELAND	L	9-1	DON LARSEN (2-7)	3071	28-54
FRI	07/10/53	AT DETROIT	W	8-4	DUANE PILLETTE (4-5)	26106	29-54
SAT	07/11/53	AT DETROIT	W	7-2	BOB CAIN (4-3)	6519	30-54
SUN	07/12/53	AT DETROIT	L	8-7	SATCHEL PAIGE (1-6)	22327	30-55
SUN	07/12/53	AT DETROIT	W	3-2	DICK LITTLEFIELD (4-7)	22327	31-55
TUES	07/14/53	AT CINCINNATI	ALL-STAR GAME				
THUR	07/16/53	NEW YORK	W	8-6	MARLIN STUART (4-1)	7901	32-55
THUR	07/16/53	NEW YORK	L	7-3	BOB CAIN (4-4)	7901	32-56
FRI	07/17/53	NEW YORK	L	6-4	DICK LITTLEFIELD (4-8)	5674	32-57
SAT	07/18/53	NEW YORK	L	13-2	DON LARSEN (2-8)	4642	32-58
SUN	07/19/53	WASHINGTON	W	5-4	HARRY BREECHEN (3-9)	4267	33-58
SUN	07/19/53	WASHINGTON	L	13-4	LOU KRETLOW (1-1)	4267	33-59
TUES	07/21/53	PHILADELPHIA	RAIN				
WED	07/22/53	PHILADELPHIA	L	11-1	DUANE PILLETTE (4-6)	2817	33-60
THUR	07/23/53	PHILADELPHIA	L	7-4(14)	SATCHEL PAIGE (1-7)	2278	33-61
FRI	07/24/53	BOSTON	L	8-0	DICK LITTLEFIELD (4-9)	3656	33-62
FRI	07/24/53	BOSTON	L	6-0	BOB CAIN (4-5)	3656	33-63
SAT	07/25/53	BOSTON	L	7-6	SATCHEL PAIGE (1-8)	1857	33-64
SUN	07/26/53	BOSTON	L	7-5	DUANE PILLETTE (4-7)	4565	33-65
SUN	07/26/53	BOSTON	W	8-5	MARLIN STUART (5-1)	4565	34-65
TUES	07/28/53	AT PHILADELPHIA	L	9-7	DON LARSEN (2-9)	2511	34-66
WED	07/29/53	AT PHILADELPHIA	L	9-3	LOU KRETLOW (1-2)	2247	34-67
THUR	07/30/53	AT PHILADELPHIA	L	5-3	MIKE BLYZKA (2-6)	1905	34-68
FRI	07/31/53	AT NEW YORK	L	11-5	MARLIN STUART (5-2)	6981	34-69
SAT	08/01/53	AT NEW YORK	W	3-2	HARRY BREECHEN (4-9)	12241	35-69
SUN	08/02/53	AT NEW YORK	RAIN				
MON	08/03/53	AT NEW YORK	L	11-3	BOB CAIN (4-6)	7117	35-70
TUES	08/04/53	AT BOSTON	L	6-2	DUANE PILLETTE (4-8)	12318	35-71
WED	08/05/53	AT BOSTON	L	5-0	DON LARSEN (2-10)	5027	35-72

THE 1953 ST. LOUIS BROWNS

DAY	DATE	OPPONENT	RESULT	SCORE	PITCHER	ATTENDANCE	RECORD
THUR	08/06/53	AT BOSTON	W	8-7(10)	MARLIN STUART (6-2)	6792	36-72
FRI	08/07/53	AT WASHINGTON	L	12-0	HARRY BREECHEN (4-10)	4337	36-73
SAT	08/08/53	AT WASHINGTON	RAIN				
SUN	08/09/53	AT WASHINGTON	W	3-0	SATCHEL PAIGE (2-8)	5991	37-73
SUN	08/09/53	AT WASHINGTON	L	12-3	BOB CAIN (4-7)	5991	37-74
TUES	08/11/53	DETROIT	W	5-2	DICK LITTLEFIELD (5-9)	2881	38-74
TUES	08/11/53	DETROIT	L	9-3	DON LARSEN (2-11)	2881	38-75
WED	08/12/53	DETROIT	L	7-3	BOB CAIN (4-8)	2001	38-76
THUR	08/13/53	DETROIT	W	1-0(11)	MARLIN STUART (7-2)	980	39-76
FRI	08/14/53	CLEVELAND	L	8-7	DUANE PILLETTE (4-9)	3209	39-77
SUN	08/16/53	CLEVELAND	W	7-6	HARRY BRECHEEN (5-10)	4862	40-77
SUN	08/16/53	CLEVELAND	W	7-5	DICK LITTLEFIELD (6-9)	4862	41-77
TUES	08/18/53	AT CHICAGO	L	3-2	LOU KRETLOW (1-3)	32638	41-78
TUES	08/18/53	AT CHICAGO	L	2-1	SATCHEL PAIGE (2-9)	32638	41-79
WED	08/19/53	AT CHICAGO	W	4-3(10)	BOB TURLEY (1-0)	9253	42-79
FRI	08/21/53	AT CLEVELAND	L	7-3	DICK LITTLEFIELD(6-10)	8717	42-80
FRI	08/21/53	AT CLEVELAND	L	3-2	HARRY BRECHEEN (5-11)	8717	42-81
SAT	08/22/53	AT CLEVELAND	L	4-1	LOU KRETLOW (1-4)	5600	42-82
SUN	08/23/53	AT CLEVELAND	L	3-1	DUANE PILLETTE(4-10)	13766	42-83
SUN	08/23/53	AT CLEVELAND	L	9-0	BOB TURLEY (1-1)	13766	42-84
THUR	08/27/53	PHILADELPHIA	W	5-4	DICK LITTLEFIELD (7-10)	2843	43-84
THUR	08/27/53	PHILADELPHIA	W	3-1	MARLIN STUART (8-2)	2843	44-84
FRI	08/28/53	PHILADELPHIA	W	8-3	DUANE PILLETTE (5-10)	2024	45-84
SUN	08/30/53	WASHINGTON	W	3-0	DON LARSEN (3-11)	4388	46-84
SUN	08/30/53	WASHINGTON	L	9-3	DICK LITTLEFIELD (7-11)	4388	46-85
MON	08/31/53	WASHINGTON	L	4-3	BOB TURLEY (1-2)	13898	46-86
WED	09/02/53	NEW YORK	L	9-1	DUANE PILLETTE (5-11)	6441	46-87
THUR	09/03/53	NEW YORK	L	8-5	BOB CAIN (4-9)	2330	46-88
FRI	09/04/53	DETROIT	W	14-6	DON LARSEN (4-11)	1744	47-88
SAT	09/05/53	DETROIT	W	1-0(12)	BOB TURLEY (2-2)	1960	48-88
SUN	09/06/53	DETROIT	L	5-2	LOU KRETLOW (1-5)	3251	48-89
MON	09/07/53	AT CLEVELAND	L	3-0	HARRY BRECHEEN (5-12)	15304	48-90
MON	09/07/53	AT CLEVELAND	L	10-7	BOB CAIN (4-9)	15304	48-91
WED	09/09/53	AT WASHINGTON	W	2-0	DON LARSEN (5-11)	4216	49-91
WED	09/09/53	AT WASHINGTON	L	2-1(12)	BOB TURLEY (2-3)	4216	49-92
FRI	09/11/53	AT BOSTON	W	2-0	DUANE PILLETTE (6-11)	3660	50-92
SAT	09/12/53	AT BOSTON	L	7-6(12)	DICK LITTLEFIELD (7-12)	10097	50-93
SUN	09/13/53	AT PHILADELPHIA	W	5-2	DON LARSEN (6-11)	8477	51-93
SUN	09/13/53	AT PHILADELPHIA	L	2-0	HARRY BRECHEEN (5-13)	8477	51-94
WED	09/16/53	AT NEW YORK	W	5-3	DUANE PILLETTE (7-11)	7771	52-94
WED	09/16/53	AT NEW YORK	L	3-2	BOB TURLEY (2-4)	7771	52-95
THUR	09/17/53	AT NEW YORK	W	7-1	DON LARSEN (7-11)	3171	53-95
SUN	09/20/53	AT CHICAGO	L	4-0	DUANE PILLETTE (7-12)	10699	53-96
SUN	09/20/53	AT CHICAGO	L	5-2	BOB TURLEY (2-5)	10699	53-97
TUES	09/22/53	AT DETROIT	W	7-3	SATCHEL PAIGE (3-9)	20072	54-97
FRI	09/25/53	CHICAGO	L	7-2	BOB TURLEY (2-6)	2068	54-98
SAT	09/26/53	CHICAGO	L	6-3	DON LARSEN (7-12)	1937	54-99
SUN	09/27/53	CHICAGO	L	2-1(11)	DUANE PILLETTE (7-13)	3174	54-100

1954 PHILADELPHIA ATHLETICS

Point of No Return

When they were good they were very very good.
But when they were bad they were horrid.

In one sense, the Philadelphia Athletics had a far more distinguished half century than the Boston Braves or St. Louis Browns. Their five World Championships and nine American League pennants were second only to the New York Yankees.

But they were hardly consistent, suffering the ignominy of finishing dead last seventeen times. No other team in either league matched that particular record of futility.

THE HISTORY—CONNIE MACK

Cornelius Alexander McGillicuddy "Connie" Mack was a good defensive-light hitting catcher with the Washington Senators and Pittsburgh Pirates from 1886 to 1896. In 1897 he purchased the Milwaukee team in Ban Johnson's Western League. In 1901, Johnson gave him fifty thousand dollars to establish an American League presence in Philadelphia and challenge the National League Phillies. Mack's career took a star turn. Mack, who managed the Philadelphia A's for almost their entire history, owned twenty-five percent of the franchise. Benjamin Shibe, also a majority stockholder in the National League Phillies, owned fifty percent. Shibe was also a partner of A.J. Reach, a

SHIBE PARK, PHILADELPHIA

Bounded by Lehigh Avenue, North 20th Street, Somerset Street and North 21st Street. Home of both the American League Athletics and National League Phillies from April 12, 1909 until Sept 19, 1954 when the Athletics left for Kansas City. The Phillies remained the sole tenants until October 1, 1970. (Photo courtesy of National Baseball Library, Cooperstown, New York.)

1954 PHILADELPHIA ATHLETICS

Front row—*Renna, Limmer, Ditmar, Hemsley, coach; Joost, manager; Moses, coach; Galan, coach; Robertson, McGhee, Power; Jacobs.* **Middle row**—*Zernial, Bollweg, Astroth, DeMaestri, W. Shantz, Valo, Suder, Finigan, McCrabb, coach; Tadley, trainer.* **Back row**—*Rozek, Fricano, Scheib, Kellner, Van Brabant, Trice, Wheat, Burtschy, Portocarrero, Martin, Upton, R. Shantz.* **Batboys** *Schmidt and Miller seated in front.* (*Photo from The Sporting News collection, St. Louis, Missouri.*)

		Games at position	Bats	Avg.	
C	Joe Astroth	71	R	.221	
1B	Lou Limmer	79	L	.231	14 HR
2B	Spook Jacobs	131	R	.258	**17 Stolen bases**
SS	Joe DeMaestri	142	R	.230	
3B	Jim Finigan	136	R	**.302**	
RF	Bill Renna	115	R	.232	13 HR
CF	Bill Wilson	91	R	.238	**15 HR**
LF	Vic Power	101	R	.255	
OF	Gus Zernial	90	R	.250	14 HR
1B	Don Bollweg	71	L	.224	5 HR
OF	Elmer Valo	62	L	.214	
IF	Pete Suder	69	R	.200	
C	Jim Robertson	50	R	.184	
C	Billy Shantz	51	R	.256	
OF	Ed McGhee	13	R	.208	
IF	Eddie Joost	19	R	.362	1 HR
OF	Joe Taylor	16	L	.224	
SS	Jack Littrell	9	R	.300	

PITCHERS

R	Moe Burtschy	**46**	W 5	L 4	3.79 ERA	
L	Bobby Shantz	2	W 1	L 0	7.88 ERA	
R	Arnie Portocarrero	45	W **9**	L **18***	4.06 ERA	
L	Alex Kellner	27	W 6	L 17	5.39 ERA	
R	Bob Trice	19	W 7	L 8	5.60 ERA	
R	Marion Fricano	37	W 5	L 11	5.16 ERA	
R	Charlie Bishop	20	W 4	L 6	4.41 ERA	
R	John Gray	18	W 3	L 12	6.51 ERA	
L	Morrie Martin	13	W 2	L 4	5.47 ERA	
R	Art Ditmar	14	W 1	L 4	6.41 ERA	
R	Ozzie Van Brabant	9	W 0	L 2	7.09 ERA	
R	Carl Scheib	1	W 0	L 1	22.50 ERA	

RELIEF PITCHERS:

R	Sonny Dixon	**38**	W 5	L 7	4.86 ERA	**4 Saves**
R	Moe Burtschy	46	W 5	L 4	3.80 ERA	**4 Saves**
L	Al Sima	29	W 2	L 5	5.272 ERA	2 Save
R	Dutch Romberger	10	W 1	L 1	11.49 ERA	0 Saves
R	Lee Wheat	8	W 0	L 2	5.72 ERA	0 Saves
R	Bill Upton	2*	W 0	L 0	**1.80 ERA**	1 Save
L	Bill Oster	8	W 0	L 1	6.32 ERA	
L	Dick Rozek	2	W 0	L 0	6.75 ERA	
R	Hal Raether	1	W 0	L 0	4.50 ERA	

MANAGER:

Eddie Joost	W 51	L 103	

Bold Type—led club
* Led league

sporting goods manufacturer. Skeptical of Mack's chances for success in Philadelphia, Baltimore manager John McGraw predicted that the A's would be the league's "white elephant". Taking note of McGraw's gloomy prediction, Mack undauntedly accepted the challenge, even using a "White Elephant" in the official team logo. He aggressively sought out and signed Phillies' second baseman Napoleon Lajoie, outfielder Elmer Flick, and pitchers Chuck Fraser, Bill Bernard, and Bill Dugglesby. The A's finished fourth in their inaugural American League season. Lajoie, whose new $6000 salary far exceeded the $2400 salary limit imposed by the National League, collected three hits in the A's five to one opening day loss to Washington in Philadelphia on April 26, 1901. Surprisingly, the game attracted 10,524 fans. The Phillies home - opener drew only 779. The American League upstarts matched or out drew their National League counterparts in attendance every year until 1915. Mack had clearly exceeded expectations. In Lajoie, a Hall of Famer, won the triple crown. batting .422 with fourteen home runs, and 125 RBIs.

THE COURT INTERVENES

Before the start of the 1902 season, however, the Pennsylvania Supreme Court junction ruled that all the players Mack pirated from his National League rivals, were the property of the Phillies, and ordered the players returned to their original club. Mack partially circumvented the court's ruling by traded Flick, Bernard, and Lajoie to Cleveland. Ohio was another state. The Pennsylvania ruling did not apply. Dugglesby and Fraser, however, were returned to the Phillies. Mack purchased pitcher Rube Waddell from Los Angeles of the California League. The left handed Waddell won twenty-four games in 1902, leading the A's to their first American League championship. Eddie Plank won twenty. In 1903, pitcher, Chief Bender, a graduate of Carlisle Indian School which also claimed the legendary Jim Thorpe as a graduate, joined the A's pitching staff. He won seventeen games. He would become the only Native American to be inducted into the Baseball Hall of Fame. The A's finished second in 1903, and slipped to fifth place in 1904, but there were notable individual accomplishments. Harry Davis led the American League with twelve homers in 1904, with eight in 1905, and with twelve again in 1906. Waddell struck out 349 batters in 1904, establishing a major record. Bob Feller of the Indians recorded 348 strike outs for the Cleveland Indians in 1946. Sandy Koufax eventually broke Waddell's mark sixty one years later, striking out 382 for the Los Angeles Dodgers in 1965.

Waddell and Plank, with twenty-six games and twenty-five victories respectively, led the A's to their second American League Pennant in 1905. Rookie Andy Coakley posted twenty wins, and Chief Bender won sixteen. Waddell missed the World Series after injuring his left shoulder while trying to grab a straw hat off Coakley's head. New York Giant ace Christy Mathewson shut out the A's, three to nothing in the opening game of the series. Plank was the loser. Bender shut out the Giants, three to nothing, defeating Joe McGinnity in the second game to even the series. But Mathewson defeated Coakley, nine to nothing, in game three. McGinnity out dueled Plank, one to nothing in game four. Mathewson then closed out the series with his third shutout, defeating Bender, two to nothing in the fifth and final game, giving John McGraw's Giants the title. Waddell won sixteen games in 1906. The A's slipped to fourth. He won nineteen games helping the A's to a second place finish in 1907. But toward the end of the season, suffering from drinking problems, his behavior became more and more violent and erratic. He blew a seven to one lead in a crucial late season game with the Detroit Tigers. The A's lost the pennant by a game and a half and traded Waddell to the St. Louis Browns in 1908. Nineteen year-old outfielder "Shoeless Joe" Jackson played in a few games for the A's in 1908. Mack recognized Jackson's phenomenal potential. But Jackson was teased unmercifully by teammates because of his rural upbringing, country manner, and lack of education. He was unhappy in Philadelphia. Reluctantly Mack traded Jackson to Cleveland for outfielder Bris Lord after the 1909 season. Jackson batted .387 for Cleveland in 1910.Lord batted only .274 for Philadelphia, although he did bat 310 for the A's in 1911.

THE BALLPARK

From 1901 to 1908 the Athletics played home games at Columbia Park on Columbia Avenue. Shibe Park, named after the majority owner of the A's, opened on April twelfth, 1909. Standing between Lehigh Avenue and Somerset Street, and North Twentieth and Twenty First streets, the first concrete and steel stadium seated twenty thousand, costing half a million dollars. From the outside, the Park looked very much like a palace. Inside, there were none of the customary billboard advertisements adorning the outfield walls because Mack didn't allow them to be posted inside the park. Consequently, there was a bland fifty foot high corrugated steel wall in right field. Extra base hits banged against this green monster made a distinctive clanging sound. Tin roofs made the dugouts uncomfortably hot in summer.

On opening day at Shibe Park on April twelfth, 1909, A's catcher Mike Powers, in pursuit of a foul pop-up, crashed into a concrete wall, suffering external and internal injuries. Surgeons attempts to save him failed. After several operations, Powers developed gangrene and died two weeks after the accident. In spite of the tragedy, the first of two glory eras for the Athletics had begun. Mack's "One Hundred Thousand Dollar Infield" : third baseman J. Franklin "Home run" Baker, shortstop Jack Barry, second baseman Eddie Collins, and first baseman Stuffy McInnis began to take shape, although McGinnis didn't actually replace the aging Harry Davis as the first baseman until the 1911 season. Right hander Charles "Chief" Bender, and left hander Eddie Plank anchored the pitching staff. The A's finished second in their inaugural season at Shibe Park.

But in 1910, the young and aggressive A's won the American League pennant, finishing fourteen and one half games ahead of the second place Yankees. They defeated the National League Chicago Cubs in a five game World Series. Collins led the regulars with a.429 average. The A's had a combined Series batting average of .317. Pitcher Jack Coombs won three games. In the 1911 Series, Baker homered in the second game, defeating the Giants' Rube Marquard. He homered again in the third game, defeating the great Christy Mathewson. In the sixth and final game, Chief Bender defeated New York, thirteen to three.

Although the 1912 A's, led the league in hitting, it finished only third. Tris Speaker batted .383 for Boston with a league leading ten homers and ninety-eight RBI's. He and Smokey Joe Wood, who won thirty-four games, led the Red Sox to 105 wins, the American League pennant, and Boston's only World Series triumph. The Washington Senators finished second. Plank won twenty-six games for the A's in 1912. Rookie outfielders Jimmy Walsh, and Eddie Murphy, purchased from the Baltimore Orioles of the International League, helped the A's back to the pennant in 1913. Collins batted .345, Baker .336 with 126 RBIs, and McGinnis .326. Joe Bush won thirteen games.

The 1913 World Series lasted five games. Philadelphia defeated the Giants again. Baker hit .450. Collins hit .421. Bender defeated Marquard in the opener, six to four. Mathewson hurled a ten inning shutout in the second game, defeating Plank and the A's, three to nothing. In a fifth game rematch, Plank defeated Mathewson and the Giants, three to one. Twenty year-old "Bullet" Joe Bush won only start in the third game, eight to two.

In 1914, the Boston Braves stunned the vaunted A's by sweeping the Series in four games. The first glory era was over. Facing competition from the upstart Federal League, Mack couldn't meet the salary demands of his top players. He sold many of his stars to other American League teams, helping the league survive. The Federal League folded. Mack turned down a substantial offer to manage the New York Yankees. He remained in Philadelphia. However, his A's finished last for seven straight years.

Chief Bender jumped to the Federal League Baltimore Orioles in 1915 but was ineffective, winning just four and losing sixteen games. He returned to Philadelphia to essentially finish his career with the National League Phillies in 1916 and 1917, compiling eight wins against two losses in his final season. He did make one appearance with the American League White Sox as late as 1925. Like Jackie Robinson three decades later, Bender endured verbal abuse from the fans and condescension from sportswriters with grace and dignity.

In 1927, Babe Ruth hit nine of his sixty home runs against the A's. Five came in Philadelphia. Ty Cobb playing for the A's, collected his four thousandth hit in Detroit against his former team, the Tigers. Nearly twenty years earlier the usually reserved Mack had once called Cobb, the "dirtiest player in history" after Cobb, playing for the Tigers, spiked third baseman Home run Baker in the arm. Baker was attempting to make a barehanded tag.

The patient Mack rebuilt his A's. In a memorable era from 1928 to 1932 one of the most dominant teams in baseball history unseated the fabled Ruth Gehrig-Yankees. They were the new home run powerhouse, and champions of the American League. Hall of Fame pitcher Lefty Grove, shortstop Jimmy Dykes, first baseman Jimmie Foxx, catcher Mickey Cochrane, and outfielder Al "Bucketfoot" Simmons led the Athletics to three consecutive pennants.

PREMIER ATHLETIC: JIMMIE "THE BEAST" FOXX

"The Beast" was one of baseball's elite performers, even among Hall of Famers. He was the most significant player in the history of the Philadelphia A's, hitting 534 career homers and finishing with a career batting average of .325. Foxx hit 58 homers in 1932.

As a team the A's peaked at one hundred and seven victories in 1931, winning at least one hundred games in each of five consecutive seasons.

THE HOWARD EHMKE SURPRISE

In the 1929 World Series, the A's easily defeated the Chicago Cubs, four games to one. Surprisingly, Howard Ehmke, at age thirty-six, opened the series for the A's despite having pitched only fifty-five innings during the regular season. Starters Lefty Grove (20-6), George "Moose" Earnshaw (24-8) and Rube Walberg (18-11)led the A's to the Pennant. But Grove and Walberg were both left handed. First baseman Charlie Grimm was the only left handed batter in the Cubs Lineup. Mack refused to name his starter in the opening game of the series, even as the players warmed up at Wrigley Field in Chicago. But he had decided to start Ehmke two weeks before the season ended, and had sent the veteran to scout the Cubs. He told Ehmke of his plan, but no one else. Mack gambled that the side armed delivery, and off speed pitches, from the right handed veteran (7-2) would be effective against the Cubs' predominately right handed lineup. It payed off. The journeyman Emhke set a new Series record by striking out thirteen batters, defeating Chicago, three to one. He struck out Chicago's toughest hitters—Rogers Hornsby (.380), Kiki Cuyler(.360), and Hack Wilson (.345)—twice each. "We were used to guys who threw hard," said Cubs shortstop Woody English. "It was beautiful to watch," said Mack. The Cubs won only the third game of the Series. Chicago, however, led, eight to nothing in the seventh inning of game four before the A's rallied for ten runs to defeat Chicago's ace, Charlie Root.

Matched against the St. Louis Cardinals, the A's won the 1930 Series in six games. The fifth game was scoreless until Foxx hit a two-run homer off Burleigh Grimes in the ninth inning. George Earnshaw had two complete game victories. The Cardinals thwarted Mack's bid for a sixth World Championship by out lasting the A's in the 1931 Series, four games to three. The second A's glory era was over.

The A's attendance figures in the first half of the 1930s were good. However, they did not support the high level of success the club achieved on the field. The World Champion A's drew a franchise record 721,663 in 1930. The last place National League Phillies, who played at tiny Baker Bowl on Broad Street, drew only 299,007. The Yankees, third place finishers in the American League, drew more than both Philadelphia franchises combined. Mack again sold his most talented players. Another prolonged down slide followed. From 1935 to 1950, the A's finished dead last ten times. Outfielders Wally Moses and Indian Bob Johnson distinguished themselves during this otherwise dismal era. Moses hit over .300 for six straight years. Johnson hit twenty or more homers nine times, driving in 100 runs seven times. Despite a last place finish in 1935, the A's led the league in home runs. Power was still an A's trademark.

The National League Phillies became co-tenants at Shibe Park in 1938.

In 1941 Joe DiMaggio hit in five straight games against the A's during his fifty-six game hitting streak. On the final day of the season, Boston's Ted Williams lashed out six hits in a double header at Shibe Park. He finished with a .406 batting average. In 1943, a sixteen year-old A's pitcher, Carl Scheib, became the youngest player ever to appear in an American League game. In time, Mack was able to restore his team to respectability. In 1948, the Athletics finished fourth, drawing a franchise record 945,076 fans.

Despite an eighth place finish, the A's drew 809,805 in 1950. Mack retired at the end of the season. He was, shortly thereafter, inducted in to the Hall of Fame. Eventually, New York's Casey Stengel broke Mack's record of nine pennants, winning his tenth in 1960. Jimmy Dykes replaced Mack as manager in 1951, guiding the A's to a sixth place finish.

The A's finished fourth under Dykes in 1952, finishing with eighty wins and seventy-four losses. It was their last winning season. Right hander Harry Byrd was the American League Rookie of the Year finishing 15-15 with a 3.32 ERA. First Baseman Ferris Fain batted .327. Five foot six inch lefty Bobby Shantz won twenty-four games. Nearly half of the total 627,100 attendance figure came in games when the stylish small southpaw pitched. An overflow crowd watched the American League's Most Valuable Player claim his twentieth victory at Connie Mack Stadium that season. After being hit by a pitch and fracturing his wrist, Shantz compiled a disappointing five and ten record in 1953. The A's drew only 362,113, their lowest attendance since 1936. It was Dykes last season as manager. Thirty-six year-old shortstop Eddie Joost took over the managerial duties for the 1954 campaign.

The National League "Whiz Kids" had taken over the town after winning the pennant in 1950. Led by the pitching of Robin Roberts, and the home run power of outfielder Del Ennis, the Phillies more than doubled the A's attendance in 1953. Even so, there was little talk of transferring the Athletics. With the relocation of the Braves and Browns so recent, Major League club owners agreed that the game needed a period of stability.

THE FINAL SEASON

In April, 1954, Joost, a veteran of fifteen big league seasons, had a modest goal in his first season as manager. He wanted to improve on a seventh place finish the previous season. Only four regulars from the fifty-three squad remained on the roster.

Prior to the start of the season the A's hired Judy Johnson, a scout for the A's since 1951, as the first black member of their instructional staff. Johnson was a former third baseban for the Negro League Hilldale Club and Philadelphia All-Stars. Connie Mack once said, "Had Johnson been white he could have named his price. The brother-in-law of the Milwaukee Braves' outfielder, Bill Bruton, Johnson's primary task was to develop the talent of pitcher Bob Trice, and outfielder Vic Power, the first black players on the A's major league roster.

Power's .349 average with the Kansas City Blues farm won the American Association batting championship in 1953. He had sixteen homers, ten triples, thirty-nine doubles. He had ninety-three RBIs. The twenty-four year old native of San Juan, Puerto Rico, had a reputation for being flamboyant. He was also thought to be combative. A band of Power's supporters picketed Yankee Stadium during the 1953 season. They demanded that he be promoted to the major league level. New York traded the first baseman to Philadelphia on December thirteenth, 1953 as part of a deal involving thirteen players.

Power was the key man in a thirteen player trade. Thirty-two year old left handed First baseman Eddie Robinson, and twenty-eight year old right handed pitcher Harry Byrd went to the Yankees along with third baseman Loren Babe, reserve outfielder Carmen Mauro, and backup first baseman, Tom Hamilton. The twenty-seven year-old Mauro retired rather than accept assignment to the Yankees' Kansas City farm team. "I just got married. I thought I was on the way," he said. "Now they are sending me back to the minors. I'm through with baseball."

In exchange, Philadelphia acquired twenty-eight year-old outfielder Bill Renna who batted .314 in forty games with the fifty-three Yankees, left handed hitting first baseman Don Bollweg, thirty-two, who batted .297, and three minor leaguers: Jim Finigan, a third baseman, Jim Robertson, a catcher, and John Gray, a right handed pitcher.

"I think the Athletics have helped themselves plenty, too," Yankee manager Stengel remarked. "They're all good men."

The trade was a precursor of the "Yankee Shuttle", a unique A's to Yankees relationship, that existed after the club moved to Kansas City. However, it wasn't the only off-season deal. Outfielder Dave Philley, a ten year veteran, was traded to Cleveland for pitchers Lee Wheat and Bill Upton. Thirty-one year old pitcher Joe Coleman was traded, along with pitcher Frank Fanovich, to Baltimore for pitcher Bob Cain.

Outfielder Gus Zernial, six year big league veteran who hit forty-two home runs in 1953, led the returning regulars. Shortstop Joe DeMaestri, outfielder Ed McGhee, and catcher Joe Astroth also returned along with left handed pitchers Alex Kellner, and Morrie Martin. The premier left hander on the staff was Shantz who was counted on to return to form. He was desperately needed to boost attendance.

Right handed veteran Marion Fricano, and rookie Arnold Portocarrero rounded out the starting rotation. The 1953 staff had a collective earned run average of 4.67. Only the Detroit Tigers' pitching staff was worse in 1953. Hall of Fame broadcaster Byrum "By" Saam was the voice of the 1954 Athletics on WCAU radio and television, as he had been since 1939.

APRIL

The "new look" Athletics began their final season at Shibe Park in Philadelphia on Tuesday afternoon, April thirteenth, with a bittersweet six to four win over the Red Sox. Gus Zernial greeted Boston southpaw Mel Parnell, a twenty-one game winner in 1953, with a two-run homer in the first inning. Right fielder Bill Renna doubled home a third run in the first. He tripled home two more runs in the bottom of the fifth inning. The A's led, five to two.

Bobby Shantz held the visiting Red Sox to just five hits. However, after throwing a curve to open the sixth inning, he winced in pain. He picked up the resin bag, slammed it down and summoned manager Eddie Joost from the dugout. He could not continue. Bowing his head in utter dejection, he trudged to the dressing room, taking much of the A's hope for a successful season with him. It was his only victory of the 1954 campaign.

Don Bollweg, another former Yankee, doubled home the A's final run in the eighth inning. Rookie second baseman Spook Jacobs had four hits in his big league debut. Vic Power singled once, and scored twice.

Despite the loss of Shantz, the A's pitching staff performed admirably for the first month of the season. On Thursday April fifteenth in New York, veteran lefty Alex Kellner allowed just six hits. But the Yankees prevailed, winning their home opener, three to nothing, on a cold, windy afternoon. There were 23,494 fans in attendance.

Hank Bauer and Bill Skowron hit back-to-back homers in the bottom of the eighth inning, sealing the Yankees' victory. Power had two of eight Philadelphia hits. He also threw out a runner at the plate in the first inning. Renna and catcher Jim Robertson each had a hit against their former team. Jacobs had two more hits. Through two games, he was six for nine.

On Sunday, April eighteenth, rookie right hander Trice pitched out of several tight spots, defeating Boston in the first game of a double-header, six to four. Doubles by Power, Bollweg, and DeMaestri highlighted a fourteen hit attack. Center fielder Jackie Jensen homered for the Red Sox in the third inning. Jensen's second homer of the day ended the second game in the fourteenth inning, giving the Red Sox a four to three win. Zernial hit two homers for the A's.

On Monday night Morrie Martin allowed only two hits through five innings at Griffith Stadium in Washington. But the Senators won, four to three. Errors by Robertson and Bollweg gave Washington three unearned runs in the seventh inning. The only earned run came off Ditmar, the loser in relief. Washington third baseman, Ed Yost, led off the bottom of the ninth inning with a game winning homer.

On Tuesday night, Kellner shut out the Senators, seven to nothing in the strongest performance of the year by a Philadelphia starting pitcher. Second baseman Wayne Terwilliger's two out single in the eighth inning was the only hit for Washington. Power drove in four runs with a pair of doubles.

However, Washington easily captured the rubber game of the series on Wednesday night, thirteen to one. Fricano took the loss. Catcher Wilmer Shantz, Bobby's brother, singled home Bollweg with the only Philadelphia run in the sixth inning.

On Saturday April twenty-fourth the A's hosted New York in the opener of their first major home stand of the Year. Trice hurled a six hit shutout. Shortstop DeMaestri hit a rare home run in the fifth inning, giving Philadelphia a one to nothing victory. Former teammate Harry Byrd suffered his second loss of the season. With two out in the ninth, Yankee's pinch hitter Joe Collins made a bid to win the game, clearing the fence with a drive down the right field line. The ball hooked foul at the last minute. Collins then lifted an easy fly ball to Power in right to end the contest.

LARGEST HOME CROWD

The first doubleheader of the Year on Sunday , April twenty-fifth, at Shibe Park, attracted 19,930 fans. It was the largest home crowd of the year for the A's. A split gave Philadelphia its only series win of the year over the Yankees. In the opener, Kellner lost to the Yankees for the second time, six to one. Former Yankees figured prominently in the A's four to two victory in the second game. Philadelphia took the lead in the second inning on a single by Renna, and a double by Finigan. Power singled in the fourth inning, scoring on a sacrifice fly by Renna. He opened the sixth inning with a walk, scoring again on singles by Zernial and Bollweg. Renna's sacrifice fly to deep center, off reliever Allie Reynolds, scored Zernial in the sixth. It was the final run of the game. Martin pitched a complete game, picking up his first victory of the year. It was the last time the A's ever defeated the Yankees in Philadelphia.

After a mid week series with Detroit was rained out, the new Baltimore Orioles, the former St. Louis Browns, played their first game ever in Philadelphia on Friday, April thirtieth. Philadelphia won, five to one. Trice won this third straight, retiring the first fifteen batters he faced before Clint Courtney opened the sixth inning with a single. Power had three hits, scoring twice. Renna tripled home a run in the sixth inning. The A's ended April with six wins and five losses. It was the only month in which they posted a winning record. They were in third place, one and one-half games behind first place Chicago.

MAY

On Saturday May first the A's completed a sweep of the brief series. Kellner defeated the Orioles, two to one. Finigan hit a two-out single off Lou Kretlow in the tenth inning, scoring Bollweg from second with the game winner. It was Kretlow's fifth straight loss to the A's over an eight year span. Kellner defeated the Orioles, two to one.

On Sunday, May second, Chicago's Don Johnson hurled a two-hit shutout in the first game of a doubleheader, defeating the A's, four to nothing before a crowd of 12,690. In the second game Elmer Valo's pinch hit single with one out in the ninth inning drove home Renna, giving Philadelphia a two to one victory. Portocarrero allowed five hits in eight innings. After Minoso walked on four pitches to open the bottom of the ninth, Marion Fricano entered the game in relief, posting his first victory of the year.

SHANTZ SHAKY IN RETURN

On Monday night Bobby Shantz pitched three innings in relief in his first starting appearance since being placed on the disabled list. He gave up five runs and five hits in the sixth inning. The A's were unable to post their third consecutive series victory. Chicago won fourteen to three. Sandy Consuegra hurled the straight two-hitter for the White Sox, retiring nineteen straight before giving up a single to Spook Jacobs with one out in the seventh. Jacobs bunt single in the ninth led to three unearned Philadelphia runs.

TRICE WINS FOURTH STRAIGHT

On Tuesday night, May fourth, Trice won his fourth straight, defeating the Indians, three to two, snapping a six game Cleveland winning streak. Zernial's eighth inning single drove home the game winner. The victory boosted the season record to nine wins and seven losses. It was the last time the club would ever be two games over the .500 mark.

The Powerful Indians routed the Athletics behind starter Bob Lemon on Wednesday night, seven to two. Former A's outfielder Dave Philley hit a three-run homer in the eighth inning. First inning errors by Zernial and DeMaestri victimized Kellner, the A's starter. Cleveland scored two unearned runs in the inning. Renna doubled home a run in fourth for Philadelphia. Power hit a lead-off homer in the eighth.

Portocarrero held Cleveland to seven hits on Thursday night. A lead-off homer by Al Smith in the eighth inning gave the Indians a three to one lead. Although Power hit his second solo homer of the series in the bottom of the inning, Cleveland held on for a three to two win.

FIRST HOME STAND SUCCESSFUL

Despite the loss, Philadelphia's first home stand of the year was a success, concluding with six victories against five losses. Home attendance, averaging more than 8000 a game through thirteen home dates, compared with an average of 6500 for the same number of dates the previous year. Shortstop Joe DeMaestri figured prominently in the club's early success with steady, and sometimes spectacular defense. He also provided some unexpected clutch hitting.

The first long road trip of the year began on Friday May seventh in New York. Morrie Martin retired thirteen straight after a first inning double by Bauer. But back-to-back homers by Mantle and Berra in the bottom of the seventh gave the Yankees a two to nothing win. Tom Morgan pitched a five hit shutout for New York.

WILMER SHANTZ HITS GRAND SLAM

In the first game of a doubleheader on Sunday afternoon, Trice lost his first decision of the year. Byrd won his first game as a Yankee, defeating his former team, seven to four. New York third baseman Andy Carey hit a three-run homer in second inning. Joe Collins and Enos Slaughter hit back-to-back homers in the third. Wilmer Shantz countered with a grand slam in the seventh, his first major league homer, ending a string of twenty-five scoreless innings by Yankee pitchers.

Darkness halted the second game of the doubleheader with the score tied one to one after the regulation nine innings. Renna victimized his former team with a homer into the left field seats in the fifth. Mantle doubled off Kellner to lead off the top of the eighth. He scored on a single by Skowron. Zernial, not known for his defense, ended the inning with a spectacular diving catch of McDougald's sinking liner to left.

Shantz told reporters that his arm wasn't responding to treatment:

It is so sore I can hardly lift it. I've been to some of the best doctors in the country. None of them have been able to help me. I haven't the slightest idea whether I'll ever be able to throw normally again."

The A's suffered two more defeats in their first ever visit to Memorial Stadium in Baltimore. A four run top of the seventh inning on Monday, May tenth, gave Philadelphia a six to three lead Trice entered the game in relief of Burtschy with one out in the ninth inning. The bases were full. He yielded a single and a double, allowing the tying runs to score. A sacrifice fly to right by Sam Mele brought home the winning run. On Tuesday night Joe Coleman shut out his former team, two to nothing. Jacobs and Renna had the only Philadelphia hits. Renna remained among the league leaders in batting with a .310 average.

On Thursday, May thirteenth Philadelphia snapped the six game losing streak, defeating Virgil Trucks in Chicago, three to two. The A's scored twice in the top of the ninth inning on a double by Bollweg, and singles by Zernial, and Pete Suder.

Chicago moved into first place in the American League on Friday, May fourteenth, nipping the A's, four to three. Daring Minnie Minoso scored from all the way first on a single in the bottom of the ninth inning. On Saturday afternoon Trice gave up four runs in the first three innings. But Bollweg and Renna doubled, leading a five run A's rally in the top of the fourth. Chicago reclaimed the lead with two runs in the bottom of the inning. Zernial homered in the sixth inning to tie the game. The White Sox won again in the bottom of the ninth. Catcher

Carl Sawatski singled home the deciding run with two out. Lee Wheat, in relief, took the loss in his first major league appearance.

In the first game of a doubleheader on Sunday, May sixteenth, at Cleveland, Bollweg singled home a run in the first, and hit a three-run homer off Bob Feller in the third. The Indians, however, answered with six runs in the fourth, winning, twelve to seven. Rosen hit his fifth homer.

DEMAESTRI SPOILS GARCIA NO-HIT BID

Mike Garcia pitched a one-hitter in the second game, shutting out the A's, six to nothing. A fourth inning single by DeMaestri was the A's only hit. Rosen hit his sixth homer.

At Briggs Stadium in Detroit on Tuesday, May eighteenth, the Tigers pounded Martin for nine hits in four innings, winning eight to three. On Wednesday night Bollweg homered to give the A's a three to two win behind Kellner. Al Kaline's bases loaded single in the ninth inning on Wednesday, May nineteenth gave the Tigers a four to three win.

SPYING ON PLAYERS IN PHILADELPHIA

The May twentieth edition of the *Philadelphia Evening Bulletin* reported that Granny Hamner, shortstop of the National League Phillies, sensed he was being followed after leaving Shibe Park after a game and called the police, who arrested Charles Leland. Leland turned out to be a private detective. "It was a case of my employing a detective to check on some of my players, said Phillies' President Bob Carpenter. "I merely want a baseball team that will be physically, and mentally prepared to play games. I have no suspicions of the behavior of my players nor do I doubt their sincerity." Hamner said calmly ,"I have nothing to worry about. My nose is clean." Despite the A's difficulties on the field, Manager Joost told reporters he wasn't aware of any such activity on the part of the Athletics' management.

On Friday, May twenty-first, in Washington, The A's lost their seventh straight game and their thirteenth loss in fourteen. The Senators took the series opener, seven to three. Bob Porterfield recorded his fifth triumph. On Saturday Zernial hit a three-run homer in the first inning. Arnold Portocarrero posted his first major league victory, ten to three. Zernial, DeMaestri, and Jacobs, had three hits apiece.

Valo hit a three-run homer in the first for Philadelphia on Sunday. Trice singled home another run in the top of the fourth. The Senators tied the game in the bottom of the inning. The Senators scored four runs in the decisive eighth inning, winning, nine to four. They took the series, two games to one.

Before 10,598 fans, the smallest crowd ever to witness a night game at Yankee Stadium, New York defeated the A's, seven to three on Monday, May twenty fourth. Finigan, Power, and Zernial each singled for the only Philadelphia hits. However, each committed an error, allowing the Yankees to score two unearned runs. The A's finished the fifteen game road trip with just two wins.

On Tuesday, May twenty-fifth, in Philadelphia Red Sox catcher Sam White hit a solo homer in the ninth to give Boston a three to two victory. On Wednesday night Zernial hit a grand slam in the third. A tenth inning single by Renna edged the Red Sox, six to five.

On Friday night Washington blasted three homers, overcoming a pair of two-run homers by Zernial. The Senators won easily, twelve to six. Lasting just three innings, Trice walked five, gave up six hits, and lost his third straight.

In the top of the seventh inning on Saturday, May twenty-ninth, Renna and Power collided while chasing a fly ball. They each, however, contributed a run scoring single in the bottom of the inning. The A's won, seven to five. Renna bruised his ribs, putting him out of the line-up for three games.

In the first game of the traditional Memorial Day doubleheader, Washington's Mickey McDermott shut out Philadelphia, six to nothing. In the ninth inning of the second game McGhee's pinch hit double with the bases loaded gave the A's a six to five win. Portocarrero allowed just two earned runs in nine innings. The A's committed three errors.

RED SOX WALLOP THE A'S TWICE

On the final day of the month, 23,255 fans at Fenway Park watched the Red Sox exploit the overworked Philadelphia pitching staff twice. Boston won, twenty to ten, and nine to nothing. The eighteen Red Sox hits in the first game included two homers by shortstop Milt Bolling. Ted Williams also homered. McGhee hit a two-run homer for Philadelphia in the second inning. The A's scored for times, and led, five to three. The A's had twelve hits. Manager Joost, Finigan, McGhee, Valo, and Zernial each had two RBIs. The Red Sox, however, scored four times in the bottom of the second, adding seven more runs in the fourth inning. The thirty runs, combined, marked the highest single game scoring total of the year in the American League. Boston's nine hits in the second game included another homer by Bolling. Jim

Piersall, and Harry Agganis all homered. Philadelphia quietly dropped into seventh place, thirteen games behind the first place Cleveland Indians.

JUNE

A'S POUND RED SOX

The smallest crowd of the season at Fenway Park, just 2342 mostly Boston fans, watched the Tuesday, June first getaway game. In a curious reversal of fortune the A's accumulated a season high twenty-three hits. They pounded the Red Sox, sixteen to six. Trice won his fifth game of the year. He also homered and doubled, driving in three runs. Zernial homered with two men on in the first inning, and homered again in the eighth inning. Those were his tenth and eleventh home runs of the season. Every Philadelphia starter hit safely. Jacobs went four for four, doubling twice. Joost hit his only homer of the year.

On Wednesday, Portocarrero allowed one earned run through seven innings. But in the top of the eighth inning, Martin, in relief, allowed four straight hits including a three-run homer. Baltimore scored six times, winning, nine to one. On Thursday night, Fricano hurled his first complete game of the season, winning, six to two. DeMaestri had three hits, including his second home run of the year. Jacobs also had three hits.

THE SMALLEST HOME CROWD

Only 1092, the smallest crowd of the year in Philadelphia watched Trice post his sixth win in the series finale on Friday, seven to six. That lifted the A's out of last place. Elmer Valo's sixth inning single scored Trice and Jacobs, with the tying and winning runs. McGhee batted in four runs. He hit a two-run homer, and a bases loaded single.

DEMAESTRI SPOILS GARCIA NO-HIT BID—AGAIN

On Saturday, June fifth, Cleveland defeated the A's, four to one, in eleven innings. In an odd coincidence, DeMaestri spoiled a no hit bid by Mike Garcia for the second time, with a fourth inning single, following a walk to Don Bollweg. Bill Shantz walked to load the bases. Bollweg scored on a sacrifice fly by Kellner, giving Philadelphia a one to nothing lead. Garcia retired the next eighteen men he faced. Meanwhile, Kellner held the Tribe scoreless until former Athletics' outfielder Dave Philley hit his second homer of the year, in the seventh inning, to tie the game. Garcia walked to open the bottom of the eleventh. He scored the deciding run on a throwing error by Finigan. Dave Philley drove in an insurance run, with a sacrifice fly.

On Sunday, June sixth, Portocarrero held the first place Indians to three hits, and homered off Bob Feller in the third inning. But it wasn't enough. The Indians won, two to one. Cleveland completed the series sweep, winning the second game of the doubleheader, seven to five. Finigan homered in the bottom of the first, offsetting a solo home run blast by the Indians Larry Doby in the top of the inning. But Indians catcher Hal Naragon tripled home three more Cleveland runs in the fourth inning.

ZERNIAL FINED

Slumping slugger Zernial angrily confronted Manager Joost after being benched for the second game. He was escorted from the dugout by security guards. Joost fined Zernial 250 dollars. It was the heaviest fine imposed on any player in the major leagues all season. Mack told reporters:

> Truthfully I don't know. Nobody tells me anything. I had Joost and Zernial in here. I couldn't get a word in edgewise. Apparently this has been smoldering for some time. As long as Joost is the manager I'll have to stand by him. After all, I put him there. I'm not going to have a ball player managing the club as long as I have a manager.

On Wednesday, June eighth, the visiting Chicago White Sox defeated Philadelphia, nine to three, scoring five times in the seventh inning. Trice took the loss. On Thursday night, Kellner yielded ten hits in six innings. The White Sox won again, nine to four.

Before a doubleheader on Friday, June eleventh, the A's traded Morrie Martin to Chicago. In return Philadelphia acquired pitchers Sonny Dixon and Al Sima, along with outfielder Bill Wilson.

THE LONGEST WINNING STREAK

The Tigers routed the A's in the first game, sixteen to five. Boone hit a two-run homer in the first inning and a grand slam in the fifth inning. Al Kaline hit another grand slam for the Tigers in the seventh. Philadelphia first Baseman Lou Limmer hit his first homer of the year. Fricano limited the Tigers to six hits in the second game, although

Boone hit his third homer of the day. Renna`s solo homer in sixth inning gave the A's a two to one victory, ending the losing streak at six games. The win sparked the A's most productive stretch of the season.

TRICE WINS HIS LAST

On Saturday afternoon, Philadelphia defeated Detroit, four to two. Dixon, in his first appearance with the A's, entered the game with two out in the ninth inning. The bases were loaded. He retired outfielder Bill Tuttle on a fly ball to center, preserving the victory. Bob Trice, the starter, claimed his seventh and last triumph in the major leagues.

Recording their first doubleheader sweep of the year on Sunday, the A's defeated the Tigers four to three, and six to three. Bobby Shantz pinch ran for Zernial who opened the ninth inning with a walk. Limmer then doubled. Both runners scored on a pinch hit single by Power. Ray Boone homered again for Detroit. Portocarrero allowed twelve hits in the second game. Boone hit his fifth home run of the series. But the A's won, six to three, to complete the sweep. They finished the home stand with a respectable six and seven record.

LARGEST CROWD TO WATCH THE A'S

The A's extended their longest winning streak of the season to five games at Comiskey Park in Chicago on Tuesday night, June fifteenth. The crowd of 26,458 was the largest to watch an A's game during their final season. Renna started the eleven to four rout attack with a two-run homer in the first. Wilson also homered, driving in three runs on the day. Finigan had a triple, double, single, and three RBIs. Jacobs had three hits, scoring all three times he reached base. The win moved the A's past Boston and Baltimore into sixth place in the American League standings, only one and one-half games behind Washington. They were four and one-half games behind the fourth place Tigers.

It looked like the streak would continue on Wednesday night. When Renna homered in the first inning, the A's led the White Sox, three to nothing. And Limmer homered in the third, giving Philadelphia a four to two advantage, and A's led six to four after six innings. But Trice could not hold the lead. In the seventh inning, the White Sox rallied for seven runs. Ferris Fain slugged an inside the park grand slam home run. Chicago won, eleven to six. On Thursday, the White Sox won the getaway game as well, six to four.

The A's began another winning streak on Friday night before 23,216 at Briggs Stadium in Detroit, winning, two to one, behind a four hitter by Portocarrero. Boone hit his sixth homer in six games against Philadelphia in the first inning. Renna answered with his third homer in three games in the second inning. Zernial, starting for the first time in a week singled home the game winner in the seventh inning. The A's posted their sixth straight victory over the Tigers on Saturday, June nineteenth, five to four. Detroit led four to nothing. But the A's rallied for five runs in the bottom of the eighth. Jacobs and Power walked. Finigan singled and Renna doubled. Zernial, DeMaestri, and Limmer followed with consecutive singles.

TAKING A SERIES IN CLEVELAND

The Indians had defeated Philadelphia seven straight times since losing in Philadelphia on May fourth. But on Tuesday night, June twenty-second, in Cleveland, the A's won for the seventh time in nine games, four to one. The Indians had defeated Philadelphia seven straight times since losing in Philadelphia on May fourth. Rosen singled with two out the first, eventually scoring on a passed ball. That was the only run allowed by starter Sima, who lasted seven and two-thirds innings, and reliever Dixon, who closed out the game. The Athletics scored three unearned runs in the fourth inning. Finigan and Renna singled Renna. Indians' third baseman Rudy Regalado booted a slow roller off the bat of Bill Wilson, loading the bases. Astroth followed with an infield hit off pitcher Early Wynn's glove, driving n a run. Sima singled home two more.

After giving up a two-run homer to Larry Doby in the first inning on Wednesday night, Trice held the Indians hitless until the sixth. But the Indians won, five to two. Nevertheless the A's completed their only series win over the Indians on Thursday, June twenty fourth, winning five to one. Portocarrero won his third straight. A triple by Wilmer Shantz, and a two-run homer by Limmer highlighted a four run second inning rally. DeMaestri hit his third, and final, homer of the year in the fourth. Although averaging five runs a game, the Indians scored just seven runs in these three games in their home park. For the much maligned Philadelphia pitching staff, it was a season high water mark.

The surprising A's were now winners of nine of their last twelve games, including five of the first eight games on the current road trip. After splitting six games against the first place Indians, and the second place White Sox, they confidently began a weekend series in Baltimore.

116

The seventh place Orioles, however, proved rude hosts. On Friday, June twenty-fifth, Baltimore scored four times in the first inning, coasting to a five to one win. The former St. Louis Browns' franchise won again on Saturday, five to four, in ten innings. Joost walked with the bases loaded to give the A's a four to three lead in the top of the tenth inning. Moe Burtschy replaced Romberger after the Orioles tied the score in the bottom of the inning. Inheriting runners on first and third, and one out, he wild pitched home the winning run. In the opener of a doubleheader on Sunday, four Philadelphia errors sabotaged a complete game performance by Trice. Trice walked only one batter and allowed no earned runs. Dick Kryhoski singled home the winning run for Baltimore in the eleventh inning. The A's won, four to three. Kryhoski also singled home the winning run in the ninth inning of the second game as the Orioles completed the sweep with a three to two win.

A'S RETURN HOME—PORTOCARRERO WINS SIXTH

After an extremely disappointing road trip, the Athletics returned to Shibe Park for a short two game home stand against the Washington Senators. In the opener outfielder Bill Renna's seventh inning triple gave the A's a three to two win. Arnold Portocarrero evened his record at six and six. In the concluding game A's catcher Bill Wilson hit two mammoth homers over Shibe Park's left field roof more than 450 feet away, giving the home team an eight to seven victory and a series sweep.

BEST FULL MONTH

The two games were again played before disappointing crowds. Despite the modest three game winning streak the Mackmen's record at month's end was just twenty-eight wins against forty one losses. However, in the month of June the A's posted fourteen wins and fourteen losses, boosting the club to fifth place in the standings. It was their best full month of the season.

CONTEMPLATING A MOVE

June was a successful month. After thirty-three home games, however, the A's had drawn only 125,000 fans. And on July first, the Mack family informed Philadelphia Mayor, Joe Clark, that they were negotiating a loan to finance club operations for the remainder of the season. They would have to sell or move the team unless they drew draw 400,000 fans in the remaining home games. The Mayor called an emergency meeting of seventy-five top community leaders. He formed a "Committee to Keep the Athletics in Philadelphia." Clark told reporters that the loss of the club would be a severe loss to the economy of the Philadelphia area. The ultimate fate of the club rested with the Mack family, the fans, and local businessmen. There would be no city subsidy. The committee suggested soliciting ten dollars each from Television viewers. All remaining A's games would be televised. The price of bleacher seats would be lowered to fifty cents. The club received ticket purchase pledges worth $55,000.

The cities of Dallas, Minneapolis-St. Paul, Houston, and Kansas City had all tentatively expressed interest in acquiring the franchise. In San Francisco city officials were going ahead with plans to build a major league baseball stadium financed by a five million dollar bond issue. After meeting with Francis McCarty, a member of the San Francisco board of Supervisors, Roy Mack, A's Executive Vice President, and middle son of owner Connie Mack, publicly declared, "the A's are not going to move."

JULY

The A's started the month in fifth place, twenty games back of the league-leading Indians. On Friday, July second, the Red Sox defeated Trice eight to four at Fenway Park. Kellner defeated the Red Sox on Saturday, seven to three. Zernial's two-run homer in the second, was his seventh homer against Boston. Joost singled home two runs in the third inning.

On Sunday, the fourth of July, Boston southpaw Leo Kiely blanked the Athletics, eight to nothing. Wilmer Shantz joined his brother on the injured list for ten days. He cut his arm while tagging out Grady Hatton at the plate in the second inning. The cut required eight stitches to close.

New York won both games of a twilight doubleheader on Monday at Yankee Stadium, seven to four, and eleven to two. In the opener, Zernial singled home Jacobs in the eighth with the first Philadelphia run after twenty-one scoreless innings. The second game was scoreless until the fifth. Sacrifice flies by Limmer and DeMaestri produced the only Philadelphia runs.

On Tuesday, July sixth, the A's returned to Philadelphia. The club announced it had agreed to play the National League Pirates in an exhibition game at Forbes Field, Pittsburgh on August ninth. The proceeds would go toward a Honus Wagner statue. That afternoon at Shibe Park, Trice lost again, this time to Washington, five to two.

With no games scheduled on Wednesday or Thursday, the well rested A's opened their final series before the All-Star break on Friday, July ninth, defeating the visiting Red Sox, nine to three, in the first of four games. DeMaestri hit two solo homers. Renna and Wilson each contributed two-run homers and Kellner won for the third time in four starts.

THE LONGEST LOSING STREAK

On Saturday, the Red Sox won, five to three, setting off the A's longest losing streak of the year. Boston slugger Ted Williams smashed a two out double in the top of the tenth inning, driving in a run and giving the Red Sox a three to two lead. Zernial's grounder to third in the home tenth scored the tying run. But Burtschy walked in the go-ahead run in the top of the eleventh.

BOSTON HUMBLES A'S AGAIN IN DOUBLEHEADER

Boston humbled the A's twice on Sunday, pounding out forty hits in an afternoon doubleheader. The Red Sox won eighteen to nothing, and eleven to one. Williams went four for six on the day, boosting his league-leading batting average to .367.

TRICE RELEASED

Trice, who gave up nine runs in three innings in the first game, was sent back to minor league Ottawa, the A's tripe-A farm club, at his own request. He pumped life into the A's in the early season, but was largely ineffective since the end of May. Right hander Ossie Van Brabant (0-2) was also optioned to Ottawa. Brabant had a 7.02 earned run average, appearing in nine games.

THE ALL-STAR BREAK

Jim Finigan represented the Athletics in the 1954 All-Star Game at Cleveland on July thirteenth. He was hitless in three trips. Rosen, of the hometown Indians, set All-Star records, hitting home runs in two consecutive at bats, knocking in five runs. The American League won, eleven to nine.

With Zernial on the injured list, the longest losing streak of the season continued after the All-Star game. Cleveland pitchers dominated the home standing A's in a three game series. Wynn pitched a three hit shutout in the opener on Thursday, July fifteenth, winning four to nothing. Only one of the Cleveland runs off Kellner was earned. On Friday night the Indians Mike Garcia picked up his twelfth victory, winning nine to three. Feller spun a masterful two-hit shutout on Saturday, posting the 256th victory of his career. The Indians won six to nothing, completing the sweep.

In the first game against the White Sox on Sunday afternoon, rookie John Gray suffered a ten to two loss in his first major league start. Chicago won the second game, four to three. The game was halted after seven innings by the Pennsylvania State curfew law that prevented any inning from starting after 6:40 P.M. on Sunday.

Tigers' starter Steve Gromek handed the A's their tenth shutout of the year in the opener of a doubleheader on Tuesday night, July twentieth, winning twelve to nothing. Harvey Kuenn's first inning grand slam highlighted a nine run Tigers' rally. DeMaestri's two-run homer in the fourth inning of the second game put the A's in front three to one. But the Tigers won again, four to three. The opposition averaged over eight runs a game during the ten game losing streak. The A's averaged less than two runs a game. The largest home crowd during the streak was less than 7500.

Just 1760 watched Limmer, DeMaestri, and Finigan all homer on Wednesday night, July twenty-first. Philadelphia ended the losing streak. Dixon, making his first start since the June 1953 streak, defeated the Tigers, four to one. Just 1675 fans watched Detroit win, nine to four, on Thursday night.

A'S FALL TO LAST

Despite the long slide, Philadelphia wasn't in the American League cellar yet. The visiting Orioles put them there, winning, seven to five, on Friday, July twenty-third.

LAST THREE GAME WINNING STREAK

The A's, however, climbed back out of the basement, claiming the final three games of the series. On Saturday they defeated former teammate Joe Coleman for the first time in four attempts, six to five. Gray, a former Yankee farmhand, earned his first major league victory. With two on, and two out, in the ninth inning, the Baltimore center fielder, Chuck Diering, singled to right. But Power threw out the lead runner at the plate to preserve the win.

On Sunday, July twenty-fifth, Philadelphia recorded it's second doubleheader sweep of the year. The A's scored seven runs in the eighth inning of the first game, winning nine to four. In the second game Don Larsen of the Orioles no-hit the A's through six innings. Consecutive seventh inning doubles by Power, Wilson, and pitcher Dixon, however, led Philadelphia to a six to four win. It was the final time the Philadelphia A's would ever win three games in a row.

The A's then embarked on a twenty-three game road trip. In the first game of a doubleheader at Briggs Stadium on Tuesday night, July twenty-seventh, consecutive home runs by Limmer and Power in the top of the ninth inning tied the score at two. A two out single by Bill Tuttle in the bottom of the ninth, however, gave Detroit a three to two victory. Limmer homered again in the third inning of the second game. The A's won, eight to three.

On Wednesday night Tigers' left fielder Steve Souchock hammered two three-run homers. Kellner suffered his twelfth loss, ten to two. Although the A's had ten hits, they didn't score until the ninth. The Tigers swept the second doubleheader of the series on Thursday night, four to two, and seven to three.

In Chicago on Friday, July thirtieth, Bob Keegan shut out the A's, four to nothing. The White Sox pitcher also singled home two runs. On Saturday, Morrie Martin, making his first start since being traded to Chicago, defeated his former teammates, seven to one. The floundering A's lost twenty-three times in July, winning only seven games. They were in last place, thirty eight and one-half games out of first.

THE A'S ARE IN DISTRESS

The effort to keep the team in Philadelphia was faring no better than the team. The committee to save the A's interim report bluntly stated that business leaders were not interested. The general public was apathetic.

Making what he called a "fair and full offer" of $4,500,000 for the franchise, C. Arnold Johnson, forty-seven-year-old Chicago real estate magnate, announced his intention to move the club to Kansas City. Johnson already owned the minor league stadium in Kansas City. A city wide referendum to approve finance the upgrading of the existing park through the sale of two million dollars in municipal bonds had already passed. Although San Francisco, and several other cities, remained interested in acquiring the franchise, they were not nearly as far along in the process.

With the reported backing of a local builder, Roy Mack wanted to purchase the stock in the club belonging to his father and brother. He told reporters from the Philadelphia Evening Bulletin, "I'm doing my utmost to keep the club in Philadelphia." Earl Mack, Roy's older brother, felt that the "Save the A's" campaign was making his brother look like a martyr at his expense. Earle told the same reporters, Roy talks big. But we don't have a dime. The Johnson offer is the only actual offer we have received. The others are a lot of rumors. It's an awfully good offer, a half million dollars more than was published in the papers. I think he'd go more if they kept on bidding." However, he and his father would sell their stock to Roy if he could raise the money. "Dad and I certainly want to keep the team in Philadelphia but there isn't a chance as far as finances are concerned. Except for one young fellow, no one in Philadelphia has made a bid for the team."

Harry Sylk, a Philadelphia based prescription drug manufacturer, had organized a Philadelphia syndicate in a bid to buy the team. "We made a very generous offer. I think it's important to have the American League represented in Philadelphia," he said. "The club would have to be reorganized from top down. This isn't a charitable venture. From a business point of view we would try to employ the kind of people who would make the club acceptable to the baseball fans of Philadelphia." Sylk said the syndicates' total package would match the Johnson offer, but admitted that the acceptance by the Macks would mean less cash in their pockets. "Nevertheless," he said, "we have given the Mack family a basis for saving the club for Philadelphia. If the Macks feel that basis is satisfactory then we will meet again."

AUGUST

The White Sox completed the four game sweep, winning twice on Sunday, August first, six to five, and two to one.

In Baltimore on Monday night, August second, the Orioles romped to a ten to two victory over the A's. Capitalizing on six Baltimore errors on Tuesday night, the A's stopped another losing streak at eight games. They defeated the Orioles, six to two. On Wednesday, August fourth, the A's climbed out of the last place , dumping the Orioles into the American League cellar. Collecting fourteen hits. they defeated Baltimore again, six to four. Bollweg homered. The other thirteen hits were all singles.

CLEVELAND FIELDS FIRST ALL BLACK OUTFIELD

The Friday, August sixth game in Cleveland had historical importance because the starting outfielders for the Indians, Larry Doby, Al Smith, and Dave Pope, represented the first all black outfield ever to play in the major leagues. The three players combined had four hits. Doby drove in two runs. He also scored twice. The A's lost again, seven to three. Thirty-five-year-old Bob Feller sunk the A's again on Saturday, five to one. Doby hit a three-run homer. The Municipal Stadium attendance for the doubleheader on Sunday, August eighth, was announced as 20,381, marking the fourth, and last, time the 1954 A's played before a crowd of more than 20,000. The A's took early leads in both games. Neither Portocarrero, nor Kellner, could hold the advantage. The Indians won seven to two, and, five to two, completing the series sweep, and increasing their lead over the second place Yankees to four games. A Monday night exhibition game with the Pirates in Pittsburgh was rained out.

The second place Yankees matched the Indians, sweeping the following four game series with the A's in New York. On Tuesday, August tenth, Jackie Price, the baseball clown and stunt man, put on a dazzling pre-game show. Then Bob Grimm posted his fifteenth win, defeating the A's five to two. But it wasn't an impressive outing. The A's out hit the Yankees, ten to eight. Demaestri led off the game with a double and scored on a single by Don Bollweg. Defensively for the A's, Bill Renna reached far into the right field stands to rob Joe Collins of a potential three run homer in the fourth inning. But the Yankees had already scored three runs in the third off Jim Bishop, and added two unearned runs in the sixth.

On Wednesday afternoon, in Philadelphia, the Board of Directors of the Philadelphia Athletics adjourned a day-long meeting without reaching a decision on the future of the club. Roy and Earle Mack refused to sit next to each other at the meeting.

That night, in New York, Harry Byrd defeated his former teammates for the second time, three to one.

In the first game of a doubleheader on Thursday night, August twelfth, Renna hit a two-run homer in the first. Irv Noren's two-run triple tied the game for the Yankees in the bottom of the inning. New York got only four more hits off Portocarrero over the final eight innings. However, Mantle singled home a run in the third inning. After Philadelphia tied the game with an unearned run in the top of the sixth, Noren homered in the bottom half of inning, putting the Yankees back on top. The A's tied the game again in the top of the eighth inning on a double by Demaestri followed by Finigan's third hit of the game. But Mantle hit his twenty-fifth homer of the year in the bottom of the inning, giving the Yankees a five to four win. In the second game the Yankees scored four times off Kellner in the first, coasting to a seven to one victory.

Philadelphia had lost twelve straight games to the top three teams in the league. A pair of victories over lowly Baltimore were the only interruptions to another long losing streak.

Philadelphia took advantage of their final visit to the Nations' Capital. They defeated the fifth place Senators on Friday the thirteenth, three to two. Finigan stole home in the eighth inning, providing the margin of victory. Don Bollweg's pinch double in the eleventh inning gave the A's a six to four win on Saturday. Charlie Bishop gained his first major league victory after five losses. Catcher Shantz, however, suffered a fractured finger in his right hand. A foul tip nicked him in the fourth inning. Washington left hander, Johnny Schmitz, defeated the A's on Sunday, four to one.

NO SYMPATHY FROM THE PULPIT

Returning home after a grueling five and eighteen road trip, the A's couldn't even count on local Christian compassion. Philadelphia Presbyterian pastor Samuel A. Jeanes was quoted in the August sixteenth edition of the New York Times:

> Your Philadelphia baseball organization is looking for somebody to buy them out of their difficult financial problems because of their declining attendance. It wasn't so many years ago that this organization played no small part in breaking down the sanctity of the Lord's day by having this city of Philadelphia legalize Sunday baseball.

In 1926 the Athletics did challenge the Philadelphia blue laws, obtaining a court injunction. The court allowed them to play a game on Sunday, August twenty-second, 1926, but the game was never played. The Pennsylvania Supreme Court eventually upheld the ban on Sunday games. However, when Mack made tentative plans to move the team to nearby Camden, New Jersey, the State Legislature interceded, allowing Sunday games with the approval of municipal officials. There were more bureaucratic delays, and it wasn't until April twenty-second, 1934, that the club became the last American League team to play a Sunday home game. They lost to Washington, four to three, in that game.

As the A's final home stand of any length began on Tuesday, August seventeenth, the Yankees, weren't in a compassionate mood, either. Unaccustomed to second place in the standings, New York routed the A's, eleven to one, behind Byrd who defeated the A's for the third straight time. The attendance of 8885 was the second largest of the home stand. On Wednesday, 7367 watched Whitey Ford defeat the A's, six to one. Only 3116, the smallest crowd ever to watch a night game in which the Yankees were involved, watched New York complete the sweep on Thursday night with an eight to five victory. Limmer committed three errors at first base. Former Yankees Bollweg and Renna doubled and singled in the bottom of the eighth inning. Each drove in two runs. The A's scored five runs in the inning. But the Yankees' Johnny Sain preserved the win in relief.

However, after Sain, and two days of rain, the A's picked up their first win of the home stand. On Sunday, August twenty-second, they beat the Senators, three to two, in the first game of a doubleheader. DeMaestri's single in the twelfth inning drove home the winning run. Portocarrero had a no hitter until Senators' right fielder Tom Wright singled to open the seventh inning. Limmer and Renna each hit their eleventh home run of the season. The A's led four to nothing lead after seven. But the Senators scored twice in the eighth inning, and twice more in the ninth.

CURFEW AGAIN HALTS SECOND GAME

For the second time during the season, the Sunday curfew halted the second game of a doubleheader with the score tied after nine innings. Washington won both ends of a second consecutive doubleheader on Monday night, eight to five, and ten to three.

A'S PLAY SPOILERS ROLE

The Indians, leading the American League by five and one-half games, began their final visit to Philadelphia on Tuesday night, August twenty-fourth. A crowd of 9175, the largest home attendance after the all-star break, watched the A's play the spoilers role to perfection. That was 290 more than the crowd that watched the opener of the final Yankee series at Shibe Park. The A's won, four to one. Rosen, the American League's most valuable player, was held hitless by John Gray. With the score tied one to one, Cleveland's Mike Garcia walked Limmer with two out in the third inning. Finigan followed with a clean single to left. Renna then beat out an infield single. Although Indians' catcher Mike Hegan fielded Renna's chop in front of the plate cleanly, his throw to first was late. And second baseman Avila's return throw to the plate bounced into the stands. Both runs scored. Power ripped a single to center, scoring Renna with the final run.

The A's led three to one after six innings on Wednesday night. However, they couldn't manage a second straight victory over the Indians. A triple by Indians' catcher Hal Naragon with two out in the tenth scored the winning run. Cleveland won, four to three, before 7311 fans.

Only 3650 saw the A's split a doubleheader with the White Sox on Thursday, August twenty-sixth. Chicago coasted to an eight to one victory in the opener. Wilson's thirteenth homer of the year accounted for the A's only run. A two-run homer by Renna followed by a two-run double by DeMaestri in the fourth inning of the second game led the A's to a four to one win. On Friday night Chicago won eleven to one, scoring eight runs in the third inning. They won again on Saturday, five to two.

The Tigers swept a doubleheader in their final visit to Philadelphia on Sunday August twenty-ninth. Tigers' starter Steve Gromek charged the mound in the ninth inning of the first game after being hit by a pitch from Fricano. A bench clearing brawl ensued. After order was restored both pitchers were ejected, although Gromek still picked up his fifteenth win of the year. The Tigers won fourteen to three. Portocarrero pitched eight strong inning in the second game. With the scored tied in the sixth inning, Boone hit his seventh homer of the year against A's pitching. Detroit won, two to one.

LAST SERIES VICTORY

Philadelphia closed out the dismal month of August on a positive note sweeping a doubleheader against the Orioles, eight to six, and six to three. An eighth inning grand slam home run by Limmer was the key blow for Philadelphia in the opener. A two-run triple by reserve outfielder Joe Taylor keyed another decisive eighth inning rally in the nightcap. The twin victories marked the third series sweep of the year by the A's, and their last series victory ever. Philadelphia was in seventh place, fifty-one games back of the Indians, and two games ahead of last place Baltimore.

SEPTEMBER

Boston again pounded A's pitching, winning eleven to one on Friday, September third. Williams hit his twenty-fifth homer of the year, and career homer 362, moving him into fifth place on the all time homer list. He trailed only Ruth, Foxx, Ott, and Gehrig.

FINAL HOME VICTORY

Only 2124 saw the Athletics defeat the Red Sox four to three Saturday afternoon. It was their final home victory ever. Consecutive first inning singles by Jacobs, Limmer, Finigan, and Zernial put Philadelphia in front, two to nothing. The Red Sox, however, led, three to two, after five and one-half innings. Limmer opened the bottom of the sixth inning with a line double into the right field corner. Zernial singled Limmer home, taking second when Ted Williams failed to come up with his hit cleanly. Joe Taylor singled home the deciding run. Boston closed the home stand with a doubleheader sweep on Sunday, August fifth, winning twelve to five, and seven to three. Joe Taylor hit his first major league homer in the second game. Boston was in fourth place in the league standings, despite being fourteen games under the .500 mark.

Only three home games, all with New York, remained. There were ten remaining road games. On Monday, September sixth, Washington and Philadelphia split a doubleheader at Washington's Griffith Stadium. The Senators' Mickey Vernon homered and tripled in the opener, driving in five runs. Washington won, eight to one. Valo's two out triple in the eighth inning of the second game drove in the deciding run in the nightcap. The A's won, three to two.Jacobs had three hits for Philadelphia.

SMALLEST AL CROWD OF THE YEAR

On Tuesday afternoon, 460 fans, the smallest crowd of the season in Washington, or anywhere in the American League, watched the Senators defeat Philadelphia, five to four. Senators' catcher Ed Fitzgerald singled home the winning run in the eighth inning.

WYNN WINS TWENTIETH—INDIANS WIN ONE HUNDREDTH

Early Wynn won his twentieth game of the year for Cleveland, defeating the A's, five to two, on Wednesday, September eighth. On

Thursday night, September, ninth, the Indians' won again, five to four, in eleven innings. It was their one hundredth win of the season. After Wilson hit a two-run homer in the second inning, the A's led four to one. In the bottom of the eighth inning, however, Dave Pope hit a homer. Then the roof caved in. Zernial and Valo each dropped fly balls, allowing the Indians to score a second run, cutting the A's lead to four to three. In the ninth inning, another catchable pop fly fell between Zernial and Wilson, allowing the tying run to score. Burtschy, the only A's pitcher with a winning record, handed the Indians the win, walking Indians' catcher Hal Naragon with the bases loaded in the bottom of the eleventh.

The A's picked up their third victory of the month at Briggs Stadium on Friday, six to five. Finigan's bases loaded single in the ninth drove in the tying and winning runs. Power and DeMaestri homered. The Tigers won, two to one on Saturday afternoon. Limmer singled home the lone A's tally in the sixth inning. Fricano was the hard luck loser.

The A's had a last opportunity to climb out of the league cellar. They needed a sweep of a Sunday, September twelfth, doubleheader in Baltimore. But the Orioles won, four to three, in the opener. After Finigan and Zernial each singled home a run in the top of the seventh inning, the A's led three to nothing. But Baltimore rallied for four runs in the bottom of the inning. In the second game Renna walked with the bases loaded in the ninth to give Philadelphia a five to four triumph.

LAST BACK-TO-BACK VICTORIES

Portocarreo closed out the four and six road trip, shutting out the White Sox at Comiskey Park, one to nothing on Tuesday, September fourteenth. It was the final time that the Philadelphia Athletics ever posted back-to-back victories. Finigan doubled in the opening inning. Zernial then singled him home, accounting for the only run of the game.

THE END

The A's returned to Philadelphia for the last time on September seventeenth. The Yankees scored five times in the top of the first, coasting to a ten to three win. The A's failed to score until the ninth inning. Berra had five RBIs for New York, increasing his league-leading total to 123. On Saturday New York again started quickly, scoring three times in the first inning. The A's, however, countered with five runs in the second inning. Bollweg hit a two-run homer. With the score tied in the ninth inning, Portocarrero walked McDougald, Noren and Mantle. Eddie Robinson's sacrifice fly drove in the winning run. The six to five victory secured second place. Casey Stengel and the Yankees had already dispatched congratulatory telegrams to Al Lopez and the Indians, who had clinched the pennant the night before.

THE FINAL HOME GAME

On Sunday, September nineteenth, just 1715 saw the final American League game ever in Philadelphia. There was no sense of occasion. The Yankees won again, four to two, and like the Indians, claimed their one hundredth victory of the season against the A's. Despite five pennants and five World Series in five seasons as Yankee manager, 1954 was Stengel's first one hundred win season. Ironically, it was also his first second place finish.

In the final game, Power robbed Mantle of a run scoring hit in the third inning with a spectacular over the shoulder catch, crashing hard into the right field wall. Suder singled home the final two runs ever for the Philadelphia A's in the fifth inning, scoring shortstop Jack Littrell and catcher Robertson. Ditmar held the Yankees scoreless for seven innings. But McDougald hit a three-run homer in the eighth to cap a four run Yankee rally. Burtchy was the loser in relief. DeMaestri, batting for Sima, flied out to Cerv in left to record final out at Shibe Park. The A's finished out their final season with six games on the road.

On Monday, September twentieth, at Fenway Park the A's lost their one hundredth game of the year, five to two. Ted Williams, who had missed thirty-seven games with a broken collar bone, slammed his twenty eighth homer of the year. Finigan hit a two-run homer with two out in the ninth.

On Tuesday night, Jackie Jensen's tenth inning single gave the Red Sox a four to three victory in the first game of a doubleheader. He hit a three-run homer in the second inning of the second game. However, he also established a dubious major league record, grounding into his thirty second double play of the year. Power, establishing himself as one of the games premier hitters, homered and tripled in the opener. He went four for eight in the doubleheader.

A'S DENY NY BEST RUNNER-UP MARK

On Friday, September twenty-fourth in New York. Behind Portocarrero, the A's thwarted second place New York's effort to establish a record for most victories by a runner-up, winning five to one. The Yankees needed a series sweep. The Dodgers, amassing 104 victories while finishing second in 1942, retained the title. Littrell completed a four for four day with a three-run homer in the ninth.

YANKEES WIN—A'S LOSE ONE HUNDRED AND THREE

The Yankees recorded their one hundred and third victory of the year on Saturday, blasting the A's, ten to two. Ironically, It was also the one hundred and third loss of the season for Philadelphia. Berra drove in a run for New York. He was still one behind Cleveland's Doby in the battle for the RBI title. Limmer homered for Philadelphia. Rookie Phil Oster made his major league debut for the A's.

A'S WIN THEIR FINAL GAME

On Sunday, September twenty-sixth the A's won the final game in their long history, eight to six, out hitting the Yankees at Yankee Stadium, sixteen to eleven. Manager Joost went three for four, finishing the season with a .362 batting average in forty-seven at bats. Suder, DeMaestri, and Renna each drove in two runs. Littrell had two hits. Power tripled. Ditmar, the winning pitcher, allowed five runs on seven hits in five and one-third innings.

MANTLE AT SHORT—BERRA AT THIRD—SKOWRON AT SECOND

The game meant little to the Yankees. Feeling thus free to experiment, or perhaps just to have fun, Stengel started regular catcher Berra at third, center fielder Mantle at shortstop, and first baseman Skowron at second base. Berra handled two chances flawlessly at third. Mantle, who began his career as a shortstop, handled eight grounders without an error. Skowron was charged with one error, handling seven chances without mishap.

The Yankees drew 1,475,171 in 1954. Cleveland drew 1,335,472. The A's drew 334,666. Twenty different A's pitchers compiled a combined era of 5.18. The club finished last, sixty games out of first.

THE FATE OF THE A'S

On Tuesday September twenty eighth in New York, President Wil Harridge met with team owners to discuss the fate of the A's.

He told reporters:

> The purpose of the meeting is to let Roy Mack explain the situation. He is operating head of the club. We have talked to him on all Philadelphia matters in that capacity. Because the club owners will be in New York for the World Series. I thought this would be an excellent time to clear up a situation that has been getting increasingly difficult for the league. There are other people who would like to make an offer for the club.

Six of eight clubs needed to approve a transfer to another city. No application to move to a minor league territory, such as Kansas City, could be made until October first. Roy Mack asked for a fourteen day grace period to raise $750,000 to buy out his father and his older brother.

At a meeting in Chicago on October twelfth, Johnson restated his offer. Then Texas oil man Clint Murchison, the future owner of the Dallas Cowboys of the National Football League, made a serious counter offer. He wanted to move the franchise to Los Angeles. The Johnson bid had a significant advantage. It was a "cash" offer while the Murchison bid involved stock and loans.

Chicago insurance investor, Charles O. Finley, backed Roy Mack, and Tommy Richardson, Eastern League President. But they could put up only $450,000. Richardson was also a member of the A's Board of Directors. President Harridge said there was no substance to the Mack offer. Another Philadelphia group, headed by Jack Renzel, sales manager for Leonard Strick tractor-trailer manufacturers, also put forward a bid. And Washington Attorney, Leo De Orsey, and plumbing contractor, Joe Tucci, bid nearly three million dollars.

VEECK MAKES A LATE BID

Even former Browns' owner, Bill Veeck, believing he had enough committed votes to block the Johnson deal, made an offer. Veeck felt that Kansas City would have difficulty supporting a major league team, and that Yankees' co-owner, Del Webb, intended to purchase the club from Johnson, and to move it to Los Angeles, at a later date. He noted that Webb and Johnson were close friends. Veeck did not expect to get the franchise, but he did want to block Johnson.

At the conclusion of the meeting, Earl Hilligan, American League publicity director, announced that the owners had authorized the sale of the franchise to Johnson, and the transfer to Kansas City by a seven to zero vote. Although Walter Briggs, owner of the Detroit Tigers opposed the move, he left the meeting early. He did not cast a vote.

Washington Vice President, Calvin Griffith, questioned the validity of the vote:

> A vote was taken. However, the Washington club, and others, do not consider it final. No mention was made of specific provisos we entered. Any announcement that we favored Kansas City, is full of misunderstandings. Kansas City was merely our third preference. Joe Cronin, representing the Red Sox, made the same provisos. A move to Kansas City would unbalance the whole league, and add considerable to the burdens of travel.

Cronin was married to the niece of the Senators' owner and President, Clark Griffith who preferred that the A's remain in Philadelphia for one more year. If the club was to be moved, he favored pre-empting a National League move to Los Angeles. Some owners, however, felt the estimated value of Los Angeles as a baseball town was inflated. Having just one team that far distant would complicate scheduling, and travel arrangements. Moreover, the Pacific Coast League was sure to fight any invasion of their territory.

Despite tentative league approval, the Macks still had not come to final terms with Johnson. Roy Mack left the meeting early. "I want to talk the whole thing over with the family. I haven't sold my stock yet," he said, agreeing to notify the league of his final decision offer by October seventeenth.

In the interim, an eight person Philadelphia syndicate quickly put together a legitimate local offer that did match the Johnson bid. Each member pledged $375,000. Jack Renzel served as spokesman for the group. "You can be sure that Roy Mack has a legitimate offer," he said. "Every member of the Mack family is happy." Others in the syndicate were radio station owner Paul T. Harron, oil executive Barry Fisher, trucking executive Arthur Gallagher, department store executive Joseph Leibman, parking lot owner Isadore Sley, grocery chain owner Arthur Rosenberg, and plumbing contractor William Anderson.

Drugstore executive Harry Sylk, who had made a tentative offer for the club in early August, reemerged as a potential local buyer. This time he was in partnership with Charlie Finley of Chicago. Finley had backed Roy Mack's earlier bid. "I have enough financial backing to match the Johnson offer," Finley said. "Our partnership could raise $1,000,000, if necessary."

On the October seventeenth deadline an exuberant Roy Mack announced to reporters, "I have notified William Harridge, president of the American League, that we have sold control of the Philadelphia Athletics to a group of eight well known Philadelphia business men. I'm very, very happy to keep the A's in Philadelphia. That has always been my goal."

Mayor Clark offered his congratulations to the group. The Mayor and the apparent new owners acknowledged they faced the tough task of rejuvenating, and restoring, Philadelphia's enthusiasm for the team.

Ernie Mehl, sports editor of the *Kansas City Star* admitted defeat, saying. "We made an honorable effort to get the franchise. If we are out of the picture then we wish the best of luck to the Philadelphia syndicate."

Johnson told reporters,"Naturally I'm terribly disappointed. I'm still puzzled about the whole thing. I still intend to call on Roy Mack tonight. Roy had a much better deal with me. I was going to make him a Vice President."

In fact, Roy had agreed to accept less from the Philadelphia group which offered him a ninth interest in the club, and an executive job at his present salary. Johnson offered Roy $450,000 for his one-third of the club stock, a guaranteed five year job with the club at a top salary, and promised to train his son, Connie Mack the third, in the business of baseball.

Johnson charged that Roy had violated a good faith agreement:

> It was a verbal agreement, true. But it stood with me as something unbreakable. It's part of the minutes of the American League meeting. I feel that I have been wronged by the Philadelphia group who so suddenly appeared on the scene, and intend to get my legal remedy. In view of the indicated advance ticket sale in Kansas City of almost two million dollars, the measure of my damages should be substantial. I'm going to be just as persistent and tenacious in this litigation as I have previously been in reaching an agreement for the purchase of the A's.

Arthur Gallagher, spokesman for the Philadelphia syndicate, branded the lawsuit unwarranted:

According to Roy Mack, no arrangements were to be considered completed until he had consulted his wife and family. The agreement was that nothing was to be done until last Monday morning.

And League President Will Harridge cautioned, "the proper time has not arrived to ask the league to approve the syndicate."

On October twenty-fourth Earl Mack signed the appropriate papers, selling his stock in the A's to the syndicate. He sent the papers across town to Roy for his approval and signature.

By noon the next day, however, the deal seem to have hit a significant snag. Roy Mack's belated demand for fifty percent ownership, brought about yet another delay. Roy Mack, heretofore referred to as the savior American League baseball for Philadelphia, was trying to get out of the deal. "If he wants to back out," said Gallagher, "let's give the story to the press. I'm so mad, I'd like to walk out of this thing now."

Chuck Comiskey of the White Sox told reporters, "I won't come back to any more meetings. The Macks have to settle this affair among themselves."

Finally, on October twenty eighth, at the Waldorf-Astoria Hotel in New York, league owners rejected the sale of the A's to the local business group. With six votes needed to approve the deal, the unofficial vote count had the owners split, four and four. Roy Mack denied casting a "no" vote. The New York Yankees and Baltimore Orioles voted against the deal. Boston was believed to be leaning against the sale. The Detroit Tigers and Washington Senators voted for the move. Cleveland and Chicago were reported to be in support of the sale.

Connie Mack criticized fellow owners for rejecting the sale of the club to the Philadelphia syndicate, rebuking his eldest son and defending his middle one. He did not mention his youngest son, Connie Jr., who had earlier unsuccessful battles with his brothers over control of the A's.

No matter what the Macks say or do the answer will be Kansas City. These good businessmen have the money. They want the club. The league owners who voted against approval simply don't want those men to have the club. The league said that they weren't rejected. They just weren't approved. Are we back in first grade? It's a runaround with an awful lot of pressure to take the A's to Kansas City. Roy's been behind everything since May, telling everybody one thing, and doing something else. I don't think it's been any fault of Earl. He's been wonderful about everything. I want to place myself on record that I'm not accepting the American League's decision as final. The citizenry of Philadelphia should join with me in this demand for a complete and public explanation of this action. The loss of the A's to our city will be a great one, not only in prestige but also sports wise, and from the business viewpoint.

Connie Mack's wife added, "New York wants this club to go to Kansas City. When New York's in the back, pushing it. Well there is your answer."

Morton Liebman, a member of the syndicate told reporters:

> I'd be willing to try again, sure. But I want to know what the ground rules are. If Roy knows, for example, that the league turned us down because one of the syndicate members was undesirable, please capitalize that. It's up to him. If he wants to keep baseball in Philadelphia, let him start the ball rolling. I can't understand why the league wouldn't tell us in public or private, the reasons for the rejection.

Harridge, who had reportedly urged Roy to withdraw from the syndicate, again urged caution:

> The Macks still own the stock. They still own the club. As far as we know now, they will continue to operate in Philadelphia.

With the deal to sell to the local syndicate fallen through, Jack Kent Cooke, owner of the International League Toronto Maple Leafs, and Toronto real estate man, L.G. Chandler expressed a belated interest in the team. Chandler was ready to build a stadium on any site suitable to the city of Toronto or to remodel the existing stadium to major league specifications. A formal offer was never presented.

For months, Johnson had waged a relentless campaign to acquire the A's franchise. And on November fourteenth he was able to announce that he had finally acquired the club, agreeing to pay the Macks approximately $3,500,000, including $2,000,000 to retire the mortgage on the ballpark, and other outstanding debts. Connie Mack received $600,000. His sons received $450,000 each.

In bed, and ailing, ninety-one year-old Connie Mack signed the final papers. Speaking on behalf of her husband, Katherine Mack told reporters:

Johnson made too strong an offer. There was nothing else we could do. Mr. Johnson is a nice man. He won out. We said that whoever got here first would be the buyer. Mr. Johnson got here at nine o'clock, the Philadelphia group dallied.

Promptness alone may not have determined the ultimate fate of the franchise. However, Johnson, a forty-seven year old former Naval Lieutenant Commander, took no chances, showing up an hour before the scheduled 9 A.M. meeting on November fourteenth. Mack's daughter had already verified Johnson's credit with a phone call. Ironically, Finley of Chicago also arrived early. "I had a check just as big as Johnson's," he said, "but I never got a chance to wave it."

When the remaining members of the Philadelphia syndicate—John P. Criscioni, Isadore Sley, Morton Lieberman, and T.R. Hang—arrived, a tearful Earl Mack told them, "We lost. The club is sold to Johnson."

The Macks sent the following letter to American League President Will Harridge:

This letter is being sent to you by Cornelius McGillicuddy, Earl McGillicuddy, and Roy McGillicuddy to inform you that we have made agreement with Arnold Johnson to sell all the outstanding stock of the American League Baseball Club of Philadelphia. We are now united in our desires. We herewith request the American League to approve the above, and would appreciate it if such approval would be obtained by you at the earliest possible date.

Washington Senators' owner Griffith, cited the "irregular tie in" between Johnson and the Yankees as a concern. Johnson was a close friend of Yankee President Dan Topping. "It takes just three votes to block the deal," said Griffith. Boston and Detroit were reportedly still opposed also.

However, Briggs relented. "I fought this until I became convinced that the move was in the best interest of baseball. The only thing that disturbed me was Johnson's connection with Yankee Stadium," he said. Johnson had purchased both Yankee Stadium and Municipal Stadium in Kansas City in December of 1953. On November eighteenth at the Commodore Hotel in New York, the sale was approved by a six to two vote. Hank Greenberg, co-owner of the Cleveland Indians, sided with Griffith in opposition. There was not a widespread expression of anguish over the loss of the A's but there were, nonetheless, loyal fans who felt betrayed.

"In August of 1954 my father promised me the A's would never leave us," said Max Silberman of the Philadelphia A's Historical Society. "Since then I trust no one."

The Union Association Unions played in Kansas City in 1884, followed by the National League Cowboys in 1886, the American Association Blues in 1888 and 1889, and the Federal League Packers in 1914 and 1915. The American League A's were returning Major League baseball to that city after an absence of forty years.

The Yankees, who enthusiastically backed Johnson from the start, asked for no compensation in return for yielding their rights to the Kansas City territory. Johnson, however, did compensate the remaining American Association teams and the Blues were subsequently transferred to Denver.

Griffith's warnings about the Yankee connection went largely unheeded, though Johnson sold Yankee Stadium at the league's request. Under Johnson the A's were never an independent Major League team. They served, for many years, as a proving ground for young Yankees' talent, not yet ready for prime time. Many established Yankee stars, periodically, spent time there on rehabilitation assignments.

The year old Baltimore franchise now became an "eastern" club for scheduling purposes, playing more home games in direct conflict with the struggling Washington franchise.

Charlie Finley eventually purchased the club from Johnson in 1965, moving the team to Oakland, California in 1967. Finley's A's matched the on the field success of the Mack glory years, winning three consecutive World Series from 1972 to 1974. But like Mack's teams, the A's struggled at the gate, failing to even approach the 1,000,000 attendance mark in eight of their first ten seasons in Oakland. And like Mack, Finley, couldn't meet the salary demands of his established stars, selling key players to meet financial obligations.

THE LAST OF CONNIE MACK STADIUM

Shibe Park, renamed "Connie Mack Stadium" in 1957, was sold to Carpenter, owner of the Phillies. The Phillies defeated the Expos in the final game there on October first, 1970. Phillies' management had intended a dignified retirement party for the old park. They sold commemorative T-Shirts and gave away souvenir seat slats to each fan in attendance. Despite beefed up security, the fans disrupted the game, littering the field with the giveaway slats, and even intruding onto the playing surface themselves. Fan interference caused Phillies' left fielder Ron Stone to miss a catch, allowing the tying run to score. After Oscar Gamble doubled home Tim McCarver with the winning run in the twelfth inning, fans poured onto the field in larger numbers. They scavenged for souvenirs. Ripping apart as much of the old stadium as they could, some even dismantled the toilets. Some ripped up pieces of the stadium turf. With security clearly overwhelmed, the Phillies wisely decided to cancel post game ceremonies.

The stadium was completely torn down in 1976. About 600 green painted wooden seats from the old park, with the original metal arm rest, were installed at Duncan Park in Spartanburg, South Carolina, home of the minor league Spartanburg Phillies. The front door of The pulpit of the Deliverance Evangelistic Church now occupies the spot that once was home plate. There is no baseball there on Sunday. The late Pastor Jeanes would be pleased.

DAY	DATE	OPPONENT	RESULT	SCORE	PITCHER	ATTENDANCE	RECORD
TUES	04/13/54	BOSTON	W	6-4	BOBBY SHANTZ (1-0)	16331	1-0
THURS	04/15/54	AT NEW YORK	L	3-0	ALEX KELLNER (0-1)	23494	1-1
SAT	04/17/54	AT BOSTON	RAIN				
SUN	04/18/54	AT BOSTON	W	6-4	BOB TRICE (1-0)	22566	2-1
SUN	04/18/54	AT BOSTON	L	4-3	MOE BURTSCHY (0-1)	22566	2-2
MON	04/19/54	AT WASHINGTON	L	4-3	ART DITMAR (0-1)	11426	2-3
TUES	04/20/54	AT WASHINGTON	W	7-0	ALEX KELLNER (1-1)	5742	3-3
WED	04/21/54	AT WASHINGTON	L	13-1	MARION FRICANO (0-1)	4175	3-4
FRI	04/23/54	NEW YORK	RAIN				
SAT	04/24/54	NEW YORK	W	1-0	BOB TRICE (2-0)	4290	4-4
SUN	04/25/54	NEW YORK	L	6-1	ALEX KELLNER (1-2)	19930	4-5
SUN	04/25/54	NEW YORK	W	4-2	MORRIE MARTIN (1-0)	19930	5-5
TUES	04/27/54	DETROIT	RAIN				
WED	04/28/54	DETROIT	RAIN				
FRI	04/30/54	BALTIMORE	W	5-1	BOB TRICE (3-0)	7327	6-5
SAT	05/01/54	BALTIMORE	W	2-1(10)	ALEX KELLNER (2-2)	3620	7-5
SUN	05/02/54	CHICAGO	L	4-0	MORRIE MARTIN (1-1)	12690	7-6
SUN	05/02/54	CHICAGO	W	2-1	MARION FRICANO (1-1)	12690	8-6
MON	05/03/54	CHICAGO	L	14-3	BOB SCHEIB (0-1)	2703	8-7
TUES	05/04/54	CLEVELAND	W	3-2	BOB TRICE (4-0)	6071	9-7
WED	05/05/54	CLEVELAND	L	7-2	ALEX KELLNER (2-3)	4275	9-8
THURS	05/06/54	CLEVELAND	L	3-2	A. PORTOCARRERO (0-1)	3170	9-9
FRI	05/07/54	AT NEW YORK	L	2-0	MORRIE MARTIN (1-2)	5805	9-10
SAT	05/08/54	AT NEW YORK	RAIN				
SUN	05/09/54	AT NEW YORK	L	7-4	BOB TRICE (4-1)	23909	9-11
SUN	05/09/54	AT NEW YORK	SUSP	1-1 (9)	ALEX KELLNER	23909	
MON	05/10/54	AT BALTIMORE	L	7-6	BOB TRICE (4-2)	7887	9-12
TUES	05/11/54	AT BALTIMORE	L	2-0	A. PORTOCARRERO (0-2)	10837	9-13
THURS	05/13/54	AT CHICAGO	W	3-2	MOE BURTSCHY (1-1)	3206	10-13
FRI	05/14/54	AT CHICAGO	L	4-3	ART DITMAR (0-2)	21613	10-14
SAT	05/15/54	AT CHICAGO	L	7-6	LEE WHEAT (0-1))	10331	10-15
SUN	05/16/54	AT CLEVELAND	L	12-7	MARION FRICANO (1-2)	21713	10-16
SUN	05/16/54	AT CLEVELAND	L	6-0	A. PORTOCARRERO (0-3)	21713	10-17
TUES	05/18/54	AT DETROIT	L	8-3	MORRIE MARTIN (1-3)	4248	10-18
WED	05/19/54	AT DETROIT	L	4-3	ALEX KELLNER (2-4)	3549	10-19
FRI	05/21/54	AT WASHINGTON	L	7-3	ART DITMAR (0-3)	3602	10-20
SAT	05/22/54	AT WASHINGTON	W	10-3	A. PORTOCARRERO (1-3)	3419	11-20
SUN	05/23/54	AT WASHINGTON	L	9-4	LEE WHEAT (0-2)	6108	11-21
MON	05/24/54	AT NEW YORK	L	7-3	ALEX KELLNER (2-5)	10598	11-22
TUES	05/25/54	BOSTON	L	3-2	MORRIE MARTIN (1-4)	4594	11-23
WED	05/26/54	BOSTON	W	6-5	MOE BURTSCHY (2-1)	4154	12-23
FRI	05/28/54	WASHINGTON	L	12-6	BOB TRICE (4-3)	2673	12-24
SAT	05/29/54	WASHINGTON	W	7-5	MORRIE MARTIN (2-4)	1412	13-24
SUN	05/30/54	WASHINGTON	L	6-0	MARION FRICANO (1-3)	6144	13-25
SUN	05/30/54	WASHINGTON	W	6-5	A. PORTOCARRERO (2-3)	6144	14-25
MON	05/31/54	AT BOSTON	L	20-10	ART DITMAR (0-4)	23255	14-26
MON	05/31/54	AT BOSTON	L	9-0	OZZIE VAN BRABANT (0-1)	23255	14-27
TUES	06/01/54	AT BOSTON	W	16-6	BOB TRICE (5-3)	2342	15-27
WED	06/02/54	BALTIMORE	L	9-1	A. PORTOCARRERO (2-4)	2717	15-28
THURS	06/03/54	BALTIMORE	W	6-2	MARION FRICANO (2-3)	2187	16-28
FRI	06/04/54	BALTIMORE	W	7-6	BOB TRICE (6-3)	1092	17-28
SAT	06/05/54	CLEVELAND	L	4-1(11)	ALEX KELLNER (2-6)	3038	17-29
SUN	06/06/54	CLEVELAND	L	2-1	A. PORTOCARRERO (2-5)	9373	17-30
SUN	06/06/54	CLEVELAND	L	7-5	MARION FRICANO (2-4)	9373	17-31
TUES	06/08/54	CHICAGO	L	9-3	BOB TRICE (6-4)	16615	17-32
WED	06/09/54	CHICAGO	L	9-4	ALEX KELLNER (2-7)	3582	17-33
THURS	06/10/54	CHICAGO	RAIN				
FRI	06/11/54	DETROIT	L	16-5	A. PORTOCARRERO (2-6)	4573	17-34

TWILIGHT TEAMS

DAY	DATE	OPPONENT	RESULT	SCORE	PITCHER	ATTENDANCE	RECORD
FRI	06/11/54	DETROIT	W	2-1	MARION FRICANO (3-4)	4573	18-34
SAT	06/12/54	DETROIT	W	4-2	BOB TRICE (7-4)	2012	19-34
SUN	06/13/54	DETROIT	W	4-3	ALEX KELLNER (3-7)	5368	20-34
SUN	06/13/54	DETROIT	W	6-3	A. PORTOCARRERO (3-6)	5368	21-34
TUES	06/15/54	AT CHICAGO	W	11-4	MOE BURTSCHY (3-1)	26458	22-34
WED	06/16/54	AT CHICAGO	L	11-6	SONNY DIXON (1-2)	5773	22-35
THURS	06/17/54	AT CHICAGO	L	6-4	ALEX KELLNER (3-8))	5339	22-36
FRI	06/18/54	AT DETROIT	W	2-1	A. PORTOCARRERO (4-6)	23216	23-36
SAT	06/19/54	AT DETROIT	W	5-4	DUTCH ROMBERGER (1-1)	7321	24-36
SUN	06/20/54	AT DETROIT	RAIN				
SUN	06/20/54	AT DETROIT	RAIN				
TUES	06/22/54	AT CLEVELAND	W	4-1	AL SIMA (1-1))	12964	25-36
WED	06/23/54	AT CLEVELAND	L	5-2	BOB TRICE (7-5)	4549	25-37
THURS	06/24/54	AT CLEVELAND	W	5-1	A. PORTOCARRERO (5-6)	4570	26-37
FRI	06/25/54	AT BALTIMORE	L	5-1	MARION FRICANO (3-5)	10160	26-38
SAT	06/26/54	AT BALTIMORE	L	5-4(10)	DUTCH ROMBERGER (1-2)	7418	26-39
SUN	06/27/54	AT BALTIMORE	L	4-3(11)	SONNY DIXON (1-3)	15792	26-40
SUN	06/27/54	AT BALTIMORE	L	3-2	AL SIMA (1-2)	15792	26-41
TUES	06/29/54	WASHINGTON	W	3-2	A. PORTOCARRERO (6-6)	2647	27-41
WED	06/30/54	WASHINGTON	W	8-7	SONNY DIXON (2-3)	4121	28-41
FRI	07/02/54	AT BOSTON	L	8-4	BOB TRICE (7-6)	12913	28-42
SAT	07/03/54	AT BOSTON	W	7-3	ALEX KELLNER (4-8)	7232	29-42
SUN	07/04/54	AT BOSTON	L	8-0	AL SIMA (1-3)	13861	29-43
MON	07/05/54	AT NEW YORK	L	7-4	A. PORTOCARRERO (6-7)	19661	29-44
MON	07/05/54	AT NEW YORK	L	11-2	MARION FRICANO (3-6)	19661	29-45
TUES	07/06/54	WASHINGTON	L	5-2	BOB TRICE (7-7)	3985	29-46
FRI	07/09/54	BOSTON	W	9-3	ALEX KELLNER (5-8)	5625	30-46
SAT	07/10/54	BOSTON	L	5-3(11)	SONNY DIXON (2-4)	3047	30-47
SUN	07/11/54	BOSTON	L	18-0	BOB TRICE (7-8)	7445	30-48
SUN	07/11/54	BOSTON	L	11-1	MARION FRICANO (3-7)	7445	30-49
TUES	07/13/54	All-Star BREAK					
THURS	07/15/54	CLEVELAND	L	4-0	ALEX KELLNER (5-9)	6209	30-50
FRI	07/16/54	CLEVELAND	L	9-3	A. PORTOCARRERO (6-8)	5525	30-51
SAT	07/17/54	CLEVELAND	L	6-0	AL SIMA (1-4)	3219	30-52
SUN	07/18/54	CHICAGO	L	10-2	JOHN GRAY (0-1)	5496	30-53
SUN	07/18/54	CHICAGO	L	4-3(7)	CHARLIE BISHOP (0-1)	5496	30-54
TUES	07/20/54	DETROIT	L	12-0	ALEX KELLNER (5-10)	4351	30-55
TUES	07/20/54	DETROIT	L	4-3	A. PORTOCARRERO (6-9)	4351	30-56
WED	07/21/54	DETROIT	W	4-1	SONNY DIXON (3-5)	1760	31-56
THURS	07/22/54	DETROIT	L	9-4	CHARLIE BISHOP (0-2)	1675	31-57
FRI	07/23/54	BALTIMORE	L	7-5	ALEX KELLNER (5-11)	1791	31-58
SAT	07/24/54	BALTIMORE	W	6-5	JOHN GRAY (1-1)	1634	32-58
SUN	07/25/54	BALTIMORE	W	9-4	AL SIMA (2-4)	4021	33-58
SUN	07/25/54	BALTIMORE	W	6-4	SONNY DIXON (4-5)	4021	34-58
TUES	07/27/54	AT DETROIT	L	3-2	CHARLIE BISHOP (0-3)	22603	34-59
TUES	07/27/54	AT DETROIT	W	8-3	MARION FRICANO (4-7)	22603	35-59
WED	07/28/54	AT DETROIT	L	10-2	ALEX KELLNER (5-12)	3535	35-60
THURS	07/29/54	AT DETROIT	L	4-2	JOHN GRAY (1-2)	4872	35-61
THURS	07/29/54	AT DETROIT	L	7-3	SONNY DIXON (4-6)	4872	35-62
FRI	07/30/54	AT CHICAGO	L	4-2	A. PORTOCARRERO (6-10)	16304	35-63
SAT	07/31/54	AT CHICAGO	L	7-1	CHARLIE BISHOP (0-4)	4581	35-64
SUN	08/01/54	AT CHICAGO	L	6-5	MARION FRICANO (4-8)	17057	35-65
SUN	08/01/54	AT CHICAGO	L	12-1	SONNY DIXON (4-7)	17057	35-66
MON	08/02/54	AT BALTIMORE	L	10-2	JOHN GRAY (1-3)	7839	35-67
TUES	08/03/54	AT BALTIMORE	W	6-2	A. PORTOCARRERO (7-10)	10134	36-67
WED	08/04/54	AT BALTIMORE	W	6-4	ALEX KELLNER (6-12)	7637	37-67
FRI	08/06/54	AT CLEVELAND	L	7-3	AL SIMA (2-5)	12560	37-68
SAT	08/07/54	AT CLEVELAND	L	5-1	JOHN GRAY (1-4)	8393	37-69

THE 1954 PHILADELPHIA ATHLETICS

DAY	DATE	OPPONENT	RESULT	SCORE	PITCHER	ATTENDANCE	RECORD
SUN	08/08/54	AT CLEVELAND	L	7-2	A. PORTOCARRERO (7-11)	20381	37-70
SUN	08/08/54	AT CLEVELAND	L	5-2	ALEX KELLNER (6-13)	20381	37-71
TUES	08/10/54	AT NEW YORK	L	5-2	CHARLIE BISHOP (0-5)	16850	37-72
WED	08/11/54	AT NEW YORK	L	3-1	JOHN GRAY (1-5)	9733	37-73
THURS	08/12/54	AT NEW YORK	L	5-4	A. PORTOCARRERO (7-12)	13890	37-74
THURS	08/12/54	AT NEW YORK	L	7-1	ALEX KELLNER (6-14)	13890	37-75
FRI	08/13/54	AT WASHINGTON	W	3-2	MARION FRICANO (5-8)	3812	38-75
SAT	08/14/54	AT WASHINGTON	W	6-4(11)	CHARLIE BISHOP (1-5)	2708	39-75
SUN	08/15/54	AT WASHINGTON	L	4-1	JOHN GRAY (1-6)	1894	39-76
TUES	08/17/54	NEW YORK	L	11-1	A. PORTOCARRERO (7-13)	8885	39-77
WED	08/18/54	NEW YORK	L	6-1	ALEX KELLNER (6-15)	7367	39-78
THURS	08/19/54	NEW YORK	L	8-5	JOHN GRAY (1-7)	3116	39-79
FRI	08/20/54	WASHINGTON	RAIN				
SAT	08/21/54	WASHINGTON	RAIN				
SAT	08/21/54	WASHINGTON	RAIN				
SUN	08/22/54	WASHINGTON	W	3-2 (12)	CHARLIE BISHOP (2-5)	3634	40-79
SUN	08/22/54	WASHINGTON	SUSP	4-4 (9)	A. PORTOCARRERO	3634	
MON	08/23/54	WASHINGTON	L	8-5	MARION FRICANO (5-9)	2094	40-80
MON	08/23/54	WASHINGTON	L	10-3	ALEX KELLNER (6-16)	2094	40-81
TUES	08/24/54	CLEVELAND	W	4-1	JOHN GRAY (2-7)	9175	41-81
WED	08/25/54	CLEVELAND	L	4-3(10)	AL SIMA (2-6)	7311	41-82
THURS	08/26/54	CHICAGO	L	8-1	A. PORTOCARRERO (7-14)	3650	41-83
THURS	08/26/54	CHICAGO	W	4-1	CHARLIE BISHOP (3-5)	3650	42-83
FRI	08/27/54	CHICAGO	L	11-0	MARION FRICANO (5-10)	2208	42-84
SAT	08/28/54	CHICAGO	L	5-2	ALEX KELLNER (6-17)	1867	42-85
SUN	08/29/54	DETROIT	L	14-3	JOHN GRAY (2-8)	3973	42-86
SUN	08/29/54	DETROIT	L	2-1	A. PORTOCARRERO (7-15)	3973	42-87
TUES	08/31/54	BALTIMORE	W	8-6	MOE BURTSCHY (4-1)	2126	43-87
TUES	08/31/54	BALTIMORE	W	6-3	SONNY DIXON (5-7)	2126	44-87
FRI	09/03/54	BOSTON	L	11-1	A. PORTOCARRERO (7-16)	2874	44-88
SAT	09/04/54	BOSTON	W	4-3	JOHN GRAY (3-8)	2124	45-88
SUN	09/05/54	BOSTON	L	12-5	CHARLIE BISHOP (3-6)	5788	45-89
SUN	09/05/54	BOSTON	L	7-3	SONNY DIXON (5-8)	5788	45-90
MON	09/06/54	AT WASHINGTON	L	8-1	A. PORTOCARRERO (7-17)	4865	45-91
MON	09/06/54	AT WASHINGTON	W	3-2	CHARLIE BISHOP (4-6)	4865	46-91
TUES	09/07/54	AT WASHINGTON	L	5-4	MOE BURTSCHY (4-2)	460	46-92
WED	09/08/54	AT CLEVELAND	L	5-2	JOHN GRAY (3-9)	14262	46-93
THURS	09/09/54	AT CLEVELAND	L	5-4(11)	MOE BURTSCHY (4-3)	6145	46-94
FRI	09/10/54	AT DETROIT	W	6-5	SONNY DIXON (6-8)	1389	47-94
SAT	09/11/54	AT DETROIT	L	2-1	MARION FRICANO (5-11)	3332	47-95
SUN	09/12/54	AT BALTIMORE	L	4-3	JOHM GRAY (3-10)	12981	47-96
SUN	09/12/54	AT BALTIMORE	W	5-4	MOE BURTSCHY (5-3)	12981	48-96
TUES	09/14/54	AT CHICAGO	W	1-0	A. PORTOCARRERO (8-17)	9128	49-96
FRI	09/17/54	NEW YORK	L	10-3	JOHN GRAY (3-11)	3047	49-97
SAT	09/18/54	NEW YORK	L	6-5	A. PORTOCARRERO (8-18)	1834	49-98
SUN	09/19/54	NEW YORK	L	4-2	MOE BURTSCHY (5-4)	1715	49-99
MON	09/20/54	AT BOSTON	L	5-2	JOHN GRAY (3-12)	1555	49-100
TUES	09/21/54	AT BOSTON	L	4-3(10)	SONNY DIXON (5-8)	2774	49-101
TUES	09/21/54	AT BOSTON	L	4-3	OZZIE VAN BRABANT (0-2)	2774	49-102
FRI	09/24/54	AT NEW YORK	W	5-1	A. PORTOCARRERO (9-18)	2032	50-102
SAT	09/25/54	AT NEW YORK	L	10-2	BILL OSTER (0-1)	9890	50-103
SUN	09/26/54	AT NEW YORK	W	8-6	ART DITMAR (1-4)	11670	51-103

THE 1957
NEW YORK GIANTS

Manhattan Transfer

We're calling all you fans
All you Giant ball fans
Come watch the home team
Going places round those bases.

Cheer for your favorites
Out at Coogan's Bluff
Come watch the Polo Grounders
Do their stuff.

The "Giant Victory March" was composed in 1946 at the suggestion of the ball club's owner, Horace Stoneham. The upbeat tune was played after each Giant victory. As fans filed out of the Polo Grounds after the final game on September twenty-ninth, 1957 the familiar trio in the left field bullpen, two trumpet players and a trombonist, once again played the song while a small crowd of onlookers sang.

"What's wrong with those guys?" asked John La Rocca, a barber from the Bronx, "It would have been more proper if they had played a funeral march! Why did they have to rub it in by playing that song?" The music also irked Jack Tausig, a steam fitter from Brooklyn. "We lost the Giants didn't we?" he asked. "Those guys must be from San Francisco."

THE POLO GROUNDS, NEW YORK

Bounded by Eighth Avenue, 157th and 158th Streets, and the Harlem River. Home of the National League Giants from April 22, 1891 to September 29, 1957 when the Giants left for San Francisco. The American League Yankees shared the ballpark from 1913 until 1922. Yankee Stadium was completed in 1923. After remaining vacant for four seasons the Polo Grounds became home to the new National League Mets during the 1962 and 1963 seasons. The stadium was razed in 1964 by the same wrecking ball that demolished Ebbets Field, Brooklyn in 1961. (Photo from National Baseball Library and Archive collection, Cooperstown, New York.)

1957 NEW YORK GIANTS

Front row—Katt, Virgil, Sarni, coach: Walters, coach; Williams, coach; Rigney, manager; Brannick, secretary; Henrich, coach; Thomas, Miller; O'Connell. **Middle row**—Logan, clubhouse custodian; Mueller, Mays, Lockman, Westrum, Spencer, Barclay; Crone, Jablonski, Antonelli, Thomson, Bowman, trainer; Sauer. **Back row**—Gomez, Rhodes, Harris, Monzant, Grissom, McCormick, Constable, Bressoud, Worthington. **Seated in front**—Batboy Logan (Photo from The Sporting News collection, St. Louis, Missouri.)

		Games at position	Bats	Avg.		
C	Valmy Thomas	88	R	.249	6 HR	
1B	Whitey Lockman	102	L	.248	7 HR	
1B	Gail Harris	61	L	.240	9 HR	
2B	Danny O'Connell	68	R	.266	7 HR	
2B	Red Schoendienst	57	SW	.307	9 HR	**78 Hits* @**
SS	Daryl Spencer	110	R	.249	11 HR	
3B	Ray Jablonski	70	R	.289	9 HR	
3B	Ozzie Virgil	62	R	.235		
RF	Don Mueller	115	L	.258		
CF	Willie Mays	150	R	**.333**	**35 HR**	**203B* 38SB***
						97 RBI
LF	Hank Sauer	98	R	.259	26 HR	
OF	Bobby Thomson	71	R	.242	8 HR	
OF	Dusty Rhodes	44	L	.205		
C	Ray Katt	68	R	.230		
C	Wes Westrum	63	R	.165		
SS	Ed Bressoud	33	R	.268	5 HR	
SS	Andre Rodgers	20	R	.244		
IF	Foster Castleman	18	R	.162		
PH	Bill Taylor	11	R	.000		
PH	Bobby Hofman	2	R	.000		
	Jim Davis		R	1.000		

PITCHERS

R	Ruben Gomez	38	W **15**	L 13	3.78 ERA	**16 Complete games**
L	Johnny Antonelli	40	W 12	L 18	3.77 ERA	**3 Shut outs**
R	Ray Crone	25	W 4	L 8	4.33 ERA	
R	Curt Barclay	37	W 9	L 9	3.44 ERA	2 Shut outs
L	Pete Burnside	10	W 1	L 4	8.80 ERA	
R	Max Surkont	5	W 0	L 1	9.95 ERA	

RELIEF PITCHERS:

R	Stu Miller	38	W 7	L 9	3.63 ERA	1 Save
R	Marv Grissom	55	W 4	L 4	2.61 ERA	**14 Saves**
R	Al Worthington	55	W 8	L 11	4.22 ERA	4 Saves
L	Mike McCormick	24	W 3	L 1	4.10 ERA	
R	Ray Monzant	24	W 3	L 2	3.99 ERA	
L	Jim Davis	10	W 1	L 0	6.55 ERA	
L	Jim Constable	16	W 1	L 1	2.86 ERA	
R	Gordon Jones	27	W 0	L 1	6.17 ERA	
R	Steve Ridzik	15	W 0	L 2	4.73 ERA	
L	Windy McCall	5	W 0	L 0	15.00 ERA	
R	Sandy Consuegra	4	W 0	L 0	2.45 ERA	
L	Joe Margoneri	13	W 1	L 1	5.24 ERA	
	Bill Rigney		W 69	L 85		

Bold Type—led club

* Led league

@ With New York and Milwaukee led league with 200 Hits.

The shift of the New York Giants and the Brooklyn Dodgers to California at the end of the 1957 season was compelling sports news. Professional football hadn't yet taken hold of the public consciousness. Professional basketball and hockey were just minor players. The term "Major League" referred almost exclusively to baseball. Baseball was king. In the 1950s, New York was the largest jewel in baseball's crown.

As early as 1845, Alexander Cartwright framed the rules for the modern game. He fielded the New York Knickerbockers, who originally played in midtown Manhattan. The team soon moved across the Hudson River to the Elysian Fields in Hoboken, New Jersey.

THE HISTORY—JOHN McGRAW

The Giants belonged to New York State for seventy-four years. They were the Troy Trojans from 1879 to 1882, moving to Manhattan in 1883, and becoming the New York Gothams. The Gothams, also known as the Maroons, played most of their games at the original Polo Grounds at 110th street and Fifth Avenue in Manhattan, with interim appearances at Jersey City, and on Staten Island. The first Polo Grounds was the home of the first World Series in 1884. The National League Providence Grays swept three games from the New York Metropolitans of the American Association. Jim Mutrie, manager of the Gothams, had negotiated the post season match up.

In 1888, its first season after formally adopting the name Giants, the ball club won its first National League title. Hosting the second World Series games at the original Polo Grounds, the Giants defeated the American Association St. Louis Browns in a ten game post season exhibition series. The Giants won six of the first eight. Pitcher Buck Keefe won four games in the series. With the final two games meaningless, Manager Mutrie sent Keefe home along with pitcher Mikey Welch, catcher Buck Ewing, and shortstop John Montgomery Ward.

After the 1888 season, the City demolished the Polo Grounds, enlarging an area known as Douglas Circle, which later became Duke Ellington Circle. Club owner, and tobacco merchant, John B. Day acquired the title to a new facility, moving the team to a horseshoe-shaped facility on Manhattan's 159th Street in an area along the Harlem River known as Brotherhood Park. The facility wasn't ready by opening day 1889, however, forcing the club to play two games in Jersey City and twenty-five more on Staten Island before settling in their permanent home.

Attired in his familiar stovepipe hat, manager Mutrie watched his "Giants" repeat as league champions in 1889, and defeat the American Association Champions, the Brooklyn Bridegrooms, in another ten game post season encounter. After losing three of the first four games, the Giants won the next five. Ward hit .417. "Cannonball" Ed Crane won four games. It was the first of many New York Subway Series. It was the only one, however, matching the Giants against Brooklyn. The Bridegrooms jumped to the National League in 1890, becoming the Dodgers.

In 1891 the Giants' new ballpark on the Harlem River was renamed the Polo Grounds, although there would never be a single game of polo at the new Polo Grounds.

First baseman Roger Connor and outfielder Willie Keeler, both Hall of Famers, were early New York heroes in the National League. Connor, the most prolific home run hitter in the game prior to arrival of Babe Ruth, had a lifetime batting average of .327. Keeler's forty-four game hitting streak for Baltimore in 1897 stood as a Major League record until DiMaggio eclipsed it in the summer of 1941.

In 1901, John McGraw, a ten-year National League veteran, joined the Baltimore Orioles of Ban Johnson's upstart American League as a player-manager. The stricter rules of personal conduct adopted by the new league cramped his confrontational style, and he had run-ins with Johnson. In 1902, he returned to the National League as manager of the Giants, at the urging of John T."Tooth" Brush, the new owner, who purchased controlling interest in the team in 1903 from Andrew Freedman for $125,000. At the urging of McGraw, Brush also imported catcher Roger Bresnahan, and pitcher Joe McGinnity from the Baltimore Orioles.

From 1903 through 1931, McGraw's Giants were the most dominant team in baseball, winning ten pennants. By the end of their tenure in New York, they had accumulated a total of seventeen pennants, and seven World Championships. Only the AL New York Yankees have won more.

Right handed Hall of Fame pitchers, Christy "Big Six" Mathewson won 373 games, and Joe "Iron Man" McGinnity won 247 games in their respective careers. Hall of Fame left hander "Rube" Marquard won 201. Mathewson was one of the first five players inducted into the Hall of Fame. Honus Wagner, Babe Ruth, Walter Johnson, and Ty Cobb were the others.

McGraw's Giants won their first pennant in 1904. But owner John T. Brush backed McGraw's decision to boycott the World Series that year. They would have faced the American League Champions, and the

Boston Pilgrims. Fans were critical of the boycott. Harboring bitterness toward Ban Johnson resulting from their relationship during his brief American League tenure, McGraw refused to lend credibility to the new league. After the Giants repeated as National League Champions in 1905, however, Brush carefully drafted a set of regulations to govern future post season competition, and agreed to meet the American League champions. The Giants easily defeated Connie Mack's Philadelphia A's, four games to one. Mathewson hurled three shutouts. The A's star pitcher, Rube Waddell was sidelined with an arm injury.

THE BALLPARK

When the original wooden stands at the new Polo Grounds burned to the ground in 1911, a new 16,000 seat concrete and steel facility was constructed by owner John T. Brush. It opened on June 28, 1911.

Coogan's Bluff, a rock outcropping sticking up through upper Harlem and lower Washington Heights, loomed over the horseshoe shaped park. The Coogan family owned the bluff and the land upon which the Polo Grounds stood. Until 1922, the path along the bluff, starting at 158th and Edgecombe Avenue, provided a free view of the field from second base to the center field score board. Picnicking spectators on the bluff could see an average of four players. The exit gate behind home plate, opened in the late innings, neatly framed the pitcher on the mound.

With home plate located at the bottom of the horseshoe curve, the distance down the line to the fence in left was just 279 feet, and it was a mere 257 feet to the right field barrier. Both bull pens were on the playing field in deep centerfield, which was cavernous. A 483 foot drive would only reach the base of the sixty foot high green blockhouse in straight away center. The team clubhouses were on the first floor of the large four story structure. A dining room for sports writers and celebrities was on the second floor. Owner Horace Stoneham maintained an office and an apartment on the upper levels.

From 1911 to 1913, the Giants won three consecutive pennants at their newly renovated facility. But McGraw's troops lost three consecutive times in the World Series. In 1911, Frank "Home run" Baker of the American League Philadelphia Athletics beat Marquard, three to one, with a two-run homer in the sixth inning of the second game. Baker beat Mathewson with another two-run blast in the in the eleventh inning of the third game, three to two.

Marquard won nineteen straight games in 1912, matching the major league record set the Giants' own Buck Keefe in 1888. In the 1912 Series, Smokey Joe Wood won three games for the American League Red Sox. In the tenth inning of the seventh and final game, Giant outfielder Fred Snograss dropped a routine fly ball. Although he made a sparkling stab of Harry Hooper's liner on the next play, Tris Speaker followed with a line single to center, driving in the tying, unearned, run. The winning run eventually scored on a sacrifice fly. In 1913, Mathewson won twenty-five games. Marquard won twenty-three, and Jeff Tesreau won twenty-two. Mathewson shut out Philadelphia in the second game of the 1913 World Series. The Giants scored three times in the top of the tenth inning to win, three to nothing. The A's, however, won the Series, four games to one.

1916 GIANTS WIN RECORD TWENTY-SIX STRAIGHT BUT FINISH FOURTH

In May 1916 the Giants won seventeen straight games on the road. In September of the same year they set a major league record, winning twenty-six straight games, all at home. Incredibly the club finished a disappointing fourth.

The Giants won another pennant in 1917. They lost again in the Series. Ed Cicotte hurled the American League White Sox to a two to one victory in the first game. Chicago won four games to two. "Shoeless Joe" Jackson, later implicated along with Eddie Ciccotte and others, in the 1919 World Series fix, batted .304. New York right fielder Dave Robertson led both teams with a .500 batting average. But he made a costly muff in the outfield that allowed the White Sox to win the final game. Charles Stoneham, a stock broker and business partner of gambler Arnold Rothestein, purchased the Giants from the Brush estate in 1919 for $1 million. Rothstein was later implicated in the Black Sox scandal of 1917.

The 1921 post season marked the first appearance of the Yankees in a World Series, and the first intra-city championship since 1889. The Giants won for the first time since 1905. All eight games were played at the Polo Grounds, where both the Giants, and the American League Champion Yankees, played their regular season games. Carl Mays and Wait Hoyt of the Yankees hurled back-to-back shutouts in the first two games. The Giants, however, won the third game, thirteen to five. Spectators on Coogan's Bluff saw center fielder Bill Cunningham haul down Babe Ruth's long drive in the first inning of game four, and somersault in celebration afterward. The Giants won again, four to two. In the fifth game, Hoyt defeated Art Nehf for the second time, winning again for the Yankees, three to one. Babe Ruth wrenched his knee, forcing him out of the line-up for the remainder of the Series. The Giants won the final three games and the Series, five games to three. Frankie Fritsch tagged out Aaron Ward of the Yankees at third base for the final out of the last game. This time Nehf defeated Hoyt, who did not allow an earned run in three starts, one to nothing.

The Giants swept all four games in the 1922 Series, holding Ruth to just two hits. Heinie Groh batted .474. Frankie Frisch batted .471. Commissioner Landis ordered the second game called because of darkness after ten innings with the score tied at three to three. There appeared to be ample daylight to complete the riveting contest. A protest by fans resulted in gate receipts being donated to local charities.

In 1923, the Giants modernized the Polo Grounds, keeping pace with their American League counterparts, who opened the palatial Yankee Stadium that year. The new extended grandstand obscured much of the view of the playing field and scoreboard from Coogan's Bluff. For the third straight year the Giants met the Yankees in the post season. The Giants won the first two World Series games ever played at Yankee Stadium. Outfielder Casey Stengel's homer in the ninth inning gave the Giants a five to four win in the opener. And his second homer of the Series in the top of the seventh inning of game three gave the Giants a one to nothing win. The Yankees, however, won all four games at the Polo Grounds. They clinched the title with a six to four victory in the sixth game, rallying for five runs in the eighth to overcome a four to one Giant lead. Babe Ruth rebounded from disappointments in his first two Series appearances, homering three times, and batting .368.

The 1924 Giants were Manager McGraw's last pennant winner. The team suffered another heart-breaking World Series loss. Aging legend Walter Johnson of the Washington Senators won the seventh, and deciding game, of the World Series in a relief appearance, four to three. In the eighth inning a ground ball bounced over Giant third baseman Fred Lindstrom's head, allowing the tying run to score. Incredibly, another ground ball took a sudden hop over Lindstrom's head in the twelfth inning, allowing the winning run to score.

Never having spent a day in the minors, seventeen-year-old outfielder Mel Ott joined the Giants in 1926. Ott became the youngest player, at twenty-five years, 144 days, to hit 200 home runs. In twenty-one seasons he hit 511 home runs, drove in 1860 runs, and batted 304 en route to the Hall of Fame. Hall of Fame pitcher Carl Hubbell, "the Meal Ticket", made his Major League debut for New York in 1928. "King Carl" had 252 career victories, winning twenty games in five consecutive seasons. Hubbell and Ott led the Giants to National League Pennants in 1933, 1936, and 1937.

The Hall of Fame first baseman, Bill Terry, became the second, and last, National Leaguer to bat .400 with a .401 average in 1930. He replaced McGraw as player manager in 1932.

In 1933, the Giants avenged their defeat in the 1924 Series, defeating the Senators in five games. Hubbell, a screwball specialist, won two games. The five foot nine inch Ott batted .389. He homered in the tenth inning to win the final game.

In the second annual Major League All-Star Game in 1934, Hubbell struck out American Leaguers Ruth, Gehrig, Jimmie Foxx, Al Simmons, and Joe Cronin in succession.

Finishing the 1936 season with twenty-six victories, Hubbell defeated the Yankees in the first game of the World Series, six to one. The Yankees hammered the Giants, eighteen to four, in game two, and again, thirteen to five, in the sixth and deciding game. Hal Schumacher posted a five to four decision in the fifth game for the Giants second win. Shortstop Dick Bartell led the Giant regulars with a 381 batting average. Ott hit .304 in the Series and homered once.

With the passing of Charles Stoneham in January, 1936, ownership of the Giants passed to his son, Horace Stoneham.

In 1937, Joe McCarthy's Yankees, behind Lefty Gomez, defeated Hubbell and the Giants, eight to one, in the opener of the World Series. Hubbell beat the Yankees, seven to three, in game four. But that was the Giants' only win as the American League Champions prevailed in five games. Outfielder Jo Jo Moore batted .391 for the Giants.

After three straight second division finishes, Ott replaced the mercurial Terry in 1942, managing the club to a third place finish. The Giants never again finished higher than fourth under his leadership. "Master Melvin" was nonetheless popular with Giants' fans. Normally exhibiting a genial demeanor, Ott, surprisingly, became the first manager ever to be thrown out of both games of a doubleheader, on June ninth, 1946. The Giants drew a record attendance of 1,219,873 in 1946, despite a last place finish.

Traded to the Giants from the Cardinals, Johnny Mize returned from military service, hitting fifty-one homers in 1947, and forty homers in 1948. Sharing the league lead each season with Ralph Kiner of Pittsburgh, Mize did, however, have the league RBI title to himself in 1947, driving in 138 Runs to Kiner's 127.

THE SHOT HEARD ROUND THE WORLD

Hall of Famer Leo "the Lip" Durocher became manager of the Giants in 1949. He led the Giants to another league title in 1951. On August twelfth, the Giants trailed Brooklyn by thirteen and one-half games. However, they won thirty-nine of their final forty-seven games, drawing even with the Dodgers on the final day of the season. On October fourth, at the Polo Grounds, they faced the Dodgers in the final game of a three game playoff. New York trailed, four to one, after eight and one-half innings. But Alvin Dark and Don Mueller singled off a tiring Don Newcombe to begin the bottom of the ninth. After Monty Irvin popped out Lockman doubled home a run. Then, with Ralph Branca on in relief, and Willie Mays on deck, Bobby Thomson hit the famed "Shot heard round the world", a three-run blast over the head of left fielder Andy Pafko. It landed in the left field bleachers, giving the Giants a five to four victory, and , of course, the pennant. It was the defining moment in franchise history.

The Giants won the first game of the 1951 World Series at Yankee Stadium, five to one. Lefty Dave Koslo defeated Yankees' ace Allie Reynolds. Monte Irvin stole home. Irvin had eleven hits in the Series, tying a record for most hits in a six game Series. Ed Lopat pitched the Yankees to a three to one victory in the second game. The Giants won again, six to two, at the Polo Grounds in game three. Whitey Lockman homered for the Giants. On a failed hit and run attempt in the fifth inning, a sliding Eddie Stanky kicked the ball out of shortstop Phil Rizzuto's hand. The Giants went on to score five runs. Rain postponed the fourth game, and cooled off the Giants as well. The Yankees won the final three games, drubbing the Giants, six to two, and thirteen to one, in their final Series appearances at the Polo Grounds. The American Leaguers clinched their fourth victory in six World Series between the two clubs with a four to three win at Yankee Stadium in game six.

Thomson was dealt to Milwaukee prior to the start of the 1954 season for left hander John Antonelli, who was in military service in Korea during the Braves final season in Boston in 1952. Having also returned from a two-year tour of military duty, Willie Mays told the New York media. "Johnny Antonelli isn't only the best pitcher I faced in service ball, he's the best pitcher I faced in any kind of ball— including the World Series."

GIANTS UPSET 1954 INDIANS

After winning their final pennant in 1954, The Giants swept the World Series from the heavily favored Indians, winners of a record one hundred and eleven regular season games. Among a handful of teams that practiced in Arizona each spring, the clubs were familiar with each other. The Giants were not in awe of Cleveland. Willie May's epic over-the-shoulder catch of an eighth inning drive off the bat of Vic Wertz, who hit .500 in the Series, preserved a two to two tie in the first game at the Polo Grounds. Pinch hitter Dusty Rhodes homered with two on in the bottom of the tenth, giving the Giants a five to two win. Rhodes drove in seven runs in six Series at bats. Antonelli, a twenty-one game winner, defeated Cleveland's Early Wynn in the second game, three to one. Antonelli also singled home the winning run in the fifth inning. Seventeen game winner Ruben Gomez defeated the Indians' Mike Garcia in game three, six to two. Finally, Don Liddle defeated Bob Lemon, seven to four, completing the four game sweep, and ending a string of seven straight Series victories by the American League champions. Durocher called shortstop Dark, who hit .412 in the World Series, "a tremendous spiritual factor, the backbone of the club."

The Giants finished third in 1955. On June fourteen, 1956, they traded Dark to the Cardinals along with catcher Ray Katt, pitcher Don Liddle, and outfielder Whitey Lockman. The marquee player that the Giants got in return was second baseman Red Schoendienst. The Giants also acquired pitchers Bobby Stephenson and Dick Littlefield, and catcher Bill Sarni. The club finished sixth.

Finishing in sixth place in 1956, under new manager Bill Rigney, the Giants drew only 629,179, the lowest attendance at the Polo Grounds since 1944. Except for the 1954 championship season, the Giants had not out drawn the Dodgers, or the Yankees, for more than a decade.

RUMBLINGS

In the spring of 1957, there were constant background rumblings concerning the shift of both New York National league franchises to the West Coast. Horace Stoneham of the Giants complained about the outmoded Polo Grounds, and the inadequate adjacent parking. Stoneham also believed that metropolitan New York's saturation with televised baseball was a factor in declining attendance.

Neither the Giants nor the Dodgers owned the land on which their home stadiums stood. Under lease agreements, both teams paid taxes on the land. The Giants paid $40,385 in 1956, plus an annual rent of $55,000. Both clubs, however, were historically good draws at the gate. Few observers felt that the National League would abandon New York altogether.

HULAN JACK'S STADIUM

Optimistic Manhattan borough president, Hulan Jack, proposed a new 110,000 seat domed stadium for the Giants to be built over the railroad tracks on the West Side. The huge triple decked structure would have adjacent parking facilities for 20,000 cars. It would be large enough to accommodate other sporting events such as the annual Army-Navy game and future Olympic games venues. The site was bounded by Sixtieth and Seventy-second streets extending from West End Avenue to the West Side Highway. Horace Stoneham, whose lease on the Polo Grounds was set to expire in 1962, expressed an interest in the project. But the land had recently been sold by New York Central to The New York Times Newspaper Company. And, in any case, Jack had no clear idea of how to raise the money to pay for the project. Other sites had been studied and dismissed as impractical. They involved the costly displacement and relocation of businesses and private residences.

Meanwhile, other cities were wooing the Giants. Minneapolis had already built a modern municipal stadium, and had been in contact with several big league teams. The Giants were clearly their first choice. Minneapolis may well have been Stoneham's first choice. The Giants' minor league team there, the Millers, led the league in attendance. The Giants' owner, however, was being strongly encouraged by O'Malley to move to San Francisco if, and when, the Dodgers moved to Los Angeles. The Giants were familiar with both cities, having played an extended series of exhibition games on the West Coast in the spring of 1953. They played against the Indians, Browns, White Sox, the Tokyo Giants, the Los Angeles Angels of the Pacific Coast League, and the University of Southern California.

THE FINAL SEASON

The average age of players on the Giants' 1957 roster was thirty. Only the Dodgers had an older roster. Three young prospects were in military service: outfielders Jackie Brandt and Willie Kirkland, and first baseman Bill White.

After five seasons with New York, knuckleball specialist Hoyt Wilhelm was traded to the Cardinals. The Giants reacquired Whitey Lockman. Cardinal general manager Frank Lane wired Giant catcher Bill Sarni, "no longer will you have to worry about Wilhelm's knucklers breaking your fingers." But the twenty-nine year old Sarni had more to worry about. He had suffered a heart attack in the previous off season.

Generously, Stoneham kept Sarni on the payroll as a coach, insuring that he qualified for the players' pension plan. Without Sarni on the active roster, the Giants were in need of a catcher. They traded left hander Dick Littlefield, and outfielder Bob Lennon to Chicago, reacquiring former Giants' catcher Ray Katt. The Giants also obtained third baseman Ray "Jabbo" Jablonski from the Cubs. And they claimed thirty-eight year old outfielder Hank Sauer from the Cardinals on waivers.

Needing to boost sagging attendance, New York had traded pitcher Dick Littlefield to the Dodgers in December, 1956 for thirty-eight year-old legend Jackie Robinson. Robinson, however, decided to retire rather than join his long time rivals.

PREMIER GIANT: WILLIE "SAY HEY" MAYS

Twenty-six year old star Willie Mays, the most significant player in the history of the New York Giant franchise, returned for his sixth season in center field. A standout defensively, Mays, the National League's 1951 Rookie of the Year, hit .345 in 1945, and finished his career with 660 home runs.

WPIX Television in New York televised selected Giants' and Yankees' home and away games in 1957. The "voices" of the Giants were Russ Hodges and Bob Delaney.

APRIL

The Giants lost the opening game of the season on a cold, rainy afternoon in Pittsburgh, nine to two, before more than 33,000 at Forbes Field. Antonelli, uncharacteristically wild, walked six, losing to the Pirates for the first time in eight starts over several seasons.

The Pirates led only three to two after seven and one-half innings. But two bad throws by third baseman Daryl Spencer in the bottom of the eighth fueled a six run Pittsburgh rally. Only one of the runs off Grissom in relief was earned. Schoendienst had three of ten Giant hits. Mays had two.

On Wednesday April eighteenth, New York Mayor Robert F. Wagner threw out the ceremonial first pitch in the Giants' home opener against Philadelphia on another cold, rainy afternoon. 8,585 shivering fans, including Baseball Commissioner Ford Frick, showed up to see New York win, six to two. First baseman Gail Harris hit a three-run homer in the fourth inning. Sauer hit a two-run shot in the sixth, the two hundred and fiftieth homer of his major league career.

GOMEZ DONS A PROTECTIVE HELMET

Umpire Bill Jackowski refused to let winning pitcher Gomez bat in the third until he donned a protective helmet, mandated by the National League. Philadelphia threatened in the top of the eighth inning. With one out, and runners at second and third, left fielder Rip Repulski singled sharply to center, scoring the lead runner. But Mays' throw to the plate held speedy Richie Ashburn at third. Grissom struck out the final two batters in the inning.

In the ninth inning, the rookie shortstop, Andre Rodgers, allowed an unearned run to score when he dropped the throw from Schoendienst on a force play at second. Despite a comfortable lead, Rigney was concerned. Determined to run a "tighter ship" than he had in 1956, he closed the doors to the Giant dressing room, explaining to reporters:

> If anyone makes a mistake—pitching, fielding, batting or running, the bases—I intend to tell him about it, right now, in front of everyone, so that we'll all understand what happened, and see that it doesn't happen again. I think Andy learned a lesson. I told him that in a situation like that, the thing to do is to make sure of one out, and then go for the double play.

The players responded positively, voting to work out at the Polo Grounds on their off day. The extra practice seemed to pay an immediate dividend. On Saturday, April twentieth, Rodgers made no mistakes in the field, and he hit his first major league home run in the sixth inning. The blast cleared the left field roof. But a three-run homer by Mays in the seventh still left New York a run behind. Dusty Rhodes led off the bottom of the ninth with a triple, but failed to score. The Phillies won, six to five.

The Giants split the first Sunday doubleheader of the season. In the first game Robin Roberts of the Phillies and Antonelli dueled to a one to one tie for eight and one-half innings. Leading off the bottom of the ninth, Mays beat out an infield grounder by sliding into first, and took second when the throw dribbled a few feet away from the first baseman, Ed Bouchee. Mays then stole third and scored on Sauer's soft liner to left, giving New York a two to one win. Philadelphia won the nightcap, eight to five, ruining rookie Curt Barclay's major league debut by scoring four runs in the first inning.

On Monday, April twenty-second, Gomez defeated the visiting Pirates three to one, backed by a three-run homer by Mays in the third inning. On Tuesday night rookie southpaw Pete Burnside, fresh out of Dartmouth College, shut out Pittsburgh, one to nothing. Mays again provided the offense, hitting a booming 450 foot double in the third that scored Sauer with the only run of the game.

On Wednesday the Giants faced the Dodgers for the first time, losing four to three at Ebbets Field. Sauer doubled home two runs off Koufax in the third inning. The Dodgers scored four runs in the fourth inning. Mays singled again in the fifth, stole second, and scored on a single by Mueller. That, however closed out the Giants' scoring.

On Friday, April twenty-sixth, at Connie Mack Stadium, Phillies' right hander Don Caldwell made his first major league start, shutting out the Giants, five to nothing. With no offensive support, Antonelli, victimized by errors by Harris and Virgil, took the loss. On Saturday Gomez, backed by two home runs by Sauer, defeated the Phillies, ten to two. But shortstop Rodgers sprained his ankle in the eighth inning.

On Sunday, April twenty-eighth, the Phillies turned the tables, humbling the Giants in the first game of a scheduled doubleheader, eleven to two. Repulski homered twice and doubled twice. Burnside failed to survive the first. The Giants led eight to seven when the second game was halted by a 7 P.M. Sunday curfew in Philadelphia. The game was scheduled to be resumed in August.

On the final day of the month, Antonelli, shut out Milwaukee, four to nothing, opening a thirteen game home stand. Striking out nine of his former Braves' teammates, he also homered to right with Darryl Spencer on base in the seventh. New York was tied for third place with Brooklyn, three and one-half games back of first place.

MAY

On Wednesday, May first, the first place Braves defeated the Giants in ten innings, five to one. With Gomez sidelined with a sinus infection, Barclay pitched seven strong innings, holding the powerful Braves to just a single run. Grissom followed with two scoreless innings. Braves' starter Warren Spahn held the Giants scoreless until shortstop Ossie Virgil led off the bottom of the ninth with a triple, and scored on a single by Jablonski, tying the game. But back-to-back homers by Bobby Thomson and Frank Torre in the top of the tenth sealed the Milwaukee win, and dealt reliever Max Surkont, a former Brave, his first defeat of the year.

In a slugfest with Cincinnati on Thursday, May second, the Reds scored three times in the top of the first and the Giants scored four in the bottom half of the inning. Gail Harris tied the score at seven all with a homer in the Giant half of the seventh. Cincinnati, however, scored twice in the top of the ninth, winning, nine to seven. On Friday, Schoendienst hit a solo homer in the bottom of the third. The Giants scored three more times in the fourth inning, and added another run in the fifth. When Sauer hit a two-run homer and Rhodes singled home two more runs in the sixth, New York led, ten to eight. But Reds' pinch hitter Pete Whisenant hit a three-run homer in the top of the ninth inning, giving the Reds an eleven to ten win. Although Antonelli pitched seven strong innings on Saturday, Grissom couldn't protect a two to nothing lead. Cincinnati scored five runs in the eighth inning. The Reds' sweep dropped New York into sixth place.

It was cool and overcast on Sunday, May fifth. In the first game of a doubleheader, the Chicago Cubs led three to one after eight and one-half innings. Virgil and Mays each hit run scoring singles in the bottom of the ninth, tying the game at three apiece. The visiting Cubs, however, ripped New York relief pitchers for five runs in the top of the tenth, ending a nine game Chicago losing streak.

GIANTS END LOSING STEAK

In the second game, Joe Margoneri pitched a complete game victory, ending the Giants' five game losing streak at five games, winning six to two. Gomez returned to the starting rotation on Monday night after missing a start with the flu but was not fully up to par. The Cubs dealt him his first defeat, six to two.

Mays, suffering from a viral infection, was recovering in Columbia Presbyterian Medical Center. But the Giants defeated the Cardinals on Tuesday night at the Polo Grounds, eight to five. Katt singled home two runs in the fifth to give New York the lead. Worthington pitched four perfect innings in relief. The win was only the second for the Giants in eight games. St. Louis routed Antonelli on Wednesday, thirteen to four. Cardinal catcher Hal Smith had six RBIs. He homered and singled twice.

DODGERS PAY FIRST VISIT

On Friday, May tenth, the defending league champion Dodgers made their first visit of the year to the Polo Grounds. Before 34,435 Gomez defeated former Giant Sal Maglie, two to one. Mays, returning to the lineup, tripled home a run in the first inning. Then Don Mueller singled him home. Mays also had two singles. After leading off the fifth inning with a walk, he scampered to third on wild pitch. The Giants' center fielder then sealed the victory with his defense, running down a mammoth 450 foot drive off the bat of Gil Hodges in the top of the ninth inning.

The Giants defeated their arch rivals again in fifteen innings on Saturday afternoon, six to five. Harris, Spencer and Lockman homered. After Brooklyn tied the game with three runs in the sixth, Worthington entered the game and pitched seven shutout innings. Third string catcher Valmy Thomas homered over the left field roof in the bottom of the fifteenth. After Johnny Podres shut out New York, five to nothing on Sunday, May twelfth, the Giants in need of pitching help, called up Stu Miller from their Minneapolis Millers farm team before beginning an eight-game road trip.

Sauer homered twice in St. Louis on Tuesday, May fourteenth, Mays reached base on an error in the fifth. He stole second and third base, scoring the go-ahead run on Cardinals' catcher Hal Smith's wild throw to third. Gomez won his fifth, five to three. The Giants scored four runs in the first inning on Wednesday night. But Antonelli gave up five runs in the fifth. Although Worthington pitched eight scoreless innings in relief, the Cardinals won, six to five, in fourteen innings.

On Thursday at Crosley Field in Cincinnati, the Giants went to extra innings again, losing to the Reds, three to two. Miller, making his first major league start, gave up a run scoring single to third baseman Gus Bell in the eighth inning. Left fielder Frank Robinson singled home the winning run in the tenth. The Reds blasted New York, eleven to one on Friday. But Gomez salvaged the final game of the series, winning six to three on Saturday.

GOMEZ MARKS BEST START BY GIANTS' PITCHER IN FIVE YEARS

His six and one start was the best for a Giant pitcher in five years. Sal Maglie began the 1952 season with seven straight wins. Mays hit his first home run in a month. He also singled twice, following up each hit by stealing second and third base. He scored three runs.

On Sunday, May nineteenth, 21,817 fans watched New York defeat the Braves, six to three, in near freezing temperatures at County Stadium in Milwaukee. For a change, Antonelli was the winner in relief of Worthington who made his first start of the year. Mays tripled home a run and scored in the sixth. Katt's bases loaded single in the eighth inning was the game winner.

On Tuesday, May twenty-first, at Wrigley Field in Chicago, Miller, in his second start, took a three to two lead into bottom of the ninth inning. With one out, the Cubs' first baseman, Dale Long, walked. Then, the Giants self destructed. Right fielder Walt Moryn grounded to Schoendienst. Schoendienst's throw to shortstop, Spencer, covering second, forced Long for the second out. Spencer's throw to Harris at first was wild. Moryn went to second. Miller seemed to have the third out in hand when Cubs' left fielder Jim Bolger hit a routine grounder to third. But Foster Castleman booted it, making the second error of the inning. Bolger reached safely. Shortstop Jack Littrell singled home the tying run, moving Bolger to second. Sandy Consuegra, recently acquired from Baltimore, relieved Miller. Consuegra yielded the game winning single to catcher Cal Neeman.

The Giants tripped the Cubs four to three on Wednesday. A sixth inning homer by Chicago first baseman Dale Long tied the score at three all. Gomez was unable to post his seventh win. But Spencer doubled to open the ninth, and scored the winning run on a single by Schoendienst.

The Giants returned east but stayed "on the road", visiting Brooklyn for the second time. On Friday, May twenty-fourth, Mays extended a hitting streak to twelve games. Antonelli, who posted three victories against Dodgers without a defeat in 1956, lost six to nothing.

MAYS JUST MISSES CYCLE

The Giants beat the Dodgers on Saturday, eight to seven. With two out in the top of the ninth inning, the score was tied at seven apiece. Starting pitcher Barclay, allowed to bat by Rigney because of a depleted Giant bullpen, singled home the go-ahead run. Barclay then set down the Dodgers in order in the bottom of the inning. Mays hit a double, triple, and a home run. Manager Alston walked Mays in his final at bat, denying him an opportunity chance to hit for the cycle. Mays singled to extend his hitting streak to fourteen games on Sunday. But Gomez lasted only three innings. Brooklyn won, five to three. New York finished the road trip with five wins and six losses.

When the Giants returned to the Polo Grounds on Tuesday, May twenty-eighth, Antonelli threw only eight pitches. But the Giants already trailed four to nothing. Philadelphia romped to a sixteen to six victory. On Thursday night the Giants rallied for four runs in the eighth inning to tie the game. But Philadelphia scored two in the tenth to win again, seven to five.

The first game of the Memorial Day doubleheader also went ten innings. Before a good crowd of nearly 20,000, Rodgers, starting at third base, homered in the second inning. Gomez allowed just three Philadelphia hits. But the opposing pitcher, Curt Simmons, opened the tenth inning with an infield hit and eventually scored the winning run. The Phillies won two to one. Mays hit an inside the park homer in the nightcap. Mueller also homered. Behind Barclay, the Giants won easily, eight to one.

MAYS SLIDES UNDER THE TAG

On Friday, May thirty-first at Forbes Field in Pittsburgh, the Giants won, three to two. After Mays doubled in the eighth inning, he immediately stole third base. Right fielder Roberto Clemente fielded Katt's sacrifice fly, making a perfect throw to the plate. Mays, however, slid under the tag. The Giants finished the month in sixth place, nine and one-half games out of first.

JUNE

New York scored another three to two victory in Pittsburgh on Saturday, June first. Mays' single in the eighth inning tied the game. Spencer doubled home the decisive run in the top of the ninth.

MAYS HITTING STREAK ENDS AT TWENTY-ONE

Pittsburgh came back to win a three to two decision in the first game of a Sunday doubleheader on Sunday, June second. Mays hit his second inside the park home run of the year, extending the longest hitting streak of the year in the National League to twenty-one games. Mays failed to get a hit in the second game. Bob Purkey shut out the visitors, two to nothing.

MAYS MAKES A SPECTACULAR CATCH

The Pirates took the series with a six to five victory on Monday. Clemente's bid for an extra base hit in the first inning was interrupted by Mays who made a spectacular, twisting, basket catch. The ball popped out of his glove when Willie crashed into the screen surrounding the light tower in left center. But the agile center fielder snared it again before it hit the ground. Mays also doubled and stole his seventeenth base in twenty-four attempts.

SUMMIT MEETING ON KEEPING THE GIANTS

There was a summit meeting between spokesman for the Giants and Dodgers and New York City officials on Tuesday, June fourth. "I still believe we have every reason to be optimistic, Mayor Wagner said afterward." "One of Mr Stoneham's major problems is the parking situation. We are looking at that." Although the Mayor promised no financial aid, He assigned Louis A. Croft, the Commissioner of Public Works, the task of studying two possible sites for a new stadium for the Giants in Manhattan. Neither the Giants or the Dodgers had yet made firm commitments to move to the West Coast. League officials had indicated they would grant permission to move if both clubs left together. They wanted a final decision by October first. Meanwhile, in San Francisco, Mayor George Christopher also commissioned a study of proposed sites for a ten million dollar stadium to house the Giants. He wanted a ten million dollar facility with parking for 12,000 cars. Christopher, a former semi-pro second baseman who once had a tryout for the San Francisco Seals of the Pacific Coast League, had been negotiating for a major league club since his election victory in 1956.

"If Stoneham and O'Malley don't take advantage of this opportunity, the other league will be looking this way," said Christopher, who had arranged a three-game exhibition series between the American League Red Sox and the hometown PCL Seals during the 1957 spring training season. The series drew than 55,000 people, impressing Joe Cronin, general manager of the Red Sox, and catching the eye of other American League officials.

TY COBB VISITS BRAVES—BRAVES VISIT NEW YORK

Before the Giants hosted Milwaukee at the Polo Grounds on the evening of June fourth, the talk in both clubhouses centered on baseball, and not on any future relocation of the Giants.

"Just before we left Milwaukee," Braves' Manager Fred Haney told gathered New York reporters, "I brought Tyrus Raymond Cobb in person into the clubhouse. I just stood back and watched. The kids stared at him in awe!" "Holy gee," said Mathews, "that guy told me things about hitting that I never dreamed of."

The Giants, however, were not in awe of first place Milwaukee, winning the first game of the series, eight to seven, in thirteen innings. The Giants trumped a four homer, twelve hit attack by the Braves with eighteen hits of their own, including homers by Schoendienst and Mays.

MAYS BOOED

Despite the homer, it was not a good night for Mays. He was picked off first base in the third inning. And, after fielding a two out single by Aaron in the fifth, he launched a high, arching throw that went into the third base dugout, allowing an unearned run to score. Unbelievably, the Giants' star center fielder was booed. The home town fans went home happy, however, when Dusty Rhodes singled home the game winner in the thirteenth inning, a little before midnight.

GOMEZ BEANED—GIANTS HIT SIX HOMERS

During pre-game warmups on Wednesday afternoon, June fifth, Gomez was hit on the left side of the head by an errant fungo, and Burnside got an emergency start. Mays and Sauer hit back-to-back home runs in the first inning. Lockman, Schoendienst, and Sauer homered in the fourth. Schoendienst homered again in the eighth, giving the Giants a season high of six homers in one game. But Adcock, Thomson, and starting pitcher Ernie Johnson, all homered for the Braves. Ironically, the winning run scored on a passed ball in the top of the eighth inning. Milwaukee won, nine to eight.

"Those last two games with the Giants were the worst games I've watched in years," said Haney, "the only thing I'm thankful for is that Cobb wasn't around to see them."

Gomez, able to resume pitching, shut out the Braves on Thursday, June sixth, two to nothing. The game took only one hour and fifty minutes to complete. A reporter suggested that Gomez ought to have somebody hit him on the head with a ball before he pitches the next time. But Gomez replied, "Oh no! That one hurt." Schoendienst homered off the photographers' rack below the upper right field tier in the third inning. It was his fourth homer in three games.

ANTONELLI FALLS DOWN STAIRS

Prior to Wednesday's loss, Antonelli had also been involved in a freak accident, falling down a flight of stairs at his home. "I guess I'm just not news anymore," he said. "I'm told I'm pitching tomorrow night anyway." When he couldn't pitch on Friday night, Barclay was pressed into service against the Cardinals, ahead of turn. The tall right hander pitched all eleven innings. But the Giants lost, five to three. It was the seventh loss in nine extra inning games for New York. A five to four loss on Saturday, and a two to one defeat in the first game of a doubleheader on Sunday, marked the Giants' tenth and eleventh one run losses, and the nineteenth and twentieth Giants' games decided by a single run. The Cardinals completed the sweep with a ten to seven win in the nightcap.

On Tuesday, June eleventh, the Giants snapped a four game losing streak, beating Chicago five to one. Gomez hurled his eighth victory and his eighth complete game. Mays backed him with a two-run triple. Ruben had now defeated each team in the National League once and the league-leading Braves twice.

MAYS, MAYS, MAYS

In the second inning of a four to three win over the Cubs on Wednesday night, Mays raced far back in center field to make a sterling catch of a long drive. He also accounted for all four Giant runs. He hit a three-run homer in the sixth inning that soared into the upper left field stands just over the 414 foot sign. In the bottom of the ninth he stole third base and scored the game winner when catcher Neeman's throw went through to left field.

THE SMALLEST HOME CROWD

And on Thursday afternoon, June thirteenth, Mays singled twice, driving in a run and scoring one. Jablonski and Lockman each hit two-run homers in a seven to four win over the Cubs. But despite the sweep and the heroics by Mays, the game attracted just 1875 fans, the lowest figure of the year. And the entire Chicago series drew less than 9000 to the Polo Grounds.

MAYS HOMER CLEARS ROOF

On Friday, June fourteenth, Mays hit one of his longest homers of the year, lining it over the left field roof in the eighth inning. But Reds' first baseman Ted Kluzewski had four hits including a two-run homer. Cincinnati won, five to four. On Saturday Gomez won his ninth decision, eight to four. The Giants scored seven runs in the eighth, their biggest inning of the season. Mueller blasted a three-run homer into the right field stands in the eighth inning on Sunday to give New York a four to three win. Each game of the series with the Reds drew more than 9000 fans.

SCHOENDIENST TRADED—THOMSON RETURNS

Mays was certainly one of the elite players who ever played the game. But he wasn't enough. The Giants needed pitching help. They also needed an immediate attendance boost.

Less than six hours before the league trading deadline at midnight on June fifteenth, club Vice President Chub Feeney announced that, after batting .307 in fifty seven games, the popular Schoendienst had been traded to the Braves.

The Giants reacquired sentimental favorite Bobby Thomson, right handed pitcher Ray Crone, and utility infielder Danny O'Connell. The twenty-five-year-old Crone, a dependable starter, had won twenty-two games in two seasons in Milwaukee. Twenty-eight-year-old O'Connell had a batting average of .266.

A butcher from Forest Hills liked the deal. "Schoendienst will win the pennant for Milwaukee this year. But he's only got one or two good years left, and we got two young players in Crone and O'Connell. And don't forget Thomson has always played well here." "We got a good pitcher," said a Manhattan dentist. He'll win ten games for us this year. Thomson gives us good protection in left. O'Connell will start hitting over here. We're not going anyplace in the pennant race this year so it's a good trade for the Giants."

But a beautician from White Plains disagreed, "We got two bums and a fair pitcher for one of the great stars of the game." A plumber from Yonkers said, "Giant fans would have been happy to take up a collection to play Red's salary and Rigney's fare back to California." "We should have traded Rigney and $100,000 to the National Broadcasting Company to get Durocher back," offered a painter from the Bronx. A housewife from the Bronx, a Schoendienst fan, said, "I felt so terrible this morning I could have cried in my coffee." At least one Dodger fan was cynical, "The Braves just gave the Giants a lot of junk, that's all," he said. And a Giant fan quickly agreed, "Sure we got robbed. But if we can't win the pennant let's do everything we can to see the Dodgers don't win it."

A VISIT TO MILWAUKEE

When the Giants began a thirteen game road trip at Milwaukee on Tuesday, June eighteenth, all three former Braves contributed to a five to four win. Crone allowed three hits in six innings of relief. O'Connell had two hits. Thomson didn't get a hit but he reached second base when Bruton dropped his 400 foot drive to the center field fence in the sixth inning. Schoendienst went hitless for the Braves.

Buhl shut out the Giants on Wednesday night, six to nothing. Mays robbed Aaron of a home run in the first inning with a leaping grab in front of the "402" marker in center, but Aaron did homer over the left field fence in the third, and left fielder Wes Covington hit a three-run homer in the fifth inning, following a double by Schoendienst.

On Thursday, June twentieth, the Giants took the rubber game of the series, winning, four to three, in twelve innings. The game lasted three and one-half hours. O'Connell tripled in the sixth inning, and scored on a double by Thomson, putting the Giants ahead, three to two. Bruton singled home Del Crandall in the bottom of the inning to tie the score. Entering the game in the ninth, Antonelli held the Braves scoreless for three innings, and drove home Gail Harris with a sacrifice fly to win the game in the twelfth. Harris opened the Giants' twelfth with a triple.

On Friday night in Chicago, New York won another extra inning thriller, twelve to ten. Chicago starter Bob Rush recorded his one thousandth career strikeout in the second inning. He struck out five in seven innings of work. In the top of the ninth, Rodgers hit his first, and only, major league grand slam. It gave New York a ten to five lead. The Cubs kept pace, scoring five in the bottom of the inning. Second baseman Spencer dropped an infield pop up with two out, allowing the tying run to score. But O'Connell and Thomson hit back-to-back homers in the tenth.

The Cubs hammered out sixteen hits in a twelve to four victory on Saturday, June twenty-second, routing Gomez in the third inning. Mercifully, the game was called because of rain after just six innings.

LONGEST WINNING STREAK

On June twenty-third, the Giants swept a Sunday doubleheader in Chicago, beginning their longest winning streak of the year. In the opener, back-to-back doubles by O'Connell and Mays keyed a four run fourth inning rally. The Giants led six to nothing, eventually winning, seven to five. In the second game, Barclay struck out eight and doubled in the first inning, driving home the first run of the game. The Giants won, five to one.

Crone suffered his second defeat as a Giant on Tuesday, June twenty-fifth, in Cincinnati. Kluzewski singled home a run in the ninth inning, giving the Reds a three to two win.

GIANTS GET TWENTY HITS

Although Gomez failed to survive the third inning for the second straight time on Wednesday night, the Giants crushed the Reds, seventeen to seven, accumulating a season high twenty hits. A home run by Thomson capped a seven run sixth inning. Thomson and Mays each had four hits.

On Thursday, June twenty-seventh, Mays became the first player ever to hit a home run over the new fifty-five foot high scoreboard in left center field at Crosley Field. Lockman also homered. Antonelli pitched a complete game, winning seven to two.

The Giants continued their curious success against the National League's best, knocking the Cardinals out of first place with a four to one win on Friday in St. Louis. Barclay posted his fourth win for the Giants. He also contributed two hits. On Saturday, Mays tripled off knuckleballer Hoyt Wilhelm to open the twelfth inning. He later scored the only run of the game on Spencer's one out single. Miller needed just one pitch of relief help from Grissom to secure his third win.

GIANTS AT .500 FOR THE LAST TIME

Winning for the twelfth time in fourteen games since the three for one trade with Milwaukee, the Giants evened their record at thirty-five and thirty-five in the first game of a double header on Sunday, June thirtieth in St. Louis. It was the last time the New York Giants would ever be at the .500 mark. Winning for the first time in four starts, Gomez posted his tenth victory. Once again, Mays paced the Giant attack, doubling, tripling, and driving in three runs. The Cardinals snapped the Giant winning streak at five games, defeating New York in the second game, seven to one. The western trip, however, was both a financial and artistic success. The Giants were ten and four. The average attendance was 18,124. Overall, New York won eighteen games in June. They lost only thirteen. They were still in sixth place. However, they were just six and one-half games out of first, trailing the fourth place Dodgers by four games.

JULY

THE LARGEST HOME CROWD

On Monday, July first the Giants began an important series against Brooklyn. The crowd of 37,409 was the largest turnout at the Polo Grounds since May twenty-ninth, 1955. On that date, 39,711 watched The Dodgers defeat New York's defending 1954 champions. This time Giants' fans again left disappointed. The Dodgers beat Antonelli for the second straight time as Drysdale shut out the Giants, three to nothing. Mays, who had two of five Giant hits, fouled a pitch of his left foot in the first inning and limped noticeably for the remainder of the game. Another good crowd, 28,667, watched Maglie shut out the Giants again on Tuesday night, six to nothing. Mays fouled a another pitch off his already sore left foot in his second at bat. This time he left the game.

ANTONELLI NAMED TO ALL-STARS

After the game, Dodger Manager Alston chose Antonelli, who had only a six and seven record, for the All-Star game, while he overlooked Gomez, who was ten and five. The choice of Antonelli over Gomez was probably due to a dearth of quality left handed pitchers in the National League. Phillies' manager Mayo Smith voiced support for the right hander. "They didn't put Gomez on the All-Stars, huh?" he asked. "He could do them some good. I sure voted for him," he told reporters.

Gomez did not disappoint Smith, pitching another complete game in the opener of a July Fourth doubleheader in Philadelphia, but losing two to one. Thomson`s triple in the seventh inning drove in the only Giants' run. Mays didn't play. "I know the club needs me," he said. "That's why I played the second game against the Dodgers. But this thing is pretty sore."

After losing the second game to the Phillies, six to two, the club limped back into the Polo Grounds with a five game losing streak, having scored only three runs in three games. Shortstop Rodgers was sent back to the minors.

A RECORD THREE PINCH HITS IN AN INNING

On Friday, July fifth, the Giants found some offense, defeating the Pirates, eleven to six. Rodgers' replacement, Eddie Bressoud, hit his first major league homer in the seventh inning. Rigney used four pinch hitters in the inning. All four reached base. Thomson, batting for Antonelli, blasted his seventh homer of the season far over the left field roof. Mays, batting for Mueller, was intentionally walked to load the bases . Jablonski, batting for Harris, and Virgil, batting for Rhodes, hit back-to-back singles. The Giants scored five times. The three successful pinch hits in one inning tied a National League record.

STAY TEAM, STAY

On Saturday afternoon, fans in the left field bleachers displayed a banner that read, "Stay Team, Stay". A small ladies day crowd saw the Giants waste a strong twelve inning pitching effort by Barclay, and a pair of homers by Spencer. The Pirates won again, three to two. Facing a three and two count from Stu Miller, with two outs, Pirates' outfielder Frank Thomas homered in the top of the thirteenth, deciding the contest. On Sunday, July seventh, Pittsburgh completed the series sweep, taking both ends of a doubleheader, eight to one, and ten to six.

THE ALL-STAR BREAK

Cincinnati hosted the 1957 All-Star Game. Hometown fans voted in large enough numbers to elect seven regular Reds' starters to the National League team. However, Commissioner Ford Frick ordered Reds' outfielders Gus Bell and Wally Post dropped from the squad. They were replaced by the Giants' Willie Mays, and the Braves' Henry Aaron. The American League won for only the second time in eight years, six to five. Mays tripled, singled, and scored the final run of the game on a wild pitch.

Taking advantage of the break in the schedule, Commissioner Frick convened a meeting with club owners, and minor league baseball officials, to address the problems surrounding possible franchise shifts. "Baseball over the next ten years faces a program of growing up with the country," he said. "We must be prepared to expand our leagues on a modernized basis. We haven't hit on any formula yet. I want to make it clear that this meeting wasn't called to discuss any imminent Dodger or Giant franchise shift to California."

When the regular season resumed, only four games separated the first five teams. Philadelphia, Milwaukee, Cincinnati, and Brooklyn were right on the heels of St. Louis. The sixth place Giants, ten games back, were certainly not out of the pennant race. They had rallied from further behind in 1951.

But the Giants were struggling. Former manager Leo Durocher blamed owner Stoneham for the general decline since the 1954 series triumph. He called the Giants' owner a "full time drunk." Stoneham, declined to respond to Durocher's remarks. But he did deny that a managerial change was imminent. Former Dodger manager Charlie Dressen had, reportedly, been approached about the job of Giants' manager. "I have no intention of removing Rigney, and I've never considered Chuck Dressen as a manager for the Giants," he said.

New York began the second half of the season with twelve games at the Polo Grounds. Antonelli beat Lindy McDaniel of the visiting Cardinals, one to nothing, on Thursday, July eleventh. Battery mate Thomas homered in the sixth.

GOMEZ-JONES EXCHANGE KNOCKDOWN PITCHES

St. Louis won, five to one, on Friday night. In the third inning, Gomez backed St. Louis starter Sam Jones off the plate with a high inside pitch. Jones retaliated with an inside chin high pitch at Gomez in the bottom half of the inning. When Gomez threw a deliberate knock down pitch at Jones in the fifth, Umpire Tom Gorman cautioned both pitchers. Mays' fourteenth homer of the year accounted for the only Giant run.

A two-run blast by Mays in the bottom of the twelfth inning of the first game of a doubleheader with the Cubs on Sunday, July fourteenth gave New York an eight to six win. Lockman hit his second homer of the game with two out in the ninth to send the game into extra innings. Thomson also homered. Mays homered again in a five to three victory in the second game. After winning his third straight, Antonelli told reporters:

> I kind of rocked back and forth before kicking my leg. It helped my control, and it also had some of the batters swinging at my motion. When I was in the army I used it once against Mays' team. The other day Willie reminded me about it so I decided to try it today.

"Whatever Johnny is doing is working well," said Rigney.

Mays himself had four hits, and Spencer hit two homers on Monday night, July fifteenth. The Giants won, six to one.

GOMEZ THROWS AT ROBINSON

Ruben Gomez was, once again, embroiled in controversy. Reds' manager Birdie Tebbetts charged that Gomez intentionally threw at outfielder Frank Robinson because he was "a Negro." He later recanted:

Robinson is being thrown at because he is a good hitter. He probably leans over the plate a bit. I should not have brought up the racial issue.

The Reds swept the final two games of the series, five to four, and two to one. Distracted Giant players were talking more frequently about the move to San Francisco. "That would be too bad, Willie. Think of all the easy homers you'll miss here," Don Mueller teased Mays, alluding to the cavernous Polo Grounds.

Nine of the Giants' next twelve games were against the front running Braves. At the Polo Grounds on Friday, July nineteenth, Milwaukee won, three to one, behind six foot nine inch pitcher Gene Conley, who played Basketball for the Boston Celtics in the off season. Thomson homered in the fourth inning. On Saturday the Giants scored five times with two out in the eighth inning to tie the score at five to five. However, Wes Covington's second homer of the game in the ninth gave the Braves the victory a seven to five win.

The Giants broke a four game losing streak in the opener of a Sunday doubleheader, defeating Milwaukee, five to four. Sauer's pinch single, with two out in the ninth, scored the tying and winning runs. Homers by Mays and Jablonski in the second gave the Giants a four to nothing lead in the second game. Milwaukee, however, rallied for three runs in the ninth inning, winning, seven to four. Schoendienst extended a hitting streak to seventeen games with three hits for the Braves.

The Giants closed out the month on the road. On Tuesday, July twenty-third at Wrigley Field, Ramon Monzant, a Venezuelan right hander who missed spring training, got his first start of the year. He pitched well. But Cubs' rookie Dick Drott shut out New York, four to nothing.

FAT FREDDY

Before the Wednesday night game, Giants' coach Dave Williams organized a group of kids along the third base foul line, heckling Cubs' rotund third base coach Freddy Fitzsimmons. "Hey buffalo," they chanted in unison. "Keep moving, you're killing the grass." Antonelli suffered a tough two to one loss to Chicago. Eighteen-year-old Mike

McCormick defeated the Cubs, five to two, in his first major league start on Thursday, July twenty-fifth. Sauer, a former Cubs' star received a warm reception in each at bat. He responded to the encouragement with three hits.

MAYS SLUMPING

Arriving in Milwaukee on Friday July twenty-sixth, the Giants pressed the Braves again before falling, six to three, in eleven innings. Schoendienst had two hits, extending his hitting streak to twenty-three games. The slumping Mays, hitless in four trips, snapped at Rigney after the game. He denied that there was any ill feeling:

> I got into this slump by myself, and that's how I'll have to get out of it. He told me I should move closer to the plate. I don't know if he is right or not. To say that I'm feuding with the manager isn't the truth.

On Saturday Buhl defeated New York, five to two. Schoendienst went hitless, ending his hitting streak. Thomson doubled home two runs in the ninth inning for the Giants.

On Sunday, July twenty-eighth, 40,503 crowded Milwaukee's County Stadium, the largest crowd to watch the Giants all season. Antonelli overpowered the Braves, two to nothing. Mays, breaking out of his slump, had four singles in the first game of a doubleheader.

THE LONGEST LOSING STREAK

Mays hit his eighteenth home run in the ninth inning of the second game. However, the Braves won, five to three, starting the Giant's longest losing streak of the year. The streak lasting into August, reached six games.

Before the final game of the series on Monday night, July twenty-ninth, Rigney predicted, "We'll probably score eight runs and beat the Braves tonight." Remarkably the Giants did score eight runs. The Braves, however, scored nine. When Jablonski hit a two-run double in the ninth inning, the Giants led eight to four. They appeared to have knocked Milwaukee out of first place. But the Braves rallied for four runs in the bottom of the ninth, tying the score. And Worthington walked Milwaukee's Felix Mantilla with the bases loaded, and two out, in the ninth inning, forcing in the winning run.

CARDINALS MOVE INTO FIRST

Joe Cunningham's pinch hit grand slam off of Gomez in the ninth inning on Tuesday night in St. Louis won the game for the Cardinals, seven to three. On Wednesday night, July thirty-first, The Cardinals won again, five to one, moving into first place, percentage points ahead of Milwaukee. The Giants were in sixth place, fifteen and one-half games back.

AUGUST

On the first of August the Cardinals' Sam Jones, backed by two homers by Stan Musial, shut out the Giants eight to nothing. Then. on Friday, August second, the Reds defeated the Giants in Cincinnati, nine to six. Mays hit his twentieth homer. Lockman's sacrifice fly tied the game in the top of the ninth. But Wally Post hit a three run homer for the Reds in the bottom half of the inning.

GIANTS PLAY BEST BALL

The Giants played their best baseball of the year during the remainder of the month. On Saturday afternoon, August third, Mays homered twice. The Giants rallied for three runs in the ninth inning, tying the Reds at four each. Antonelli held the Reds hitless in three innings of relief, and homered in the eleventh inning to give New York a five to four win, and end the six game losing streak. The Giants won again, seven to six, in the first of two games on Sunday. The game lasted fourteen innings. There were 26,026 fans on hand in Cincinnati. Mays hit two more homers. Although the Giants had thirteen hits, a bases loaded walk in the top of the fourteenth inning proved decisive. The Reds won the nightcap however, three to two.

Prior to the game on Monday, August fifth, at Ebbets Field Mays was involved in an automobile accident en route to the game. He was uninjured. The Giants' center fielder had four hits, including his twenty-fifth home run of the year. The Dodgers won, however, five to two.

LONGEST WINNING STREAK MATCHED

On Tuesday night, Thomson had a pair of triples, driving in three runs. Barclay shut out the Dodgers, five to nothing. On Wednesday night, Thomson and Jablonski each had three hits. Hank Sauer hit a three-run homer in the top of the ninth inning, giving New York an eight to five win. And on Thursday, the Giants took the series, three games to one, scoring four runs in the first inning, three more in the second, and coasting to a twelve to three victory. Sauer and Mays homered.

Mays stole home in the bottom of the first inning on Friday night against Philadelphia. The Giants scored three times and added three more runs in the third to win, six to two, at the Polo Grounds. After a rain out on Saturday, Barclay hurled his second consecutive shutout on Sunday, beating the Phillies five to nothing.

MAYS HAS .630 SLUGGING PERCENTAGE—BEST IN NL

A good crowd, 13,880 at the Polo Grounds, saw the Giants match their longest winning streak of the year with their fifth straight win. Mays tripled twice, raising his slugging percentage to .630, the highest in the National League. Aaron of the Braves was second, at .628. Boston's Ted Williams led the Major Leagues at .728. Mickey Mantle, at .708 of the Yankees was second in the American League. The Phillies avoided a sweep, ending the Giant victory string in the second game of the doubleheader. Philadelphia won, two to nothing. Mays had two of only three Giant hits off Jack Sanford.

On Tuesday, August thirteenth, New York defeated Brooklyn, for the fourth straight time, four to two. Gomez hurled his fourteenth complete game. Mays singled, continuing a nineteen game hitting streak. McDevitt, Labine, and Roebuck combined to end Mays' hitting streak on Wednesday. The Dodgers won, seven to six.

GIANTS SPOIL DODGER HOPES

On Thursday evening, 7,587, the smallest Giant-Dodger crowd in recent history, saw the Giants take their second straight series from their intra-city rivals. New York drove another spike in the fading Brooklyn pennant hopes, winning nine to four. In the top of the first, the Dodgers scored the first two earned runs allowed by Barclay in twenty innings. Thomas hit a pair of two-run homers for the Giants.

On Friday night in Philadelphia, the Phillies and the Giants completed the final two and two-thirds innings of the suspended second game of the May twenty-eighth doubleheader. There was no further scoring. Grissom preserved an eight to seven victory. Jablonski smashed a two-run homer off Roberts in the top of the ninth inning of the regularly scheduled game, giving Barclay a two to one victory.

Posting his sixteenth victory, Sanford beat the Giants for the second time in a week, three to one, on Saturday, striking out five, and upping his league-leading total to 147. Giants' starting pitcher Gomez left after straining his shoulder on a fielding play in the third inning.

On Sunday, August eighteenth, the Giants swept a doubleheader from the Phillies, five to four, and one to nothing. Sauer hit his eighteenth and nineteenth home runs of the year in the first game. Worthington limited Philadelphia to three hits in the second.

On Tuesday, August twentieth, the Cardinals beat the Giants four to three in the opener of a doubleheader. In the second game, eighteen year-old rookie Von McDaniel won in his first, and last, appearance at the Polo Grounds, defeating Antonelli, for whom the Giants had not scored an earned run in nineteen innings, three to two. "All games are pressure games when you're pitching for the Giants," Antonelli told reporters. Musial homered in both games.

THE GIANTS VOTE TO MOVE

After months of speculation, the Giants' Board of Directors finally voted to move the club to San Francisco. Voting for the move were Stoneham, his son, Charles Stoneham, his nephew Charles S. "Chub" Feeney, his brother-in-law Charles Aufderhar, Vice Presidents Edgar P. Feeley, Dr. Anthony M. Palermo, and Max Schneider, and treasurer Joseph J. Haggerty. The lone no vote, M. Donald Grant, a partner in the Wall Street firm of Fahnestock & Co, said, "It just tears my heart to see them go. I've been a Giant rooter all my life. Then too, as a business man, I think they would do better staying here. I would rather have a National League franchise here than in any other city." Mayor Wagner said only that he was "very sorry."

Mrs. John McGraw, the diminutive widow of the Giants' legendary manager, was saddened but still hopeful:

> A miracle may happen. They may not leave. I'm praying that something will happen to make them stay. They'll always be the New York Giants to me, even if they leave New York. The Giants have been my life.

The final eleven million dollar package accepted by the Giants included a thirty-five year lease on a new 45,000 seat stadium with 12,000 parking spaces to be built in the Bayview Park area, south of the city. The token annual rental would be just five percent of after tax revenues from ticket sales concessions. Profits from a stadium club and restaurant sales were also included.

The Giants had to pay one million dollars to the Pacific Coast League for invasion of its territory, and another $125,000 to the American League Red Sox, parent club of the San Francisco Seals. The Seals would move to Salt Lake City. Because of the evening chill and fog in the Bay area, the Giants planned to play mostly day games in San Francisco, scheduling night games only on Tuesday and Friday nights.

Julius November, a Brooklyn lawyer who owned only ten of the 11,751 units of common and preferred stock then outstanding, filed suit in New York Supreme Court. November claimed the move violated the rights of all minority stockholders. Although he had lived in Brooklyn for two decades, he referred to himself as a "dyed-in-the-wool" Giant fan. Mr. November called the Board of Directors' vote, "an extraordinary corporate act beyond its authority." Judge George Tizler directed the Giants to "show cause" why the move should not be restrained. However, he eventually ruled in favor of the Board of Directors.

Former manager and Hall of Fame first baseman Bill Terry had made a serious offer to purchase the Giants. But there weren't many offers. "We could sell the club," said Chub Feeney, "but my uncle Horace doesn't want to sell the club." Stoneham intended to keep the Giants whether they played in New York or San Francisco.

BACK ON THE FIELD

In the game with the Cardinals on Wednesday, August twenty-first, at the Polo Grounds, the Giants' own eighteen-year-old rookie left hander, Mike McCormick, relieved Miller after Musial and Moon homered in the top of the first inning. Mays homered in the bottom of the inning, and the Giants scored six runs in the third, en route to a thirteen to six victory.

Mays homered again in the first inning on Thursday night. He also doubled twice on the night, raising his batting average to .332. Only 2,614 watched the now lame duck Giants win, six to two, in the Polo Grounds.

CUBS' RUSH HAS LONGEST OUTING FOR AN NL PITCHER

The Giants tripped the Cubs again, three to two, in a sixteen inning marathon on Friday night, August twenty-third. Right hander Bob Rush pitched all fifteen and one-third innings for the Cubs, the longest outing of the year for any National League pitcher. Mays singled with two out in the final inning, stole second, and raced home on a single by Jablonski. Miller was the winner in relief as the Giants climbed to within seven games of the .500 mark.

On Saturday afternoon, the Cubs avoided a sweep. Antonelli held a two to one lead through seven innings. But Banks twenty-ninth home run tied the game in the eighth. And Cubs' center fielder Bob Speake hit a two-run homer in the ninth for a four to two win.

On Sunday, August twenty-fifth, the Giants beat the fading Reds, ten to one. Mueller hit his fifth sixth home runs of the year. Gomez posted his fourteenth win and his fifteenth complete game. Only Billy Pierce of the American League White Sox had as many complete games.

TEBBETTS ORDERS CURFEW

Cincinnati had been in first place on July fifth. Looking for answers, manager Tebbetts ordered an eleven o'clock curfew for the Reds after Sunday's loss. He banned smoking, and beer drinking, in the clubhouse.

GIANTS SCORE SEVENTEEN RUNS

The ban had no immediate effect. The Giants pounded Cincinnati again on Monday, scoring a season high seventeen runs. The final score was seventeen to three. O'Connell homered for the second straight day. Sauer contributed a three-run homer.

On Tuesday, August twenty-seventh, homers by Schoendienst, Mathews, and Torre helped Milwaukee to a four to three win at the Polo Grounds. Mays went two for three, raising his average to .337.

BIGGEST INNING OF THE YEAR

On Wednesday afternoon, August, twenty-eighth, the Giants defeated the league-leading Braves, twelve to six. An eight run third, the biggest inning of the year for the Giants, highlighted the easy victory. Barclay, the winning pitcher, singled twice in the inning.

WACHAGGA CHIEF ATTENDS GAME

Thomas Marealle, Paramount Chief of the Wachagga Tribe of British East Africa, attended the game as a guest of the Giants and the U.S. State Department.

The Giants closed out their final August in New York at Ebbets Field. On Friday, August thirtieth, the Dodgers won ten to nothing. And on Saturday Brooklyn won again, seven to five. August was the most productive month of the season for the Giants who won nineteen games, losing only thirteen. However, they were still in sixth place, nineteen and one-half games behind first-place Milwaukee.

SEPTEMBER

Brooklyn scored two unearned runs in the second inning on Sunday, September first. But the Giants salvaged the series finale, winning, seven to five. Mays hit his twenty-ninth home run in the fourth inning. He hit his nineteenth triple in the sixth inning. Lockman also tripled, contributing to a five run Giants' rally in the seventh inning.

DOUBLE DIGITS FOR THE LAST TIME

On their return to the Polo Grounds on Monday September second, the Giants scored ten or more runs for the fifth time in eleven games, defeating the Pirates, eleven to five, in the first game of a doubleheader. Sauer homered twice. Virgil, pinch hitting for Sauer in the eighth inning, hit a three-run homer. It was the last time the New York Giants' offense would ever produce as many as ten runs. Mays hit his thirtieth home run in the second game, leading the Giants to a four to three win. Antonelli posted his twelfth win, four to three.

LAST WINNING STEAK

Still hopeful of a fourth place finish, the Giants defeated the Pirates again on Tuesday night, six to five in ten innings. The win pushed the club's last winning streak ever to four games. Home runs by O'Connell, Mays, and Thomas pushed the team total to 146, surpassing the club's 1956 season total, with eighteen games left.

Matched against the Pirates again in Pittsburgh on Wednesday September fourth, the Giant bats went silent. Bob Friend dealt McCormick his first setback, shutting out New York, two to nothing. McCormick, who had two of the seven Giant hits, gave up nine hits but only two for extra bases. The left hander struck out six. His season performance impressed Rigney. "You didn't waste any of that bonus money you gave this boy," he told Stoneham. "That lad is going to be a standout pitcher."

On Thursday the Giants stranded fourteen base runners against Pittsburgh's "Whammy" Douglas. Douglas, who lost his right eye in a 1949 auto accident, struck out eight Giants, winning four to two decision.

THE END OF A CLASSIC RIVALRY FROM THE GIANTS' PERSPECTIVE

The *New York Times* reported on the fan behavior at the first regular season meeting between the two clubs at the Polo Grounds on April twentieth 1901:

> It was the same appreciative crowd that made New York one of the most popular cities with ball players. It was always ready to cheer a good play, whether made by a home player, or even one of the visiting team.

The lights were turned on at the stadium for the first time on May twenty-fourth, 1940. On Friday, September sixth, the Dodgers defeated the Giants in the last night game at the Polo Grounds, three to nothing. Brooklyn won again on Saturday afternoon, five to four.

Clearly the New York fans had become more boisterous over the years. The rivalry had become more intense. The Giants won the final encounter between the two teams ever played within New York City limits on Sunday, September eighth, three to two. Gilliam's two-run homer in the second gave Brooklyn an early two to nothing lead. Mays singled to lead off the fourth inning, scoring on Jablonski's triple into the right field corner. Then, thirty-eight-year-old Sauer slammed his twenty-fifth homer. With one out in the seventh inning Barclay gave up a walk and a single. Thirty-nine-year-old Grissom, another veteran, relished the last of these battles. Entering the game in relief, he induced Reese to hit into a inning ending double play. He retired the last six Dodgers in order. The win gave the Giants an overall 650 to 606 edge in the remarkable series. They claimed victory in the final encounters at both Ebbets Field, and at the Polo Grounds.

One of the last of the 22,376 fans filing out of the park remarked, "If the Giants had played this well more often in the past, they wouldn't be heading to California. There would be no worrying about attendance here." With two home games remaining, the total home attendance figure, 637,278, actually exceeded the 630,278 figure for the entire previous season.

Thomson, whose famous 1951 homer was probably the greatest memory connected with the Dodger-Giant rivalry, told reporters, "I've had my happy moments at this park. I can't think about what I did that far back. I'll be paid next year for what I do this season. I'm not getting a salary now from that homer."

WE USED TO HATE THEM

Rigney said of the rivalry, "We used to hate them. We still do. It'll carry over if the Dodgers end up in Los Angeles next season."

"I got no use for them bums," said a shoe repairman from Brooklyn. "If they wanna move, I say let 'em go. I used to be a great fan, sold soda pop so I could sit out in left field, watching Zach Wheat. There was a ballplayer."

New York won only two of its final twelve games on the road. Before the smallest crowd of the year at Crosley Field, the Reds won, four to one, on Tuesday, September tenth.

REDS DENY MOVE TO NEW YORK

Reds' General Manager Gabe Paul denied a rumor that the Reds would move to New York if the Giants moved to San Francisco. "Even now we are negotiating to let contracts to paint the seats at Crosley Field for the 1958 season. If we were contemplating moving, we wouldn't be doing that," he told reporters. The Reds, who may once have coveted the New York market, had drawn a million fans for the first time in club history in 1956. "We are happy in Cincinnati. We have no intention of initiating a proposal for any shift," said the Reds' vice president, Gabe Paul.

After two off days, the rested Giants beat the Cardinals in St. Louis seven to three, surpassing their 1956 win total of seventy-six. Mays went four for four, doubling twice. He announced after the game that he would participate in an October barnstorming tour of Venezuela, along with Hank Aaron, Don Newcombe, Frank Robinson, Elston Howard, Al Smith, and George Crowe.

YOU NEED ME MORE THAN BASEBALL NEEDS YOU

Mays smashed his thirty second homer on Saturday, September fourteenth. But the second place Cardinals, still in pursuit of Milwaukee, won six to one. Before the game, a preoccupied Bobby Thompson initially ignored the request of a ten-year-old fan for an autograph. "You need me more than baseball needs you—better sign," said the kid. Thompson, grinning sheepishly, complied.

In their final visit to Wrigley Field on Sunday, September fifteenth, the Giants lost both games of a doubleheader, six to two, and seven to six. Mays, Sauer, and Harris all homered in the second game.

The Giants' final trip to County Stadium in Milwaukee proved no help at all to the pennant contending Dodgers. Despite a strong effort by Barclay on Tuesday, September seventieth, the Braves won three to one. Although Mays hit this thirty-fifth home run on Wednesday night, the Braves won again, eight to two. Antonelli, who had beaten the Braves four straight times , couldn't survive the first inning.

New York Times' columnist Arthur Daley lamented in his September twelfth column:

> A night game on the coast will finish so late that morning newspapers in the East will barely make the last editions with the results. The average fan may be unconcerned with journalistic problems, but he can't help but be concerned if he never knows who is leading whom in the team standings. Everyone—or almost everyone—insists that San Francisco is the loveliest city on earth. But it is a trifle on the chilly side. 'I once pitched there on the Fourth of July,' said Bill McCorry, the traveling secretary of the Yankees. 'I still can remember a guy in a box seat wearing a raccoon coat.' What does San Francisco have to offer? The first major league game in all history ever to be called on account of fog was on June sixth in Brooklyn this season. (See "THE FOG" page 210.)

The Giants played a doubleheader in Pittsburgh on Saturday, September twenty-first.

HARRIS' SEVEN RBIS IN GAME—NL SEASON HIGH

The Pirates won the first game, five to four. In the second game Harris homered twice, tripled, and singled, driving in seven runs, a National League season high. Gomez posted his fifteenth, and final, victory of the year, nine to five. He also singled twice. Rigney was ejected for arguing with the second base Umpire, Stan Landes. Rigney felt that Gomez had not interfered with Mazerowski on a force play at second base. Mays was moved up to second in the batting order in order to help him win the National League batting title. After going two for four in the opener, he had only one hit in six trips in the second game. His average dipped to .337. Pittsburgh won the final game on Sunday, five to one.

McCormick was excused from Tuesday's game in Philadelphia so that he could register for college. Relief pitcher Grissom was also permitted to end his season a few days early because of a sore arm. Mays had homered in every National League park for the past three seasons. He homered in every park, except Philadelphia's Connie Mack Stadium, during the 1957 season. And he was still in contention for the batting title. In the final game against the Phillies, on Tuesday, September twenty-fourth, Rigney put Mays in the lead-off spot. The extra turn at bat didn't help. Phillies' ace Curt Simmons held Mays homer less, and hitless, hurling a five to nothing shutout. Mays' average dropped to .333. He had only one hit in his final eleven times at bat. Rigney also started Barclay in place of Antonelli, giving him a shot at his tenth victory.

Although the Giants returned to New York on Wednesday, they didn't play again until Saturday afternoon, finishing the season with two games against the Pirates.

GOMEZ HURLS SIXTEENTH COMPLETE GAME

In the last ladies day at the Polo Grounds on Saturday afternoon, Gomez lost, one to nothing, to Pittsburgh's Ron Kline. However, he completed his sixteenth game. Milwaukee's Spahn led the league with eighteen. Pittsburgh's Bob Friend had seventeen. Gomez also doubled twice, getting two of six Giant hits. A crowd of 3200 saw Pittsburgh's Frank Thomas homer in the ninth to account for the only run of the game. Gomez doubled twice.

THE END

On Sunday September twenty-ninth, Russ Hodges, voice of the Giants, hosted the pre-game ceremonies before the Giants last game at the Polo Grounds. Virtually every generation of stars in Giant history was represented, including eighty-six-year-old Jack Doyle, who managed the club in the pre-McGraw era. Stars from previous Giant teams introduced at home plate on a warm sunny afternoon were Red Murray, George Burns, George "Hooks" Wiltse, Moose McCormick, Frank Frisch, Rosie Ryan, John "Hans" Lobert, Larry Doyle, Rube Marquard, Carl Hubbell, Mel Ott, Hal Schumacher, Billy Jurges, Monte Irwin, Sal Maglie, Buddy Kerr, and George "Kiddo" Davis. Recently retired players included Sid Gordon, and Willard Marshall, who also played for the Braves in their last season in Boston. Eighty-one-year-old George

Levy, former stadium announcer who once used a megaphone to announce, "the 'batreez' for today's game," was also introduced. Each former Giant received a noisy ovation.

With a sense of occasion, Rigney started as many of the 1951 and 1954 pennant winners as he had available. Antonelli was on the mound with Wes Westrum behind the plate. Thomson and Lockman occupied opposite infield corners. Rhodes and Mueller flanked Mays in the outfield. Between innings Rosemary Clooney's hit song, *This Old House,* played over the Public Address System.

If it mattered, the Pirates won, nine to one, behind Bob Friend. The Giants finished in sixth place, twenty-six games back of the League-Champion Milwaukee Braves. Rhodes sacrifice fly in the first inning scored Mueller with the final New York Giant run ever. The loss went to Antonelli. His eighteen losses were the most in his eight year career. The final out was recorded at four thirty-five Sunday, when Dusty Rhodes grounded a three two pitch to Dick Groat at short. Before the infielder's throw reached first base, fans were leaping barriers, and surging toward the Giant clubhouse in center field.

The players fled for the safety of the center field clubhouses with Mueller, and a puzzled Rigney, puffing, and bringing up the rear. The fans chanted, "Hang Horace, Hang Horace." The Giants' owner, who maintained an apartment on the fourth floor of the blockhouse in center field. The chants soon turned to "We want Willie, we want Willie." The usually accessible Mays, who still sometimes played stick ball with the kids in the streets outside his Harlem apartment, did not make a farewell appearance either.

The post game demonstration was motivated by a curious blend of anger, affection, annoyance, nostalgia, excitement, and curiosity. Most fans remained in the stands. Those on the field were mainly souvenir hunters. They ripped up home plate, the pitcher's rubber, the bases, and even gouged out sections of outfield grass. Will Anderson, now a publisher in Portland, Maine, was at the game. Then a high school senior from Ardsley, New York, he claimed a heavy orange and black sign reading "To Upper Stands" as a souvenir. "What do those people in California know about baseball," he mused. There was no heavy vandalism, or violence. The New York Police mostly monitored the activities, without intervention. They did, however, retrieve the bronze plaque that was removed from the Eddie Grant Memorial in center field from three teenage boys. The memorial, placed in 1921, honored the late Giant infielder who died in World War I. He was the only Major League baseball player ever killed in military service prior to the War in Viet Nam.

New York Times' columnist Milton Bracker reported:

> Officially, the last fan to leave the Polo Grounds was a woman: Mrs. Blanche S. McGraw. She had attended games at least three times a week when her husband, perhaps the greatest single figure in Giant history, managed the team. Her right eye moistened a little as she was asked what she remembered with greatest joy at the Polo Grounds. 'Why Mr. McGraw winning pennants,' she smiled. And which pennants? "All of them."

Mrs. McGraw witnessed every Giant opening game, except one, since 1903, and home games at all fourteen Giants' World Series from her complimentary box seat in section nineteen, just to the left of the Giants' dugout.

While she was leaving, workmen were already digging up turf in center field. It would transplanted at Seals stadium in San Francisco. The final line of *New York Times'* coverage of the game read, "Coogan's Bluff will feel mighty lonesome come next spring."

In his book *Veeck as in Wreck,* Bill Veeck accused Stoneham of inattention to his franchise, and lack of promotion:

> Stoneham had the best franchise in the National League. He had, potentially, the best drawing card in Willie Mays. He was in New York, the center of the communications industry. What did he do about it? He not only refused to go two steps out of his way to sell his team, he resisted the publicity that was thrust upon him. In the end, he picked up his franchise, and moved to San Francisco, indignant because his attendance had fallen. When the Polo Grounds began to fall apart, Stoneham moved on to his new wind blown castle by the sea.
>
> The feudal barons of old used to throw their garbage on the floor, and keep covering it over, until the stench became so unbearable that they had to move on to another castle.

In 1962, the National League Baseball returned to New York and to the partially renovated Polo Grounds. The fledgling New York Mets, owned by M. Donald Grant, former member of the Giants' Board of Directors, and the lone dissenting member over the move to the West Coast, moved his club to the new Shea Stadium in 1964. The new park was constructed on the same site in Flushing Meadows that proposed as a home for the Dodgers by Robert Moses, six years earlier. Although the city took over the facility in 1961, the Coogan family had not received proper compensation by the time the Mets abandoned their offices at the old park in 1964. The

State Supreme Court directed the city to hasten condemnation proceedings and to establish a fair market value on the property.

DEMOLITION OF THE POLO GROUNDS

Demolition of the Polo Grounds began on April ninth, 1964, making way for a public housing project, known at the Polo Grounds Apartments. The Wrecking Corporation of America, tasked with destroying the grand old park had gotten so much publicity that it had changed its logo to a baseball, and its slogan to "On the Ball." Harry Avirom, Vice President of the company, wielded a sledgehammer himself for the occasion. "One thing I'll say for this place," he said. "No collapse action here, very well built. It could have lasted forever." But it didn't. A two ton steel ball, painted like a baseball for the occasion, smashed into the concrete walls.

"Those chairs over there are for sale, three bucks each," Avirom said, pointing to piles of green seats on the infield. The Birmingham Blue Dukes minor league team took five hundred seats. Yonkers Raceway purchased six hundred seats. The city of St. Augustine, Florida, took two thousand. Some went to the Hall of Fame in Cooperstown. Others went to local schools.

The thirty foot flag poles sold for fifty dollars each. A couple of hundred spectators at the park looked for their own free souvenirs. A man from Yonkers took just an envelope of dirt.

Workers, wearing Giants' baseball shirts, pounded the roof of the visitor's dugout with sledgehammers. A black cat who had taken up residence there scrambled out of the dugout, paused for a last look, and ran off to search for a new home. "Cats and dogs who live here will be able to care for themselves," said Avirom. "We slug harder than the Giants ever did in this park. Slug, bang, slam! Gotta make the right moves. Gotta take calculated risks. Yeah, yeah, something like baseball you could say. Getting at the Polo Grounds was something I've always wanted to do. This makes up for the sad day we went after Ebbets Field in 1960." Avirom, a die hard Dodger fan, reveled in the destruction.

Crew member Stephen McNair, also a Dodger fan, pointed to the section of the left field fence below the "Section thirty-three" sign. "I'm going to take that down myself. History was made there." Bobby Thomson hit the "Shot heard round the world" over that fence in 1951, keeping the Dodgers out of the World Series.

The scoreboard clock, one of the last items of historical importance to be removed, was frozen at ten twenty-four. It wasn't clear whether it was morning or evening.

The demolition was completed on May thirtieth. On that same Saturday afternoon before a crowd of 38,472 at Shea Stadium in Flushing Meadows, the New York Mets defeated the San Francisco Giants, six to two. Willie Mays, in center field for San Francisco, tripled and singled.

TWILIGHT TEAMS

DAY	DATE	OPPONENT	RESULT	SCORE	PITCHER	ATTENDANCE	RECORD
TUES	04/16/57	AT PITTSBURGH	L	9-2	JOHNNY ANTONELLI (0-1)	33405	0-1
THURS	04/18/57	PHILADELPHIA	W	6-2	RUBEN GOMEZ (1-0)	8585	1-1
SAT	04/20/57	PHILADELPHIA	L	6-5	AL WORTHINGTON (0-1)	9809	1-2
SUN	04/21/57	PHILADELPHIA	W	2-1	JOHNNY ANTONELLI (1-1)	14230	2-2
SUN	04/21/57	PHILADELPHIA	L	8-5	CURT BARCLAY (0-1)	14230	2-3
MON	04/22/57	PITTSBURGH	W	3-1	RUBEN GOMEZ (2-0)	5403	3-3
TUES	04/23/57	PITTSBURGH	W	1-0	PETE BURNSIDE (1-0)	3445	4-3
WED	04/24/57	AT BROOKLYN	L	4-3	CURT BARCLAY	21998	4-4
THURS	04/25/57	AT BROOKLYN	PPD RAIN	0			
FRI	04/26/57	AT PHILADELPHIA	L	5-0	JOHNNY ANTONELLI (1-2)	14718	4-5
SAT	04/27/57	AT PHILADELPHIA	W	10-2	RUBEN GOMEZ (3-0)	7557	5-5
SUN	04/28/57	AT PHILADELPHIA	L	11-2	AL WORTHINGTON (0-2)	31222	5-6
SUN	04/28/57	AT PHILADELPHIA	SUSP	8-7	7TH INNING GIANTS LED	0	
TUES	04/30/57	MILWAUKEE	W	4-0	JOHNNY ANTONELLI (2-2)	13833	6-6
WED	05/01/57	MILWAUKEE	L	5-1(10)	MAX SURKONT (0-1)	5961	6-7
THURS	05/02/57	CINCINNATI	L	9-7	MARV GRISSOM (0-1)	3011	6-8
FRI	05/03/57	CINCINNATI	L	11-10	PETE BURNSIDE (1-1)	5352	6-9
SAT	05/04/57	CINCINNATI	L	5-2	JOHNNY ANTONELLI (2-3)	7389	6-10
SUN	05/05/57	CHICAGO	L	8-3(10)	GORDON JONES (0-1)	9765	6-11
SUN	05/05/57	CHICAGO	W	6-2	JOE MARGONERI (1-0)	9765	7-11
MON	05/06/57	CHICAGO	L	6-2	RUBEN GOMEZ (3-1)	1604	7-12
TUES	05/07/57	ST LOUIS	W	8-5	AL WORTHINGTON (1-2)	4934	8-12
WED	05/08/57	ST LOUIS	L	13-4	JOHNNY ANTONELLI (2-4)	3263	8-13
FRI	05/10/57	BROOKLYN	W	2-1	RUBEN GOMEZ (4-1)	34435	9-13
SAT	05/11/57	BROOKLYN	W	6-5 (15)	AL WORTHINGTON (2-2)	7434	10-13
SUN	05/12/57	BROOKLYN	L	5-0	PETE BURNSIDE (1-2)	17696	10-14
TUES	05/14/57	AT ST LOUIS	W	5-3	RUBEN GOMEZ (5-1)	9301	11-14
WED	05/15/57	AT ST LOUIS	L	6-5 (14)	AL WORTHINGTON (2-3)	8642	11-15
THURS	05/16/57	AT CINCINNATI	L	3-2 (10)	STEVE RIDZIK (0-1)	7337	11-16
FRI	05/17/57	AT CINCINNATI	L	11-1	CURT BARCLAY (0-3)	9367	11-17
SAT	05/18/57	AT CINCINNATI	W	6-3	RUBEN GOMEZ (6-1)	11721	12-17
SUN	05/19/57	AT MILWAUKEE	W	6-3	JOHNNY ANTONELLI (3-4)	21817	13-17
TUES	05/21/57	AT CHICAGO	L	4-3	STU MILLER (0-4)	1967	13-18
WED	05/22/57	AT CHICAGO	W	4-3	AL WORTHINGTON (3-3)	5731	14-18
FRI	05/24/57	AT BROOKLYN	L	6-0	JOHNNY ANTONELLI (3-5)	27299	14-19
SAT	05/25/57	AT BROOKLYN	W	8-7	CURT BARCLAY (1-3)	21607	15-19
SUN	05/26/57	AT BROOKLYN	L	5-3	RUBEN GOMEZ (6-2)	22971	15-20
TUES	05/28/57	PHILADELPHIA	L	16-6	JOHNNY ANTONELLI (3-6)	4977	15-21
WED	05/29/57	PHILADELPHIA	L	7-5 (10)	MARV GRISSOM (0-2)	2216	15-22
THURS	05/30/57	PHILADELPHIA	L	2-1 (10)	RUBEN GOMEZ (6-3)	19887	15-23
THURS	05/30/57	PHILADELPHIA	W	8-1	CURT BARCLAY (2-3)	19887	16-23
FRI	05/31/57	AT PITTSBURGH	W	3-2	AL WORTHINGTON (4-3)	13070	17-23
SAT	06/01/57	AT PITTSBURGH	W	3-2	AL WORTHINGTON (5-3)	5301	18-23
SUN	06/02/57	AT PITTSBURGH	L	3-2	CURT BARCLAY (2-4)	12793	18-24
SUN	06/02/57	AT PITTSBURGH	L	2-0	PETE BURNSIDE (1-3)	12793	18-25
MON	06/03/57	AT PITTSBURGH	L	6-5	JOE MARGONERI (1-1)	7504	18-26
TUES	06/04/57	MILWAUKEE	W	8-7 (13)	AL WORTHINGTON (6-3)	10390	19-26
WED	06/05/57	MILWAUKEE	L	9-8	STEVE RIDZIK (0-2)	4892	19-27
THURS	06/06/57	MILWAUKEE	W	2-0	RUBEN GOMEZ (7-3)	4787	20-27
FRI	06/07/57	ST LOUIS	L	5-3 (11)	CURT BARCLAY (2-5)	8419	20-28
SAT	06/08/57	ST LOUIS	L	5-4	AL WORTHINGTON (6-4)	8649	20-29
SUN	06/09/57	ST LOUIS	L	2-1	STU MILLER (0-2)	16403	20-30
SUN	06/09/57	ST LOUIS	L	10-7	PETE BURNSIDE (1-4)	16403	20-31
TUES	06/11/57	CHICAGO	W	5-1	RUBEN GOMEZ (8-3)	4440	21-31
WED	06/12/57	CHICAGO	W	4-3	AL WORTHINGTON (7-4)	2203	22-31
THURS	06/13/57	CHICAGO	W	7-4	JIM DAVIS (1-1)	1875	23-31
FRI	06/14/57	CINCINNATI	L	5-4	STU MILLER (0-3)	9917	23-32
SAT	06/15/57	CINCINNATI	W	8-4	RUBEN GOMEZ (9-3)	9095	24-32

THE 1957 NEW YORK GIANTS

DAY	DATE	OPPONENT	RESULT	SCORE	PITCHER	ATTENDANCE	RECORD
SUN	06/16/57	CINCINNATI	W	4-3	MARV GRISSOM (1-2)	11242	25-32
TUES	06/18/57	AT MILWAUKEE	W	5-4	RAY CRONE (4-1)	33945	26-32
TUES	06/18/57	AT MILWAUKEE	W	5-4	RAY CRONE (4-1)	33945	26-32
WED	06/19/57	AT MILWAUKEE	L	6-0	RUBEN GOMEZ (9-4)	29380	26-33
THURS	06/20/57	AT MILWAUKEE	W	4-3 (12)	JOHNNY ANTONELLI (4-6)	28737	27-33
FRI	06/21/57	AT CHICAGO	W	12-10(10)	STU MILLER (1-4)	6462	28-33
SAT	06/22/57	AT CHICAGO	L	12-4	RUBEN GOMEZ (9-5)	12118	28-34
SUN	06/23/57	AT CHICAGO	W	7-5	JOHNNY ANTONELLI (5-6)	26732	29-34
SUN	06/23/57	AT CHICAGO	W	5-1	CURT BARCLAY (3-5)	26732	30-34
TUES	06/25/57	AT CINCINNATI	L	3-2	RAY CRONE (4-3)	13824	30-35
WED	06/26/57	AT CINCINNATI	W	17-7	STU MILLER (2-3)	14097	31-35
THURS	06/27/57	AT CINCINNATI	W	7-2	JOHNNY ANTONELLI (6-6)	8025	32-35
FRI	06/28/57	AT ST LOUIS	W	4-1	CURT BARCLAY (4-5)	15388	33-35
SAT	06/29/57	AT ST LOUIS	W	1-0 (12)	STU MILLER (3-3)	16209	34-35
SUN	06/30/57	AT ST LOUIS	W	5-3	RUBEN GOMEZ (10-5)	26090	35-35
SUN	06/30/57	AT ST LOUIS	L	7-1	RAY CRONE (4-3)	26090	35-36
MON	07/01/57	BROOKLYN	L	3-0	JOHNNY ANTONELLI (6-7)	37409	35-37
TUES	07/02/57	BROOKLYN	L	6-0	CURT BARCLAY (1-4)	28667	35-38
THURS	07/04/57	AT PHILADELPHIA	L	2-1	RUBEN GOMEZ (10-6)	30442	35-39
THURS	07/04/57	AT PHILADELPHIA	L	6-2	STU MILLER (3-4)	30442	35-40
FRI	07/05/57	PITTSBURGH	W	11-6	JOHNNY ANTONELLI (7-7)	4998	36-40
SAT	07/06/57	PITTSBURGH	L	3-2 (13)	STU MILLER (3-5)	6530	36-41
SUN	07/07/57	PITTSBURGH	L	10-6	AL WORTHINGTON (7-5)	10625	36-42
SUN	07/07/57	PITTSBURGH	L	8-1	RUBEN GOMEZ (10-7)	10625	36-43
TUES	07/09/57	All-Star GAME	L	6-5	AT ST LOUIS		
THURS	07/11/57	ST LOUIS	W	1-0	JOHNNY ANTONELLI (8-7)	6021	37-43
FRI	07/12/57	ST LOUIS	L	5-1	RUBEN GOMEZ (10-8)	11617	37-44
SAT	07/13/57	ST LOUIS	RAIN				
SUN	07/14/57	CHICAGO	W	8-6 (12)	ARV GRISSOM (2-2)	5727	38-44
SUN	07/14/57	CHICAGO	W	5-3	JOHNNY ANTONELLI (9-7)	2675	39-44
MON	07/15/57	CINCINNATI	W	6-1	RUBEN GOMEZ (11-8)	9111	40-44
TUES	07/16/57	CINCINNATI	L	5-4	CURT BARCLAY (4-7)	6117	40-45
WED	07/17/57	CINCINNATI	L	2-1	STU MILLER (3-6)	4007	40-46
FRI	07/19/57	MILWAUKEE	L	3-1	JOHNNY ANTONELLI (9-8)	11628	40-47
SAT	07/20/57	MILWAUKEE	L	7-5	MARV GRISSOM	9214	40-48
SUN	07/21/57	MILWAUKEE	W	5-4	STU MILLER (4-6)	13768	41-48
SUN	07/21/57	MILWAUKEE	L	7-4	JOHNNY ANTONELLI (9-9)	13768	41-49
TUES	07/23/57	AT CHICAGO	L	4-0	RAY MONZANT (0-1)	9589	41-50
WED	07/24/57	AT CHICAGO	L	2-1	JOHNNY ANTONELLI (9-10)	8908	41-51
THURS	07/25/57	AT CHICAGO	W	5-2	MIKE MCCORMICK (1-0)	7587	42-51
FRI	07/26/57	AT MILWAUKEE	L	6-3 (11)	STU MILLER (4-7)	33743	42-52
SAT	07/27/57	AT MILWAUKEE	L	5-2	RAY CRONE (4-4)	34430	42-53
SUN	07/28/57	AT MILWAUKEE	W	2-0	JOHNNY ANTONELLI(10-10)	40503	43-53
SUN	07/28/57	AT MILWAUKEE	L	5-3	AL WORTHINGTON (7-6)	40503	43-54
MON	07/29/57	AT MILWAUKEE	L	9-8 (10)	AL WORTHINGTON (7-7)	24170	43-55
TUES	07/30/57	AT ST LOUIS	L	7-3	RUBEN GOMEZ (11-9)	16140	43-56
WED	07/31/57	AT ST LOUIS	L	5-1	RAY CRONE (4-5)	15192	43-57
THURS	08/01/57	AT ST LOUIS	L	8-0	JOHNNY ANTONELLI(10-11)	15763	43-58
FRI	08/02/57	AT CINCINNATI	L	9-6	AL WORTHINGTON (7-8)	17896	43-59
SAT	08/03/57	AT CINCINNATI	W	5-4 (11)	JOHNNY ANTONELLI(11-11)	8854	44-59
SUN	08/04/57	AT CINCINNATI	W	7-6 (14)	MARV GRISSOM (3-3)	26026	45-59
SUN	08/04/57	AT CINCINNATI	L	3-2	STU MILLER (4-8)	26026	45-60
MON	08/05/57	AT BROOKLYN	L	5-2	RAY CRONE (4-6)	15070	45-61
TUES	08/06/57	AT BROOKLYN	W	5-0	CURT BARCLAY (5-7)	18202	46-61
WED	08/07/57	AT BROOKLYN	W	8-5	MARV GRISSOM (4-3)	25913	47-61
THURS	08/08/57	AT BROOKLYN	W	12-3	RUBEN GOMEZ (12-9)	18753	48-61
FRI	08/09/57	PHILADELPHIA	W	6-2	RAY CRONE (5-6)	6247	49-61
SAT	08/10/57	RAIN					

TWILIGHT TEAMS

DAY	DATE	OPPONENT	RESULT	SCORE	PITCHER	ATTENDANCE	RECORD
SUN	08/11/57	PHILADELPHIA	W	5-0	CURT BARCLAY (6-7)	13880	50-61
SUN	08/11/57	PHILADELPHIA	L	2-0	JOHNNY ANTONELLI(11-12)	13880	50-62
TUES	08/13/57	BROOKLYN	W	4-2	RUBEN GOMEZ (13-9)	27234	51-62
WED	08/14/57	BROOKLYN	L	7-6	RAY CRONE (5-7)	13704	51-63
THURS	08/15/57	BROOKLYN	W	9-4	RAY MONZANT (1-1)	7587	52-63
FRI	08/16/57	AT PHILADELPHIA	W	8-7	STU MILLER (5-8)	11804	53-63
FRI	08/16/57	AT PHILADELPHIA	W	2-1	CURT BARCLAY (7-7)	18433	54-63
SAT	08/17/57	AT PHILADELPHIA	L	3-1	RUBEN GOMEZ (13-10)	7928	54-64
SUN	08/18/57	AT PHILADELPHIA	W	5-4	MIKE MCCORMICK (2-0)	14591	55-64
SUN	08/18/57	AT PHILADELPHIA	W	1-0	AL WORTHINGTON (8-8)	14591	56-64
TUES	08/20/57	ST LOUIS	L	4-3	JIM CONSTABLE (0-1)	13196	56-65
TUES	08/20/57	ST LOUIS	L	3-2	JOHNNY ANTONELLI(11-13)	13196	56-66
WED	08/21/57	ST LOUIS	W	13-6	MIKE MCCORMICK (3-0)	5296	57-66
THURS	08/22/57	CHICAGO	W	6-2	RAY CRONE (6-7)	2614	58-66
FRI	08/23/57	CHICAGO	W	3-2 (16)	STU MILLER (6-8)	4148	59-66
SAT	08/24/57	CHICAGO	L	4-2	JOHNNY ANTONELLI(11-14)	6389	59-67
SUN	08/25/57	CINCINNATI	W	10-1	RUBEN GOMEZ (14-10)	8768	60-67
MON	08/26/57	CINCINNATI	W	17-3	RAY MONZANT (2-1)	2383	61-67
TUES	08/27/57	MILWAUKEE	L	4-3	AL WORTHINGTON (8-9)	14897	61-68
WED	08/28/57	MILWAUKEE	W	12-6	CURT BARCLAY (8-7)	11543	62-68
FRI	08/30/57	AT BROOKLYN	L	10-0	RUBEN GOMEZ (14-11)	16113	62-69
SAT	08/31/57	AT BROOKLYN	L	7-5	MARV GRISSOM (4-4)	14222	62-70
SUN	09/01/57	AT BROOKLYN	W	7-5	RAY CRONE (7-7)	17936	63-70
MON	09/02/57	PITTSBURGH	W	11-5	RAY MONZANT (3-1)	10310	64-70
MON	09/02/57	PITTSBURGH	W	4-3	JOHNNY ANTONELLI(12-14)	10310	65-70
TUES	09/03/57	PITTSBURGH	W	6-5 (10)	STU MILLER (7-8)	3172	66-70
WED	09/04/57	AT PITTSBURGH	L	2-0	MIKE MCCORMICK (3-1)	8909	66-71
THURS	09/05/57	AT PITTSBURGH	L	4-2	AL WORTHINGTON (8-10)	5189	66-72
FRI	09/06/57	BROOKLYN	L	3-0	RAY CRONE (7-8)	21373	66-73
SAT	09/07/57	BROOKLYN	L	5-4	RUBEN GOMEZ (14-12)	11629	66-74
SUN	09/08/57	BROOKLYN	W	3-2	CURT BARCLAY (9-7)	22376	67-74
TUES	09/10/57	AT CINCINNATI	L	4-1	JOHNNY ANTONELLI(12-15)	4715	67-75
FRI	09/13/57	AT ST LOUIS	W	7-3	JIM CONSTABLE (1-1)	16843	68-75
SAT	09/14/57	AT ST LOUIS	L	6-1	JOHNNY ANTONELLI(12-16)	11723	68-76
SUN	09/15/57	AT CHICAGO	L	6-2	RAY CRONE (9-8)	9294	68-77
SUN	09/15/57	AT CHICAGO	L	7-6	STU MILLER (7-9)	9294	68-78
TUES	09/17/57	AT MILWAUKEE	L	3-1	CURT BARCLAY (9-6)	25390	68-79
WED	09/18/57	AT MILWAUKEE	L	8-2	JOHNNY ANTONELLI(12-17)	31566	68-80
FRI	09/20/57	AT PITTSBURGH	RAIN				
SAT	09/21/57	AT PITTSBURGH	L	5-4	AL WORTHINGTON (8-11)	8110	68-81
SAT	09/21/57	AT PITTSBURGH	W	9-5	RUBEN GOMEZ (15-12)	8110	69-81
SUN	09/22/57	AT PITTSBURGH	L	5-1	RAY MONZANT (3-2)	19574	69-82
TUES	09/24/57	AT PHILADELPHIA	L	5-0	CURT BARCLAY (9-9)	7019	69-83
SAT	09/28/57	PITTSBURGH	L	1-0	RUBEN GOMEZ (15-13)	3206	69-84
SUN	09/29/57	PITTSBURGH	L	9-1	JOHNNY ANTONELLI(12-18)	11606	69-85

THE 1957 BROOKLYN DODGERS

Why Not Take All of Me

It ain't official yet. We hope official it don't get.
But beware, my friend , and let me warn ya,
they're thinkin' a takin' the Bums to California.

from *Let's Keep the Dodgers in Brooklyn*
by Sam Denhoff and Bill Persky
Sung by Phil Foster

I t wasn't the smallest opening day crowd ever at Ebbets Field. 11,202 watched the Dodgers beat the Pirates, six to one, on Friday, April eighteenth, 1957. But the winners of back-to-back National League pennants deserved better in spite of the overcast skies, and fifty-five degree temperature. Sal Maglie allowed just four Pittsburgh hits. The Dodgers unleashed a fourteen hit attack. Not that Brooklyn fans, often filling the smallish park close to its 32,111 capacity, had to prove their loyalty. The Dodgers were the most profitable operation in the Major Leagues in their last five seasons in the borough. Before the game, woebegone tramp clown Emmett Kelly planted seeds behind home plate. It's doubtful that Charles "Hercules" Ebbets, who built the grand stadium in 1913 for $750,000, would have approved. Perhaps a vegetable garden or rhubarb patch was a reasonable alternative use for the old ballpark should the Dodgers' move to Los Angeles.

EBBETS FIELD, BROOKLYN

Bounded by Sullivan Place, Bedford Avenue, Montgomery Street and McKeever Place. Home of the National League Dodgers from April 9, 1913 until September 24, 1957. (Photo from the National Bseball Library and Archive Collection, Cooperstown, New York.)

THE BROOKLYN DODGERS

Front row—*Erskine, Gilliam, Labine, Zimmer, Cimoli, Herman, coach; Mulleavy, coach; Reese, Alston, manager; Becker, coach; Pitler, coach; Campanella, Furillo.* **Middle row**—*Griffin, clubhouse custodian; Scott, traveling secretary; Valdez, Craig, Jackson, Kennedy, Hodges, Drysdale, Roebuck, Bessent, Wendler, trainer; Buhler, assistant trainer; Roseboro.* **Back row**—*Valo, Harris, McDevitt, Collum, Walker, Pignatano, Neal, Newcombe, Amoros, Podres, Snider, Koufax, Kipp, Gentile.* **Seated in front**—*Clubhouse assistant DiGiovanna and Batboy Lehan .* (*Photo from The Sporting News collection, St. Louis, Missouri.*)

		Games at position	Bats	Avg.	
C	Roy Campanella	100	R	.242	13 HR
1B	Gil Hodges	150	R	.299	27 HR 98 RBI
2B	Jim Gilliam	148	SW	.250	**26 Stolen bases**
SS	Charlie Neal	100	R	.270	12 HR 11 Stolen bases 62 RBI
3B	Pee Wee Reese	75	R	.224	
RF	Carl Furillo	107	R	.306	12 HR
CF	Duke Snider	136	L	.274	**40 HR** 92 RBI **104 Strike outs***
LF	Gino Cimoli	138	R	.293	10 HR 57 RBI
OF	Sandy Amoros	66	L	.277	7 HR
IF	Don Zimmer	84	R	.219	6 HR 19 RBI
OF	Elmer Valo	36	L	.273	
C	Rube Walker	50	L	.181	
3B	Randy Jackson	34	R	.198	
C	Johnny Roseboro	19	L	.145	
OF	Bob Kennedy	9	R	.129	
C	Joe Pignatano	6	R	.214	
1B	Jim Gentile	2	L	.167	
PH	Rod Miller	1	L	.000	

PITCHERS

R	Don Drysdale	34 W 17	L 9	2.69 ERA	**148 Strikeouts**
L	Johnny Podres	31 W 12	L 9	**2.66 ERA***	3 Saves
R	Don Newcombe	28 W 11	L 12	3.49 ERA	
L	Danny McDevitt	22 W 7	L 4	3.25 ERA	
R	Sal Maglie	19 W 6	L 6	2.93 ERA	
R	Carl Erskine	15 W 5	L 3	3.55 ERA	
L	Sandy Koufax	34 W 5	L 4	3.88 ERA	

RELIEF PITCHERS

R	Clem Labine	58 W 5	L 7	3.44 ERA	**17 Saves***
R	Ed Roebuck	44 W 8	L 2	2.71 ERA	8 Saves
R	Roger Craig	32 W 6	L 9	4.61 ERA	
R	Don Bessent	27 W 1	L 3	5.73 ERA	
R	Rene Valdez	5 W 1	L 1	5.54 ERA	
L	Jackie Collum	3 W 0	L 0	8.31 ERA	
L	Ken Lehman	3 W 0	L 0	0.00 ERA	
R	Don Elston	1 W 0	L 0	0.00 ERA	
L	Fred Kipp	1 W 0	L 0	9.00 ERA	
R	Bill Harris	1 W 0	L 1	3.86 ERA	

MANAGER

Walter Alston   W 84 L 70

Bold Type—led club
* Led league

EMMETT KELLY AT EBBETS FIELD

THE BALLPARK

Although the seating capacity was increased to 32,000 in 1932, Ebbets Field remained one of the leagues smaller ballparks. The brown stone exterior was distinguished by numerous arched windows and porticos. There were twelve gilded ticket windows. The home plate entrance was at the intersection of Sullivan Place and McKeever Place. The familiar "EBBETS FIELD" label curved around the top of the park, high above this entrance. Those entering here came upon a spectacular rotunda with an Italian marble floor patterned to resemble the stitches on a baseball. A chandelier with twelve baseball bat arms and twelve light globes shaped like baseballs hung from the ceiling.

The roof, and double-decked grandstand, extended all the way down the right and left field foul lines providing upper and lower deck seating. There was bleacher seating beyond the left field wall. The field dimensions measured 348 feet from home plate to the fence along the left field foul line. It was 297 feet down the line in right, and 389 feet to the fence in dead center field. Balls hit into the screen above the ten foot high concrete wall in left were in play. There were bleachers beyond the left field wall. Caroms off the nineteen foot concrete wall in right field were unpredictable because the lower half of the concave barrier sloped away from the field at a forty-five degree angle. The right field wall was topped by nineteen feet of screen mesh. At the junction with the center field fence, a large scoreboard, topped by a red "Shaefer Beer" sign and a "Bulova" clock, stood five feet in front of the wall. The "h" and the "e" in the "Schaefer" sign would light up to indicate a hit or an error. A black arrow on a yellow "Abe Stark" clothiers advertisement at the bottom of the scoreboard pointed to the words "Hit here, Win suit."

On Memorial Day, 1946, a long drive to right field by Boston second baseman Bama Rowell shattered the "Bulova" clock, showering Dodger outfielder Dixie Walker in broken glass, and inspiring the fictional home run by Roy Hobbs in the film, "The Natural." Bernard Malamud, the author of the book on which the film was based, was a Dodger fan.

The area around the stadium, bounded by Sullivan and McKeever Place, Montgomery Street and Bedford Avenue, was deteriorating rapidly. Prior to the construction of the stadium, the site was known as "pigtown" because local residents frequently dumped their garbage there. Local farmers fed their pigs on the refuse. On October twenty-ninth, 1956, Dodger owner Walter O'Malley sold Ebbets Field to real estate developer Marvin Kratter for three million dollars. Kratter planned to build a middle income residential and commercial community on the site. A lease-back arrangement called for the Dodgers to pay annual rental with the team permitted to play there for five more seasons. The rent would increase substantially after three years. Finding a new home for the Dodgers was, therefore, a top priority. O'Malley had recently sold ballparks owned by the Dodgers in Montreal and Dallas-Fort Worth for a million dollars each. He was willing to invest five million dollars in a new facility.

Dodgers' assistant General Manager Arthur E. Patterson told reporters, "No serious offer from another city is being entertained." But the City of New York was already trying to counter proposals made to the Dodgers by the City of Los Angeles. For the immediate future, the Dodgers would remain in Brooklyn, but for the second straight year the club had a contract to play at least seven games a year at nearby Roosevelt Stadium in Jersey City, New Jersey, which had a larger seating capacity than Ebbets Field.

THE HISTORY

The National League Hartfords played a single season in Brooklyn in 1877. In 1844 the Trolley Dodgers began play there. Playing home games at Washington Park, the Dodgers, also known as the Bridegrooms won the American Association pennant in 1889. They jumped to the National League in 1890, beginning a continuous sixty-seven year run. They were known as the "Superbas" from 1899 to 1905. The club took the nickname "Robins" from 1914 to 1931 in honor of manager Wilbert Robinson, who managed the franchise to its first National League pennant in 1916. Hall of Fame left handed pitcher Rube Marquard won thirteen games that season. Right hander Jeff Pfeffer won twenty-five. Hall of Fame outfielder Zack Wheat batted 312. First baseman Jack Daubert batted .316. The American League Boston Red Sox defeated Brooklyn in the 1916 World Series, four games to one. A fourteen inning struggle in the second game was the longest contest in Series' history. After yielding a first inning home run to Brooklyn outfielder Hy Myers, Boston's Babe Ruth shut out the Dodgers the rest of the way, winning two to one. Brooklyn right hander Jack Coombs defeated the Red Sox in the third game, four to three, posting Brooklyn's first ever victory in a Series' game.

The Robins won the league title again in 1920. Hall of Fame right hander Burleigh Grimes, who won twenty-three games, joined Wheat, Myers, and Marquard. Wheat batted .328. Myers hit .304. But the

Robins lost to the American League Cleveland Indians in the 1920 post season five games to two. Cleveland spit ball pitcher Stanley Coveleski won three games in the Series. Robinson managed the team through the end of the 1930 season. The permanent name "Dodgers" was adopted in 1932.

Casey Stengel managed the Dodgers from 1934 to 1936. However, Brooklyn finished no higher than fifth during his tenure. Burleigh Grimes managed the team the next two seasons. But the club finished sixth in 1937 and seventh in 1938.

In October, 1937, the Brooklyn Trust Company, who held the mortgage on Ebbets Field and had loaned the Dodgers over $500,000, was concerned. The company encouraged National League President Ford Frick to recommend a qualified baseball person to act as President of the Dodgers and to restore the franchise. When Cardinals' General Manager Branch Rickey declined the position, Frick turned to Larry McPhail, recently fired by the Cincinnati Reds. Using $400,000 from Brooklyn Trust, McPhail overhauled Ebbets Field and installed lights at Ebbets Field as he had done at Crosley Field in Cincinnati. Replacing the old green and gold uniforms with new white uniforms trimmed in "Dodger" blue, McPhail hired Leo Durocher to manage the 1939 Dodgers. He also acquired slugging first baseman Dolph Camilli from the Philadelphia Phillies, and outfielder Ernie Koy from the Yankees. The Dodgers finished third in 1939. Brooklyn climbed to second place in the standings, twelve games back of Cincinnati, in 1940.

In 1941, under Durocher, the club completed the rebuilding process and finally won another pennant. First baseman Camilli, the league's Most Valuable Player, led the Dodgers, hitting thirty-four homers. Mickey Owen was the National League All-Star catcher. Right fielder Pete Reiser batted .343. Left fielder Dixie Walker batted .311, and Hall of Fame outfielder, Joey Medwick, batted .318. Another Hall of Famer, former Cubs' second baseman Billy Herman, hit .291. It was shortstop Pee Wee Reese's first year in the Majors. Right hander Van Lingle Mungo was in the last of eleven seasons in Brooklyn. The Dodgers lost their first "Subway" Series with the Yankees, four games to one.

PREMIER DODGER: JACKIE ROBINSON

When McPhail resigned at the end of the 1942 season, sixty-one year-old Branch Rickey took over as President of the Dodgers. Durocher was a shortstop with Rickey's Cardinals from 1933 to 1937, during the successful Gas House Gang years. Rickey and Durocher were responsible for breaking baseball's color line by bringing Jackie Robinson, the most significant player in the history of the Dodgers, to Brooklyn. The two men restored the farm system and rebuilt the Dodgers, winning the National League pennant in 1947.

In 1947, his rookie season, Hall of Famer Robinson batted .297, and led the league with twenty-nine stolen bases. Reiser batted .309, and Walker batted .306. Ralph Branca won twenty-one games. Having won their fourth pennant, the Dodgers lost to the Yankees again in the 1947 World Series. Although, this time it took the American Leaguers the full seven games to accomplish the task.

In 1949 Robinson was the National League's Most Valuable Player, leading the league with a .342 average, and again in stolen bases with 37. Right fielder Carl Furillo from Reading, Pennsylvania was nicknamed the "Reading Rifle" because of his strong throwing arm. He batted .322. Don Newcombe was the Rookie of the Year, winning seventeen games. The Dodgers edged the Cardinals by only a single game to win the pennant. Once more the Yankees prevailed in the Series. Preacher Roe shut out New York, one to nothing in the second game, claiming the only Dodger victory. Reese batted .316 in the Series.

Walter O'Malley succeeded Rickey as President of the Dodgers, purchasing the team in October, 1950.

Bobby Thomson's playoff homer claimed the 1951 pennant for the Giants. But Joe Black, National League Rookie of the Year, won fifteen games with a league-leading 2.15 ERA, putting Brooklyn back on top in 1952. The Giants finished four and one-half games back. Robinson led the regulars with a .308 batting average. Reese stole a league-leading thirty bases. Black started three games in the 1952 Series, facing Allie Reynolds of the Yankees each time. He won the opening game, four to two. Reynolds, posting a Series ERA of 1.77, shut out the Dodgers, two to nothing in the fourth game, and won the deciding seventh game for the Yankees, four to two.

Second baseman Junior Gilliam was the National League Rookie of the Year in 1953, batting .278 for the defending league champs. Furillo batted .344, Robinson .329, Duke Snider .336, and first baseman Gil Hodges .302. Carl Erskine won twenty games. However, the Yankees again conquered the Dodgers, four games to two. Erskine struck out a Series record fourteen batters in the third game to give the Dodgers their first victory. The Dodgers won the fourth game also, defeating Whitey Ford, seven to three.

Brooklyn finished five games back of the Giants in 1954. But in 1955, their second year under manager Walter Alston, the Dodgers again won the pennant. Snider led the league with 136 RBIs. Catcher Roy Campanella batted .318. Newcombe won twenty games.

BROOKLYN FINALLY BEATS THE YANKEES

In 1955, Brooklyn finally defeated the Yankees, winning the World Series in seven games. It was their first, and only, World Series triumph. The Dodgers became the first club ever to win the Series after losing the first two games. Johnny Podres, the Series' Most Valuable Player, was the winning pitcher in both the third and seventh games. Duke Snider hit four homers. With the Dodgers leading, two to nothing, in the bottom of the sixth inning of the seventh game, Sandy Amoros speared Yogi Berra's sinking drive into the left field corner. Reese's relay throw doubled Gil McDougald off first. That killed a potential Yankee rally, and sealed the victory.

The Dodgers claimed their ninth and last pennant for Brooklyn in 1956, edging the Milwaukee Braves by only a single game. Second baseman Gilliam was the only regular to bat .300. Newcombe won twenty-seven games.

LAST SUBWAY SERIES

Snider and Hodges each batted .304 in the 1956 Series. After losing the first two games in Brooklyn, the Yankees won the Series in seven games. Don Larsen pitched the only perfect game in World Series history, winning the fifth game, two to nothing. Snider tied a Series record, hitting his tenth homer in post season competition.

LOOKING FOR A HOME

Just days before the 1957 season opener, recommendations were presented to New York Mayor Robert Wagner concerning potential sites for a new Dodger stadium. There was strong local opposition to each of the proposed sites.

New York City Council President Abe Stark proposed that a new stadium be built on the thirty-nine acre Parade Grounds site in Prospect Park, Brooklyn. That tract of land was bounded by Parade Place, Parkside, Caton Avenue, and Coney Island Avenue. However, the Brooklyn City council, preferred to keep the park open for public use.

That left two sites under consideration. The downtown site favored by Brooklyn Borough President Cashmore was bounded by Warren Street, Fourth, Flatbush and Fifth Avenues. The area covered 480 acres and 110 city blocks. Including a 50,000 seat stadium, a new subway concourse at Flatbush and fourth, renovation of the area, and a projected 100 million dollar loss to the city in real estate taxes, the total cost of building a new home for the Dodgers there was projected to be a staggering 200 million.

Dodger owner O'Malley, however, expressed a preference for a second site in downtown Brooklyn, just north of the one proposed by Cashmore. "We want the air rights over the Long Island Railroad station. The Dodgers don't want anything else. We'll pay for a new ballpark by ourselves," he said.

O'MALLEY WANTS DOMED STADIUM

Fascinated by historical accounts that the Roman Coliseum had a canopy, O'Malley envisioned a covered stadium. Immediately after the Dodgers' victory in the 1955 World Series he announced that he had commissioned Buckminster Fuller of Princeton to design a geodesic dome for the Dodgers to play in. "A dome worked in Rome. It will work in Brooklyn," he told skeptical reporters. However, the problem of getting grass to grow indoors under a permanent dome had not yet been solved.

If there was to be a downtown ballpark, Parks Commissioner Robert Moses, the principal negotiator for the City of New York, agreed with O'Malley's choice of the Long Island Railroad property. That site, encompassing the Fort Green Street Meat Market, was bounded by Hanson Place, Portland Atlantic and Flatbush Avenues. But Moses was also in charge of city highways and preferred a suburban site for a new stadium. "I really just don't want to see a baseball field in downtown Brooklyn at all. The streets will never handle all those cars," he said, proposing a futuristic plastic domed stadium be built on the 1939 Worlds Fair site in Flushing Meadows, Queens, bounded by Northern Boulevard, Roosevelt Avenue, Grand Central Parkway and 126th street. The future site of Shea Stadium was then only in use as a commuter parking lot. Moses proposed a twenty year lease arrangement to enable the city to recover construction costs.

O'Malley was intrigued that Moses had followed up on his preference for a domed stadium, but was not impressed with the suburban location. "If my team is forced to play in the borough of Queens, they will no longer be the Brooklyn Dodgers," he said.

THE FINAL SEASON

Despite the Dodgers' loss in the 1956 World Series, memories of the 1955 triumph lingered. Although the aging 1957 Brooklyn squad didn't exactly qualify as the "Nine Old Men of Summer", they were not the fabled "Boys of Summer" any longer. Legendary Hall of Fame second baseman Jackie Robinson had retired in the off season rather than be traded to the rival Giants. He was thirty-eight. Among those players returning, Reese was thirty-eight, Campanella, thirty-five, Furillo, thirty-five, Hodges, thirty-three, and Newcombe, twenty-nine. Erskine, Labine, and Snider were each thirty. Maglie was thirty-nine.

FIVE FUTURE HALL OF FAMERS ON SQUAD

Even with Robinson retired, the Dodgers began the 1957 campaign with five future Hall of Famers on the roster. 1957 was the final season for Hall of Fame catcher Roy Campanella, the league MVP in 1952, 1954, and 1956. Roy was injured in a tragic automobile accident following the 1957 season. He would always be a Brooklyn Dodger, and only a Brooklyn Dodger.

After playing eleven seasons in Brooklyn, Hall of Fame center fielder Snider played five more in Los Angeles. Pee Wee Reese, finally inducted into the Hall in 1996, played a single season on the Coast. Sandy Koufax entered his third season for Brooklyn. Don Drysdale entered his second. Both later firmly established their Hall of Fame credentials in Los Angeles.

Although the Dodgers' everyday players were veterans, the starting pitchers were primarily young. Drysdale was only twenty. Koufax was twenty-one. Left hander Johnny Podres returned from military service at the age of twenty-four. Ed Roebuck was also twenty-four. The fifth starter, Danny McDevitt, was twenty-five.

A collection of aging and emerging stars, the Dodgers figured to be a pennant contender in their final season on the east coast. The team was still a big draw, at home and on the road.

SPRING TRAINING

In early April, 1957, the Dodgers were confident, and loose. While batting in a spring training game in Tampa just prior to the season opener, Pee Wee Reese fouled a ball off his shin, falling to the ground in pain. "If this happened to an ordinary man," remarked a droll Gil Hodges, "he'd go to the hospital. But you, indomitable one, intend to play ball."

"Not me," said Pee Wee, "I'm going to the hospital!" "Alston has been saying all along that he wanted to get Don Zimmer into the lineup. Here is one problem that resolves itself for him," quipped Dodger Vice President, Emil J."Buzzy" Bavasi.

The New York "voices" chronicling the exploits of the 1957 Dodgers on WOR-TV, and WMGM Radio, were Vin Sculley, Al Helfer, and Jerry Doggett. Longtime Dodger announcer Red Barber had been broadcasting New York Yankees' games on TV and radio since 1954. Barber became the first announcer ever inducted into the Baseball Hall of Fame in 1978.

APRIL

On Tuesday night, April sixteenth, 1957, the Brooklyn Dodgers opened their final season on the road at Philadelphia. Prior to the game a statue of Connie Mack erected in a small park across the street from the stadium was officially unveiled by Baseball Commissioner Ford Frick. With American League President Will Harridge also in attendance, Shibe Park was officially renamed "Connie Mack Stadium." The crowd of 37,667 was the largest ever to see a season opener in Philadelphia up to that time. The game lasted twelve innings.

In the third inning, rookie shortstop Don Zimmer homered, delivering Brooklyn's first run of the season. Hodges homered in the eighth to tie the score at six all. Clem Labine, in relief of starter Newcombe, held Philadelphia scoreless over the last four innings. Phillies' starter Robin Roberts pitched all twelve innings despite being hit in the chest by a wicked line drive off the bat of Hodges in the tenth. Left fielder Gino Cimoli homered in the top of the twelfth to give Brooklyn a seven to six victory.

Starting pitcher Maglie posted the one hundred and ninth victory of his Major League career, defeating the Pittsburgh Pirates in the Dodgers' home opener on Thursday, six to one. Maglie allowed just four hits. The Dodgers collected fourteen. Johnny Podres shut out the Pirates' on Saturday, April twentieth, hurling the first complete game by a Dodger pitcher since Koufax shut out the Pirates in September 1955. Snider and Furillo homered back-to-back off Pirates' starter Bob Friend, giving the Dodgers their third straight win. Brooklyn already had a total of seven homers for the young season.

The visiting Pirates won the opener of the first Sunday double-header of the season, six to three, behind right hander Bob Purkey. Furillo's three-run homer in the ninth off relief specialist Elroy Face came too late. The Dodgers won the second game, seven to four.

JERSEY CITY OPENER

On Monday April twenty-second, 11.629, slightly larger than the attendance at the home opener at Ebbets Field, watched Roger Craig defeat the Phillies, five to one, in the first of seven Dodger "home" games at Roosevelt Stadium in Jersey City, New Jersey.

Back at Ebbets Field on Wednesday, 21,998 fans watched the Dodgers beat the Giants, four to three. Eager for the annual renewal of this cross-town rivalry, Dodger fans booed every Giant batter. The contingent of Giant fans retaliated in kind. Hodges doubled home two runs in the decisive fourth inning.

PURKEY'S A MYSTERY

At Forbes Field in Pittsburgh on Friday, April twenty-sixth, Bob Purkey, the only pitcher to beat the Dodgers through eight games, completely baffled them again, winning seven to one. The usually calm manager Alston complained, "He held the ball as much as forty seconds while my man was in the box."

But pinch hitter Elmer Valo complained that Purkey had quick pitched him in the seventh inning. "The pitch to me," he said, "was right down the pipe. If it had happened to be at my head I'd be in the hospital now, for I didn't see it until it was by me."

Newcombe, backed by the second fourteen hit Dodger attack of the year, defeated Pittsburgh, six to two in the second game on Saturday. In Sunday's series' finale, Bob Friend shut out the Dodgers, three to nothing. Hodges doubled and tripled.

On Tuesday, April thirtieth, at Ebbets Field, Zimmer had five hits, homering in the tenth to defeat Chicago, ten to nine. Sandy Amoros hit a pinch homer in the ninth inning to tie the game. Campanella homered twice. Hodges contributed a three-run blast in the eighth. The Dodgers were a game behind first place Milwaukee in the standings.

MAY

On Wednesday, May first, a two-run double by Hodges in the fifth inning marked his one thousand four hundredth career hit. The Dodgers beat the Cubs again, seven to two.

A sixteen inning game on Thursday night, eventually won by the Cardinals, three to two, took four hours and fifty-four minutes to complete. A double by Cimoli, and a single by Hodges produced a Dodger run in the first. Snider doubled home Gilliam with the tying run in the eighth. Podres pitched seven strong innings, allowing only one earned run. Labine and Bessent held the Cardinals scoreless until second baseman Don Blasingame singled home the game winner in the sixteenth.

In the second game of the year at Roosevelt Stadium in Jersey City on Friday night, May third, a surprisingly large crowd of 14,470 braved drizzling rain and gusty winds. Newcombe shut out St Louis, six to nothing. Furillo tripled home Cimoli and Snider in the bottom of the first inning. On Saturday Charley Neal blasted a two-run homer with one out in the ninth. Cardinal right fielder Stan Musial entered the series with a gaudy .468 batting average, but had just two hits in thirteen at bats.

FIRST SHOWDOWN SERIES

On Sunday, May fifth, the defending champion Dodgers (12-4), hosted the league-leading Braves (13-3) at Ebbets Field. Separated by just a game in the standings, the two clubs began the first of several dramatic showdown series. The Braves drew first blood, winning the first game ten to seven. Milwaukee, having finished just a game back of the NL champion Dodgers in 1956, took a two to nothing lead in the first. But Campanella's three-run homer capped a five run Dodger rally in the bottom of the first. Brooklyn scored two more in the third. Henry Aaron's three-run homer in top of the fourth inning cut the Dodger lead to a single run. The Braves scored three more times in the top of the fifth and a single run in the eighth. Relief pitcher Ernie Johnson retired the first sixteen Dodgers he faced.

CIMOLI HOMERS IN FOURTEENTH

On Monday, May sixth, the Dodgers, playing in already their third extra inning game of the month, defeated the Braves, five to four, in fourteen innings. Third baseman Eddie Mathews homered twice for the Braves. Milwaukee first baseman Joe Adcock's eighth inning homer tied the game at three apiece. In the top of the twelfth, Mathews singled, went to third on a single by Joe Adcock, and scored the go-ahead run on a sacrifice fly by shortstop Johnny Logan. Cimoli doubled and scored the tying run in the bottom of the twelfth. Cimoli's fifth hit of the game, a homer in the fourteenth inning, gave the Dodgers the win shortly after midnight.

The split of the two game series left the Dodgers a game behind the Braves. Third place Cincinnati, the next visitors to Ebbets Field, was within two and one-half games of the league lead. On Tuesday, May seventh, the Reds, leading the league in home runs, collected fourteen hits, scoring five runs in the ninth inning en route to a nine to two victory. None of the Cincinnati hits was a home run.

THE LONGEST LOSING STREAK

However, Reds' first baseman Ted Kluzewski hit two home runs on Wednesday, May eighth, and third baseman Don Hoak hit a decisive grand slam in the eighth inning. Although Hodges hit a three-run homer for the Dodgers in the bottom of the ninth, the Reds held on to win their ninth straight, seven to six. The Dodgers dropped into third place.

Brooklyn produced a modest five wins and four losses on its first significant home stand. The pitching staff was overworked. Podres had a pulled tendon in his left elbow and an inflammation of the bone in the upper arm. Koufax had a strained muscle in the left forearm. Labine had a sore left shoulder. Maglie had a bruised right thumb, and right hander Randy Jackson had a sore left knee.

Normally supportive fans were clearly distracted by the talk about the transfer of the club. Attendance for the first fifteen home dates of the 1957 season was 33,703 below that for a comparable number of dates in 1956. The Dodgers' attendance figures were significantly higher than those for the rival Giants, however.

MAYS ISSUES A CHALLENGE

Before their first series of the year at the Polo Grounds on Friday, May tenth, there was plenty of lighthearted bantering. Watching the Dodgers take batting practice, a grinning Willie Mays challenged Dodger catcher Rube Walker to a foot race. As Walker left the batting cage, Mays insisted, "You owe me five bucks, Rube. If you ain't gonna pay me, I'll ask the man to put in the paper that you welshed on a bet." "I'll race you for the money," responded the slow-footed Dodger reserve. "I want a piece of that bet," said Duke Snider. "You bettin' on Walker?" said Mays. "I'm betting on you," said Duke. "C'mon, I'll race you, Rube," said Mays, "and I'll run backwards." "I'll still bet on you Willie," said Duke. The race never actually took place.

Podres, taking his cuts next, told Reese, "See that spot in the upper right field stands? I hit one up there once." "I can't see the plaque," said Pee Wee Reese covering his eyes, searching for the spot. "See what?" asked Podres. "I naturally assumed that public spirited citizens would put a bronze plaque on the seat with the inscription, 'this marks the spot where Johnny Podres hit a home run.'" "Oh I didn't hit it in a game," said Podres sheepishly, "I hit it in batting practice."

MAGLIE'S SCORELESS INNING STREAK ENDS

When the game started, 34,543 saw Mays end Maglie's string of twelve and one-third scoreless innings against his old club by tripling home a run in the first inning. He later scored on a sacrifice fly. The Giants defeated the Dodgers, two to one. Reese doubled home the only Dodger run in the eighth inning. Mays ran down a 450-foot drive by Hodges in the ninth to seal the Giants' victory.

It took the Giants fifteen innings to defeat the Dodgers again on Saturday afternoon, May eleventh. In the sixth inning Campanella singled home two runs. Elmer Valo, pinch hitting for Roebuck, singled home another to tie the score, five to five. Though the Dodger bull pen could have used a rest, Labine and Bessent kept the Giants at bay until the fourteenth inning. Reserve catcher Valmy Thomas homered with two out in the fifteenth to deal the Dodgers their third consecutive one run loss, six to five, dropping the Dodgers two full games behind the Braves. The four game losing streak was a modest one, but alarming to Dodger fans, unaccustomed to losing.

However, on Sunday afternoon, May twelfth, Podres shut out New York, five to nothing, salvaging the series' finale. Brooklyn scored three times in the first inning. Snider hit his fourth homer of the year in the third.

SECOND SHOWDOWN SERIES

On Tuesday, May fourteenth, the Dodgers traveled to Milwaukee for the first time. Before 34,731 enthusiastic fans, the Braves dealt Newcombe his first defeat on the road in thirteen starts over a two year span, three to two. Braves' center fielder Bill Bruton tripled home the game winner in the sixth inning.

LONGEST WINNING STREAK
COMBINED STRIKEOUT RECORD SET

Zimmer homered in the tenth inning on Wednesday, May fifteenth to give Brooklyn a three to two victory. Labine hurled three perfect innings in relief.

On Thursday, May sixteenth, at Wrigley Field in Chicago, Koufax fanned thirteen. Moe Drabowski of the Cubs struck out ten. The combined total of twenty-three strikeouts tied the National League record. The Dodgers won three to two.

On Sunday, May nineteenth, in St. Louis, Brooklyn scored seven runs in the top of the ninth inning, beating the Cardinals. The Dodgers crushed St. Louis again, ten to three on Monday night. Then, on Tuesday in Cincinnati, Podres hurled the third straight complete game by a Dodger pitcher, defeating the league-leading Reds, six to one, and moving the club into a second place tie with Milwaukee. The winning streak was at five games. But the Reds rebuffed the Dodgers, eight to one, on Wednesday in the final game of the road trip.

FINAL MAYORS TROPHY GAME

On Thursday May twenty-third, over 30,000 watched the Dodgers host the American League Yankees in the Annual Mayor's Trophy exhibition game supporting sandlot baseball and other charities in the New York metropolitan area. Mayor Wagner threw out the ceremonial first pitch in this final encounter between these perennial post season rivals. The Dodgers lost, ten to seven.

Erskine, who injured his shoulder in spring training, made his first start for the Dodgers. After the Yankees scored two runs in the first inning, Amoros doubled home two Brooklyn runs in the fifth. A two-run homer by center fielder Mickey Mantle keyed a seven run New York rally in the sixth inning. Brooklyn rallied, scoring a single run in the bottom of the sixth inning, and four more in their half of the seventh.

STILL LOOKING FOR A NEW HOME

The search for a new home for the Dodgers continued. City Council President Abe Stark proposed that the city build a new stadium on the current Ebbets Field site, creating parking space for an additional 5000 vehicles by acquiring five acres of blighted land adjacent to the park. O'Malley expressed no enthusiasm for that plan, telling reporters he couldn't remain at Ebbets Field. But either of two other downtown Brooklyn sites under consideration were acceptable to him. "I told John Cashmore I'd carry him piggyback to Macy's window if I could get either one of them," he said.

SNIDER REACHES FIFTEEN HUNDRED HITS

The Dodgers hosted the Giants again on Friday, May twenty-fourth, winning six to nothing. Campanella clouted two homers off Antonelli, who had beaten the Dodgers three times in 1956. Newcombe recorded his second straight shutout, and sixth consecutive complete game. Furillo homered to take the league lead in RBIs with thirty-one to Aaron's thirty. When pitcher Curt Barclay was called upon to pinch hit in the top of the ninth inning on Saturday, he slapped a single to right, giving the Giants an eight to seven win. Second baseman Gilliam leaped high to rob Mays of a hit in the ninth inning on Sunday. The Dodgers held on to win, five to three. Snider's homer to center in the third inning was fifteen hundredth hit of his career. Zack Wheat held the Brooklyn record with 2894 career hits. The recently retired Robinson had 1815. Reese and Furillo were the only active Dodgers ahead of Snider. Reese had 2077. Furillo had 1682.

CAMPY STEALS A BASE

On Monday, May twenty-seventh, the Dodgers began an extended baseball tour of Pennsylvania with a five to one win over the Phillies. Cimoli and Snider each hit two-run homers, backing Drysdale's two-hit pitching. The astonished Phillies watched slow-footed Campanella steal second base in the second inning. Campy took second, without even drawing a throw.

The Dodgers lost to Pittsburgh at Forbes Field, three to two, in eleven innings on Tuesday. With one out, and Pirates' pitcher Roy Face on third, in the bottom of the eleventh, Roberto Clemente grounded to short. Reese's throw to the plate was late. "The ball stuck in the webbing of my glove," said the disconsolate shortstop. Podres shut out the Pirates on Wednesday night, one to nothing. On Thursday afternoon a two-run homer by Snider gave the Dodgers a four to three win in the opener of the traditional Memorial Day doubleheader. Reese, however, pulled a muscle his right side. He was placed on the injured list.

ANOTHER FOUR GAME LOSING STREAK

In the nightcap, Bob Purkey beat the Dodgers for the third straight time. Pittsburgh won, three to one, and Brooklyn spiraled downward into another four game losing streak.

On Friday, back in Philadelphia, Drysdale and Roberts faced each other for the second time in five days. Roberts won this time, two to one. Campanella hit his seventh homer of the year. The Dodgers won fifteen and lost twelve during the month. They were in second place, one and one-half games behind the red-hot league-leading Cincinnati Reds.

JUNE

Before 30,6621 on Saturday, June first, the Phillies' Jack Sanford allowed just two hits, struck out eleven, and shut out Brooklyn, three to nothing. With the Phillies in contention, attendance in Philadelphia was up more than 50,000 for the same number of dates the previous year. The win moved the Phillies into a second place tie with the Dodgers. Philadelphia won again on Sunday, five to three.

DODGER MANAGEMENT PREOCCUPIED?

Local sports writers charged Dodger management with being pre-occupied with relocating the franchise, and inattention to current Dodgers' problems on the field. With four infielders on the disabled list, the front office had made no moves to find replacements. Alston, still focused on the pennant race, put the nearby New York race tracks off limits to the Dodger players. The manager also clamped down on clubhouse card-playing. "I don't think there's anything wrong in going to the track or with playing cards. But right now we can use a little less distraction, and a little extra batting practice," Alston said.

LONGEST WINNING STREAK MATCHED

On Monday night, Podres, again, was the Dodgers stopper. He shut out the Phillies, four to nothing, salvaging the final game of the road trip. Podres had two of the three Brooklyn victories in the last eight games. The Dodgers followed with four more wins, matching their longest victory string of the year. They would never again win five consecutive games as the Brooklyn Dodgers. On Tuesday, June fourth, at Ebbets Field, Koufax struck out twelve to up his league-leading total to fifty-nine. Brooklyn defeated Chicago, seven to five. On Wednesday night, June fifth, in Jersey City, Drysdale hurled his first major league shutout, winning four to nothing. Hodges, hitting .359, had three hits. It was the Dodgers' seventh straight triumph over the Cubs. Roosevelt Stadium was eerily shrouded in fog at game's end, a harbinger of things to come.

THE FOG

The dense sea fog, swirling in off the Atlantic coast, settled in for an extended stay. It had a larger effect on the Thursday night, June sixth, contest against Chicago at Ebbets Field. Balls that stayed low could be seen. But with two out in the top half of the first inning and a runner on second base, Cubs' first baseman Dale Long hit a high infield pop up. Shortstop Don Zimmer, seemingly the only Dodger to have a vague idea where the ball was, made a lunging last minute catch, saving a run.

The fog got worse. When the Dodgers came to bat in the bottom of the inning, Hodges walked. Campanella lined out to right. Walt Moryn made that catch easily. But when Charlie Neal then hit a high fly ball, center fielder Bob Spence circled, searching desperately for the ball. Without radar he had very little chance of finding it. It fell for a double, scoring Hodges. "I knew it was up there somewhere," said Spence, "but that was all I knew." Cubs' second baseman Bob Morgan shouted to second base Umpire Tom Gorman, "Call time. It's impossible out there. This inning will never end if they keep hitting the ball into the air."

Morgan summoned the managers, plate umpire Ken Burkhart, and third base umpire Dusty Boggess. Boggess, the senior member of the crew, ordered play halted. Tex Rickards, the announcer at Ebbets Field for thirty-two years, told the fans, "The game will be delayed pending the results of the fog. So please be patient while Gladys Goodding entertains you." Curiously, the organist at Ebbets field for nineteen years, started her medley of songs with "California here I come." Goodding was also the organist at Madison Square Garden for the basketball New York Knicks and the hockey New York Rangers.

After a one hour and twenty-six minutes later the game was officially postponed and ordered replayed in its entirety. In 1931 fog had forced the cancellation of a Pacific Coast League game at Wrigley Field in Los Angeles. This was the first time fog had forced cancellation of a major league game, although in 1947, a game between the Dodgers and Cubs at Ebbets Field was postponed because of swarming gnats.

THE ORIGIN OF THE NAME "DODGERS"

A letter appearing in the Saturday, June eighth, *New York Times,* written by A. Hoyt, Jr. of Atlantic Beach, New York, enlightened readers on the origin of the nickname "Dodgers":

> Unless I'm mistaken, the name 'dodgers' is definitely associated with Brooklyn, and no other city. In its earlier day, when the horse cars were replaced by trolley cars, Brooklynites complained that to cross the street they had to dodge the speedy trolleys, a menace as compared to the jogging horse cars. It followed that Brooklynites became known as 'dodgers'. So what better name for their ball team? Under the circumstances, in the

event that their ball team is moved to another town, the name 'dodgers' should rightly be held in Brooklyn for the team which will inevitably take the place of the late lamented.

FIRST PLACE FOR THE LAST TIME

The Dodgers defeated the leading Cincinnati Reds on Friday, June seventh, six to three, and again on Saturday, June eighth, nine to two. The two victories moved the Dodgers into first place. On Saturday, Podres won his sixth straight. Light hitting reserve catcher Rube Walker, playing in place of a resting Campanella, homered in both games. It was the last time the Dodgers would ever lead the National League standings as representatives of the Borough of Brooklyn.

THE LARGEST HOME CROWD
STILL ANOTHER FOUR GAME SLIDE

The largest crowd of the season at Ebbets Field—33, 850—watched Cincinnati regain the league lead by sweeping both games of a doubleheader on Sunday, June ninth. Hodges produced the only Dodger run of the afternoon, homering into the upper deck in left field in the sixth inning of the opener. Ten-year veteran Hal Jeffcoat shut out Brooklyn, three to nothing, in the nightcap, pitching his second complete game victory of the year over the Dodgers. It was the sixth complete game effort of his career, and his fourth against the Dodgers.

BRAVES VISIT AGAIN—CAMPY SETS A RECORD

Milwaukee, now in second place, defeated Brooklyn, three to one on Monday, June tenth. A two-run homer by Mathews in the fourth inning dealt the Dodgers their second defeat ever at the Roosevelt Stadium. Hodges had three of four Dodger hits. On Tuesday, June eleventh, at Ebbets Field, a grand slam by Dodger nemesis Bobby Thomson offset solo homers by Cimoli and Campanella, giving the Braves a seven to two victory.

Campanella's homer, the two hundred thirty-seventh of his career, gave him the National League career mark for homers by a catcher, surpassing Gabby Hartnett of the Cubs. After Gilliam singled in the bottom of the first inning on Wednesday night, Braves' starter Conley fielded a bunt by Reese cleanly. But his throw to first was wild, eluding the first baseman. The error led to four unearned Dodgers' runs. Podres staked to

212

an early nine run lead, didn't survive a four run Milwaukee outburst in the fourth. Although Frank Torre, Mathews, and Aaron all homered off Roebuck in the ninth, Labine recorded the final two outs, preserving an eleven to nine Dodger triumph. Reese celebrated his return to the line-up with a double, and two singles. Hodges singled and walked three times raising his league-leading batting average to .372. He also contributed a sacrifice fly. However, he bruised his ribs in a collision with Bob Malkmus at second base, joining Furillo, Labine, and Podres on the disabled list. The ninth inning homer by Braves' third baseman Eddie Mathews was the two hundredth of his career.

DRYSDALE VS LOGAN—THE FIGHT

On Thursday, June thirteenth, lead-off batter Bill Bruton homered on the first pitch of the game, and again with a man on in the second, to give the Braves a four to nothing lead. After his second blast cleared the pro-truding wing of the center field upper deck, Drysdale, hit the next batter, Johnny Logan, in the back. With Alston on his way to the mound to make a pitching change, Logan, at first base, taunted, "I'll get you when you come into second base." "If you've got a beef with me, come on. Get it over with now!" responded the right hander. Logan charged the mound. Hodges, in hot pursuit of Logan, was tackled from the rear by Milwaukee first base coach John Riddle. A surge of players from both benches filled the infield. Drysdale landed a clean right hand to Logan's head. The Braves' shortstop retaliated with body punches before being restrained by Alston and others. Mathews, however, reached Drysdale and wrestled him to the ground. Now back on his feet, Hodges, a gentle giant with particularly huge hands, forcibly separated the two remaining antagonists and dragged Mathews by his ankles across the third base line to the edge of the Braves' dugout. "Here," said Gil to the startled Braves remaining in the visitors' dugout, "where shall I deposit him?" Meanwhile, Newcombe bear-hugged Drysdale, the disheveled Dodgers' pitcher, escorting him to the home team dugout.

"I'm sorry it happened. I was mad about the homer, but I didn't throw at Logan," said Drysdale. "It was just a close pitch. My fast ball runs in on a right handed batter." While Logan, sporting an obvious cut above his left eye, unconvincingly told reporters, "That's an old cut from my last fight, with Hal Jeffcoat."

When the game resumed, Ken Lehman, in relief, pitched five scoreless innings. Cimoli hit a two-run homer in sixth. In the bottom of the seventh, Reese singled home the tying run. But catcher Carl

Sawatski homered off Labine, following a double by Bobby Thomson. That keyed a four run Milwaukee rally in the top of the eighth. The Braves won, eight to five.

League President Warren Giles assessed Logan one hundred dollars. He fined Drysdale only forty dollars. "It's an injustice. It wasn't an even settlement. He started the fight when he threw at me," said Logan.

On Friday, June fourteenth, Gilliam stole home with two out in the bottom of the tenth to beat St. Louis, two to one. Newcombe pitched all ten innings on his thirtieth birthday. The Cardinals won on Saturday, six to five. St. Louis closed out the Brooklyn home stand with a doubleheader sweep on Sunday, June sixteenth.

REESE, ALSTON EJECTED

The Dodgers led six to one after five innings in the opener. Campanella and Drysdale homered. St. Louis rallied to tie the game in the sixth. A seventh inning homer by third baseman Ken Boyer gave them a seven to six victory. In the ninth inning, Reese and manager Alston were both ejected by the home plate umpire, Frank Secory, for protesting a called third strike. Alston decided to rest Reese in the second game, starting Neal at short. Leading three to two after five innings, the Cardinals chased Podres with four runs in the sixth St. Louis posted an eight to four win. President Giles suspended Alston for three games, fining the Dodgers' manager seventy-five dollars. He fined Reese fifty dollars.

Coach Billy Herman filled in for Alston on Monday, June seventeenth, as the Dodgers opened a road trip in Cincinnati. Left hander Danny McDevitt, in his first major league start, pitched a sparkling seven hitter. He struck out eleven, winning seven to two. Cimoli homered in the first. Neal, still at shortstop, had three hits. On Tuesday, Newcombe shut out Cincinnati, seven to nothing. He also homered and doubled. The win lifted Brooklyn into a virtual tie for second place with the Cardinals, and the Phillies. All were only a game behind first place Milwaukee.

SNIDER SUED

After the game Snider had papers served on him naming him a defendant in a law suit concerning a 1954 incident in which a foul ball fractured the arm of Mrs. Dovie Green. Mrs. Green was suing for $75,000 in damages.

Drysdale led three to nothing after pitching six shutout innings on Wednesday, June nineteenth. But in the seventh inning, Reds' third baseman Don Hoak hit his fourth homer of the year against Dodger pitching, rallying the Reds to only their second win in ten games, four to three. "Sure I called for the wrong pitch. The catcher always calls for the wrong pitch when it ends up in the stands," said Campanella. Alston returned from suspension to guide the Dodgers on Thursday night. Cincinnati gained a split of the four games, winning, six to one in the final game of the series.

On Friday in St. Louis, eighteen year-old Von McDaniel, in his third big league start, shut out Brooklyn, two to nothing, allowing just two hits. With the score tied four to four in the ninth inning on Saturday, Neal and Reese hit back-to-back doubles. Snider tripled home Reese, giving the Dodgers a six to four win. Hodges hit a three-run Homer in the third. St. Louis won the first game of a doubleheader on Sunday, June twenty-third. In the fourth inning, former Dodger Wally Moon tripled and stole home. The Dodgers recovered, scoring six runs in the top of the seventh inning of the second game, and routing St. Louis, ten to four. Erskine, coming off the disabled list to make his first regular season start, allowed just one run in six innings.

DODGERS-BRAVES AGAIN

The fourth series of the year between the Dodgers and the Braves began on Tuesday, June twenty-fifth, at County Stadium in Milwaukee. McDevitt, in his second outstanding outing in a week, shut out Milwaukee, two to nothing. After Snider homered in the first, the Dodgers didn't get another hit off loser Burdette until Neal singled in the eighth.

On Wednesday night, Milwaukee rallied for six runs in the eighth, defeating the Dodgers, thirteen to eight. Mathews homered twice for Milwaukee. Campanella and Neal homered in the losing effort for the Dodgers. On Thursday night Aaron tripled home both Milwaukee runs in the eighth, giving the Braves a two to nothing lead. Hodges and Cimoli opened the Dodger ninth with singles. But the Dodgers scored only once, losing, two to one. Buhl out-dueled Drysdale, picking up his ninth win of the year. The Braves led the season series six games to three.

DODGERS STILL A ROAD DRAW

The Dodgers were still a big drawing card on the road. The three games in Milwaukee drew 104,185. Four in St. Louis drew 101,609, and four in Cincinnati drew 70,172 in the middle of the week.

On Saturday, June twenty-ninth, Erskine, in his second straight start stopped the Cubs at Wrigley Field, two to one, with relief help from Labine. Campanella homered with Furillo on board in the fifth inning. In the first game of a doubleheader on Sunday, June thirtieth, Ernie Banks doubled in a run in the bottom of the ninth inning to give Chicago a three to two victory.

CUBS FAN 27—DODGERS FAN 12

Brooklyn concluded the long road trip with a five to one victory in the second game behind a another strong effort by McDevitt. Cubs' pitchers fanned twenty-seven Dodger batters on the afternoon, establishing the major league record for strikeouts by one team in a doubleheader. Don Ellston fanned eleven Dodgers in the first game. Dick Littlefield struck out four in the first game, and one in the second. Lown had one strikeout in the first game. Jim Brosnan had one. Drabowski struck out nine in the second. McDevitt and Newcombe each had six strike outs for the Dodgers. The combined total of thirty-nine strikeouts established the major league record for strikeouts by both teams in a doubleheader. Drabowski and Koufax had already combined to tie the league record for most strikeouts in a single game six weeks earlier.

The fourteen and seventeen record in June marked the Dodgers' poorest monthly performance in several seasons. They were in fourth place. But they were only three and one-half games behind the first place Braves.

JULY

DODGERS FACE SURGING GIANTS

With Snider sidelined with an injured finger on his left hand, Brooklyn faced the Giants at the Polo Grounds on Monday, July first. Cimoli started in center. A crowd of more than 37,000 welcomed the Giants home after a successful western road trip that had brought them back into contention. They were just four games back of Brooklyn. The Dodgers, who had not lost to a left hander all year defeated Johnny

Antonelli for the second straight time, three to nothing. Junior Gilliam homered in the first to provide all the offense Drysdale would need. Maglie, starting for the first time in a month, followed with another shutout on Tuesday night, winning six to nothing.

Pittsburgh visited Ebbets Field for the traditional fourth of July doubleheader. The Dodgers won the first game, five to one. The Pirates won the second game, eight to two. The split left Brooklyn in fourth place, two and one-half games behind league-leading Cincinnati.

On Friday night, July fifth, Campanella hit a three-run homer off Robin Roberts, giving Brooklyn a six to five win over Philadelphia. Jack Sanford, chosen by Alston for the National League All-Star pitching staff, defeated the Dodgers, nine to four.

SNIDER BOOED

In the first game of the doubleheader on Sunday, July seventh, Phillies' first baseman Ed Bouchee, leading off in the ninth inning, homered off Sal Maglie, giving Philadelphia a two to one victory. The home fans booed Snider for not running out a double play grounder in the first inning. (Snider thought second baseman Granny Hamner had caught the ball.) In the second game, Philadelphia shortstop Chico Fernandez, a former Dodger, doubled home three runs with two out in the sixth inning to give the Phillies a five to two win. The three game sweep by the Phillies was the Dodgers' only real lull in the month of July. Brooklyn, now in fifth place, had not been in the second division at the All-Star break since 1948.

THE ALL-STAR BREAK

Though Reds' fans successfully voted seven home team players onto the 1957 National League All-Star roster for the game at Busch Stadium in St. Louis, Alston added Cimoli, Hodges, and Labine to the squad. Labine, was charged with three earned runs in the top of the ninth inning. After the National League rallied for three runs in the bottom of the inning, Hodges lined sharply to left with the tying run on to end the game. The AL won, six to five. League President Warren Giles seemed unconcerned about rumors that the National League was on the verge of abandoning New York entirely. "We left all of New England to the American League when the Braves moved to Milwaukee, and we don't regret that," he told reporters.

GILLIAM VS SANCHEZ—THE FIGHT

Opening the second half of the season at Ebbets Field on Thursday, July eleventh, Snider hit a pair of two-run homers to defeat Cincinnati, five to four. When Raul Sanchez brushed Gilliam back with a pitch in the seventh, the Dodger second baseman dragged a bunt down the first baseline. Gilliam bowled over Sanchez, who was covering first base on the play. The two players squared off, exchanging punches. The benches emptied.

Campanella quickly got between the two initial combatants. Hodges separated Charlie Neal of the Dodgers, and Don Hoak of the Reds. The melee persisted for fifteen minutes. Gilliam, Sanchez, Neal, and Hoak were all ejected. Although Chief Justices from every state in the union were attending the game as his guest, League President Giles adjudicated the incident. He fined all players involved one hundred dollars each. "Any revival of this incident, on the field or off, will be considered a serious offense," he said. "It will be dealt with accordingly."

THE BOYS OF SUMMER ARE BACK
THE DODGERS BEGIN ANOTHER RUN FOR THE PENNANT

Newcombe defeated the Reds, three to one, at Jersey City on Friday, July twelfth. Cimoli singled home the game winner with two out in the eighth inning.

ANOTHER VISIT FROM MILWAUKEE

Maglie defeated Bob Buhl of the Braves in a good pitching duel on Sunday, July fourteenth, three to two. Schoendienst, recently acquired from the Giants, homered on the fourth pitch of the game for Milwaukee. Charlie Neal led off the bottom half of the first with a double. He scored on a sacrifice fly by Snider. Former Dodger Andy Pafko doubled home Joe Torre in the top of the ninth inning to put Milwaukee ahead. But Hodges hit a dramatic two-run homer to win the game in the bottom half of the inning. Alston, wearing a broad grin, was the first to greet the Dodger first baseman at home plate.

CRUSHING THE BRAVES—THE BIGGEST INNING

There was a lot more to smile about at Ebbets Field on Monday night, July fifteenth as the Dodgers crushed Milwaukee, twenty to four. Neal homered to lead off the bottom of the first. Snider. Amoros homered in the third. In the fourth inning, Neal hit his second homer of the game, and Drysdale hit his second homer of the season. The Dodgers scored four more runs. Adding insult to injury, the Dodgers finished the rout by scoring a season high nine runs off relief pitcher Taylor Phillips in the eighth. On the same night, 33,906 fans at Connie Mack Stadium In Philadelphia, watched the Phillies beat the Cardinals, six to two, and move past the Braves into first place in the National League standings.

CONTEMPLATING A MOVE

Braves' owner Lou Perini, traveling with his team, had moved his own club from Boston to Milwaukee five years earlier. He told Brooklyn reporters at Ebbets Field that the old ballpark was antiquated, had too few desirable seats, and extremely limited parking:

> O'Malley can't live here. Whether he'll move to Los Angeles or some other location I wouldn't say. You tell me. I'll tell you I'd like to see Moses build that park at the Flushing Meadows site. He'd have everything there. He'd have parking, and a lot of other things. He's a visionary man. I'd venture to say that sometime in the future the Yankees will be playing in the new Moses' park instead of at Yankee Stadium.
>
> We can't be selfish about the matter. Suppose it does cost each club another $25,000 or $35,000 in additional transportation. Baseball has to go to the Pacific coast. It has to expand. But I think that by all means the National League should retain the New York territory. New York is the greatest sports town, the greatest baseball town, I think, in the country.

Perini, however, was skeptical about the rosy predictions for Dodger success on the West Coast:

> They have a lot of things in Los Angeles: a lot of sun, a lot of racing, a lot of big sports events, and big football games, and shows. The folks out there want to see champions. The Dodgers would draw well there. They would have to be champions to do it all the time.

IN BROOKLYN, YOU'RE FIRST OR YOU'RE BANKRUPT

Ironically, the enormous success of Perini's Braves in Milwaukee following the transplant from Boston, was perhaps the biggest single motivation for moving the Dodgers. "This is a very serious problem,"

O'Malley told writer Roger Kahn. "With the Braves making more money than we are, they'll hire the best scouts away from us and before you know it, they'll have a better team. That would be ruinous. You know what I say. In Brooklyn, you're first or bankrupt." However, the Dodger owner told Mayor Wagner, "My roots are New York. People in Los Angeles want the Dodgers to move. They've made flattering offers. But I am in no way committed at this point."

O'Malley could legitimately cite a decaying, obsolete playing facility, and poor parking as reasons for leaving. He certainly couldn't point to poor attendance. The Dodgers had drawn over a million fans for twelve straight years, a record unmatched by any other team.

Blunt, outspoken Hall of Famer Rodgers Hornsby, in town with the incoming St. Louis Cardinals, didn't mince words when asked what he thought of the Dodgers and Giants moving to California. "I would consider it a disgrace if the National League gave up New York," he told reporters.

THE DODGERS STAY HOT

On Tuesday, July sixteenth, at Ebbets Field, Brooklyn defeated Cardinal ace Lindy McDaniel for the third time, winning seven to five. The loss left St. Louis one-half game back of first place Milwaukee. Snider hit his twentieth homer. Newcombe had beaten the Cardinals twelve straight times in a streak interrupted by a tour of military service. But on Wednesday night, he lost to St. Louis, seven to three. The Brooklyn winning streak ended at five games. On Thursday night, the Cardinals rallied for seven runs in the top of the ninth, taking a nine for four lead. But a grand slam by Hodges in the bottom of the inning tied the score. A suicide squeeze bunt by Cimoli scored Snider from third in the eleventh inning, giving Brooklyn a ten to nine win.

GIL HODGES APPRECIATION NIGHT

There were 28,724 fans on hand Friday, July nineteenth, for a twilight doubleheader billed in advance as "Gil Hodges Appreciation Night." Cubs' outfielder Lee Walls hit his second homer of the game in the top of the tenth to give Chicago a temporary three to two lead. Snider tied the game with a solo homer in the bottom of the tenth. Catcher Johnny Roseboro followed with a three-run homer, giving the Dodgers a six to three victory. Between games, Hodges was showered with a variety of gifts, ranging from a Dodge convertible automobile to a years supply of dill pickles. There were salutary telegrams from personal friends, former teammates, and even one from President Eisenhower.

After Hodges' first inning single in the second game scored Jim Gilliam, the one thousandth run batted in of his Dodger career, the cheering was louder than the ovation at the between game ceremonies. The Dodgers won, five to three.

SNIDER GETS THREE HUNDREDTH HOMER

Snider hit his three hundredth career homer on Saturday. Brooklyn beat the Cubs again, seven to five. Chicago outfielders Walt "Moose" Moryn, Chuck Tanner, and Lee Walls all homered in the first game of a Sunday doubleheader. Shortstop Ernie Banks drove home the winning run with a line single in the sixth. The Cubs won, four to three. The Dodgers defeated Bob Rush with a five run fifth inning in the final game, winning seven to two.

Brooklyn was on the road for the rest of the month. On Monday, July twenty-third in St. Louis, Podres shut out the Cardinals, one to nothing, allowing five hits. Losing southpaw Sam Jones only allowed three hits. Rube Walker, starting in place of Snider in center field, singled home Hodges in the second inning. The win left the Dodgers just a game behind the first place Braves, increasing their lead over the third place Cardinals to a game and one-half. Brooklyn was two games ahead of the fourth place Cincinnati Reds.

DODGERS REMAIN A GAME BACK

St. Louis moved past Brooklyn again in the standings, winning the final two games of the series, three to nothing, and three to two. The Cardinals were now just one-half game behind Milwaukee. The Braves had lost two straight in Philadelphia. The Dodgers were still just a game out of first. Cincinnati, having defeated Pittsburgh twice, was tied with Brooklyn for third place.

In Cincinnati on July twenty-sixth, the Dodgers lost, six to five, in eleven innings. Reds' relief pitcher Hershel Freeman doubled home the winning run in the bottom of the eleventh. Hodges, who had three hits, was thrown out at the plate in the top of the eleventh. Hodges and Furillo homered to back a five to three win by McDevitt on Saturday. Furillo hit a grand slam on Sunday. The Dodgers beat the Reds again, seven to two.

With the Dodgers making a serious charge at the league lead, Maglie and Labine combined for a one to nothing shutout in the first game of a doubleheader in Chicago on Tuesday, July thirtieth. Furillo scored Snider with a sacrifice fly in the fourth inning. Defensively, Furillo and Amoros both threw out runners at the plate. Drabowski, who struck out eleven Dodgers, was the hard luck loser for Chicago. Brooklyn dropped the nightcap, four to three. Roebuck was credited with both victories in another doubleheader on Wednesday night. Brooklyn rallied in the ninth inning of each game to beat the Cubs, three to two, and two to one.

In third place, two games back of Milwaukee, the Dodgers were twenty-one and ten in July, besting the Cardinals twenty and ten record. The Braves, Reds, Cardinals, and Phillies each took turns atop the league standings during the month. Brooklyn fought its way back into contention. It was a classic pennant race.

CIMOLI AND LABINE

Cimoli's .295 average was second only to Furillo's .306. He had emerged as the regular left fielder. He was one of six Dodgers to drive in more than fifty runs during the 1957 season. Minor league scouts reported that the twenty-six year-old prospect an outstanding fielder with a strong throwing arm. He was rated a weak hitter. However, his performance, during a postseason tour of Japan in October 1956, impressed Alston who told reporters:

> Some of those Japanese pitchers were tough, too. One of them fanned fifteen of us in one game. So, as he kept hitting, especially to left, I decided then and there we could start him right off, playing every day. Now, I'm not saying that, had we not gone to Japan, we would never have found out what a real fine ballplayer Cimoli is. It might have taken a little longer.

Labine led all National League relief pitchers in 1957, with seventeen saves. A fractured index finger on his right hand had failed to heal properly. The crooked finger altered his delivery, causing his sinker ball to take a sudden drop. He appeared in fifty-eight games, second only to the sixty-seven appearances made by Turk Lown of the Cubs.

AUGUST

HODGES GETS RECORD GRAND SLAM
DODGERS GET EIGHTEEN HITS AGAINST CUBS, BRAVES

The Dodgers finished the five game series in Chicago with their third straight win on Thursday, August first. Hodges hit his thirteenth career grand slam, setting a new major league record. The Dodgers collected a season high eighteen hits, posting an easy twelve to three win.

On Friday in Milwaukee, Gene Conley outlasted Podres, one to nothing. On Saturday Campanella singled home two runs in the eighth inning, breaking up a pitching duel between Maglie and Lew Burdette. Brooklyn won, seven to one. Hodges homered again on Sunday. The Dodgers got eighteen hits again. Mathews, Aaron, Logan, and Rice all homered for Milwaukee. The Braves won, nine to seven. The series was a great financial success, drawing 128,317 for the three games.

DODGERS HOST GIANTS WITH FADING PENNANT HOPES

After a mediocre eight and six record on the road trip, the Dodger pennant hopes were fading. However, Brooklyn's thirty-one and twenty home record was the best in the National League. And they had twenty-six games remaining to be played at Ebbets Field.

At Ebbets Field on Monday August fifth, Drysdale turned back the visiting Giants, five to two. Relishing the spoilers role, the Giants won the final three games of the series, five nothing, eight to five, and three to two. Only one of the four games drew more than 20,000 fans. The talk about moving the clubs to the West Coast was trying the patience of fans. They were growing increasingly ambivalent toward both teams.

In Pittsburgh on Friday, August ninth, Snider's twenty-seventh homer defeated the Pirates, four to two. On Saturday, his twenty-eighth home run backed a three to nothing shutout by Drysdale. In the ninth inning of the first game of a doubleheader on Sunday, Pirates' right fielder Paul Smith homered with a man on, tying the game, three to three. In the bottom of the tenth, Snider leaped high against the "435" foot sign in center to haul down a long drive by Pittsburgh left fielder Bob Skinner. The reprieve was only temporary, however. The Pirates' shortstop, Bill Mazerowski, followed with a single, driving home the winning run. Pittsburgh won the nightcap, six to two, behind Douglas. The Dodgers stranded ten base runners.

Neal's third inning homer staked Maglie to a two to nothing lead at the Polo Grounds on Tuesday, August thirteenth. But the Giants won, four to two. Homers by Hodges, Elmer Valo, and Zimmer led the Dodgers to a crucial seven to six win on Wednesday night. The Giants rallied for five runs in the bottom of the seventh inning, chasing McDevitt. However, Labine and Roebuck managed to preserve the victory.

The Giants gave the Dodgers another downward nudge on Thursday night. The Dodgers led four to three after five and one-half innings. But the Giants scored three times in the bottom of the sixth inning, and added three more in the eighth, claiming a nine to four victory.

Podres won the opener of a four game series with the Pirates easily enough on Friday, August sixteenth, four to one. But the Pirates overcame an early three to nothing Dodger lead on Saturday, winning seven to three. Snider's thirtieth home run in the seventh inning gave Maglie a two to one victory in the first game of a doubleheader on Sunday, August eighteenth. His thirty-first homer tied the second game at four to four in the seventh inning. The Pirates scored four in the top of the eighth. Pittsburgh held on to win, eight to six. Hodges opened the ninth with a home run. The rally fell short. Ironically, the last place Pirates were the first team to win ten games against Brooklyn in its final season.

MORE ON THE MOVE

The Dodgers had a day off on Monday, August nineteenth. Across town, the New York Giants officially declared that they were moving to San Francisco that afternoon. O'Malley told anxious reporters, "Nothing has happened to the Dodgers. There's no announcement to make." However, he said he intended to confront city officials with the facts of the deal that lured the Giants to San Francisco compared with his own prerequisites for keeping the Dodgers in Brooklyn:

> There is hardly any comparison. Whether the people want to consider me a villain or not, they have to admit that no one has ever offered what the Brooklyn club is offering, in its desire to stay in New York. If the land near Atlantic and Flatbush Avenues can be made available properly, and at a common-sense figure, we have a standing offer to put $5,000,000 into a new stadium, and to pay an annual rental of $500,000 plus a New York City amusement tax of 5 percent of the gross admissions. We only need the help of the City in condemning the land. If all efforts fail locally, the Dodgers

could buy the land on which to build a new stadium in Los Angeles, which will be on the tax rolls there.

On both coasts negotiations concerning the future of the club were continuing. Mayor Wagner offered the full cooperation of the City. O'Malley conceded to Moses that the cost of build a new stadium would be higher than the five million dollars he had to offer up front. The City Board of Estimates put the cost of constructing a new facility anywhere in Brooklyn at a minimum of fifty million dollars. The cost of the stadium alone would be seven million, and nine million if the stadium was domed. But O'Malley proclaimed, "The Dodgers are prepared to sell a bond issue to the Citizens of Brooklyn, backed by the full faith and credit of the Dodger franchise, and to show games on subscription Television. I have no doubt, Mr. Moses, none whatsoever, about our ability to finance ourselves." He told reporters once again that the Flushing Meadows site favored by Moses was, "a great place for a new stadium. Not for the Dodgers though. Fans in Brooklyn couldn't get there."

MEANWHILE IN LA

Los Angeles did not have a suitable ballpark. Either the Coliseum or Wrigley Field, home of the Pacific Coast League Los Angeles Angels, would have to be renovated. Harold McClellan, millionaire paint manufacturer, and former Assistant Secretary of Commerce, was the primary negotiator for Los Angeles. He favored the construction of a new stadium at Chavez Ravine. The Dodgers' request for a 350 acres was a major stumbling block. McClellan told the LA City Council that the city did not own 350 acres in the designated area. The Dodgers' original request had been for 200 acres. The new Giants' Stadium in San Francisco was being built on a 90 acre site. There were other questions to be resolved. "Who gets what, concessions, parking, and the like?" McClellan asked. "Where, and when, are the returns due? We want the Dodgers to come, but it has to be an equitable plan before we'll consider it. The worst thing that could happen wouldn't be to have the proposed transfer fail, but to wind up with a bad deal. I'm not going to give away the City Hall to get them here."

DODGERS PREPARE FOR STRETCH RUN

With six games left to play against first place Milwaukee, the Dodgers still had a mathematical chance to win their third straight pennant. Showing the competitive nature that had won them four of the last five league titles, Brooklyn put themselves into position to make a run at Milwaukee. They swept three games from Cincinnati at Ebbets Field. The opener of a doubleheader on Tuesday, August twentieth, lasted three hours and six minutes before the Dodgers won, eleven to five. Alston complained that Sanchez, the Reds starter and a key figure in the July brawl between the two clubs, was throwing a spitter. Umpire Dusty Boggess, however, found no conclusive evidence. Chased after yielding four Brooklyn runs in the eighth inning, the Cuban right hander was loudly booed. He angrily tossed his glove into the crowd as he approached the Reds' dugout. Snider hit his thirty-second homer. The Brooklyn center fielder hit his thirty-third homer in the twelfth inning of the second game, giving the Dodgers a six to five victory. That game lasted three hours and thirty-two minutes. It was allowed to continue past the normal league 12:50 a.m. curfew, finishing at 1:07 a.m. In a final tuneup for the incoming Braves, the Dodgers showed no signs of fatigue from the previous days grueling doubleheader, blasting Cincinnati in support of a five hit shutout by Newcombe, eight to nothing, on Wednesday night.

FINAL SHOWDOWN SERIES IN BROOKLYN

On Thursday August twenty-second at Ebbets Field, the Braves quickly avoided the possibility of the sweep the Dodgers desperately needed, winning the opener of a three game series, six to one. Aaron homered off Maglie in the first with two aboard.

On the brink of elimination, Brooklyn trailed two to nothing in the top of the eighth inning on Friday night. With the bases loaded and one out, Roebuck struck out Aaron and Mathews, ending the inning. Amoros doubled off the right field screen to open the ninth inning. Neal singled him home. Furillo and Zimmer walked to load the bases. Cimoli then singled sharply to center driving in two runs, giving the Dodgers a three to two victory.

The Braves held a commanding eight to three lead on Saturday. But Hodges and Snider both homered in a desperate four run seventh inning rally, cutting the Milwaukee lead to a single run. Burdette held the Dodgers scoreless over the last two innings, however. And the Braves scored five more in the ninth inning. The final score was thirteen to seven.

With the bases loaded, and two out in the ninth inning, on Sunday, August twenty-fifth, Maglie, the fourth Dodger pitcher, struck out

Cardinal third baseman Ken Boyer on three pitches, preserving a six to five Dodger win. After the game, the Dodgers traded the veteran right hander to the Yankees for thirty seven thousand dollars and two minor league players to be named later. The "sale" of Maglie was widely viewed as a concession of the pennant to the Braves.

On Tuesday night at Ebbets Field, Chicago shortstop Ernie Banks stroked his thirtieth home run, a three-run shot off Dodger starter Newcombe in the first inning. Newcombe stormed off the mound to a chorus of boos after being removed. The Dodgers lost, nine to four.

CARL FURILLO NIGHT

On Wednesday, August twenty-eighth, "Carl Furillo night" ceremonies at Ebbets Field delayed the start of the game for more than forty minutes. The game itself took fourteen innings. It lasted four hours and fourteen minutes. Furillo responded with two hits. Brooklyn won, four to three. Roebuck pitched nine scoreless innings in relief. Valo, pinch hitting for Cimoli, delivered the game-winning single at exactly 1 a.m.

THE GIANTS FINAL VISIT

In the Friday night opener of the final Dodger-Giant series ever at Ebbets Field, Brooklyn romped to a ten to nothing win behind a three hitter by Drysdale. Only three Giants got as far as second base. It was the Brooklyn mound staff's sixteenth shutout of the season. Hodges hit his sixth home run in eleven games. Neal and Furillo also homered. Snider left the game in the sixth. He had continuing soreness in his left knee. Campanella was forced out of the line-up also, after injuring his right thumb in the pre-game infield practice.

The Dodgers closed out August, defeating the Giants again, seven to five on Saturday. Reliever Roebuck, who stopped the Giants over the last three and one-third innings, singled with two out in the sixth inning to touch off a two-run rally. Brooklyn took a six to five lead. Roebuck homered in the eighth inning, providing the Dodgers with an insurance run.

SEPTEMBER

The Giants won the final game between the two clubs ever played in Brooklyn on Sunday, September first, seven to five. Brooklyn scored three runs in the ninth. With two out in the last inning, and Furillo on first, Umpire Boggess ruled Campanella out on a called third strike, ending the game abruptly. Campanella, who ducked away from the pitch, argued vehemently that the pitch was inside.

As 18,895 fans watched, the Phillies won both ends of a double-header at Ebbets Field on Monday night, collecting a season-high seventeen hits off Dodger pitching in a ten to four triumph in the first game. They had fourteen more hits in a seven to four victory in the nightcap. Snider hit his thirty-fifth homer in the opener, and his thirty-sixth in the second game.

DODGERS TOP MILLION MARK IN FINAL AT ROOSEVELT STADIUM

10,190 Dodger fans at Roosevelt Stadium watched the final Dodger game ever on Tuesday night, September third, putting the Dodgers over the one million mark in attendance for the thirteenth straight year. Philadelphia completed the sweep with a three to two triumph. Phillies' outfielder Harry Anderson homered with an man on, and two out, in the ninth, tying the score. Drysdale battled Jack Sanford, who allowed just three Dodger hits, even through eleven innings. Shortstop Chico Fernandez tripled in the twelfth. Willie Jones, pinch hitting for the pitcher, Dick Farrell, scored Fernandez with a sacrifice fly to Snider, giving the Phillies their sixth straight triumph over the Dodgers.

In the seven games at Jersey City, the Dodgers drew 117,678 fans, averaging 16,811. Jersey City Commissioner of Parks, Bernard C. Berry, announced that he had offered the use of Roosevelt Stadium in 1958, part-time or full time, to the Philadelphia Phillies, Cincinnati Reds, and Pittsburgh Pirates. None of the three teams responded to the offer.

In the opener of their final extended road trip on Wednesday, September fourth, the Dodgers finally defeated the Phillies, twelve to three, in Philadelphia. Hodges hit his twenty-fifth home run with two men on in a seven run eighth inning. On Thursday evening, Erskine won for the fourth time in five starts, three to one.

THE END OF A CLASSIC RIVALRY FROM THE DODGERS' PERSPECTIVE

21,373 watched the opener of Brooklyn's final series ever at the Polo Grounds on Friday night. Podres shut out New York, three to nothing. Valo's three-run homer, in the first inning, provided all the scoring. On Saturday the Dodgers tripped the Giants, five to four. Snider, back in the lineup, hit a three-run Homer in the sixth inning, his thirty-seventh of the year. Roger Craig pitched five scoreless innings in relief. The victory was the twelfth for Brooklyn in twenty-one meetings with New York, clinching the season series between the two clubs, with one game left to play.

The first regular season game ever played between Brooklyn and New York opened the National League season at the Polo Grounds on April twentieth, 1901. Brooklyn won, three to two. The *New York Times* reported, "The score does not fully tell how close, and interesting the game was."

22,376 watched as the last game of the most fascinating rivalry in baseball history was played at the Polo Grounds on September eighth, 1957. The score was again three to two. This time the Giants won a brief, final encounter in just one hour and fifty-three minutes. Gilliam homered in the second inning, following a two out walk to pitcher Drysdale. Giants' Left fielder Sauer homered off the left field scoreboard in the fourth, capping a three-run New York rally, and closing out the scoring. The game may have meant more to the Dodgers, who were technically still in the pennant race. The contest, itself, was worthy of the great rivalry, producing the best elements of any baseball game: sparkling defense, timely hitting, and good pitching.

On Tuesday, September tenth, in Chicago, Ernie "let's play two" Banks hit his ninth and tenth home runs of the year off Brooklyn pitching, leading the Cubs to a nine to two win. Looking ahead to the last-ditch show down in Milwaukee, Podres gained a split for the Dodgers, defeating Chicago nine to one, on Wednesday night, despite another home run by Banks. The Dodgers collected fifteen hits. Podres, himself, had two.

LAST DITCH SHOWDOWN WITH MILWAUKEE AND THE UMPIRES

Leading the Dodgers by seven games, the Braves clearly established themselves as a team of destiny, winning a two to one decision behind Bob Buhl on Thursday, September twelfth, that was controversial, even bizarre.

A sacrifice fly by Neal brought home the first Dodger run in the top of the second inning. Pafko singled home Mathews with the tying run in the bottom half of the inning. With one out in the top of the fourth inning, Neal singled. Campanella and McDevitt walked, loading the bases. Gilliam followed, hitting a sinking liner to right. When Pafko appeared to make a diving catch off his shoe tops, Neal tagged and scored the apparent go-ahead run. Campanella held at second. However, right field umpire Ed Sudol claimed that Pafko had trapped the ball, overruling second base umpire Hal Nixon. Nixon had made the out signal. In the confusion, Schoendienst tagged Campanella, and stepped on the bag at second for a inning ending double play. Neal's run didn't count. After a consultation among the umpires, the "no catch" ruling was upheld. General Manager Bavasi made a gesture of disgust from a box near the Brooklyn dugout.

With the score still tied, one to one, Reese singled to open the top of the ninth inning. Snider hit a two out double into the right field corner. But Reese, representing the potential go-ahead run, stumbled rounding third and had to retreat to third. Hodges struck out to end the inning.

After Logan walked to open the bottom of the ninth, Wes Covington fouled off two unsuccessful bunt attempts. Covington then called for time. Umpire Boggess granted his request. McDevitt had not seen the umpire grant time and threw a pitch. Covington, staying in the box, grounded sharply to third. Gilliam handled it easily, turning an apparent double play. Boggess, however, who had his differences with the Dodgers all season, nullified the play. He ruled that time had been called. There was more ranting from the Dodgers' bench. Someone threw a towel out of the dugout. Given a second chance, Covington singled. Logan raced to third on the hit, and scored the winning run on a sacrifice fly by catcher Del Crandall.

BAVASI FILES A PROTEST

In frustration, Bavasi implored league President Giles to order the game replayed:

> In the interest of justice, and the integrity of baseball, action should be taken in fairness to all clubs in contention for the pennant.

Giles failed to overturn the ruling. The loss overshadowed a strong effort by McDevitt who struck out seven, enabling the Dodger staff to break its own National League record of 817 set in 1953.

The Dodgers won pyrrhic victories in the final two games of the series, five to one, and seven to one. Furillo had four RBIs in the two games. Hodges went three for four in the last game, hitting his twenty-sixth home run of the season. The Dodgers won the final battle, but

Milwaukee won the season series, twelve games to ten. A series sweep would have left the Dodgers just four games out of first. Over 113,000 fans watched the three games at County Stadium.

Moving on to Cincinnati on Sunday, September fifteenth, the dispirited club committed four errors, losing eleven to six, despite Snider's thirty-eighth homer. In a three to two loss on Monday night, Roebuck walked in the winning run in the tenth inning.

Before the Dodger game in St. Louis of Tuesday, September seventeenth, Cardinal manager Fred Hutchinson said, "We think we can win the pennant." Just three games back of the Braves, the Cardinals rallied past the Dodgers, scoring seven runs in the seventh to win, twelve to seven, before 24,000 fans at Busch Stadium. They clinched second place.

DODGERS PLAY SPOILERS ROLE

On Thursday, September eighteenth, in the last game of any pennant race significance for Brooklyn, the Dodgers played spoilers, defeating St. Louis, six to one. Drysdale gained his sixteenth victory. He reduced his already impressive ERA to 2.67.

KEEP THE DODGERS IN BROOKLYN

After conferring with O'Malley, other baseball officials, and Mayor Wagner, Nelson Rockefeller made a last-minute offer to purchase a percentage of the Dodgers. He wanted to participate in the building of a new stadium. Both Mayor Wagner and Republican Mayoral candidate Robert Christenberry both praised Rockefeller's action. "It is fortunate," said Christenberry, "that you as a private citizen stepped in to prevent further municipal deterioration. The matter should have been handled more effectively by the Wagner Administration."

"Mr. Christenberry is trying to manufacture political capital," replied the Mayor. "Everybody is anxious to keep the Dodgers in Brooklyn. We are very grateful to Mr. Rockefeller for his interest." Donald O'Toole, Deputy State Commissioner of Commerce suggested that the City acquire Fort Hamilton as a site for the new stadium proposed by Rockefeller.

THE SMALLEST HOME CROWD

The lame duck franchise began it's final home stand on Friday evening, September twentieth. Early in the afternoon, the Dodgers were officially eliminated from the pennant race by a nine to three Milwaukee victory in Chicago. The smallest crowd of the year, 6,749, watched Hodges hit his twenty-seventh, and final, homer of the year with Cimoli on board in the first. Erskine took a two to one lead over the Phillies into the top of the ninth. With a runner on third, and one out, Zimmer, finishing out the season at short in place of the popular Reese, fielded a slow roller barehanded. His throw to the plate was late. The tying run scored. After Stan Lopata then singled to center, Snider's throw to the plate was in time. Campanella appeared to have tagged Hamner out. Umpire Vic Delmore, however, ruled Hamner safe, turning aside Campanella's protest. Philadelphia won, three to two.

A final Ladies Day crowd of 12,000, watched Podres take a two to one lead into the ninth inning on Saturday. But successive doubles by the Phillies' catcher Granny Hamner and right fielder Bob Bowman tied the score. For the second time in four games, Roebuck walked in the winning run. In the final day game at Ebbets Field on Sunday, September twenty-second, the Dodgers defeated Philadelphia, seven to three. Drysdale posted his seventeenth, and final, victory of the season. Rookie first baseman Jim Gentile hit his first major league homer.

SNIDER SETS HOMER, RBI MARKS

Snider hammered his thirty-ninth and fortieth home runs of the year, tying Ralph Kiner's National League record of forty or more homers in each of five consecutive seasons. Snider also passed the one thousand career RBI milestone. Only three active National Leaguer players had more: Gil Hodges, Stan Musial, and Del Ennis. The Dodger win snapped a streak of eight straight Phillies' victories at Ebbets Field.

THE END

New York Times' columnist Arthur Daley wrote in his September twenty-second column:

> The richest of all baseball legends is the one that has flowered in Flatbush. It cannot be transplanted to alien soil, such as Los Angeles. It's a tree that grew in Brooklyn, a nut tree, if you will. There it must forever remain, gnarled and withered from lack of nutrition and affectionate care. The Dodgers are indigenous to Brooklyn. When, and if, they go, they must leave the glorious legend behind. 'Everything

happens to Brooklyn,' is the oldest, and truest, of baseball maxims. Name one zany, or out of the ordinary, happening. The odds are a million to one that the Dodgers were involved in it.

HODGES, CAMPANELLA, KOUFAX HONORED AT FINAL GAME IN BROOKLYN

Before the final game ever played at forty-four year old Ebbets Field on Tuesday, September twenty-fourth, Hodges, Campanella, and Koufax were honored by the National Conference of Christians and Jews. Although each received an inscribed humidor, the ceremony didn't seem to have any added significance. Most of the 6,702 fans were curiously reserved. Some were, seemingly, resigned to losing the Dodgers. Others, perhaps, just refused to accept or couldn't accept that it was really the last game.

CIMOLI SCORES FINAL RUN

Gilliam walked in the opening inning. He scored on Valo's double off the right field wall. Cimoli singled in the third inning. He scored the final Dodger run ever scored at Ebbets Field on a single by Hodges. That was enough for McDevitt who shut out Pittsburgh, two to nothing. Zimmer had two of just five hits allowed by Pittsburgh rookie Bennie Daniels. The experience had a déjà vu quality for Elmer Valo, who had also played in the final game for the 1954 Philadelphia A's.

Between innings, organist Gladys Goodding played numerous appropriate selections: *Am I Blue, After You're Gone, Thanks for the Memories, Que Sera Sera, When I Grow Too Old to Dream, How Can You Say We're Through, Don't Ask Me Why I'm Leaving,* and *When the Blue of the Night Meets the Gold of the Day.* When Pee Wee Reese at third base cleanly handled Pirate first baseman Dee Fondy's grounder in the ninth, and threw to Hodges at first for the final out, Goodding affectionately played *May the Lord Bless You and Keep You,* competing with the recorded tune, *Follow the Dodgers* that always played after Dodger games. She concluded with *Auld Lang Syne.* Fondy remembers: "There was no rush to tear the place apart like there was at the Polo Grounds a few days later. The fans treated the game like any other." The Pirates were the visitors in the final Giants' game in New York as well, winning nine to one.

Stadium announcer, Tex Rickards calmly intoned the usual post game instructions, "Please do not go onto the playing field. Use any exit that leads to the street." Optimistically, the grounds crew perfunctorily raked the infield, covered the mound and home plate, performing all the other routine chores done in preparation for the next game.

There was no notice of the final game in Brooklyn on the front page of the September twenty-fifth edition of the *New York Times*. There were, however, quotes from the Dodgers' manager. and longtime favorites in the sports section. "When I came here, I heard this was a tough town, that the fans could get on you. But they treated me good. I'm slow making friends. When I make them, I hate to leave them," said Alston." Reese echoed his manager. "I don't think any ballplayer anywhere ever had better treatment than I had in Brooklyn." "It was a funny feeling. Every play you watched, you realized that you'll never see the same thing at Ebbets Field again," said Erskine. "It's an eerie feeling," agreed Duke Snider.

There was no baseball in New York in either league on Monday, September twenty-third. At Yankee Stadium, Carmen Basilio defeated Sugar Ray Robinson on a split decision to win the World Middle Weight Championship. There was, however, baseball at County Stadium in Milwaukee. At 11:34 P.M. Hank Aaron of the Braves followed a two out single by Johnny Logan in the bottom of the eleventh inning with his forty-third homer. The 400 foot blast cleared the center field fence to defeat the second place Cardinals, four to two. 40,926 fans celebrated. The win clinched the National League pennant. Former Giant Red Schoendienst singled in the bottom of the seventh and scored the tying run on a double by Mathews. As Braves' owner Perini left the stadium, the words embroidered on a dress handkerchief in his left suit pocket read, "Life is Sweet". Wisconsin Governor Vernon Thomson wired President and Mrs. Eisenhower, and Vice President and Mrs. Nixon an invitation to the World Series opener in Milwaukee. It read, "We would enjoy the opportunity to show you the unexcelled hospitality of our state, and the unmatched spirit, and ability of our Milwaukee Braves." For the first time in seven years, the National League representative in the World Series would not be either the Dodgers or the Giants.

CAMPANELLA SETS ENDURANCE MARK

On a chilly Friday evening, September twenty-seventh, the Phillies beat the Dodgers in Philadelphia, three to two, clinching the season series with Brooklyn for the first time since 1952. Sanford, the National League strikeout leader, fanned nine Dodgers. Only a two-run homer by Amoros in the top of the ninth avoided a shutout. Campanella set a National League record, having caught one hundred games in nine straight seasons.

FINAL VICTORY—FINAL GAME

Brooklyn posted its final victory on Saturday afternoon, defeating the Phillies, eight to four, before a crowd of 18,789 in Philadelphia. Reserve third baseman Randy Jackson's three-run homer capped a five run third inning.

The Dodgers lost their final game as representatives of the Borough of Brooklyn, two to one, on Sunday, September twenty-ninth. Uninspired, they lost to a left hander for the first time all season. Twenty-three year old rookie Seth Morehead, making his first major league start, held the Dodgers to just four hits.

Cimoli singled to open the game, went to third on a single by Furillo. He scored Brooklyn's last run ever on a sacrifice fly by Hodges. It was the ninety eighth RBI of the season for Hodges. Because Phillies' left fielder Harry Anderson misplayed Furillo's hit, he was charged with an error. Thus the final Dodgers' run was scored as unearned. Hodges had the distinction of driving in the final run for the Dodgers both at home and on the road. The Dodgers finished in third place, eleven games back of the new National League Champion Milwaukee Braves, and three games back of the second place St. Louis Cardinals.

The Braves defeated the American League New York Yankees in a seven game World Series, becoming the first team in history to rally from a three games to one deficit.

Walter O'Malley finalized his agreements with Los Angeles. He announced that the beloved Dodgers were, in fact, turning their backs on the Borough of Brooklyn.

New York Times' columnist Daley noted:

> And a bitter end it was for those faithful Brooklyn fans who enabled the Dodgers to amass a profit of $1,800,000 over a five-year span. That's the one ugly, and inescapable fact that sets this deal apart from all the other franchise transfers. Other teams were forced to move by apathy or incompetence. The only word that fits the Dodgers is greed.
>
> Baseball is a sport, eh? It may be for Tom Yawkey of the Red Sox, Phil Wrigley of the Cubs, and one or two others. The crass commercialism of O'Malley and Horace Stoneham of the

Giants presents the disillusioning fact that it's big business, just another way to make a buck.

Baseball cannot be run with the coldness of an I.B.M. machine. It has to be run with heart, and sentiment, and emotion, or maybe we've been worshiping false gods for these many years.

International League President, Frank Shaughnessy approached Baseball Commissioner Ford Frick about putting a Triple-A team in Brooklyn. "We were told we couldn't go in there," he said. Frick told reporters that New York was now an American League territory. "It would take consent of the American League clubs to permit a team to invade that territory," he said.

Razing of Ebbets Field began on February twenty-third, 1960 to make way for a twenty-two million dollar housing project, the largest of its kind in any of New York's five boroughs, to be built by the Kratter Corporation. New York Times' columnist Gay Talese eloquently reported:

> An iron ball crashed, like Pete Reiser, against the wall. After forty-four years as the home of the Dodgers, and a monument to daffiness, the park began to vanish. 200 spectators, and some former Brooklyn Dodger players gathered to watch a two ton iron ball hammer against this arena where, between 1913 and 1957, baseball was played in a manner never before imagined or recommended. It was here that a fan once exclaimed, 'We got three men on base.' His neighbor asked, 'Which base?' It was here that Leo Durocher snarled, and Hilda Chester cheered. A little lady always bought one seat for herself, and one for her grey tabby cat that sat behind first base and slept.

The wrecking ball was decorated like a baseball for the occasion. Appropriately, the flag was raised upside down, an international sign of distress. Lucy Munroe sang the National Anthem on this chilly bleak February day as she had many times before Dodger games.

Roy Campanella, Carl Erskine, Tommy Holmes, and old catcher Otto Miller, who caught the first game at the park on April ninth, 1913 were present for the nostalgic occasion. A band played. Public address announcer Tex Rickards performed his task one final time, "Ladies and Gentlemen, now coming in to pitch for the Dodgers, number thirteen. Ralph Branca." Branca, an insurance salesman in a camel's hair coat, emerged from the crowd, smiling. Campanella, at home plate in a wheel chair, was awarded his locker, his familiar number thirty-nine uniform, and a pot full of Ebbets Field dirt.

At a past game on a hot August afternoon Rickards announced in true Brooklynese malapropos worthy of comedian Norm Crosby, "Will the fans along the railing in left field please remove their clothes." The Brooklyn fans were noted for hanging white clothing, including shirts, and underwear, along the left field railing to distract opposition batters. They understood they were not being asked to disrobe. Such curious moments were very much a part of the Ebbets Field experience.

Harry Avirom, the President of the Wrecking Corporation of America, a die hard Dodger fan, oversaw the destruction insisting he was "not insensitively tearing up Ebbets Field." He told reporters that almost everything, including flagpoles, railings, stadium seats, dugout telephones and benches, clubhouse locker, and other souvenirs items were available to fans. "Some people might like this stuff for a game room or patio. They just have to come out to the ballpark to get them. Even Giant fans are welcome." Avirom would also supervise the destruction of the Polo Grounds four years later.

THE SYM-PHONEY BAND

The comical top hatted seven piece Sym-phoney Band was a part of an evening's entertainment at Ebbets Field. The band's dual purpose since its formation in 1938 was to amuse the crowd and harass opposing players. Brother Lou Soriano on snare drum, a civilian driver for the First Army stationed on Governors Island by day, served as the Sym-Phoney conductor. Pat Palma, a beer distributor, played the bass drum. William "Cally" Califano, a student at Brooklyn's Lafayette High School, played tenor sax. Ziggy Rullo, a lithographer, played trumpet. Frank Ambro, a Parks Department employee, played clarinet. Louis Dallojacono, a Williamsburg Savings Bank clerk, crashed the cymbals during tunes like *How Dry I Am* and when an opposition player sat down, and Pete Dellaiacono, Parks Department tree pruner and former amateur lightweight boxing champion, played trombone. All seven were from the Greenpoint section of Brooklyn.

Longtime band member, Shorty Laurice, who joined the Sym-Phoney as a trombonist in 1941, died in 1954. Courtesy of Dodger business manager, Harold F. Parrott, the band always sat in Section eight, row one, seats one through seven, midway between Catcher Campanella and Hodges at first.

The Sym-Phoney did not travel. "We went to Jersey City once last year," said Brother Lou. "There's no fans over there. What they didn't throw at us! What they didn't say to us! So now we stay out." If they tormented the opposition players, the Sym-Phoney didn't razz umpires. "We used to play *Three Blind Mice* when the umpires took the field (a tradition started by the organist Gladys Goodding) but now they got four umps. What!—we can't come up with the fourth mouse. So Na, we leave 'em alone." If we don't, they holler at us," said Brother Lou. The band faded into history along with their beloved "bums".

DEMOLITION OF EBBETTS FIELD

It would take ten weeks to destroy Ebbets Field. 2,200 seats from the old park were donated along with some of the lights to the baseball field at the Hart Island prison facility off the Bronx. Inmates would sit on the memory soaked seats in a new setting, during future summers, watching the Hart Island Wildcats play.

At the end of the demolition, the 1000-pound Ebbets Field corner-stone was broken open with a sledge hammer in front of about 600 sentimental spectators on April twenty-fourth, 1960. The stone, simply inscribed, "Ebbets Field–1912" contained a time capsule—a copper box filled with newspapers, baseball publications, personal cards, coins and other mementos of the day it was placed, July sixth, 1912. The moisture dampened periodicals made reference to Mayor William J. Gaynor, President William Howard Taft, and the Brooklyn Superbas baseball team. Auctioneer Saul Leisner had already sold the corner-stone to National League President Warren Giles for $600. Giles intended to bequeath the stone to the Baseball Hall of Fame. The stone may have been forgotten, except for the memory of a sixty-three-year-old New York building inspector, Edward A. Duval, who had been present on the misty morning when Colonel Charles H. Ebbets laid the stone. Duval recalled that Ebbets swore he'd never leave the place until his team won a championship. The Brooklyn Dodgers won their only World Championship, thirty years after his death in 1925.

Prior to this last official ceremony at the old park, an assortment of items were sold at auction, including pictures, signs, bases, and auto-graphed balls and bats. Flower pots filled with infield dirt were given away to those in attendance. And as a part of the preliminary build up to the opening of the real corner stone, workers exploded a dummy block and five circus clowns emerged wearing Dodger uniforms. It was an ignoble but somehow appropriately bizarre farewell to the ballpark, that, more than any other, has come to symbolize baseball in the 1950s.

In time it would seem normal to see the Dodgers playing in Los Angeles. "They are going to be very big out here," said comedian Bob

Hope. "I can't wait to see Duke Snider in a bare-midriff uniform". The Los Angeles Dodgers have been enormously successful. But the Dodger tree was nourished, and grew, in Brooklyn. Few professional sports teams have ever had the kind of bond with a community that the Brooklyn Dodgers did. Emmett Kelly, the sad but loyal Ringling Brothers clown, announced that he didn't intend to accompany the team to Los Angeles, telling reporters that the Los Angeles Coliseum was "too big for one clown."

The old Ebbets Field site is now the site of the Jackie Robinson Apartments, a curious if fitting tribute to the former Dodger legend.

When National League Baseball returned to New York for the 1962 baseball season, the fledgling New York Mets wore uniforms trimmed in both Dodger blue and Giant Orange. In 1964 the Mets moved from their temporary home at the Polo Grounds into a new ballpark, Shea Stadium, at Flushing Meadows, seven years after Robert Moses proposed that site as a home for the Dodgers.

Forty-two years later, O'Malleys choice of sites, the Long Island Railroad terminal site, at Atlantic and Flatbush avenues, remains undeveloped.

It is impossible to overstate or forget the importance of the Dodgers to the community of Brooklyn. Today, on Third Avenue in the Bay Ridge section of Brooklyn, there is a Brooklyn Dodger bar. On one wall there is a huge mural of Ebbets Field. On another there is a reproduction of the famous "Hit Sign, Win Suit" sign that made up part of the right field fence. Jackie Robinson's bat is also there.

O'Malley, and the Dodgers, bad guys to the end in Brooklyn, unsuccessfully sued the bar owners, Kevin and Brian Doyle, for trademark infringement in 1989. "They shoulda never picked a fight with Brooklyn," said Kevin. "I was born a short time after the Dodgers and the New York Giants pulled their two-team gold rush to California. So I grew up with second hand heartache. I had to listen to the stories. Brooklyn has two million people, and as many characters. The borough took its pain, absorbed it, and made it part of its lore."

The pain still lingers. No other former team has been so lamented. At the Brooklyn Historical Society, visitors are asked to recall memories. One entry reads in part:

> When the Dodgers left, I was nineteen. I've since become
> a priest, and God forgive me, I didn't pray for Walter O'Malley
> when he went to our maker.

DAY	DATE	OPPONENT	RESULT	SCORE	PITCHER	ATTENDANCE	RECORD
TUES	04/16/57	AT PHILADELPHIA	W	7-6 (12)	CLEM LABINE (1-0)	37667	1-0
THURS	04/18/57	PITTSBURGH	W	6-1	SAL MAGLIE (1-0)	11202	2-0
SAT	04/20/57	PITTSBURGH	W	2-0	JOHNNY PODRES (1-0)	15939	3-0
SUN	04/21/57	PITTSBURGH	L	6-3	DON NEWCOMBE (0-1)	19635	3-1
SUN	04/21/57	PITTSBURGH	W	7-4	DON DRYSDALE (1-0)	19635	4-1
MON	04/22/57	PHILADELPHIA JC	W	5-1	ROGER CRAIG (1-0)	11629	5-1
WED	04/24/57	NEW YORK	W	4-3	RENE VALDES (1-0)	21998	6-1
THURS	04/25/57	NEW YORK	PPD RAIN				
FRI	04/26/57	AT PITTSBURGH	L	7-1	JOHNNY PODRES (1-1)	26918	6-2
SAT	04/27/57	AT PITTSBURGH	W	6-2	DON NEWCOMBE (1-1)	12826	7-2
SUN	04/28/57	AT PITTSBURGH	L	3-0	ROGER CRAIG (1-1)	11317	7-3
TUES	04/30/57	CHICAGO	W	10-9 (10)	DON BESSENT(1-0)	8379	8-3
WED	05/01/57	CHICAGO	W	7-2	DON DRYSDALE (2-0)	3214	9-3
THURS	05/02/57	ST LOUIS	L	3-2 (16)	DON BESSENT (1-1)	8311	9-4
FRI	05/03/57	ST LOUIS JC	W	6-0	DON NEWCOMBE (2-1)	14470	10-4
SAT	05/04/57	ST LOUIS	W	4-2	CLEM LABINE (2-0)	9423	11-4
SUN	05/05/57	MILWAUKEE	L	10-7	RENE VALDES (1-1)	26599	11-5
MON	05/06/57	MILWAUKEE	W	5-4 (14)	SANDY KOUFAX (1-0)	15885	12-5
TUES	05/07/57	CINCINNATI	L	9-2	JOHNNY PODRES (1-2)	9830	12-6
WED	05/08/57	CINCINNATI	L	7-6	DON NEWCOMBE (2-2)	10820	12-7
FRI	05/10/57	AT NEW YORK	L	2-1	SAL MAGLIE (1-1)	34435	12-8
SAT	05/11/57	AT NEW YORK	L	6-5 (15)	DON BESSENT (1-2)	7434	12-9
SUN	05/12/57	AT NEW YORK	W	5-0	JOHNNY PODRES (2-2)	17696	13-9
TUES	05/14/57	AT MILWAUKEE	L	3-2	DON NEWCOMBE (2-3)	34731	13-10
WED	05/15/57	AT MILWAUKEE	W	3-2 (10)	CLEM LABINE (3-0)	19599	14-10
THURS	05/16/57	AT CHICAGO	W	3-2	SANDY KOUFAX (2-0)	3105	15-10
FRI	05/17/57	AT CHICAGO	RAIN				
SAT	05/18/57	AT CHICAGO	RAIN				
SUN	05/19/57	AT ST LOUIS	W	10-3	DON NEWCOMBE (3-3)	10482	16-10
MON	05/20/57	AT ST LOUIS	W	10-4	DON DRYSDALE (3-0)	13724	17-10
TUES	05/21/57	AT CINCINNATI	W	6-1	JOHNNY PODRES (3-2)	21036	18-10
WED	05/22/57	AT CINCINNATI	L	8-1	SANDY KOUFAX (2-1)	18624	18-11
THURS	05/23/57	NEW YORK YANKS	L	10-7	MAYORS TROPHY GAME	30000	EXHIB
FRI	05/24/57	NEW YORK	W	6-0	DON NEWCOMBE (4-3)	27299	19-11
SAT	05/25/57	NEW YORK	L	8-7	DON DRYSDALE (3-1)	21607	19-12
SUN	05/26/57	NEW YORK	W	5-3	SANDY KOUFAX (3-1)	22971	20-12
MON	05/27/57	AT PHILADELPHIA	W	5-1	DON DRYSDALE (4-1)	20673	21-12
TUES	05/28/57	AT PITTSBURGH	L	3-2 (11)	DON NEWCOMBE (4-4)	13259	21-13
WED	05/29/57	AT PITTSBURGH	W	1-0	JOHNNY PODRES (4-2)	3610	22-13
THURS	05/30/57	AT PITTSBURGH	W	4-3	SAL MAGLIE (2-1)	24263	23-13
THURS	05/30/57	AT PITTSBURGH	L	2-1	SANDY KOUFAX (3-2)	24263	23-14
FRI	05/31/57	AT PHILADELPHIA	L	2-1	DON DRYSDALE (4-2)	24381	23-15
SAT	06/01/57	AT PHILADELPHIA	L	3-0	ROGER CRAIG (1-2)	30621	23-16
SUN	06/02/57	AT PHILADELPHIA	L	5-3	DON NEWCOMBE (4-5)	20259	23-17
MON	06/03/57	AT PHILADELPHIA	W	4-0	JOHNNY PODRES (5-3)	16218	24-17
TUES	06/04/57	CHICAGO	W	7-5	SANDY KOUFAX (4-2)	9300	25-17
WED	06/05/57	CHICAGO JC	W	4-0	DON DRYSDALE (5-2)	9712	26-17
THURS	06/06/57	CHICAGO	FOG				
FRI	06/07/57	CINCINNATI	W	6-3	ROGER CRAIG (2-2)	22149	27-17
SAT	06/08/57	CINCINNATI	W	9-2	JOHNNY PODRES (6-2)	15841	28-17
SUN	06/09/57	CINCINNATI	L	3-1	DON DRYSDALE (5-3)	33850	28-18
SUN	06/09/57	CINCINNATI	L	3-0	ED ROEBUCK (0-1)	33850	28-19
MON	06/10/57	MILWAUKEE JC	L	3-1	DON NEWCOMBE (4-6)	22412	28-20
TUES	06/11/57	MILWAUKEE	L	7-2	ROGER CRAIG (2-3)	18491	28-21
WED	06/12/57	MILWAUKEE	W	11-9	ED ROEBUCK (1-1)	18180	29-21
THURS	06/13/57	MILWAUKEE	L	8-5	CLEM LABINE (3-1)	14778	29-22
FRI	06/14/57	ST LOUIS	W	2-1	DON NEWCOMBE (5-6)	16341	30-22
SAT	06/15/57	ST LOUIS	L	6-5	ROGER CRAIG (2-4)	18580	30-23

THE 1957 BROOKLYN DODGERS

DAY	DATE	OPPONENT	RESULT	SCORE	PITCHER	ATTENDANCE	RECORD
SUN	06/16/57	ST LOUIS	L	7-6	CLEM LABINE (3-2)	23674	30-24
SUN	06/16/57	ST LOUIS	L	8-4	JOHNNY PODRES (6-3)	23674	30-25
MON	06/17/57	AT CINCINNATI	W	7-2	DANNY MCDEVITT (1-0)	4596	31-25
TUES	06/18/57	AT CINCINNATI	W	7-0	DON NEWCOMBE (6-6)	18551	32-25
WED	06/19/57	AT CINCINNATI	L	4-3	CLEM LABINE (3-3)	18809	32-26
THURS	06/20/57	AT CINCINNATI	L	6-1	ROGER CRAIG (2-5)	18217	32-27
FRI	06/21/57	AT ST LOUIS	L	2-0	DANNY MCDEVITT (1-1)	27972	32-28
SAT	06/22/57	AT ST LOUIS	W	6-4	DON NEWCOMBE (7-6)	19441	33-28
SUN	06/23/57	AT ST LOUIS	L	4-3	DON DRYSDALE (5-4)	27780	33-29
MON	06/24/57	AT ST LOUIS	W	10-3	CARL ERSKINE (1-0)	26416	34-29
TUES	06/25/57	AT MILWAUKEE	W	2-0	DANNY MCDEVITT (2-1)	33901	35-29
WED	06/26/57	AT MILWAUKEE	L	13-9	CLEM LABINE (3-4)	39233	35-30
THURS	06/27/57	AT MILWAUKEE	L	2-1	DON DRYSDALE (5-5)	31051	35-31
FRI	06/28/57	AT CHICAGO	RAIN				
SAT	06/29/57	AT CHICAGO	W	2-1	CARL ERSKINE (2-0)	16653	36-31
SUN	06/30/57	AT CHICAGO	L	3-2 (11)	DON BESSENT (1-3)	29208	36-32
SUN	06/30/57	AT CHICAGO	W	5-1	DANNY MCDEVITT (3-1)	29208	37-32
MON	07/01/57	AT NEW YORK	W	3-0	DON DRYSDALE (6-5)	37409	38-32
TUES	07/02/57	AT NEW YORK	W	6-0	SAL MAGLIE (3-1)	28667	39-32
THURS	07/04/57	PITTSBURGH	L	5-1	CARL ERSKINE (2-1)	20664	39-33
THURS	07/04/57	PITTSBURGH	W	8-2	DON NEWCOMBE (8-6)	20664	40-33
FRI	07/05/57	PHILADELPHIA	W	6-5	ROGER CRAIG (3-5)	13324	41-33
SAT	07/06/57	PHILADELPHIA	L	9-4	DON DRYSDALE (6-6)	11353	41-34
SUN	07/07/57	PHILADELPHIA	L	2-1	SAL MAGLIE (3-2)	16805	41-35
SUN	07/07/57	PHILADELPHIA	L	5-3	CLEM LABINE (3-5)	16805	41-36
TUES	07/09/57	All-Star GAME AT ST LOUIS					
THURS	07/11/57	CINCINNATI	W	5-4	ROGER CRAIG (4-5)	16350	42-36
FRI	07/12/57	CINCINNATI J.C.	W	3-1	DON NEWCOMBE (9-6)	23472	43-36
SAT	07/13/57	CINCINNATI	RAIN				
SUN	07/14/57	MILWAUKEE	W	3-2	JOHNNY PODRES (7-3)	20871	44-36
MON	07/15/57	MILWAUKEE	W	20-4	DON DRYSDALE (7-6)	18262	45-36
TUES	07/16/57	ST LOUIS	W	7-5	CARL ERSKINE (3-1)	15449	46-36
WED	07/17/57	ST LOUIS	L	7-3	DON NEWCOMBE (9-7)	17000	46-37
THURS	07/18/57	ST LOUIS	W	10-9 (11)	ROGER CRAIG (5-5)	17569	47-37
FRI	07/19/57	CHICAGO	W	6-3 (10)	CLEM LABINE (4-5)	28724	48-37
FRI	07/19/57	CHICAGO	W	5-3	SAL MAGLIE (4-2)	28724	49-37
SAT	07/20/57	CHICAGO	W	7-5	DON DRYSDALE (8-6)	14866	50-37
SUN	07/21/57	CHICAGO	L	5-4	CARL ERSKINE (3-2)	13303	50-38
SUN	07/21/57	CHICAGO	W	7-2	CLEM LABINE (5-5)	13303	51-38
TUES	07/23/57	AT ST LOUIS	W	1-0	JOHNNY PODRES (8-3)	29416	52-38
WED	07/24/57	AT ST LOUIS	L	3-0	SAL MAGLIE (4-3)	24347	52-39
THURS	07/25/57	AT ST LOUIS	L	3-2	DON NEWCOMBE (9-8)	27892	52-40
FRI	07/26/57	AT CINCINNATI	L	6-5 (11)	ROGER CRAIG (5-6)	30514	52-41
SAT	07/27/57	AT CINCINNATI	W	5-3	DANNY MCDEVITT (4-1)	19230	53-41
SUN	07/28/57	AT CINCINNATI	W	7-2	JOHNNY PODRES (9-3)	28524	54-41
TUES	07/30/57	AT CHICAGO	W	1-0	SAL MAGLIE (5-3)	15576	55-41
TUES	07/30/57	AT CHICAGO	L	4-3	DON NEWCOMBE (9-9)	15576	55-42
WED	07/31/57	AT CHICAGO	W	3-2	ED ROEBUCK (2-1)	17163	56-42
WED	07/31/57	AT CHICAGO	W	2-1	ED ROEBUCK (3-1)	17163	57-42
THURS	08/01/57	AT CHICAGO	W	12-3	SANDY KOUFAX (5-7)	8075	58-42
FRI	08/02/57	AT MILWAUKEE	L	1-0	JOHNNY PODRES (9-4)	45840	58-43
SAT	08/03/57	AT MILWAUKEE	W	7-1	ED ROEBUCK (4-1)	39368	59-43
SUN	08/04/57	AT MILWAUKEE	L	9-7	SAL MAGLIE (5-4)	43109	59-44
MON	08/05/57	NEW YORK	W	5-2	DON DRYSDALE (9-6)	15070	60-44
TUES	08/06/57	NEW YORK	L	5-0	JOHNNY PODRES (9-5)	18202	60-45
WED	08/07/57	NEW YORK	L	8-5	DON NEWCOMBE (9-10)	25913	60-46
THURS	08/08/57	NEW YORK	L	12-3	SAL MAGLIE (5-5)	18753	60-47
FRI	08/09/57	AT PITTSBURGH	W	4-2	DANNY MCDEVITT (5-1)	14100	61-47

TWILIGHT TEAMS

DAY	DATE	OPPONENT	RESULT	SCORE	PITCHER	ATTENDANCE	RECORD
SAT	08/10/57	AT PITTSBURGH	W	3-0	DON DRYSDALE (10-6)	24751	62-47
SUN	08/11/57	AT PITTSBURGH	L	4-3(10)	CLEM LABINE (5-6)	18350	62-48
SUN	08/11/57	AT PITTSBURGH	L	6-2	ROGER CRAIG (5-7)	18350	62-49
TUES	08/13/57	AT NEW YORK	L	4-2	ED ROEBUCK (4-2)	27234	62-50
WED	08/14/57	AT NEW YORK	W	7-6	DANNY MCDEVITT (6-1)	13704	63-50
THURS	08/15/57	AT NEW YORK	L	9-4	DON DRYSDALE (10-7)	7587	63-51
FRI	08/16/57	PITTSBURGH	W	4-1	JOHNNY PODRES (10-5)	9592	64-51
SAT	08/17/57	PITTSBURGH	L	7-3	SANDY KOUFAX (5-3)	8665	64-52
SUN	08/18/57	PITTSBURGH	W	2-1	SAL MAGLIE (6-5)	14416	65-52
SUN	08/18/57	PITTSBURGH	L	8-6	CLEM LABINE (5-7)	14416	65-53
TUES	08/20/57	CINCINNATI	W	11-5	ED ROEBUCK (5-2)	16132	66-53
TUES	08/20/57	CINCINNATI	W	6-5(12)	DON DRYSDALE (11-7)	16132	67-53
WED	08/21/57	CINCINNATI	W	8-0	DON NEWCOMBE (10-10)	8125	68-53
THURS	08/22/57	MILWAUKEE	L	6-1	SAL MAGLIE (6-6)	19082	68-54
SAT	08/23/57	MILWAUKEE	W	3-2	DON DRYSDALE (12-7)	21945	69-54
SAT	08/24/57	MILWAUKEE	L	13-7	JOHNNY PODRES (10-6)	22671	69-55
SUN	08/25/57	ST LOUIS	W	6-5	DON DRYSDALE (13-7)	10863	70-55
TUES	08/27/57	CHICAGO	L	9-4	DON NEWCOMBE (10-11)	7283	70-56
WED	08/28/57	CHICAGO	W	4-3(14)	ED ROEBUCK (6-2)	18019	71-56
FRI	08/30/57	NEW YORK	W	10-0	DON DRYSDALE (14-7)	16113	72-56
SAT	08/31/57	NEW YORK	W	7-5	ED ROEBUCK (7-2)	14222	73-56
SUN	09/01/57	NEW YORK	L	7-5	JOHNNY PODRES (10-7)	17936	73-57
MON	09/02/57	PHILADELPHIA	L	10-4	DANNY MCDEVITT (6-2)	18895	73-58
MON	09/02/57	PHILADELPHIA	L	7-4	ROGER CRAIG (5-8)	18895	73-59
TUES	09/03/57	PHILADELPHIA JC	L	3-2(12)	DON DRYSDALE (14-8)	10190	73-60
WED	09/04/57	AT PHILADELPHIA	W	12-3	DON NEWCOMBE (11-11)	17615	74-60
THURS	09/05/57	AT PHILADELPHIA	W	3-1	CARL ERSKINE (4-2)	18087	75-60
FRI	09/06/57	AT NEW YORK	W	3-0	JOHNNY PODRES (11-7)	21373	76-60
SAT	09/07/57	AT NEW YORK	W	5-4	ROGER CRAIG (6-8)	11629	77-60
SUN	09/08/57	AT NEW YORK	L	3-2	DON DRYSDALE (14-9)	22376	77-61
TUES	09/10/57	AT CHICAGO	L	9-2	SANDY KOUFAX (5-4)	3489	77-62
WED	09/11/57	AT CHICAGO	W	9-1	JOHNNY PODRES (12-7)	3461	78-62
THURS	09/12/57	AT MILWAUKEE	L	2-1	DANNY MCDEVITT (6-3)	32353	78-63
FRI	09/13/57	AT MILWAUKEE	W	5-1	DON DRYSDALE (15-9)	40637	79-63
SAT	09/14/57	AT MILWAUKEE	W	7-1	CARL ERSKINE (5-2)	40775	80-63
SUN	09/15/57	AT CINCINNATI	L	11-6	DON NEWCOMBE (11-12)	11972	80-64
MON	09/16/57	AT CINCINNATI	L	3-2 (10)	JOHNNY PODRES (12-8)	4351	80-65
TUES	09/17/57	AT ST LOUIS	L	12-5	DANNY MCDEVITT (6-4)	23473	80-66
WED	09/18/57	AT ST LOUIS	W	6-1	DON DRYSDALE (16-9)	22468	81-66
FRI	09/20/57	PHILADELPHIA	L	3-2	CARL ERSKINE (5-3)	6749	81-67
SAT	09/21/57	PHILADELPHIA	L	3-2	JOHNNY PODRES (12-9)	12075	81-68
SUN	09/22/57	PHILADELPHIA	W	7-3	DON DRYSDALE (17-9)	6662	82-68
TUES	09/24/57	PITTSBURGH	W	2-0	DANNY MCDEVITT (7-4)	6702	83-68
FRI	09/27/57	AT PHILADELPHIA	L	3-2	BILL HARRIS (0-1)	11595	83-69
SAT	09/28/57	AT PHILADELPHIA	W	8-4	ED ROEBUCK (8-2)	19789	84-69
SUN	09/29/57	AT PHILADELPHIA	L	2-1	ROGER CRAIG (6-9)	9885	84-70

THE 1971 WASHINGTON SENATORS

Another One Bites The Dust

*First in War, First in Peace, and
Last in the American League.*

A fitting epilogue to the end of the Washington Senators era in the American League occurred on Wednesday evening May 10, 1972. Seven months after the final Senators' game in Washington, the remnants of that team, the Texas Rangers, opened their first series at Memorial Stadium in Baltimore against the American League Champion Orioles. Only a few hundred former fans bothered to mark the homecoming of sorts by traveling thirty-five miles up the expressway from Washington. Some hung signs deriding the Rangers, and club owner Bob Short, throughout the bleachers, and the upper deck.

Short, who transferred the franchise to Texas in 1971, was the target of heckling throughout the night. He felt secure enough to sit in the open with Orioles' owner Jerold Hoffberger behind the first base dugout.

The chilly spring night was relatively uneventful until a young woman came down the aisle, undeterred. She poured a beer over Short's blond hair. Beer spilled over onto his topcoat, and onto Hoffberger as well. Short dried his hair with a towel tossed from the Texas dugout. And two security guards took up residence nearby for the remainder of the evening. Too late, however. The woman had

GRIFFITH STADIUM, WASHINGTON

Bounded by Georgia Avenue, U Street, Fifth Street and W Street NW. Home of the original and expansion American League Senators from 1892 through 1899 and from 1902 until September 21, 1961. (Photo from The National Baseball Library and Archive Collection, Cooperstown, New York and the Martin Luther King Library.)

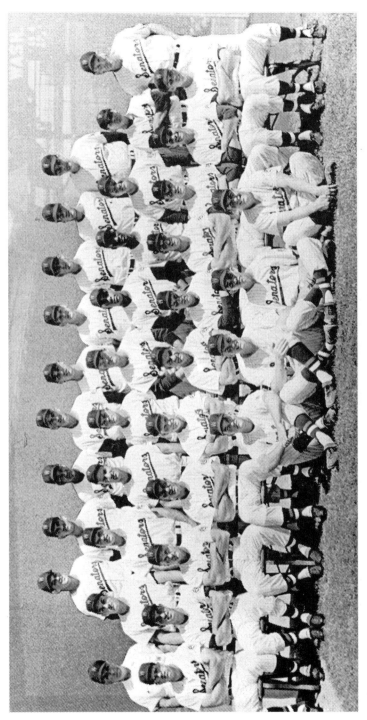

1960 WASHINGTON SENATORS

Front row—Throneberry, Consolo, Clary, coach; Mele, coach: McCullough, coach; Lavagetto, manager; Swift, coach; Allison, Kralick, Hernandez, Lee. **Middle row**—Lentz, trainer; Killebrew, Dobbek, Fischer, Gardner; Whisenant, Battey, Green, Valo, Stobbs, Lemon. **Back row**—Ramos, Pascual, Becquer, Moore, Bertoia, Naragon, Clevenger, Valdivielso, Woodeshick. **Seated in front**—Batboy Baxter and ballboys Frazier, McWhorter, and Hubscher. (Photo from The Sporting News collection, St. Louis, Missouri.)

RFK STADIUM, WASHINGTON

Located at East Capitol and 22nd Streets SE between Independence Avenue and North Carolina Avenue along the Anacostia River. Home of the Washington Senators from April 2, 1962 until September 30, 1971. (Photo from the National Baseball Library and Archive

1971 WASHINGTON SENATORS

Front row—*Howard, Bosman, Hudson, coach; Zarilla, coach; Williams, manager; Burke, vice-president; Fox, coach; Susce, coach; Camacho, coach; Zeigler, trainer; Hawkins, traveling secretary.* **Middle row**—*F. Baxter, equipment manager; Cox, Burroughs, Randle, Harrah, Nelson, Maddox, Shellenback, McCraw, Broberg, Pina.* **Back row**—*Casanova, Lindblad, Thompson, Unser, Allen, Cullen, McLain, Billings, Mincher, Grzenda, Gogolewski, Riddleberger.* **Seated in front**—*Batboys Matheson and E. Baxter.* **Not pictured**—*Coach Wayne Terwilleger. (Photo courtesy of the Texas Rangers Baseball Club and Don Wingfield.)*

President John F. Kennedy throwing out the first ball at the expansion Senators home opener, Monday, April 10, 1961. Vice President Lyndon Johnson is to Kennedy's right and Senators' manager Mickey Vernon is to Kennedy's right. The White Sox won 4–3 before 26,725 fans.

		Games at position	Bats	Avg.		
C	Paul Casanova	83	R	.203	5 HR	
C	Dick Billings	62	R	.246	6 HR	
1B	Don Mincher	88	L	.291	10 HR	
1B	Mike Epstein	24	L	.247		
2B	Tim Cullen	78	R	.191		
2B	Lenny Randle	66	SW	.219		
3B	Dave Nelson	84	SW	**.280**	5 HR	**17 Stolen bases**
3B	Joe Foy	37	R	.234		
LF	Frank Howard	100	R	.279	**26 HR**	**83 RBI**
CF	Del Unser	151	L	.255	9 HR	
RF	Elliott Maddox	103	R	.217		
OF	Jeff Burroughs	50	R	.232	5 HR	
OF	Tommy McCraw	60	L	.213	7 HR	
OF	Larry Biittner	40	L	.257		
OF	Richie Scheinblum	13	SW	.143		
IF	Don Wert	20	R	.050		
SS	Toby Harrah	116	R	.230		
IF	Bernie Allen	97	L	.266		
OF	Curt Flood	13	R	.200		
C	Jim French	14	L	.146		
2B	Frank Fernandez	18	R	.100		
2B	Tom Ragland	10	R	.174		
SS	Jim Mason	3	L	.333		
C	Dick Stelmaszek	6	L	.000		
C	Bill Fahey	2	L	.000		

PITCHERS

R	Dick Bosman	34	W **12**	L 16	3.73 ERA	**113 Strike outs**
R	Denny McLain	33	W 10	L **22***	4.28 ERA	
L	Jim Shellenback	40	W 3	L 11	3.53 ERA	
R	Bill Gogolewski	27	W 6	L 5	2.75 ERA	
R	Pete Broberg	18	W 5	L 9	3.47 ERA	
R	Jackie Brown	14	W 3	L 4	5.94 ERA	
R	Mike Thompson	16	W 1	L 6	4.86 ERA	
R	Jerry Janeski	23	W 1	L 5	4.96 ERA	1 Save

RELIEF PITCHERS

R	Paul Lindblad	43	W 6	L 4	2.58 ERA	**8 Saves**
R	Casey Cox	54	W 5	L 7	3.99 ERA	7 Saves
R	Horacio Pina	56	W 1	L 1	3.59 ERA	2 Saves
R	Joe Grzenda	46	W 5	L 2	**1.92** ERA	5 Saves
L	Denny Riddleberger	57	W 3	L 1	3.21 ERA	1 Save
L	Darold Knowles	12	W 2	L 2	3.52 ERA	2 Saves

MANAGER
Ted Williams W 63 L 96

Bold Type—led club
*Led league

already committed her bold act of civil disobedience in the name of all Senators' fans.

Earlier, another fan of the late Washington team had an usher deliver a hot dog, and a beer, to Mr. Short with her compliments. She told the usher to note that the beer was "cold", and that the hot dog was "hot", implying that wasn't always the case at Short's former home at Robert F. Kennedy Stadium.

The 1971 move marked the first time since the 1903 agreement setting up the dual league structure, that Major League Baseball completely abandoned a charter member city. The general expansion guideline of leaving the stronger franchise in a two team city didn't apply unless the Washington/Baltimore area was considered one market. It also marked the first time since 1900 that any city had lost two franchises.

Calvin Griffith, adopted son of longtime Senators' owner Clark Griffith assumed the ownership of the club after his father died on October twenty-seventh, 1955 at the age of eighty-five. Calvin quickly began maneuvering to move the original Senators out of Washington. He shared Clark's love of the game, and had learned some of his father's management and player acquisition skills. But he did not share his father's love of the City of Washington. The team, which had not had a winning season in ten years, finished last in 1955, and attendance had dipped to a ten year low of 425,238. This figure was not as low as the final season figures for the Braves, the Browns, or the Athletics in their final seasons. But it was certainly cause for concern. There were no teams south of Washington. Until the Browns moved to Baltimore in 1954, Philadelphia was the closest city to the north with major league baseball. But despite their relatively exclusive market area, attendance had dwindled steadily since 1946, the only season that the Senators topped the one million mark. They finished fourth that year. The Senators had finished in second place in 1945, just one and one half games behind the pennant winning Detroit Tigers.

Though attendance had shown a modest increase yearly since 1955, Calvin Griffith cited the usual reasons for wanting to move in 1960. With a maximum seating capacity of about 29,000, aging Griffith Stadium was the smallest park in the Major Leagues. The area surrounding the park was deteriorating. There was practically no adjacent parking. Broadcast revenues were inadequate.

In 1958, Metropolitan Stadium in Bloomington, Minnesota was completed. But Minnesota was still seeking a major league franchise to play in the facility. In 1960 Griffith asked the American League for permission to move the Senators to Minneapolis before a new

Continental League, being formed by New York lawyer William Shea, and former Dodger President Branch Rickey placed a team there.

At congressional hearings concerning Major League Baseball's antitrust exemption, Senator Estes Kefauver publicly warned Griffith against moving. Fearing hostile legislation, other owners pressured Griffith to stay in Washington. Gabe Paul, owner of the Cincinnati Reds, called the Senators' owner, "baseball dumb, and a terrible operator." Nevertheless, in 1961, the American League finally allowed Griffith to move to Minnesota. The Senators thus became the sixth original Major League franchise to move within a decade. The team changed their nickname to the "Twins", in reference to the adjacent twin cities of Minneapolis and St. Paul.

Under immediate threat of Congressional action to remove Major League Baseball's exemption from antitrust legislation, the American League placed a new team in Washington in 1961. They also awarded an expansion franchise to Los Angeles, making Los Angeles a two-team city. To prevent the imminent formation of the proposed Continental League, the National League also expanded to ten teams for the 1962 season, placing a new franchise in New York, and a new team in Houston. Franchise shifts and expansion since 1952 had put Major League Baseball in seven new cities. No city had lost Major League Baseball altogether. The talent pool, however, was stretched very thin by the addition of four new teams.

THE OLD BALLPARK

Each April from 1910 to 1961 tiny Griffith Stadium was the most famous ballpark in the land. Presidents from Taft to Kennedy inaugurated each new season by throwing out the "first pitch." The "Presidential Opener" was scheduled a day earlier than opening day contest in other American League cities. Cincinnati, home of the oldest professional baseball team, still has the honor of hosting the ceremonial season opener in the National League, getting a one day head start on other National League teams.

Located at Georgia and Florida Avenues, NW, the Washington ballpark was constructed in 1892. Originally known as "National Park", it was rebuilt after a destructive fire prior to the 1911 season. The ballpark was renamed "Griffith Stadium" when Clark Griffith purchased the team in 1920. It also served as a home for the Negro Baseball League's Homestead Grays, and for the National Football League's Washington Redskins. The fences were a long way from home plate. It was 407 feet down the left field line, and 421 feet to the center field fence. It was 320 down the right field line to the most prominent feature, a thirty foot high green wall. The Washington Monument was visible beyond the wall which featured a large manual scoreboard on which the scores of all out of town games were posted. A National Bohemian Beer advertisement topped the scoreboard. As a boy Commissioner Bowie Kuhn updated the scores from behind this wall. The center field fence joined the right field fence at a right angle, and then moved back almost immediately, at another right angle, joining the left field bleachers. The intersection of the fences pointed towards home plate, providing a suitable location for the flag pole. An oak tree, the largest of a handful of trees remaining from an oak forest that existed on the site before the park was built, stood just beyond the flag pole. The phrase "Meet me by the tree", not only referred to a convenient rendezvous point but was shorthand for "Let's skip work and go to the stadium." Frequently, the aroma of baking bread from the Bond Bakery on nearby Seventh Street wafted over the park.

The classic left field bleachers, separated from the main grandstand by a "beer garden" concession stand, was the only area of the park where beer could be purchased. Other vendors wishing to service those left field fans were required to pass through fair territory. Mickey Mantle's massive 565 foot clout in 1953 was the only major league home run to clear the bleachers. But two homers by star catcher Josh Gibson of the Negro League Homestead Grays cleared the bleachers.

In a 1998 article in the *Washington Post*, columnist John Holway recalled that Gibson's blast certainly got the attention of the Senators' owner, Griffith.

> Clark Griffith often came to the Grays dugout. "You gonna hit a home run for me today?" he'd ask. "I'll try, Mr. Griffith," Josh would answer.
>
> When Gibson hit the top of the Briggs hot dog sign above the bleachers, "old man Griffith almost swallowed his cigar," old-time writer Ric Roberts laughed.
>
> In 1942, amid a Communist party campaign to open white baseball to blacks, Griffith called Gibson and first baseman Buck Leonard into his office. "If I take you boys, it will break up your league," he said prophetically. They never heard from him again.

In 1956 Calvin Griffith had a six foot high screen placed in front of the left field stands accommodating right handed Senators' sluggers Roy Sievers, Jim Lemon, and Harmon Killebrew. The distances to the fences were shortened to 350 feet down the line in left and 407 feet to center.

Abandoned after the 1961 season, Griffith Stadium was sold to Howard University in 1964. University Hospital was built on the site. The demolition of the park in 1965 received little notice. Some of the seats from the old ballpark were transferred to Rosecroft Raceway, a horse trotting track, in Temple Hills, Maryland. David Gough, a long-time Senators fan, has two in the basement of his home in Alexandria, Virginia.

Howard University held a two-day symposium on Griffith Stadium in October, 2001. A baseball museum was added to the hospital muse-um. Original plans to mark home plate were abandoned when survey-ors concluded it was located in the emergency room. First base was eventually marked with a brass tile. But that is in a passenger elevator.

THE ORIGINAL SENATORS

The Nationals of the American Association, the first Washington franchise, began play in 1873, joined the Union Association in 1884, and moved to the Eastern league in 1885. They eventually joined the National League in 1886, and began to use the name "Senators". But the team folded after the 1899 season. Another National League franchise, also known as the "Senators", began play in 1892, and folded in 1899.

The nickname "Nats", used by the old National League franchise, was picked up by the original American League Senators, when they began play in 1901.

Connie Mack played catcher for the Senators prior to 1900. Hall of Famers Ed Delahanty, Tris Speaker, George Sisler, Heinie Manush, and Al Simmons played briefly for the Senators at the end of distinguished careers. Delahanty set a franchise record with a .376 average in 1902.

PREMIER SENATOR: WALTER "BIG TRAIN" JOHNSON

Pitcher Walter Perry Johnson, the "Big Train", was the premier Senator in franchise history. One of the first five "Select" players inducted into the Hall of Fame, Johnson won thirty-two games in 1912, thirty-six in 1913, and over twenty games twelve times. In a twenty-one year career the "Big Train" posted 414 wins. Only Cy Young, with 507, won more.

CLARK GRIFFITH

Owner Clark Griffith managed the team from 1912 through 1920. The team finished second twice, third twice, and fourth once. Outfielder Sam Rice stole a franchise record sixty-three bases in 1920.

Griffith was not one of the League's wealthier owners. Like Connie Mack of the A's, he often traded or sold his best players in order to survive. "Both Connie and me pawned our life insurance to stay in business," said Griffith. "A few years back the American League was trying to help Bill De Witt stay alive with his St. Louis Browns. The owners voted to give him a penny of every American League admission. But if he couldn't take the heat, baseball didn't need him." Affectionately known as "The Old Fox", Griffith relied on guile and clever trades. At the end of the 1914 season, Walter Johnson accepted an offer of a $16,000 salary and a $10,000 dollar signing bonus from the Chicago Whalers of the new federal league. Griffith was willing to match the salary but not the bonus. White Sox owner Charles Comiskey was initially unconcerned with Griffith's dilemma. "How would you like to see Walter Johnson pitching on Chicago's south side for the Feds and ruining your attendance?" Griffith asked. Comiskey chipped in the $10,000. Johnson stayed put in Washington. In 1915, Griffith acquired Hall of Famer Sam Rice from a minor league team in Portsmouth, Virginia, simply by canceling a $600 debt that the Portsmouth team owed the Senators.

During the war years, Griffith was as wiley as ever, patching and filling. *Washington Post Sports* Columnist Shirley Povich recalls:

> Illustrative of the manner of Griffith's dealings is the Mike Chartak story. Chartak was a surplus outfielder with the Yankees, who put him on the market in 1942. Griffith made a $10,000 offer, only to be told by Yankees general manager Ed Barrow that 'the Browns have already offered me $13,000 for Chartak.' Griffith pleaded with Barrow, pointing out that 'the Browns don't draw peanuts.' He said Chartak would make the Senators a better team and the Yanks would profit from better attendance in Washington. Barrow was persuaded and sold Chartak to Griffith for $10,000. Two months later, Griffith sold Chartak. To whom? The Browns. And for how much? Thirteen thousand dollars.

TWO BAD HOPS AND A WORLD CHAMPIONSHIP

Twenty-seven-year-old second baseman Bucky Harris managed Griffith's Senators to their first two pennants in 1924 and 1925. In 1924, first baseman Joe Judge batted .324. Hall of fame outfielders Sam Rice and Leon "Goose" Goslin, hit .334 and .344 respectively. The "Big Train" contributed twenty-three victories.

Johnson, in his eighteenth season, lost the first game of the 1924 World Series to Art Nehf of the New York Giants in twelve innings. However, in a relief appearance, he held the Giants scoreless over the final four innings of the twelve inning seventh game, picking up his first World Series victory. In the eighth inning, shortstop Bucky Harris hit a bad hop double over the head of the Giants' Fred Lindstrom at third, scoring two runs, and tying the game, three to three. Then, in the twelfth inning, Senators outfielder Earl McNeeley hit a grounder that also bounced over Lindstrom's head, allowing the winning run to score. Washington won the game, four to three. It was Washington's only World Series triumph. Judge led all the regulars in the Series with a .385 average. Goslin hit .344. Rice hit a career high .350 in 1925. Goslin hit .334. Johnson and Stanley Coveleski each won twenty. Shortstop Roger Peckinpaugh, the American League's Most Valuable Player, committed eight errors in the World Series. When Johnson defeated the Pittsburgh Pirates in the opening game of the 1925 World Series, four to one, and shut them out in the fourth game, four to nothing, the Senators led three games to one. The Pirates, however, won the fifth game, six to two, and the sixth game, two to one. In the seventh game, played in a constant rain, the Senators scored four runs in the first inning. But Pittsburgh rallied for three runs in the bottom of the ninth to win, nine to seven. Johnson was the losing pitcher.

In 1927 Babe Ruth collected eight of his sixty homers against Washington. Finishing the season with a series against the Senators at Yankee Stadium, Ruth hit his fifty-eighth home run off "Hod" Lisenbee and his fifty-ninth homer off Paul Hopkins of the Senators on the next to last day of the regular season. Then he hit his sixtieth off Senators' left hander Tom Zachary in the final game of the season.

Outfielder Tris Speaker hit .327 for the Senators in 1927. Washington finished third. In 1928, Goslin won the league batting title in with a .379 mark, hitting over .300 for the seventh consecutive season. He finished with a career batting average of .316. third baseman Ossie Bluege batted .297. The Senators finished fourth.

The legendary Johnson replaced Harris as manager, guiding the team to ninety four wins in 1930 and a second place finish, behind the Philadelphia Athletics, but ahead of the Ruth-Gehrig Yankees. Hall of Fame shortstop Joe Cronin, batting .346, was the American League's Most Valuable Player. Sam Rice batted .349. Five pitchers posted fifteen or more wins, establishing a Major League record. Left hander Lloyd Brown won sixteen. Right handers Firpo Marberry, Sad Sam Jones, General Crowder and Bump Hadley each won fifteen. The

Senators held that major league record exclusively until the 1998 Atlanta Braves pitching staff matched it, also producing five starters with at least fifteen victories. Tom Glavine won twenty, Greg Maddox won eighteen, John Smoltz and Kevin Millwood each won seventeen, and Denny Neagle won sixteen.

The Senators finished a solid third in 1931 and again 1932, behind only the powerful Athletics and Yankees. But feeling his team lacked discipline under Johnson, Griffith named shortstop Joe Cronin player-manager in 1933. Pushing for a pennant, he acquired catcher Luke Sewell, outfielders Goose Goslin and Fred Schulte, left handed pitchers Earl Whitehill and Lefty Stewart, and right hander Jack Russell in trades. But he had to give up pitchers Firpo Marberry, Carl Fischer, and Lloyd Brown in trade. All had performed well in Washington. The Senators also had to part with outfielders Sammy West and Carl Reynolds, catcher Roy Spencer and cash. Reynolds batted .305 with Washington in 1932. West batted .287 that year. The collective result was that Washington won its final American League Pennant in 1933. Rice and Bluege, the only Senators to play on all three Washington pennant winners, batted .294 and .261 respectively. Bluege hit six homers and drove in seventy-one runs. The Senators lost to the New York Giants in their final World Series appearance, four games to one. Losing the first two games at the Polo Grounds in New York, Washington posted its final post season victory ever in game three. However, Carl Hubbell won his second game of the Series, defeating the Senators, two to one, in game four, out dueling Jack Russell in an eleven inning struggle. It took the Giants ten innings to win the fifth game, four to three, at Griffith Stadium.

After a seventh place finish in 1934, Cronin, who was married to the Clark Griffith's niece, was traded to Boston as a player manager for a record $250,000. "No ballplayer is worth that kind of money," said Griffith. Griffith may have been right but Washington had only eight winning seasons in the twenty-seven years that followed Cronin's departure.

In 1938 outfielder Taffy Wright hit .350, the highest average in the league. Mostly used as a pinch hitter, he marginally qualified for the batting title playing in the minimum 100 games required. The Baseball commissioner, however, awarded the title to Boston's Jimmie Foxx who hit .349. Foxx had nearly twice as many at bats.

CECIL TRAVIS

Unheralded shortstop Cecil Travis hit .359 for Washington in 1941, a remarkable performance overshadowed by both the .406 mark compiled by Ted Williams, and the fifty-six game hitting streak by Joe DiMaggio. Dimaggio hit in five straight games against Washington.

Speedy outfielder George Case, who led the league in stolen bases five times, batted .320 in 1942. He stole sixty one bases in 1943.

Having spent seventeen years as a player in Washington, Ossie Bluege replaced Bucky Harris as manager in 1943 leading Washington to a second place finish. Case stole sixty-one bases, batting .294. Hall of Famer Early Wynn, who spent his first eight seasons with the Senators, won eighteen games.

The Senators fell back into the American League basement in 1944. However, they finished second in 1945, despite hitting only twenty-seven home runs as a team. An inside-the-park homer by first baseman Joe Kuhel was the only one in Washington. Bluege's Senators fell only a game and a half short of first place Detroit. The club drew 652,660, their highest mark since the 1925 pennant winning season. With many players in military service, one-armed Pete Gray was playing regularly in St. Louis, and left handed pitcher Bert Shepard, who lost a leg after being shot down over Germany, pitched one game in relief for Washington wearing a prosthesis. He gave up three hits, allowing one run, in five innings.

The 1946 Senators finished fourth, drawing over a million fans for the first time in club history. First baseman Mickey Vernon won his first of two league batting titles, hitting .353. Joe Kuehl replaced Bluege as manager after the Senators finished seventh in 1947. But the club finished seventh in 1948 and last in 1949 before Harris returned in manage the Club from 1950 to 1954. Fifth place finishes in 1952 and 1953 were the best the team could do under Harris. Vernon won his second batting title in 1953, hitting .337. The club would never again finish higher than fifth in Washington. Even with former Dodger manager Chuck Dressen at the helm, the club finished last in 1955 and only seventh in 1956.

Although Eddie Yost, the Senators' third baseman from 1944 through 1957 had a mediocre career batting average of .254, he had an uncanny batting eye, drawing 1614 career walks, seventh on the all time list. Yost led the league with hundred and forty-one bases on balls in 1950, batting .295 with an on base percentage of .541.

THE CUBAN CONNECTION

The original Senators had a unique Cuban connection. Super scout Joe Cambria brought Cuban pitchers Connie Marrero, Camilo Pascal, and Pedro Ramos to the Senators, along with shortstops Jose Valdivielso and Zolio Versalles, outfielder Carlos Paula, and first baseman Julio Becquer. He even attempted to sign pitcher Fidel Castro. The talent in Cuba had a special virtue. It cost Griffith, virtually nothing except what he paid Cambria.

In 1957, Washington's Roy Sievers led the league with forty-two home runs. Jim Lemon hit thirty-nine in 1958. In 1959 Harmon Killebrew tied Cleveland's Rocky Colavito for the league title, hitting forty-two homers. Killebrew hit 573 career home runs, eighty-two as a Washington Senator.

Despite three consecutive years in the American League cellar from 1957 until 1959 the Senators attendance actually increased minimally each year. When the club finished fifth in 1960 in Manager Cookie Lavagetto's third season as manager, attendance was up over 130,000. The original Senators were the only one of the five shifted franchises in the 1960's to show an increase for five consecutive years prior to the move. The team on the field was improving too, winning seventy-three games, the most in eight years. Lemon, the All-Star left fielder in 1960, hit thirty-eight homers, and third baseman Killebrew hit thirty-one. Catcher Earl Battey and right fielder Bob Allison each hit fifteen. Camilo Pascual posted seventeen victories and Pedro Ramos won thirteen.

On Monday evening, October third, 1960 Griffith's Senators played their final game in Washington, losing to Baltimore, two to one. Milt Pappas out dueled Ramos. Catcher Hal Naragon opened the bottom of the fifth inning with a single. Billy Consolo tripled him home. It was the final run ever scored by the original American League Washington Senators.

The line-up and batting order for that last game was:

SS	Zolio Versalles
CF	Lenny Green
3B	Harmon Killebrew
LF	Jim Lemon
1B	Julio Becquer
RF	Bob Allison
C	Hal Naragon
2B	Billy Consolo
P	Pedro Ramos

There were only 4758 fans at the game. Neither of the two daily newspapers paid significant attention to the event the next morning.

THE NEW BALLPARK

The *Washington Star* did have an article on the new District of Columbia Stadium complete with artist renditions. Located on the banks of the Anacostia River in south east Washington, the 50,000 seat ballpark was intended to house both the National Football League Redskins and the Senators. It would have adjacent parking for 12,500 cars. The first symmetrical dual purpose facility built for both football and baseball, the new stadium had lighting fixtures affixed directly to an undulant circular grandstand roof. There were no unsightly light poles. There were also no true bleachers. Outfield seating was available high above, and beyond, a twenty-five foot high green wall. An old style scoreboard, sponsored by the Washington Post newspaper, covered the entire right field wall. Out of town scores were posted, and continually updated. Because the ballpark was built on swamp land, the natural grass playing surface never drained well.

Washington Star columnist John McKelway reported: "Still undecided is the role of the Washington Baseball Club in the new stadium pending the outcome of a law suit over the sale of Griffith Stadium." Griffith could no longer complain about inadequate parking. His demand for a new stadium had been met. However, he moved to another new stadium, in Bloomington, Minnesota.

Hall of Fame broadcaster Bob Wolff, the longtime radio voice of the original Senators, followed the club to Minneapolis.

DAMN YANKEES

In the hit Broadway musical *Damn Yankees,* Joe Hardy led the downtrodden Washington Senators team to victory over the mighty New York Yankees. The mythical Senators won the American League pennant in 1964. Ironically, the Minnesota Twins, only four years removed from Washington, did win the American League pennant a year later, ending a long era of Yankees' domination. Versalles was the league's Most Valuable Player in 1965. Killebrew hit twenty-five homers, and Allison hit twenty-three.

THE NEW SENATORS

Muting Congressional opposition to the move of the original franchise to Minnesota, the new expansion baseball team in Washington, began play in 1961, retaining the nickname "Senators".

VALO AND WHISENANT FAMILIAR WITH FINAL SEASON ROUTINE

Senators' outfielders Elmer Valo and Pete Whisenant had already been on teams in their final season prior to franchise relocation. The 1960 Season in Washington marked the third time that Valo, who played for both the 1954 A's and 1957 Dodgers, had gone through the experience. It was the second time that Whisenant, who played for the 1952 Boston Braves, had done it. By coincidence, both were claimed by the new Washington franchise in the expansion draft. Left handed pitcher Hal Woodeshick, a left handed pitcher with the 1960 Senators, was also drafted and thus remained in Washington.

MINCHER PLAYS IN FINAL SEASON FOR BOTH WASHINGTON FRANCHISES

Don Mincher, a first baseman with the 1960 Senators, went with the original franchise to Minnesota. In 1971, he was traded back to Washington by the Oakland A's. He thus had the singular distinction of playing out the final season for both Washington franchises.

Other players who played for both Washington franchises included Camilo Pascual, Zoilo Versalles, and Roy Sievers.

On September twenty-first, 1961 the next generation Senators finished out their first season against the former Senators, the Minnesota Twins in the final game ever played at Griffith Stadium. The Twins won, six to three, before less than two thousand fans. Under manager Mickey Vernon the surprising next generation Senators had thirty-one victories, and thirty-one defeats, after sixty-two games. Threatening to go over the .500 mark in their sixty-third game, the Senators led the Boston Red Sox, twelve to five, with two outs in the ninth inning of the second game of a Sunday afternoon doubleheader at Fenway Park. The Red Sox, however, rallied for eight runs to win. The team collapsed after that, winning only thirty one of its last one hundred games. Roger Maris hit nine of his record sixty-one homers against the 1961 expansion team.

CHENEY STRIKES OUT TWENTY-ONE ORIOLES

In 1962, Senators played home games at the new District of Columbia Stadium. They won only sixty games. However, on September twelfth, Tom Cheney struck out a record twenty-one batters in a sixteen inning game at Memorial Stadium in Baltimore. Chuck Cottier, a second baseman with a career batting average of .220 hit two home runs in a game off the Yankees' ace southpaw, Whitey Ford, finishing the season with just six homers. Ford told reporters after the game, "A good hitter would have fouled those pitches off."

In 1963 the Senators won just fifty-six games. Their attendance, 535,604 was the lowest in the major leagues. However, the Senators improved every year under new manager Gil Hodges, the former first baseman for the Dodgers. They won sixty-two games in 1964, seventy in 1965, seventy-one in 1966, and seventy-six in 1967. Prior to the 1965 season, Washington traded promising left hander Claude Osteen, and third baseman John Kennedy, to the Los Angeles Dodgers in return for six foot-seven inch slugger Frank Howard, third baseman Ken McMullen, pitchers Phil Ortega and Pete Richert, and first baseman Dick Nen. The deal gave the struggling Senators instant credibility. Howard's soaring long distance blasts awed fans. Stadium maintenance workers painted the seats to mark the spots, in the far reaches of the upper deck, where his home runs landed.

In 1968, Hodges was lured back to New York to manage the Mets. The Mets sent right handed pitcher Bill Denehy to Washington in compensation, making it probably the first major league player for manager trade. Denehy pitched in just three games for the 1968 Senators, who reverted to pre-Hodges era form, finishing tenth under their new manager, Jim Lemon. Proving to be a silver lining in a very dark cloud, Howard hit a record ten home runs in just six games played from May twelfth through May nineteenth, 1968. That was certainly the most significant individual accomplishment in the history of the expansion Senators. Howard finished the season with a league-leading, and franchise record, forty-four homers.

BOB SHORT BUYS THE SENATORS

In 1969 Minnesotan Robert Short, President of Motor Freight Inc, owner of the Beamington Hotel and Motor Inn in Minneapolis, unsuccessful 1966 candidate for Lieutenant Governor, and 1968 Democratic National Committee chairman purchased the Senators for a reported ten and one-half million dollars outbidding comedian Bob Hope's offer for the team.

Short had purchased the Minneapolis Lakers of the National Basketball association in 1956. In 1960, at the same time Calvin Griffith was moving the original Senators to Minneapolis, Short moved the Lakers to Los Angeles. In 1965, he sold the NBA franchise to businessman Jack Kent Cooke, a twenty-five percent stockholder in the Washington Redskins, for over five million dollars, the highest amount ever paid for a major sports franchise. He used that money to purchase the Senators franchise. With a flair for the dramatic, the persuasive Short convinced a reluctant Ted Williams, a baseball legend, to manage the Senators. Short promised, "It's a whole new ball game." The improvement was stunning.

The ballpark was renamed "Robert F. Kennedy Stadium". The Senators finished fourth, ten games above .500, recording the most wins for a Washington team since 1933. 1969 marked the first winning baseball season in the Nation's Capital since 1952. Even golden glove shortstop Ed Brinkman, who hit just .187 the previous year, batted a respectable .266. Howard hit a career high forty-eight home runs. First baseman Mike Epstein reached a career high, too, hitting thirty homers. Pitcher Dick Bosman also posted a career best, winning fourteen games, and leading the American League with a 2.19 ERA.

1969 was the only winning season in the ten year history of the expansion Senators. In sight of another in 1970, the team closed out the year with fourteen straight losses.

THE FINAL SEASON

At the end of the 1970 season, the Senators traded the popular shortstop Brinkman, and third baseman Aurelio Rodriguez, to Detroit along with pitcher Joe Coleman, for controversial pitcher Denny McLain. McLain, a thirty game winner in the in 1968, and a twenty-four game winner in 1969, had since been suspended twice by Commissioner Bowie Kuhn for gambling. Detroit also sent Washington outfielder Elliott Maddox, infielder Don Wert and pitcher Norm McRae to complete the deal.

Short persuaded thirty-two-year-old Curt Flood, a former St. Louis Cardinal center fielder with a career batting average of .293, and a three time National League All-Star, to play for Washington in 1971. Making the first serious modern day challenge to baseball's reserve clause, Flood filed suit in federal court after refusing to accept a 1969 trade to the Philadelphia Phillies. He sat out the entire 1970 season. With Del Unser, the 1968 American League Rookie of the Year, flanking Flood in right, the outfield defense promised to be outstanding. The Senators had also acquired left handed first baseman Tom McCraw from the White Sox in exchange for outfielder Ed Stroud.

The Senators headed into their final season with McLain and Bosman as the only dependable starting pitchers. However, right handed Casey Cox, and left handed Darold Knowles were dependable in relief. Epstein and Howard were expected to be the heart of the offense. The rookie shortstop, Toby Harrah, was a question mark.

Tony Roberts, Ron Menchine, and Johnny Holliday did play by play on WWDC radio, 1260 kHz, for the 1971 Senators on radio. National broadcasting veteran Ray Scott was the TV voice of the Senators on WTOP, Channel nine, replacing Shelby Whitfield, the voice of the Senators since 1969. Whitfield provided a personal account of the Short era in Washington in his book, *Kiss it Goodbye*. The owner's personal choice as announcer, Whitfield effectively promoted the club during broadcasts. No longer willing to be Short's "company" man in the booth, he was fired after the 1970 season.

APRIL

OPENING DAY
THE LARGEST HOME CROWD BUT NO PRESIDENT

In an event of no small importance, the Senators won their first opening day game in nine years before a capacity crowd of 45,061 at RFK Stadium on Monday, April fifth. The Senators easily defeated Vida Blue, and the powerful Oakland Athletics, eight to nothing. The twenty-one year old Blue finished the 1971 season with twenty-four victories, and an ERA of just 1.92, capturing the American League's Cy Young award. On this day, however, he gave up a lead-off single to Toby Harrah. Opposite field singles by first Baseman Mike Epstein and catcher Paul Casanova drove in two first inning runs. An error by A's shortstop Bert Campaneris led to two unearned runs in the second. Then Flood contributed a perfect bunt single in a two-run fourth. Washington added two more runs in the fifth. Howard drove in two runs with a single, and a sacrifice fly. Although Epstein had only one hit, he walked once with the bases loaded. Bosman pitched a six hit shutout.

Defensive highlights on this sunny, warm afternoon included two fine catches in left field by lumbering Frank Howard. New third baseman Joe Foy started two double plays, and Toby Harrah flawlessly handled the one ground ball hit to him at short.

President Richard Nixon missed the opening game ceremonies. Secretary of Defense Melvin Laird, and Army Master Sergeant Daniel

Pitzer, recently released from a North Viet Namese prison, represented the President. Pitzer threw out the first ball.

On Wednesday afternoon, the defending World Champion Baltimore Orioles hosted Washington in their own home opener. Left hander Dave McNally, twenty and four lifetime against the Senators, out dueled Casey Cox for a three to two victory. Third baseman Foy, and right fielder Elliott Maddox, hit run scoring singles in the third inning, giving Washington a two to nothing lead. But Orioles' right fielder Frank Robinson drove in the winning run with a double to right in a three-run Oriole fifth inning.

McLAIN WINS IN DEBUT

On Friday, April ninth Washington returned to RFK Stadium for their first night game of the year. McLain, in his debut as a Senator, defeated the visiting New York Yankees, five to four, in ten innings. The crowd of 25,079 was the best for the second home game in Washington in twenty-three years. Horace Clarke singled home two runs in the top of the ninth to put the Yankees ahead, four to three. But Maddox singled home the tying run in the bottom of the ninth. McLain held the Yankees in the top of the tenth. Pinch hitting for McLain in the bottom of the tenth inning, McCraw smashed a one and one pitch over the right field fence to give Washington the win.

On Saturday Mel Stottlemeyer posted his twenty-third career shutout, defeating Washington, six to nothing. Epstein had two of only three Senators' hits. After scoring the final run of the game in the ninth inning, Yankee outfielder Ron Woods was rushed to Doctor's Hospital to have an inflamed appendix removed by Washington team physician, Dr. George Resta.

Posting the first shutout of his career, Steve Klein defeated Bosman, one to nothing, in the opener of the first doubleheader of the year on Sunday before 24,358. In the second inning, Curt Blefary hit a sinking liner to left that eluded Flood's diving catch attempt. The ball rolled to the 410 foot marker. Blefary circled the bases, barreling into catcher Jim French. French received Epstein's relay throw in plenty of time, but Blefary jarred the ball loose. He was ruled safe at home, completing an inside the park home run.

With the bases loaded in the bottom of the sixth inning of the second game, however, the Senators received poetic justice. Bernie Allen's fly ball to right eluded Blefary's diving catch attempt. The ball rolled to the wall for a three-run double. The Senators rallied from a three to nothing deficit for a four to three win. Knowles pitched four scoreless innings in relief.

On Monday, April twelfth, Boston survived a five run Senator rally in the bottom of the ninth, holding on to win, ten to seven. Washington eventually collected fifteen hits off Boston starter Ray Culp. But Culp himself singled home two runs in the sixth inning, keying a six run Boston rally. Epstein and Foy had three hits apiece for Washington. Boston handed McLain his first loss of the year on Wednesday night, winning five to three. On Thursday night, however, Tim Cullen capped a six run seventh inning rally with a two-run single. That lifted Washington past the Red Sox, six to five.

HOWARD BUNTS—McLAIN HURLS A SHUTOUT

On Saturday, April seventeenth the Senators began their first extended road trip of the season rallying from behind again to beat the Indians in Cleveland, five to three. Howard led off the seventh inning with a surprise bunt single starting a four run rally. McLain pitched a three hit shutout, defeating the Indians four to nothing in the opener of a doubleheader on Sunday. Cleveland's Steve Dunning hurled a one-hitter in the second game handing Washington it's second one to nothing loss of the season. Hard luck loser Casey Cox yielded only three hits to the Indians.

On Tuesday, April twentieth in New York, Shellenback defeated the Yankees, seven to two. Howard finally hit his first home run of the year. Light hitting Tim Cullen, who had never hit a home run at Yankee Stadium, also homered. "I haven't hit any anywhere," he said. "We haven't been hitting too many homers so I figured I had better get the team moving."

The Senators had a total of only three home runs through twelve games, all against New York. But they added three more against the Yankees on Wednesday night. McCraw, Allen, and Unser all connected in a nine to six win over nemesis Stottlemeyer.

McLAIN LOSES HIS COOL

McLain pitched five hitless innings in his fourth start against Milwaukee at RFK stadium on Friday, April twenty third. He retired the first fourteen batters in order. However, the Brewers won, four to nothing. There was no score until the top of the sixth inning. Ted Kubiak opened the sixth with a single to left, and rookie pitcher Bill

Parsons moved him to second with a sacrifice bunt. Brewer second baseman Tommy Harper grounded to short for the second out. McLain had kept his reputed temper in check as a Senator. But when his three and two pitch to the next batter, first baseman Mike Hegan, was ruled ball four, he raged at plate umpire Art Franz. 17,149 fans cheered in support of their pitcher, and directed a wave of boos at the umpire. One hurled a full can of beer at Franz. After the Brewers rallied for four runs with two out, McLain engaged in another heated exchange with Franz, earning his first ejection of the year. "I warned him about using abusive language once. When he used it again, I threw him out," Franz told reporters. McLain differed with the umpire's version of events.

I didn't use any abusive language directly at him until after he threw me out. I didn't question his ancestry, like I did the umpire who threw me out in Oakland last year. But the guy was missing pitches all night. That pitch to Hegan wasn't even close. The guy is taking bread out of my mouth when he misses pitches, and money out of my pocket when he misses them in critical situations. It's a shame. He's a major league umpire. He should have the ability to bear down when the pressure is on, just like a player does.

The crowd remained surly after McLain's expulsion. In the last inning, a beer can, thrown from the upper deck, struck left fielder Frank Howard in the head, opening a small cut above his left eye.

FLOOD MAKES A SMALL CONTRIBUTION

On Saturday, April twenty-fourth, the Senators trailed the Brewers again, four to one, after six innings. But they rallied for two runs in the bottom of the seventh, setting the stage for another dramatic comeback win. With runners at first and second and two out in the eighth, Flood singled home the tying run. Still batting less than .200, he received a gratifying standing ovation from 6597 fans on a very chilly evening at RFK. Howard bounced a two out single to right in the ninth. Cullen, who led off the inning with a double, scored from third to give the Senators a five to four win. The Milwaukee defensive alignment for Howard had three players to the left of second base. In his normal position, second baseman Ted Kubiak would easily have made the play. Deflecting attention from himself, Howard talked to reporters about Flood's game-tying hit. "That was great," he said. "I think the whole team is happy for him." "Great," added Williams. "Hell, give the guy a chance. He's been away from the game for a year." "It delights me to be able to contribute something to the club," Flood said. "I just try to hit the ball. After a while you don't know what you're doing wrong, you just try and feel your way around. So far it hasn't worked out. Things can't go wrong forever."

The only disappointed member of the Senators' organization was promotions director Oscar Molomot, who gave away only 2390 pairs of panty hose, well below the record of 9000.

On Sunday, April twenty-fifth. Washington came from behind again. Dick Billings singled home the tying run in the ninth inning. McCraw singled home the game winner in the tenth, giving the Senators a three to two win. Unser, who had two hits, was batting .343 on the young season.

On Monday, April twenty-sixth, Minnesota's Jim Perry defeated Washington for the twenty-fifth time in his career, winning seven to two. Killebrew and Tony Oliva homered for Minnesota.

SENATORS HIT HIGH WATER MARK

On Tuesday night, McLain pitched his second shutout, defeating the Twins, two to nothing. On Wednesday night, April twenty-eighth, the Senators came from behind again, rallying for three runs in the bottom of the eighth inning to win, four to three, in a game that was delayed twice by rain. Killebrew's two-run single in the seventh gave the Twins a three to one lead. With the bases loaded and two out in the bottom of the eighth, Washington still trailed, three to two. But when Casanova chopped a grounder to third, the ball took a high bounce. The speedy Casanova beat Killebrew's throw to first. Running on the pitch with two out, both Foy and McCraw raced home, giving the Senators their ninth win in twelve games, four to three. Their twelve and eight record was the season's high water mark.

CURT FLOOD'S DEPARTURE

At the end of April, Flood, hitting only .200, and struggling in the field, quit, returning to Copenhagen, Denmark, where he lived during his 1970 baseball sabbatical. He wired Short:

> I tried. A year and one-half off is too much. Very serious personal problems mounting every day. Thank you for your confidence and understanding.

Short told reporters:

> I've been working with him to try and solve his personal
> and financial problems. I'd like him to know from both me and
> Ted Williams that we'd like to have him back with the club. I
> think he's a great person. I'd sign him again.

Joe Reichler, an assistant to Commissioner Kuhn, was immediately dispatched to talk to Flood. He caught up to him at John F. Kennedy
Airport in New York. "He told me he was in a hurry," said Reichler:

> He said he had to catch a flight to Washington. 'By way of
> Barcelona?' I asked. He laughed and said, 'You know.' I told
> him that he can't expect to come right back to playing form.
> The fans didn't expect him to come back and hit .400. I told
> him Bob Short would stand by him.

Flood responded hesitantly, "I know I owe Bob Short a great deal.
He stuck his neck out for me. All right, I'll give it some thought." But
he reversed himself suddenly. "No," he said. "I'm not going to do it.
I've reached the end. I'll go crazy if I don't get out!" He didn't return.

"He didn't get off to a good start and I sat him down," said Williams.
"But no one on this club had a better attitude. I wasn't thinking of sending him to Denver or anything. As far as I'm concerned he was big
league. His eyes yesterday looked like he hadn't slept very good."

Although Epstein hit is first homer of the year on Thursday April
twenty-ninth, Chicago won, five to four. On the final day of the month,
former Senator Rick Reichart homered against his former team. Ed
Stroud, another former Senator, had two hits. The Senators finished the
month in third place, just a game and one-half behind the first-place
Red Sox.

MAY

HOWARD PROTESTS A CALL

In his poorest outing in five starts, McLain lost, five to three on
Saturday, May first. After Maddox reached on an error to open the
sixth inning, Howard hit a fly ball that appeared to clear the fence in
left. After umpire Jim Odom indicated home run, Howard circled the
bases, touching home plate with what would have been the tying run.
However, after a consultation with the first and third base umpires,
Odom ruled the hit a ground rule double. Odom reversed his decision
upon consultation with the third base umpire. He supported a Chicago

protest, ruling the hit a ground rule double. Howard charged out of the dugout making the circular home run sign with his hand above his head. The crowd booed loudly, and hurled bottles. After the game Odom told reporters, "I could have been bullheaded and not asked. But we're out there to get things right."

PITCHERS FACE LACK OF SUPPORT

With a man on in the top of the ninth inning on Sunday, Reichart homered again, giving the White Sox a three to one victory. Outfielder Lee Maye was happy about the sweep of his former team. "I enjoyed playing in Washington, and I like to beat everybody. But winning four here was just a little something extra for me," he said. Cox, the loser, had a 2.63 ERA, the lowest on the Washington staff. Cox told reporters, "This is a team game, and we need runs."

After losing, two to nothing, in Milwaukee on Tuesday, Bosman echoed Cox's frustration. "I've been through this no run bit before. You just have to bear down, and hope we come up with a run in the late innings," he said. Howard didn't play because of a sore elbow.

On Wednesday, the Brewers rallied from a three-run deficit to win four to three. McLain left the game in the fourth with a stiff neck.

The team batting average was only .167. Howard and Epstein were not driving in runs. "Maybe just going to a ballpark that we haven't seen since last year, and getting some extra batting practice swings will help," said Williams. It did.

On Friday night, May seventh, at Metropolitan Stadium in Minnesota, Washington snapped the six game losing streak. With two out and nobody on in the ninth inning, the Senators rallied for four runs, defeating the Twins, six to five. Epstein singled to open the inning. McCraw tripled home a run, and Casanova hit a two-run homer. Harrah then legged out an infield hit. When Tony Oliva dropped Epstein's routine fly ball hit to short right center, Harrah scored the game winner. "That's about the worst game I ever managed," said the embarrassed Twins manager, Bill Rigney.

THE TRADE

Moments after the game, Knowles and Epstein learned they had been traded to Oakland. The Senators acquired first baseman Don Mincher, left handed reliever Paul Lindblad, reserve catcher Frank Fernandez, and substantial cash. The team had been a player short since the Flood defection. The two players for three deal filled the roster. Short promised to spend the cash involved on the club's number one pick in the free agent draft, scheduled for June.

Batting .239 with the A's, left handed Mincher, a member of the original Senators in their final season prior to the move to Minneapolis, had two homers. Epstein, batting .247 for the Senators had just one. But he had a total of fifty homers over the past two seasons in Washington. Epstein regretted the deal calling Short "the greatest owner in the game." In a phone call to A's owner Charlie Finley, Short referred to Epstein as "my son." Knowles, two and two, with three saves and an ERA of 3.60, had no regrets. "I'm happy, It's great! I wanted to get away from here," he said. Lindblad had one victory and no defeats, posting an ERA of 3.94 with Oakland.

Williams told reporters, "This is a great opportunity for Mike and Darold to be with a winner. It will make it a little easier for us to put Frank Howard on first base. Another catcher will give us more room to maneuver."

ASSESSING THE McLAIN DEAL

The deal invited assessments of the unpopular off season deal with Detroit. McLain had pitched well through the first month of the season, posting two shutouts, and a respectable 3.00 ERA. Foy, the regular third baseman, was batting .270. Maddox, McRae, and Wert had not yet made significant contributions.

Brinkman had already committed four errors as the Tigers' shortstop. He was batting only .191. Rodriguez was batting .253. Coleman, struck on the head with a batted ball in spring training, was still on the disabled list. Hannan had one victory, without a defeat, and a 4.50 ERA.

Despite losing six of seven games, the Senators were just a game below the .500 mark. They trailed first place Boston by only three games.

GAME OF THE WEEK

The players obtained from Oakland had not reported in time for the NBC TV *Game of the Week* on Saturday, May eighth. Minnesota chased Bosman early, winning nine to two. Howard hit his third homer although he was still bothered by a sore shoulder. On Sunday, McLain tripled and Unser homered in the third inning. Later in the same inning Maddox, trying to score on a sacrifice fly, was thrown out at the plate. Twins catcher Tom Tischinski, appeared to have tripped him prior to receiving the throw. Maddox, feeling he was never tagged, argued heatedly with the umpire. Manager Williams joined the argument, which lasted several minutes. The game marked the second time on the season that McLain had completed a ten inning game. However, with the bases loaded and two out in the bottom of the tenth, reserve catcher George Mitterwald singled, giving Minnesota a six to five win, and McLain his fifth loss.

The White Sox swept a doubleheader on Wednesday night, winning five to nothing, and nine to five, extending their mastery over the Senators to six straight.

McLAIN'S FIRST START AGAINST THE TIGERS

On Friday, May fourteenth, the Senators first home game since the Epstein trade. McLain won a three to two decision in his first start against his former teammates before 18,694. Howard hit his fourth home run to give Washington a two to nothing lead. After Detroit rallied to tie the game in the top of the ninth, Harrah doubled in the bottom half of the ninth, and scored the game winner on Casanova's sacrifice fly.

With two out in the bottom of the fifteenth on Saturday, Mincher blasted a pinch hit homer, giving Washington a five to four win over Detroit. Mickey Lolich did not allow a hit before Casanova singled with one out in the eighth inning. With two out in the ninth inning, Casanova homered to tie the game. Lindblad held the Tigers scoreless for the final five and one-third innings.

BRINKMAN-COLEMAN RETURN TO DC

On Sunday, May sixteenth, Coleman triumphed in his first start against his former club. Howard's two-run homer in the bottom of the fifth tied the game. Center fielder Mickey Stanley hit his second homer of the game in the eighth inning, giving the Tigers a five to four win.

On Wednesday, May seventeenth, twenty-one year-old right hander Mike Thompson made his major league debut. He walked the first three Orioles he faced in the top of the first, and wild pitched a run home. But a two-run double by Frank Robinson was the only hit Thompson allowed in seven strong innings. However, Baltimore won, four to one.

Dean Chance shut out the Senators, one to nothing, at Detroit on Friday. Brinkman doubled home the only run of the game. On Saturday afternoon, Northrup and Rodriguez hit back-to-back homers in the first inning, leading the Tigers to a three to one win.

McLAIN RETURNS TO DETROIT

Sunday's first game marked McLain's return to Detroit. 53,337 fans gave him a standing ovation when he was announced as the starting pitcher. He got another when he came to bat for the first time. McLain struck out five. However, Norm Cash and Al Kaline both homered off their former teammate, and Mickey Lolich shut out the Senators, five to nothing. Cash hit two more homers off Thompson in the second game of the doubleheader, including a grand slam. Les Cain shut out the Senators, eleven to nothing. It was the third shutout loss in four games for Washington.

The Senators finally broke the eight game losing streak on Monday, May twenty-fourth, defeating the division leading Red Sox, eight to six at Fenway Park. Howard hit his sixth homer. Foy and Casanova hit consecutive doubles in the seventh inning to break a six all tie.

BIITTNER ARRIVES

On Tuesday night, Foy's fourth hit, a bases loaded single in the eleventh inning, gave Cox his first win of the year. Larry Biittner, recently called up from the Senator's Denver farm team, had three hits, and three RBIs in the six to five win. The Senators posted back-to-back wins for only the second time during the month. The Red Sox won the last two games at Fenway, three to two, and six to two.

On Friday May twenty-eighth in Washington, Kansas City's Ken Wright shut out the Senators, defeating McLain five to nothing, before a small crowd of 4,139.

On May thirty-first, before a good Monday night crowd of 13,289 at RFK, Biittner had three more hits, lifting his batting average to .379. Three Washington pitchers combined to shut out California, four to nothing. Thompson, who allowed just one hit in three innings, left the game with a dislocated finger. Riddleberger pitched five innings, allowing two hits. Cox set down the Angels in order in the ninth inning. The Senators were in last place in the American League east, eleven and one-half games behind first place Boston. They were two and one-half games behind the fifth place Indians.

McLAIN IS ONLY STARTER TO WIN IN MAY

Washington starting pitchers had won only two games since April twenty-seventh. McLain had both victories. Noting that fact, Williams remarked, "Impossible, impossible. Not only impossible. It's unbelievable."

JUNE

Bosman took his manager's frustration to heart, defeating California, six to five, on Tuesday, June first, retiring the first thirteen batters he faced. He took a three to two lead into the top of the seventh. With two out, the game was interrupted for thirty-two minutes by a power outage. When play resumed, Cleveland's Sandy Alomar was caught stealing to end the inning. A three-run homer by Maddox in the bottom of the seventh gave Washington a six to two lead. Pinch hitter Tony Gonzales singled to open the Cleveland eighth. After center fielder Roger Repoz followed with a double, Williams pulled Bosman. Pina, Grzenda, and Cox were all ineffective in relief, allowing three Indian runs. Lindblad, however, got his first save as a Senator. Entering the game in the ninth inning with runners on first and third and two out, he struck out American League batting champion Alex Johnson to end the game.

WRIGHT AND WRONG

On Wednesday, McLain lost to Angel left hander Clyde Wright, two to one. Told that he had now lost more games than any pitcher in the American League, McLain said, "When you're going good, you're going good. A guy named Wright beat me tonight. A kid named Wright beat me last Friday night. But everything I do is wrong. I thought I was throwing the ball by hitters pretty well. The first two batters I faced today were my kids. They couldn't touch me. They're a little young though. One is just two. The other is three."

THE LONGEST GAME

On Friday, June fourth, the Senators and Athletics played the sixth longest game in league history. It was a twenty-one inning marathon game, lasting five hours and nineteen minutes. The start was delayed seventeen minutes by rain. The final inning started just prior to a 1 A.M. curfew, imposed after a twenty-two inning game between Minnesota and Washington on June twelfth, 1967. That game lasted six hours and thirty-eight minutes.

The Senators put together five hits in the ninth, scoring their only three runs in the inning. Harrah's two-run single tied the game. It was a remarkable night defensively for Larry Biittner. He threw out Gene Tenace at the plate in the second inning, and threw out Reggie Jackson at first in the thirteenth after Jackson singled to right and rounded first base too aggressively. And Biittner later threw out Dick Green at the plate in the top of the twenty-first inning. That was the second out. Shellenback, however, walked the next two batters, loading the bases, and then walked Jackson to force in the winning run. He then threw a wild pitch, allowing the final run of the game to score. In a cruel irony, Biittner popped up with two runners on in the bottom half of the inning for the final out of the game.

MINCHER-KNOWLES RETURN

Mincher had four singles on the night. Lindblad worked four score-less innings in relief. In his first appearance in Washington since being traded to Oakland, Epstein went hitless. Knowles was charged with two runs in the ninth. It was his third appearance in a twenty or more inning game. He pitched ten innings for the Senators in a twenty inning game against the Twins in 1967, and hurled six innings for Washington in a twenty-two inning contest against Chicago the same year.

Bando and Monday homered on Saturday. Catfish Hunter beat Washington, six to one. Again Bosman got little offensive support. Mincher had three of the seven hits for the Senators who had scored in only two of the past thirty-two innings.

BLUE VS McLAIN

On Sunday, June sixth, 40,246, the second largest crowd of the season watched Oakland's Blue, who had eleven straight victories since being shelled by Washington on opening day, defeat McLain, the last thirty game winner, eight to one, in the Eighth Annual Children's Hospital Benefit game. Williams used an all right handed hitting line-up against the A's star, even though catcher Frank Fernandez, and third baseman Don Wert were both batting less than .100. Blue fanned seven to raise his league-leading strikeout total to 115. "He showed me a good fast ball. He's fast, has a great arm, he's going to be a good pitcher," said Howard who singled once in four trips. Maddox singled home the only Washington run in the third inning.

LOOKING FOR HELP FROM THE FARM

The Senators got a firsthand look at their top minor league talent in a June seventh exhibition game with the Triple-A Bears in Denver. Despite three errors by Harrah, and one by Cullen, the Senators defeated Denver on Monday June seventh, fourteen to eleven. Speedy third baseman Dave Nelson had two hits, and four RBIs for Denver. Second baseman Lenny Randle had three hits. First baseman Dick Nen, right handed pitcher Jackie Brown, and catcher Dick Billings also impressed Williams.

SENATORS INEFFECTIVE AGAINST SOUTHPAWS

Because the Senators' offense continued to be ineffective against left handers, Royals manager Bob Lemon called up southpaw Paul Splittorff from the Royals Triple-A farm at Omaha to pitch against Washington on Tuesday, June eighth, in Kansas City. Splittorff won, four to two, dropping the Senators' record against southpaws to five and ten. Jackie Brown, in his major league debut, allowed four hits and one run in two and one-third innings, relieving Cox in the third inning. The Senators committed two errors in the third inning, and another in the seventh. Howard's sixth inning double was the first extra base hit in fifty-two innings for Washington. McCraw hit his fifth homer in the ninth.

PATEK IRRITATES COX

Royals shortstop Fred Patek singled and stole second in the third inning. Then he relayed the catchers' signals to Kansas City batters. "There is another way for him to do it other than stand there and wave," said a very angry Casey Cox. If I had faced him again, we might have crossed him up. I might even have knocked him down. He could get another hitter hurt." Casanova warned Patek to watch out, the next time he came to the plate.

Lindblad, who Williams felt deserved to be selected to the All-Star team, pitched two and two-third strong innings in relief on Wednesday night. But in the ninth inning Royals first baseman Chuck Harrison hit a line drive at Billings in left. Billings broke in on the ball. It sailed over his head. "It was a tough play," said Williams. "Another outfielder might have caught it, I don't know. It was a hell of a try." Howard hit his seventh home run.

SNAKE BIT

On Friday, June eleventh, McLain lost again in Anaheim, four to two. Howard homered in the third. He also singled twice, lifting his batting average to .309. Harrah was charged with his thirteenth error of the season. After Losing to the Angels Clyde Wright for the second time, McLain said:

> I've never seen a club as snake-bit as this one. I can't let it get me down. I can't pitch any better than I did tonight. I've got to keep pitching. I can't let the mental part get to me. This can't go on much longer.

Billings doubled home two runs in the sixth inning on Saturday, giving the Senators a three to two victory over the Angels. Bosman lasted seven and one-third innings to get the win. It was his first win after seven straight defeats. Nineteen year-old rookie Andy Hassler was the fifth left hander to start against Washington in a week. Harrah hit his first major league homer on Sunday, June thirteenth. Cox held the Angels scoreless over the last four and two-thirds innings, protecting a five to two victory.

Before the road trip concluded in Oakland, Wert and Foy were sent to Denver. Second baseman Lenny Randle, and third baseman Dave Nelson were called up.

EPSTEIN SETS CONSECUTIVE HOMER MARK

The A's swept a brief two game series. Epstein tied an American League record for most consecutive homers in two games, homering in his last two at bats in an eight to two victory on Tuesday, June fifteenth, and in his first two at bats on Wednesday, June sixteenth. Oakland won again, five to one. "There was no additional satisfaction because I hit the homers off Washington," he said, grinning broadly. "It was unbelievable, unbelievable," said McLain, who gave up five homers on Wednesday night. "I've never had anything like that happen to me. It was either a strikeout or a home run. That Epstein is really hot. He can't make a mistake. I've never seen a hitter hotter than he was in this series." Randle and Nelson both made their Major League debut against Blue. Randle had a single in four trips. Nelson was hitless.

On Friday, June eighteenth, Bosman was staked to a big lead for the first time since opening day. Washington defeated Boston, eight to five. There were nearly 10.000 fans at RFK to witness he unveiling of the "new" Senators. In the first inning, third baseman Dave Nelson walked, stole second, and scored the first run of the game. Then, with two men on in the fourth, he hit his first major league home run. That gave the Senators a six to nothing advantage. Second baseman Lenny Randle singled twice, scored a run, and batted in one. He also participated in three double plays.

On Saturday afternoon, Brown picked up his first major league win, combining with Cox on a two to nothing shutout of the Red Sox. Mincher tripled home Unser in the first inning. Billings, making his debut as a catcher, threw out two runners. He also singled home an insurance run in the seventh.

PETE BROBERG'S DEBUT

Owner Short used some of the money he received in the Epstein trade to out bid Oakland to sign pitcher Pete Broberg, a junior at Dartmouth College in New Hampshire, and the club's number one draft pick. "You have to be impressed with an arm like that. He's going to scare some hitters in this league," said Williams.

Broberg made his major league debut against Boston before nearly 20,000 on Sunday, June twentieth, in Washington. The hard throwing right hander struck out seven, holding the Red Sox to two hits through the top of the sixth inning. Howard hit a three-run homer in the bottom of the inning, giving him a three to nothing lead. After Tony Conigliaro doubled home two runs with one out in the top of the seventh, Lindblad entered the game in relief. He yielded a run scoring single that tied the game. In the top of the ninth inning, former Senator John Kennedy singled off Horacio Pina, giving Boston a four to three triumph.

Before only 5,000 fans at RFK on Monday night, the Orioles pounded out eighteen hits, defeating McLain, seven to two. In the first game of a doubleheader on Tuesday night, Nelson had three hits. He scored twice. Washington defeated the Orioles, eight to six. Mincher also had three hits, including his fifth home run. Lindblad was the winner in relief.

Grant Jackson pitched a two to nothing shutout in the second game for Baltimore. Shellenback held the Orioles scoreless until Merv Rettenmund homered with a man on in the fifth inning. Palmer defeated

Washington, seven to five, on Wednesday night. McNally defeated the Senators in the final game, six to one, on Thursday night.

In New York on Friday, June twenty-fifth, the Yankees roughed up Broberg in his first road start, winning twelve to two. Stottlemeyer shut out Washington, four to nothing on Saturday. McLain lost for the ninth straight time. Bobby Murcer homered twice. The Senators swept their first doubleheader of the season on Sunday. Jerry Janeski walked the first two batters he faced in the first game before being replaced by Joe Grzenda. Grzenda allowed just one run in six and one-half innings. Unser's two-run homer in the third inning provided all the Senators' offense. Washington won, two to one. In the second game Shellenback, who had not won a game since defeating the Yankees in New York on April twentieth, shut out the Yankees, eight to nothing.

At Fenway Park on Monday, June twenty-eighth, Boston exploded for seven runs in the eighth inning of the first game to win, ten to four. Boston won again on Tuesday night, six to two.

SHORT'S FINANCIAL PROBLEMS

When the Senators returned to Washington, the D.C. Armory Board threatened to seize gate receipts if past due rent on RFK Stadium wasn't paid promptly. Short owed the city $135,000. Claiming that he was overcharged, he asked for a takeover of the stadium by the federal Department of Interior, and demanded a rent free lease, unless the team drew more than a million fans. He told reporters he had made an honest effort. It was time to quit:

> All I want is the nine million I paid for the club, plus the six hundred thousand dollars I lost the first year, the one million I lost last year, and what I've lost so far this season. Except for a few loyal fans, Washington is a bad baseball town. It was bad when I came here. It's still bad. I had to do something. Here the greatest active pitcher was available. Hell, I wasn't happy about trading Rodriguez and Brinkman. I would have paid a million dollars in cash for McLain with no complaints if I could have kept my infielders. How was I to know Flood couldn't play the game anymore. I was trying.
>
> I've had offers from would-be purchasers in Dallas, Toronto, Denver, New Orleans, Phoenix, and Honolulu. I didn't buy this club to move it, or to lose money. The problem of keeping baseball in Washington isn't Bob Short's. In fact, they ought to pay me to play ball here.

Short expressed his displeasure with the prominent business people in the District of Columbia who had made public offers to invest in the Senators, and bail him out of bankruptcy:

If they would put their money where their mouths are, the Senators would be in better shape.

And Short was clearly upset with his fellow American League Club owners:

These other guys are supposed to be my partners, aren't they? I was ready to throw in fifty thousand dollars to help bail out the Seattle franchise. Why can't they lend me money?

Short didn't blame Mayor Walter Washington. "He has the good of the ball club, and the city at heart," he said. Former Senators' owner Calvin Griffith, who moved the original franchise to Minnesota, was sympathetic. "The city doesn't deserve a baseball team," he said. "The people there do not go see it played." Manager Williams readily agreed, "there is a hard core of fans here all right. There are only six or seven thousand of them. Basically Washington is a city of transient people. Most people don't give a damn. The way things are set up in this town—bad rent, bad concessions, no television market—hell, nobody could make it." Mayor Washington said, generously, "I know Mr. Short is a deeply troubled man. He is trying to find a solution."

HIGH TICKET PRICES

Targeted at affluent Washington suburbs, the Senator's 1971 ticket prices were among the highest in either league. They were nearly twice the prices charged by the nearby Orioles. And Baltimore was in first place.

THE LONGEST WINNING STREAK

The struggle to keep the team in Washington was failing. The Senators, however, began to play their best baseball of the year. The began their longest winning streak of the season at RFK on the final day of June. McLain showed flashes of his past brilliance, holding the Yankees scoreless for eight innings. After Roy White hit a solo homer in the top of the ninth inning, however, Stottlemeyer was positioned to record his third shutout win of the year over Washington. With two out in the bottom of the ninth, he had one to nothing lead.

NEVER GIVE UP

Then, with Randle on first and two outs in the bottom of the ninth, Howard, Allen, and Biittner all singled, giving Washington a sudden two to one win. "I just sat there and stared for a couple of minutes," said a stunned McLain. "You never give up until the last man is out." The Senators were in fifth place, nineteen and one-half games behind the Orioles, who had now taken over first-place in the standings. They were six games ahead of last place Cleveland.

JULY

On Thursday, July first, Shellenback posted his second complete game win over the Yankees in a week, three to one. "The big thing is that he has proved to me that he can throw," said Williams. Mincher singled twice, driving in two runs.

The Senators won again on Friday night, in Cleveland, six to three. Mincher homered with a man on in the eighth inning. Biittner, who had five hits in seven at bats over two games, hit a three-run homer in the second inning.

On Saturday July third, Jackie Brown shut out the Indians through five innings, allowing only two hits. He also singled home a run in the fourth inning. Bernie Allen followed with a homer. When Biittner, who had a run scoring single in the first, beat out an infield hit in the top of the fifth, driving in Howard, Washington led, four to nothing. The Indians rallied for three runs after two were out in the sixth. But relievers Riddleberger, Pina, and Grzenda protected a four to three Senators' victory.

BROBERG'S FIRST WIN

On Sunday, the fourth of July, Broberg posted his first major league victory, defeating the Indians, nine to four. He pitched a complete game, allowing six hits. Cleveland ace "Sudden" Sam McDowell, the American League leader in strikeouts, commented on Broberg. "He throws as hard as I do. He hides the ball well. All of a sudden it's on you," he said.

On Monday, July fifth, the "Big Ted Machine" steam rolled the Indians, fifteen to six. McLain lasted just two innings. "We didn't think he was throwing well enough," said Williams. Unser and Howard both homered for the second game in a row. Billings went three for three, with a home run and four RBIs.

WILLIAMS PRAISES BILLINGS

"If I had to pick a man who has been our inspiration, it would be Billings. He has given us a big lift with his catching, and with his bat," said Williams. Facing an upcoming series with the first place Orioles in Baltimore, the manager told reporters, "We're going in there with our heads up."

In the first game of a doubleheader on Thursday July sixth, McNally defeated Washington, six to two, ending the winning streak at six games. Shellenback gave up three home runs in the first inning. The Senators earned a split, breaking the Orioles' own modest three game winning streak in the second game with a three to two victory. Starter Bill Gogolewski and Casey Cox combined to hold the Orioles to just five hits. Randle scored the winning run on Dick Hall's wild throw to the plate in the seventh inning. Howard homered in both games, running his consecutive game homer streak to four. The Orioles swept the final two games in Baltimore, four to nothing, and seven to three.

BRINKMAN AGAIN BEATS WASHINGTON

On Friday, July ninth, the Tigers began a three game visit to the Nation's Capitol. Brinkman drove in the only run of the game with a suicide squeeze bunt in the top of the eleventh inning. Coleman pitched all eleven innings for the Tigers, shutting out the Senators, one to nothing.

Broberg received a standing ovation when he pitched out of trouble in the seventh inning. "I'd hate to make a living facing Broberg," said Brinkman. "The Senators have found a pitcher. What a future he has ahead of him," said Detroit manager Billy Martin.

McLain lost his fifteenth game, four to two, on Saturday. With two out in the tenth inning on Sunday, July eleventh, McCraw stretched a single into a double. After Howard and Maddox walked to load the bases, Nelson hit a one hopper up the middle. Although Brinkman gloved the ball, he had no chance to get the speedy Nelson. Maddox beat his throw to second. McCraw scored to beat the Tigers, four to three.

THE ALL-STAR BREAK

Despite losing two of three games to the Tigers, Williams was upbeat about the Senators' future. Going into the All-Star break, he told reporters, "We have the best bullpen in the league. I'm convinced of that. McLain is still the key. A lot depends on him. If he can pitch like he did, he would give us a stopper. Bosman can back him up. But a lot depends on Denny." The manager also praised the play of shortstop Cullen.

Frank Howard was the Senators' lone representative to the 1971 All-Star game at Tiger Stadium. Oakland's Reggie Jackson hit a mammoth home run off of the light tower high above the right field stands, leading the American League to their first victory in eight years.

SHORT'S SENATORS AND
EDWARD BENNETT WILLIAMS' REDSKINS

When Short bought the Senators in 1969, it had been at least a decade since either the Senators or National Football League Redskins posted a winning season. Redskins president Edward Bennett Williams dramatically turned to legendary Green Bay Packer coach Vince Lombardi to coach the football team. In an equally bold move, Short persuaded legendary Boston outfielder Ted Williams to manage the baseball team. The Redskins finished 7-5-2, and the Senators finished with eighty-six wins, and only seventy-six losses.

After Lombardi died of cancer in 1970, the Redskins slipped back to a seven and nine mark. Edward Bennett Williams turned to new coach George Allen for inspiration. Using the slogan "The Future Is Now!" Allen promised, and delivered, immediate success. He traded current, and future draft choices for proven stars and veterans.

After the Senators fell back to seventy wins, and ninety-two losses in 1970, Short brought in his own established veterans, Curt Flood and Denny McLain. The moves were bold. But Short's team didn't improve. There was high interest in the Redskins as they opened training camp in mid July. There was little interest in the Senators who were in last place, twenty games behind Baltimore.

On Thursday July fifteenth, the Senators began the second half of the season as they had the first. They scored eight runs and won behind Bosman at RFK. This time they defeated Chicago, eight to three. It was their first triumph over the White Sox in seven meetings. Nelson homered in the first inning, and singled home two more runs in the sixth inning. In an excellent Friday night pitching duel, Tommy John defeated Broberg, two to nothing.

Behind Jim Kaat, a member of the 1960 Senators, the Twins defeated Washington Saturday, five to three. The final two Minnesota runs were unearned. On Sunday afternoon, July eighteenth, three straight hits in the ninth gave Washington two runs, and a three to two win. When the

Twins caught Maddox in a run down between first and second, Harrah, on third base with the score tied at two, broke for home. Carew's throw to the plate was in time, but Harrah slid under the tag. Cox was the winner in relief. A two-run homer by Billings gave Brown a five to two win in the rubber match of the series on Monday night.

BOSMAN PERFORMS FOR THE PRESIDENT

Bosman singled home a run just as President Nixon, Mrs. Nixon, and daughter Julie arrived at the stadium on Tuesday, July twentieth, with one out in the home second. He doubled home two more runs in the sixth inning. On the mound he struck out a career high ten batters. The Senators defeated the Brewers, five to one.

BROBERG'S FIRST HOME WIN

Broberg posted his first home victory on Wednesday, July twenty-first, defeating the Brewers, six to one, on a five hitter. In his previous two starts, the Senators had been shut out. "The first time I saw him pitch, I thought maybe he didn't belong here. Since then I've changed my mind," said Billings. "He throws equal to or better than Jim Palmer. I don't think he'll ever spend a day in the minors."

The Brewers ended the winning streak at four games on Thursday night, shutting out the Senator's, two to nothing, despite another strong starting effort by Shellenback.

CITY COUNCIL PRESSURES SHORT

The Senator's owed the city over one hundred and sixty thousand dollars. When City Council Chairman Gilbert Hahn again threatened to seize the clubs' assets, an emotional Short told reporters:

> The outlook for baseball in Washington is dimmer than dim, bleaker, than bleak. I've been turned down by the Armory Board and by Congress. The bankers won't lend me any more money, and I'm faced with the prospect of not having a radio contract for next year. I've got no more money to put into it. When I go there will be no Ted Williams either.

Award winning *Washington Post* sports columnist Bob Addie also saw little hope that the Senators would remain in Washington:

Among the possible solutions to Short's dilemma are selling the club, moving the club, or going bankrupt. It isn't a buyer's market for baseball franchises at the moment. So that's out unless the price is lowered. And Short has said he won't do that. He has a fascination for the second solution. He does not quake at the possibility of bankruptcy. There are some who insist Short's 'partners' would stop him from moving the club. The national pastime should be in the Nation's Capital, and all that sort of thing, you know. Commissioner Kuhn has said that even if Short moves his club, a replacement would be sought. That indicates Short either has the votes or knows there is no legal way to stop him.

The Senators' radio and TV contracts were already among the least lucrative in the Major Leagues. And their radio flagship station, WWDC, had informed them that it wouldn't match it's current offer for the 1972 season.

After Short pleaded his case to his fellow American League club owners, Commissioner Kuhn and American League President Joe Cronin formed a committee to investigate the club's finances. Leery of congressional intervention, they were clearly hoping to find a local buyer, and to keep the team in the District of Columbia. Short, however, felt no obligation to sell to a local buyer or syndicate.

Washington Star baseball columnist Merrill Whittlesey lamented the probable loss of the Senators:

We would still have the Capital, the Washington Monument, the Lincoln and Jefferson Memorials, the Redskins, and the Smithsonian, but people say when you don't have a major league team you're a bush town and who wants to live in a bush league town. Everybody likes Miami. Dallas has Nieman-Marcus. New Orleans has Ramon Fizz. Omaha is nice, Indianapolis is growing and Denver is a mile high, but they are not big league cities. Washington is one of five charter cities in the American League, dating back to 1901 with Detroit, Chicago, Cleveland and Boston. The Yankees didn't come in until 1903. What has Washington done to deserve to be kicked out except be the victim of suspect ownership. Last in the American League is better than not being in the American League at all!

HOWARD GETS HOT

On Saturday, July twenty-fourth in Chicago, the White Sox won the opening game of a doubleheader, six to five in ten innings. Howard, who had six hits on the day, hit his seventeenth home run. His eighteenth home run, a two-run blast in the seventh inning of the second game, landed on the roof of the left field stands some 450 feet from home plate. His two-run double in the ninth inning gave Washington a five to three win. Knuckleballer Wilbur Wood defeated Washington, five to one, in the first game of another doubleheader in Chicago on Sunday. Howard homered into the center field upper deck in the second game. Reichardt hurt his former team again, homering twice in the second game. His three-run blast in the seventh gave Chicago a nine to six win, and a sweep.

On Tuesday night in Minnesota, Oliva hit a home run off Lindblad in the ninth inning to beat Washington, four to two. On Wednesday night Gogolewski won his first major league game, defeating the Twins seven to one.

Nelson hit a lead-off homer in Milwaukee on Friday, July thirtieth. Bosman won his fourth game of the month, three to two. Then on the final day of the month, Billings' eighth inning single drove in the winning run in the eighth inning. Cox was the winner, four to three. The Senators were in fifth place, a game and one-half ahead of last place Cleveland.

AUGUST

COOKE NOT INTERESTED

Bob Addie reported in the Sunday, August first edition of the *Washington Post* that Short had tried to sell the Senators to Jack Kent Cooke, minority owner of the Redskins. In 1954, Cooke attempted to purchase the Philadelphia A's and move them to Toronto. But he firmly declined Short's offer. "I'm looking for a way to move the Redskins out of town," Cooke said, probably in jest.

BURROUGHS GETS A BIG HIT

The Brewers swept a doubleheader at County Stadium that afternoon, three to two, and four to three. Broberg yielded five runs in the first inning at Detroit on Monday. Rookie Jeff Burroughs hit a three-run homer to tie the game in the seventh. "It was a big hit for the kid. Too bad we ruined it," said Williams. The Tigers, however, scored another run in the bottom of the seventh inning, and added three more in the eighth. Detroit won, eleven to seven.

McLAIN DENIES HE IS WASHED UP

The Senators faced the Tigers again on Tuesday night. Washington won this time, four to two. Appropriately, McLain claimed the Senators' final victory ever at Tiger Stadium. It was his second win over his former team, in four starts. Looking for a Detroit reporter who had written of his demise, he said, "I think I've dispelled the thought that I'm washed up. Tell him I'll meet him in the alley if he doesn't have the guts to show here." Washington trailed two to one after eight innings. But Allen led off the top of the ninth with a single, and McCraw doubled. Cullen then singled off Brinkman's glove, driving home the tying run. The go-ahead run scored when Burroughs hit a sharp grounder to third that handcuffed Rodriguez. Nelson then singled home an insurance run. Howard hit his twentieth home run in the second inning.

Lolich out dueled Bosman in the series finale on Wednesday, two to one. Lolich struck out fourteen. Bosman allowed just four hits, but Casanova singled home the only Senators' run in the second inning.

In a battle to avoid last place. Cleveland defeated Washington, seven to one, at RFK on Thursday, August fifth. On Friday, however, Gogolewski pitched his first complete game victory in two seasons, winning seven to three. The win snapped a five game losing streak. Then, on Saturday, Broberg pitched his first major league shutout, He also drove in two runs with his first major league hit. Washington won again, seven to nothing.

THE HOT PANTS DAY PROMOTION

On Sunday, August eighth, 13,921 watched Cleveland beat McLain, six to two. McLain, who now led the league in defeats, was probably not the major attraction. In the Sunday morning edition of the *Washington Post,* Columnist Bob Addie took note of the unusual promotion in advance.

Not all of our citizens share the Senators' enthusiasm for Hot Pants Day at the stadium. Among the sample telephone calls, and letters to this desk protesting bad taste is this one from a man who insists he isn't a prude: 'I think of the vulnerable youngsters who will be out at the game Sunday. It seems to me just another way to make a cheap buck.'

Tasteless or not, the advertising gimmick was successful, attracting the largest crowd of the home stand. It was the second largest crowd during the second half of the season.

After Kansas City swept the first three of a five game series, the Senators had nine losses in eleven games. On Thursday, August twelfth, Broberg won the second game of a doubleheader, defeating the Royals, two to one.

BACK TO BACK SHUTOUTS

The Senators won two straight from the visiting California Angels. On Friday, McLain won four to nothing, pitching his first shutout since April twenty-seventh. On Saturday, Thompson shut out the Angels again, two to nothing. Burroughs homered with a man on in the seventh inning. The Angels defeated the Senators, four to three, in ten innings on Sunday afternoon, ending the three game winning streak.

OPENING DAY REPRISE

On Tuesday, August seventeenth, the Senators nearly reprised their opening day victory over Oakland, defeating the A's, eight to one at RFK, ending a string of twelve straight road victories by Oakland. "Blue Moon" Odom was the loser this time, not Vida Blue. Gogolewski was the winner, not Bosman. There were less than 9000 fans this time. Home runs by Howard and Mincher keyed a ten hit Washington attack. Epstein had no hits in three at bats for Oakland. On Wednesday night Washington exploded for seven runs the eighth inning, winning ten to three for Broberg, completing an improbable sweep of the league leaders. Mincher homered again. Unser and Nelson each had three hits.

LAST WINNING STREAK

On Friday Washington began a fourteen game road trip with a doubleheader sweep at Royals Stadium in Kansas City, six to three, and eight to two. The victories pushed the Senators' last significant winning streak to four games. They gave the club seven victories in eight games. Howard had six hits. Burroughs drove in five runs in the doubleheader. McLain and Bosman each pitched a complete game. The Royals won eight to five on Saturday, snapping the winning streak.

On Sunday, Splittorff defeated the Senators for the third time, four to one, losing a shutout when Burroughs homered with two out in the ninth inning.

Broberg lost, two to one, on Tuesday, August twenty-fourth in California. McLain won his third straight victory on Wednesday night, five to four. And on Thursday Biittner sparked a five run rally with a tie breaking single in the ninth inning that carried Washington to an eight to three win. Lindblad was the winner in relief.

Avenging the two game sweep in Washington, Oakland swept a four game series in Oakland. On Friday, August twenty-seventh, reserves Curt Blefary Angel Mangual each hit three-run homers, leading the A's to a six to two win. Burroughs hit his fourth homer for Washington. On Saturday Unser hit a two-run double in the top of the second to put the Senators in front, three to two. But Sal Bando hit his fourth career grand slam off Thompson in the bottom half of the inning. The A's coasted to a ten to six win. Mincher homered with a man on in top of the fifth for Washington. Blue posted his twenty-third victory, beating Broberg, four to three, in the first game of a doubleheader on Sunday. Washington committed five errors. Jim Hunter posted his seventeenth win in the nightcap, hurling a nine to nothing shutout.

On the last day of August, a sixth inning grand slam by Mincher highlighted a six to five win in the opener of Washington's final series at Yankee Stadium. The Yankees rallied for four runs in the bottom of the eighth inning to tie the game. Then Unser led off the top of the ninth with a single, and went to second on a ground out. He scored the winning run when a grounder by Burroughs went through the legs of rookie shortstop Frank Baker. Washington remained in fifth place, thirty games behind the league-leading Orioles.

SEPTEMBER

A 205 PITCH SHUTOUT

On Wednesday, September first, six foot four inch Gogolewski hurled his first major league shutout. Amazingly, he needed 205 pitches to defeat the Yankees, two to nothing. Nonetheless, it was the tenth shutout of year by the Washington pitching staff. McCraw tripled home a run in the first inning. After three straight losses to Shellenback, New York finally beat him on Thursday night. It was a laugher, eleven to one. The Yankees, only five and ten against Washington, were three games over the .500 mark against the rest of the league.

ORIOLES' WEAVER IMPRESSED WITH BROBERG

Seven of Washington's next ten games were with the division leading Orioles. Baltimore began its final visit to RFK on Friday, September fourth. Broberg lost a shutout bid in the eighth as the Orioles rallied from a two to nothing deficit to win four to two. Baltimore manager Earl Weaver was impressed. "With a curve ball over the plate, he's Vida Blue," he said. On Saturday Palmer defeated the Senators again, six to two. Howard hit his eleventh career homer off McNally with a man on in the first inning.

A FINAL VICTORY OVER BALTIMORE

On Sunday, September fifth, before nearly 10,000, the second largest crowd in the final month of the season, Bosman defeated Baltimore, five to three, in the Orioles final appearance in Washington. Robinson hit a two-run homer in the second inning. Billings answered with a three-run homer in the third. With a runner on first, and one out in the top of the eighth, pitching coach Sid Hudson went to the mound. "I'll fight you if you take me out," said Bosman who then retired Frank Robinson, and Elrod Hendricks to end the inning. Cullen doubled home two runs in the bottom of the inning. Howard went four for four.

THE LONGEST LOSING STREAK

The longest losing streak of the season followed. On Labor Day Monday, September fifth, Mickey Lolich of the Tigers shut out the Senators, three to nothing, posting his twenty-third victory. The win tied him with Oakland's Vida Blue for the league lead. It was the Detroit left handers' fourth win over Washington.

THE SMALLEST HOME CROWD

On Tuesday, September sixth, Jim Northrup's homer in the eleventh, his second of the game, gave the Tigers a three to two win before 2369, the smallest crowd of the season. Gates, Brown, Bill Freehan, and Rodriguez all homered in the Tigers' final game in Washington on Wednesday night. Detroit dealt Broberg his fourth straight loss, five to three. Casanova homered for Washington.

After losing four to two on Wednesday in Baltimore, McLain told reporters, "I may jump off a roof." The Senators were averaging less than two runs a game in support of McLain. Palmer won his nineteenth for the

Orioles. Teammate Cuellar won his eighteenth on Thursday, seven to one. The final three games of the series were rained out, and never made up.

Rain also postponed the start of a series in Cleveland. The Indians won the opener of a doubleheader on Tuesday, September fourteenth, three to one. Rookie Vince Colbert, a graduate of Washington's Eastern High didn't allow a run until Mincher homered in the ninth inning.

A FIFTEEN INNING STANDOFF

The second game was suspended with the score tied five to five after a grueling fifteen innings. Working with the worst records in the American League, Steve Hargan (1-12) pitched five scoreless innings for the Indians, and Shellenback (3-10) pitched five scoreless innings for the Senators. Billings tied the game with a two-run homer in the top of the ninth inning.

LAST DITCH EFFORTS TO KEEP BASEBALL IN DC

Throughout September, Kuhn ,and Tigers' owner John Fetzer, continued searching for new ownership that would keep the team in the capital city. They sought out affluent businessmen connected with General Motors, Chrysler, and Ford.

Giant supermarket owner Joe Danzansky, President of the Metropolitan Washington Board of Trade, had a steady stream of encouraging phone calls. "I'm flattered and gratified, over the response. It shows me that the people in Washington do want major league baseball here, and prefer local ownership as well," he said. His highest offer was nine million dollars for complete ownership. He offered proportionally less for ninety, or eighty percent control. Fearful that National League San Francisco Giants or San Diego Padres might move to Washington, Orioles' owner Hoffberger offered his support to Danzanky.

Bill Veeck, who had tried to acquire the team from the estate of former owner James. M. Johnston in 1969, made Short an offer through attorney Edward Bennett Williams in late August.

CONTACTING THE PADRES

Washington attorney Earl Foreman, owner of the professional Virginia Squires, an American Basketball Association team, and the Washington Whips, a professional soccer team, had absolutely no interest in an American League baseball franchise. He made a bid for thirty to fifty percent ownership of the San Diego Padres, intending to move the National League team to Washington. Admittedly underfinanced, he called C. Arnoldt Smith's fifteen million dollar asking price, "ridiculous". "They have our proposition. It will be a quick yes or no," he said.

Attorney Williams, and former U.S. Senator Thomas Kuchel, contacted the Padres. They went to San Diego as emissaries of Mayor Washington. The immediate response from San Diego owner C. Arnoldt Smith was negative. Horace Stoneham, president of the San Francisco Giants also said he had "absolutely no interest" in the Washington offers.

SPECULATION IN TEXAS

Speculation in Texas over the potential success of the franchise in Dallas wasn't all positive. Clint Murchison, owner of the NFL Dallas Cowboys, said, "Frankly, I think they'd bomb here. Any baseball team would." Blackie Sherrod, sports editor of the Dallas *Morning Herald,* wrote, "Texas, in summer, isn't a place for a sports promoter to get rich."

Lamar Hunt, owner of the current Dallas-Fort Worth Texas League baseball team, and Fred Scovell, Chairman of the Arlington Sports Commission, both believed Short's twelve million dollar asking price was too high. "It sure ain't no damn bargain," said Scovell.

Nonetheless, Arlington Mayor Tom Vandegriff told reporters, "We understand he wants twelve million dollars. We think that would be a bargain. We got folks that would put it up in a minute, and we could easily better the Washington broadcast revenues. Our stadium is paid for. It could be upgraded easily by spring to accommodate 35,000, and more, if we need it." The area was free of baseball competition though selected Houston Astros' games were broadcast over local stations. "I think you folks up there are pretty lucky to have two American League teams closer than Dallas is to Fort Worth," he said. Low interest credit extended by Texas banks enabled Short to make back payments, overcoming the last obstacle to the transfer of the Senators to Texas.

THE COST OF RFK STADIUM

Robert F. Kennedy Stadium cost ten million dollars annually in interest alone. The city still owed the entire nineteen million dollar principle, severely compromising Washington's bargaining position. In desperation, city officials considered invoking a local statute that stipulated that any business incorporated in the District of Columbia must have it's principle place of business in Washington. However, the existing "Washington Baseball Club" was incorporated in Minnesota. In 1960, H. Gabriel Murphy, a Washington insurance man, owned forty per cent of the original Senators' franchise. He contended that Calvin Griffith's move to Minnesota violated the same statue. His court challenge was not upheld.

McLAIN LOSES HIS TWENTIETH

As a Tiger in September of 1968, Denny McLain won his thirtieth game before a full house in Detroit. As a Senator, on Wednesday, September fifteenth, 1971, he lost his twentieth at Tiger Stadium before only 3,066. Detroit won four to two, behind Joe Coleman, who won his eighteenth. And Aurelio Rodriguez homered again for Detroit, further accentuating the deficit resulting from the unpopular off season trade.

After losing to the Tigers, three to one on Thursday, Bosman echoed McLain, "Unbelievable, unbelievable. How could so many things go wrong every time out? It's depressing, really depressing." He had even more to be depressed because a thief had stolen his wallet from his hotel room.

Williams told reporters that, despite the losing record, he appreciated his teams effort:

> Our spirit is good, our attitude is good, the bench is lively. We just can't seem to get the hit when it counts or make the big play.

In Washington on Friday, September seventeenth, the losing streak reached nine games, not including the suspended game in Cleveland. The Red Sox rallied for five runs in the fifth inning to win ten to seven. On Saturday, the Senators finally won, beating the Red Sox for the final time, six to one, behind Gogolewski. Howard homered and tripled. On Sunday afternoon, Broberg hit his first major league homer. But he surrendered two home runs, losing to the Red Sox, four to three. "He must get the breaking ball over to be a winner," said Williams.

REACHING TWENTY INNINGS AGAIN
McLAIN WINS, THEN LOSES

Monday, September twentieth, the home team began the night as the visiting team, resuming the game that was suspended in Cleveland a week earlier. The Senators finally rallied for three runs in the top of the twentieth inning. McLain, claimed his tenth, and final, victory of the year. He held the Indians scoreless for four innings. Cleveland scored a run in the bottom half of the final inning. But Washington held on to win, eight to six. Although the game started in Cleveland, it was the second twenty or more inning game of the year completed in Washington.

Twenty minutes later McLain started the regularly scheduled game. This time he lost, three to one. Harrah had the only three hits off Cleveland's Allan Foster. With two runners on in the eighth inning, Mincher hit a long drive to right that cleared the wall in right field. But it landed inches foul. "That was as disheartening as anything that has ever happened to me," Mincher said. Satisfied with the split, McLain told reporters, "The evening wasn't a waste." He expressed concerned with the club's future. "I hope Washington doesn't lose this team. I really hope that," he said.

However, in Boston, the next morning American League Club owners voted ten to two to approve the move to Texas. Milwaukee was placed in the eastern division. The new Texas Rangers were placed in the western division. Only Chicago and Baltimore dissented.

After presenting his case, Danzanky told Mayor Washington:

> I have a feeling that the cards were stacked against us. We never really had a chance. I made my last offer in good faith. They never once asked us to put up more money. If more were needed, we might have put it up. It is my honest feeling that the owners had decided in advance that the team was going to Dallas.

On Capitol Hill, Maryland Senators J. Glenn Beall and Charles Mathias expressed regret. Senators William Spong of Virginia and Sam Erwin of North Carolina requested an immediate investigation of baseball's antitrust exemption. Predictably, a happy Texas Senator John Tower cabled Short and Williams with congratulations. "I'm confident that the sports community in Dallas, Fort Worth will provide the support and spirit, which are an integral part of a winning ball club." Representative Jim Wright of Texas cabled Mayor Vandergriff. "You did it. It is a great day for our entire north Texas area. We are all indebted to you."

LAMENTS

"No, I won't go to Dallas," said heartbroken broadcaster Ron Menchine. "I thought Short would sell the team. But I think the support here has been admirable. Washington hasn't won a pennant since nineteen thirty-three. All it takes to draw here is a contender." Publicity director Burton Hawkins said, "It's been a bad season all around. Howard and Bosman had below par years, and the kids weren't ready." Public address announcer Sherman Brodey said, "I hurt inside. This tears me up. I never thought it would really happen." Former manager Bucky Harris lamented, "I'm very, very sorry it happened."

Williams, the current manager, said, "Short tried everything to make a go of it. He promoted, he spent money for bonus players, and none of it worked."

NIXON COMMENTS

President Nixon, an avid baseball fan, called the news "heartbreaking." He told reporters that Washington was a good sports town, and hoped the Baltimore Orioles would schedule some of their games in Washington. He felt the tradition of the "Presidential Opener" should continue, indicating that he might throw out the first ball on the next opening day at Anaheim, California. He considered the Los Angeles Angels his new "home" team.

That evening, the now lame duck franchise defeated Cleveland, nine to one. Nelson had three hits, including his fifth home run. Unser also had three. Bosman won his twelfth.

LAST BACK-TO-BACK WINS

A three to two win over the Indians on Wednesday completed the last back-to-back victories ever posted by Washington. Gogolewski won his sixth against five losses, becoming the only Senators' pitcher with a winning record. Gogolewski also hit a bases loaded double in the second inning, driving in three runs. Most of the 1458 fans in attendance talked amongst themselves about the move of the franchise to Texas.

Charles Hawkins, a blind student at D.C. Teachers College, usually sat in the upper deck. This time he found a front row seat. From there he could hear the ball pop into the catcher's mitt, and the crack of the bat, clearly. He listened to the play-by-play coverage on his portable radio. "I like this team. I see them getting some better players. I'd hate to be without them," he said.

Wilfre Milofsky, a Bethesda attorney, attending the game on his son's fourteenth birthday said, "It's not much of a present. You can't print what I really think. I got interested when Ted Williams joined the team. I haven't missed a night game this season." John Adams, another Bethesda fan, blamed Williams. "He left his pitchers in too long, and they lost too many games."

"I thought lightning never strikes twice. I still can't believe it," said Dr. George Resta, team physician for over twenty years.

The *Washington Star* editorial page on Wednesday, September twenty-second reflected:

> It's a dumb game, anyway—particularly dumb in Washington. Good Riddance. And yet it was a thrill to sit out in the early spring sunshine at the opening game—every bit as meaningful as an inauguration. Bob Short was not worthy of us. He spent too much, cared too little, and thought he could buy his way out of his mistakes with high priced tickets and panty hose. Let him go. To hell with it. And yet...

New York Time's columnist Arthur Dailey agreed:

> Short undercut Williams with his dreadful deals. There is reward for mismanagement in modern baseball though. The delinquent is given permission by his lodge brothers to seek instant prosperity elsewhere.

TWENTY-FIRST SHUTOUT LOSS

The Red Sox swept a three game series in Boston. Roger Moret dealt the Senators their twenty-first shutout loss of the year, four to nothing on Friday, September twenty-fourth. Although Howard hit his twenty-fifth homer at Fenway Park on Saturday, McLain lost his twenty-second game, six to three. On Sunday the Red Sox broke open a close game with a four run seventh, defeating Bosman, eight to one.

LAST OFFICIAL HOME VICTORY

The Senators posted their last official victory in Washington on Tuesday, September twenty-eighth, at RFK, topping the Yankees, four to two, before an intimate gathering of 3,242 fans. Consecutive singles by Mincher, Billings, and Burroughs broke a two to two tie in the seventh. Battling the Twins Tony Oliva for the American League batting title, Yankee right fielder Bobby Mercer had only one hit in four at bats, dropping his average to .331. Oliva was hitting .337.

Murcer singled once on Wednesday night to extend a hitting streak to fourteen games. Stottlemeyer turned back the Senators, six to three, defeating Washington for the fifth time during the season. Harrah, who had three hits, was the only batter with any success against the Yankees' righthander.

VEECK ON WASHINGTON

Bill Veeck, the former owner of the Browns, who inadvertently set in motion the parade of now seven franchise moves, was a paying customer at the Senators' final game on Thursday, September thirtieth. In his baseball autobiography, *Veeck as in Wreck*, published in 1962, he offered his opinion about the move of the 1960 Senators:

> My feelings were that it would be basically wrong, and even worse, stupid for the American League to leave Washington. If Presidents are going to toss out baseballs on opening days, better in an American League park than a National League one. If I couldn't make a club go in Washington I would turn in my shield.

THE END

It was an usually warm and humid evening for late September. A haze hung over the stadium. Banners adorned the upper deck. The "Short Sucks" sign hanging vertically from the upper deck in right center remained untouched throughout the game. A "Fuck Short" sign overhanging center field was removed quickly by security guards. A "Bob Short Fan Club" banner was draped below a completely empty section in the upper left field stands.

As he suited up for the last time, Frank Howard told teammates and reporters:

> I've been playing for the Senator's for seven years. I think of this city as my own. I enjoyed everyday of it, no matter how bad we were.

Souvenir caps, cups, shirts, balls, and copies of Ted Williams' book, *My Turn at Bat*, were among the leftover Senators' promotional giveaway items available in boxes as patrons entered the stadium for the last time. Since Short wasn't available, Williams was greeted with a chorus of boos as he exchanged the lineup card with Yankee manager Ralph Houk. Fans hurled copies of Williams' book onto the field.

FANS CHEER THE PLAYERS

The fan response varied as each Senator came to bat. In general, they displayed affection for the team. Caught by surprise, Cuban born catcher Casanova's legs buckled when he received a long, warm ovation that was clearly out of proportion to his .225 career batting average. The official announced attendance was 14,460. An estimated 4000 more late arriving fans passed through unattended turnstiles as the game continued.

Starter Bosman left the field with his head down in the fifth with the Senators behind, five to one. He had given up three homers among eight hits. "I wanted this one so badly," he said.

Eighty-one year-old Loddy May Lively, wearing a red suit, and a hat which had the red cardboard letters S-E-N-A-T-O-R-S stapled to the brim, shook her finger. "Come on boys. Got to play catch-up now," she said. Concerned about her favorite players, she said sweetly, "I'll pray for them."

The fans saved their loudest applause for Howard. When he hit the Senator's final home run in a dramatic sixth inning, the standing ovation was thunderous. Rounding third, Hondo doffed his cap to Yankees' pitcher Mike Kekich. The moment was so emotional that he came out of the dugout twice to salute the fans, waving his batting helmet, and tossing his red cap into the crowd, and blowing kisses from the top of the first base dugout. He wiped away tears using part a towel that remained draped over his right arm. "He's the greatest man I know," said Bosman, who was among those who greeted the slugger at home plate.

Howard, lingering in the trainers room long after the game, told reporters:

> Kekich gave me a healer for which I thanked Munson. A two and nothing count, so I knew it would be a fast ball. I knew I would get a good pitch to hit, because the game didn't mean that much. I still had to lay wood on it.

> "It's okay," explained a grinning Kekich. "Let's just say I tried to throw him a straight pitch."

Howard offered this humble assessment of himself and his contribution to the Senators:

> I'm not an ordinary player. But I'm not a great player. I put out a hundred percent just like everybody on this club. This was the fan's game, not the players game, not the farewell game for the press. This one was for the fans. We finished

right. I'd like to stay here, and finish my career. I got my chance to play regularly here, and to make big money. Hell, it's my home. I'm going to meet with Bob Short and see how I fit into their plans. Dallas may deserve baseball, but so does Washington.

For the record, Maddox doubled home the tying run in the sixth inning. McCraw singled home Unser with the go-ahead run in the eighth. When McCraw later scored the final Senators' run ever on a sacrifice fly by Maddox, Washington led seven to five.

Between innings the scoreboard flashed "Thanks to Bernie, Paul, Bos, Denny..." Promotions director Oscar Molomot vetoed the playing of *Auld Lang Syne*. Despite the continuous chant, "We want Hondo," Williams, who had dramatically homered in his own final at bat as a player at Fenway Park, had a proper sense of occasion. When New York came to bat in the top of the ninth, Mincher replaced Howard at first base.

The Yankees Felipe Alou grounded out to shortstop Toby Harrah to open the final half inning. Bobby Murcer tapped one to pitcher Grzenda who threw to first for the second out.

FINAL OUT NEVER RECORDED

But with Horace Clarke at bat, a young man ran onto the field. Unrestrained by security personnel, he uprooted first base from its moorings. There was a brief moment of stunned silence, before hundreds of other fans, facing no resistance, swarmed onto the field. Bosman, the departed starting pitcher, left the safety of the dugout, and frantically tried to restore order, personally beseeching fans to return to their seats only to lose his cap to a souvenir snatching fan.

The stern public address announcement, "Unless the field is cleared, the game must be forfeited," was absurdly futile. The game was officially declared a forfeit, the first in the majors in seventeen years. All the records were logged into the record book. There was no winning, or losing, pitcher indicated. The final out was never recorded.

Fans roamed the stadium for hours after the players had left the field. While security officers monitored events from a distance, they dug up home plate, and removed the remaining bases, grabbing anything that had souvenir value, including scoreboard numbers, light bulbs, and the distance markers hanging from the outfield fences. They even dug up sections of grass.

In a curiously festive atmosphere, many fans just ran around the base paths. The bases themselves, of course, were no longer there. Although one threw up after sliding head first into third, those following him on the base paths merely ran around the unfortunate mess, heading for home plate. Several practiced sliding into home. The improvisational theater resulted in only minimal damage to the field.

"This has always been a good town. It has a nice stadium," said Yankees' coach Elston Howard. "First Calvin Griffith wanted to move. And now Short. I don't understand these owners."

"I sure as hell don't want us to go to Dallas," said Casey Cox.

Manager Williams, talking to Washington reporters for the last time, said:

> It isn't that I mind moving to Texas as much as having to meet new newspaper guys. How do I know they won't be like those guys in Boston? You guys here in Washington aren't so bad considering. Oh hell, of course I'm going to Dallas. I haven't been fired as manager.

The Senators finished in fifth place in the American League Eastern Division, four and one-half games ahead of the last place Cleveland Indians.

POSTSCRIPTS

Several Major League exhibition games have been played at RFK Stadium since the departure of the Senators. The Orioles and Pirates met there in an exhibition game in 1972, and the Mets played Red Sox in another exhibition there the following year.

In May, 1973, it appeared that Major League Baseball would return to the Nation's Capital. Debt ridden San Diego Padres owner, C. Arnhold Smith, agreed, pending league approval, to sell the franchise to Washington's grocery chain owner Joe Danzanky, accepting a $100.000 deposit. But League officials delayed a vote on the sale, and after an eight month search, Smith sold the team to to San Diego businessman Ray Kroc, the McDonald's hamburger king.

In 1982, at the age of 75, Hall of Fame shortstop Luke Appling briefly became famous again when he hit a home run off Warren Spahn in the first of several Cracker Jack Old-Timers' games in Washington. That may have been the final baseball thrill to grace the Nation's Capital.

Since RFK Stadium was permanently reconfigured for football in 1974, it has been restored to its intended baseball alignment, only twice, for pre-season games between the Orioles and the Red Sox in April 1990, and the Cardinals and Expos in 1999, part of an effort to bring professional baseball back to Washington. But leery of more scrutiny by the national legislature and acknowledging the DC area constitutes twenty-five percent of the Baltimore Orioles fan base, Major League Baseball is reluctant to return to Washington.

BOB SHORT SELLS THE RANGERS

In 1978 in Minnesota, Bob Short lost a hotly contested race for the United States Senate seat. He sold his interest in the Texas Rangers to Brad Corbett in 1980, making a substantial profit on the sale. Short died on November twentieth, 1982.

SENATORS' REUNION

On August tenth, 1986 there was a reunion game at Baltimore's Memorial Stadium, pitting members of the 1966 Orioles against members of the 1966 Senators. In 1966, the amazing Orioles, American League champions, swept four straight games from the heavily favored Dodgers in the World Series. The Senators had finished one and one-half games out of last place.

But twenty years later, the Senators won this symbolic old timers game, three to one. Seven former Washington pitchers combined to pitch three scoreless innings. Unser, Cullen, Lindblad, Cox, Hannan, Epstein, French, and Nen represented the final 1971 squad. Members of the 1966 team included: Pete Richert, Ken McMullen, Fred Valentine, Benny Daniels, and Don Lock. Former Orioles included Frank Robinson, Brooks Robinson, Boog Powell, and Moe Drabowsky.

After Dave McNally and Wally Bunker gave up first inning singles to Don Lock and Mike Epstein, Drabowsky, a prankster of some note, came in to pitch. He lobbed a bright red tomato to Fred Valentine, who hit it as it sailed over the plate like a hanging curve ball. Catcher Andy Etchebarren picked up the remains of the splattered tomato. After walking to the mound, he wiped his glove clean, on Drabowsky's uniform. "Quit throwing trick pitches," a laughing Valentine protested.

TOO BAD IT HAS TO END

Outfielder Chuck Hinton, a 1964 all-star, once allowed two Kansas City runners to score on a single sacrifice fly in a game at RFK. They were the tying and winning runs for the Royals. But Hinton was firmly convinced that there were two out when he made the catch. No amount of screaming by teammates, or fans, could persuade him otherwise. He ran resolutely, head down, toward the Senator's dugout. However, on this day in 1986, his ringing single to left off Tom Phoebus in the fourth, and final, inning scored Buster Narum and Dick Nen with the deciding runs. "Fantastic!" Hinton exclaimed, celebrating with his teammates at home plate. "We just clinched the pennant. Way to go gang! Too bad it has to end."

TWILIGHT TEAMS

DAY	DATE	OPPONENT	RESULT	SCORE	PITCHER	ATTENDANCE	RECORD
TUES	04/06/71	OAKLAND	W	8-0	DICK BOSMAN (1-0)	45061	1-0
WED	04/07/71	AT BALTIMORE	L	3-2	CASEY COX (0-1)	34811	1-1
FRI	04/09/71	NEW YORK	W	5-4 (10)	DENNY MCLAIN (1-0)	25079	2-1
SAT	04/10/71	NEW YORK	L	6-0	DICK SHELLENBACK (0-1)	6412	2-2
SUN	04/11/71	NEW YORK	L	1-0	DICK BOSMAN (1-1)	24358	2-3
SUN	04/11/71	NEW YORK	W	4-3	DAROLD KNOWLES (1-1)	24358	3-3
MON	04/12/71	BOSTON	L	10-7	JERRY JANESKI (0-1)	7392	3-4
TUES	04/13/71	BOSTON	L	5-3	DENNY MCLAIN (1-1)	12154	3-5
WED	04/14/71	BOSTON	W	6-5	DAROLD KNOWLES (2-0)	4286	4-5
SAT	04/17/71	AT CLEVELAND	W	5-3	DICK BOSMAN (2-1)	5108	5-5
SUN	04/18/71	AT CLEVELAND	W	4-0	DENNY MCLAIN (2-1)	11400	6-5
SUN	04/18/71	AT CLEVELAND	L	1-0	CASEY COX (0-2)	11400	6-6
TUES	04/20/71	AT NEW YORK	W	7-2	DICK SHELLENBACK (1-1)	6851	7-6
WED	04/21/71	AT NEW YORK	W	9-6	JERRY JANESKI (1-1)	5415	8-6
FRI	04/23/71	MILWAUKEE	L	4-0	DENNY MCLAIN (2-2)	17149	8-7
SAT	04/24/71	MILWAUKEE	W	5-4	HORACIO PINA (1-0)	6597	9-7
SUN	04/25/71	MILWAUKEE	W	3-2 (10)	JOE GRZENDA (1-0)	9780	10-7
MON	04/26/71	MINNESOTA	L	7-2	JIM SHELLENBACK (1-2)	3931	10-8
TUES	04/27/71	MINNESOTA	W	2-0	DENNY MCLAIN (3-2)	7971	11-8
WED	04/28/71	MINNESOTA	W	4-3	JOE GRZENDA (2-0)	3804	12-8
THURS	04/29/71	CHICAGO	L	5-4	DAROLD KNOWLES (2-1) 3681	12-9	
FRI	04/30/71	CHICAGO	L	8-1	JERRY JANESKI (1-2) 6502	12-10	
SAT	05/01/71	CHICAGO	L	5-3	DENNY MCLAIN (3-3)	12073	12-11
SUN	05/02/71	CHICAGO	L	3-1	DAROLD KNOWLES (2-2) 8684	12-12	
TUES	05/04/71	AT MILWAUKEE	L	2-0	DICK BOSMAN (2-2)	3457	12-13
WED	05/05/71	AT MILWAUKEE	L	4-3	DENNY MCLAIN (3-4)	4769	12-14
FRI	05/07/71	AT MINNESOTA	W	6-5	DENNY RIDDLEBERGER(1-0)	7606	13-14
SAT	05/08/71	AT MINNESOTA	L	9-2	DICK BOSMAN (2-3)	9091	13-15
SUN	05/09/71	AT MINNESOTA	L	6-5 (10)	DENNY MCLAIN (3-5)	28980	13-16
WED	05/12/71	AT CHICAGO	L	5-0	DICK BOSMAN (2-4)	7333	13-17
WED	05/12/71	AT CHICAGO	L	9-5	JOE GRZENDA (2-1)	7333	13-18
FRI	05/14/71	DETROIT	W	3-2	DENNY MCLAIN (4-5)	18694	14-18
SAT	05/15/71	DETROIT	W	4-3 (15)	PAUL LINDBLAD (2-0)	6237	15-18
SUN	05/16/71	DETROIT	L	5-4	DENNY RIDDLEBERGER(1-1)	7923	15-19
MON	05/17/71	CLEVELAND	L	6-3	DICK BOSMAN (2-5)	3186	15-20
TUES	05/18/71	CLEVELAND	L	7-3	DENNY MCLAIN(4-6)	5690	15-21
WED	05/19/71	BALTIMORE	L	4-1	MIKE THOMPSON (0-1) 6833	15-22	
THURS	05/20/71	RAIN					
FRI	05/21/71	AT DETROIT	L	1-0	JERRY JANESKI (1-3)	25833	15-23
SAT	05/22/71	AT DETROIT	L	3-1	DICK BOSMAN (2-6)	24342	15-24
SUN	05/23/71	AT DETROIT	L	5-0	DENNY MCLAIN (4-7)	53337	15-25
SUN	05/23/71	AT DETROIT	L		11-0 MILT THOMPSON (0-2)	53337	15-26
MON	05/24/71	AT BOSTON	W	8-6	JOE GRZENDA (1-3)	14331	16-26
TUES	05/25/71	AT BOSTON	W	6-5 (11)	CASEY COX (1-2)	13760	17-26
WED	05/26/71	AT BOSTON	L	3-2	JERRY JANESKI (1-4)	13526	17-27
THURS	05/27/71	AT BOSTON	L	6-2	DICK BOSMAN (2-7)	14995	17-28
FRI	05/28/71	KANSAS CITY	L	5-0	DENNY MCLAIN (4-8)	4139	17-29
SAT	05/29/71	KANSAS CITY	RAIN				
SUN	05/30/71	KANSAS CITY	RAIN				
MON	05/31/71	CALIFORNIA	W	4-0	DENNY RIDDLEBERGER(3-1)	13289	18-29
TUES	06/01/71	CALIFORNIA	W	6-5	DICK BOSMAN (3-7)	3675	19-29
WED	06/02/71	CALIFORNIA	L	2-1	DENNY MCLAIN (4-9)	3606	19-30
FRI	06/04/71	OAKLAND	L	5-3 (21)	DICK SHELLENBACK (1-3)	6159	19-31
SAT	06/05/71	OAKLAND	L	6-1	DICK BOSMAN (3-8)	6221	19-32
SUN	06/06/71	OAKLAND	L	8-1	DENNY MCLAIN (4-10)	40246	19-33
MON	06/07/71	AT DENVER (EX)	W	14-11	DICK SHELLENBACK	5061	EXHIB
TUES	06/08/71	AT KANSAS CITY	L	4-2	CASEY COX (1-3)	13207	19-34
WED	06/09/71	AT KANSAS CITY	L	5-4	PAUL LINDBLAD (2-1)	9242	19-35

THE 1971 WASHINGTON SENATORS

DAY	DATE	OPPONENT	RESULT	SCORE	PITCHER	ATTENDANCE	RECORD
THURS	06/10/71	AT KANSAS CITY	RAIN				
FRI	06/11/71	AT CALIFORNIA	L	4-2	DENNY MCLAIN (4-11)	6445	19-36
SAT	06/12/71	AT CALIFORNIA	W	3-2	DICK BOSMAN (4-8)	12836	20-36
SUN	06/13/71	AT CALIFORNIA	W	5-2	CASEY COX (2-3)	20051	21-36
TUES	06/15/71	AT OAKLAND	L	8-2	JERRY JANESKI (1-5)	8392	21-37
WED	06/16/71	AT OAKLAND	L	5-1	DENNY MCLAIN (4-12)	19873	21-38
FRI	06/18/71	BOSTON	W	8-5	DICK BOSMAN (5-8)	9420	22-38
SAT	06/19/71	BOSTON	W	2-0	JACKIE BROWN (1-0)	8954	23-38
SUN	06/20/71	AT BOSTON	L	4-2	HORACIO PINA (1-1)	19884	23-39
MON	06/21/71	BALTIMORE	L	7-2	DENNY MCLAIN (4-13)	5106	23-40
TUES	06/22/71	BALTIMORE	W	8-6	PAUL LINDBLAD (3-1)	11072	24-40
TUES	06/22/71	BALTIMORE	L	2-0	DICK SHELLENBACK (1-4)	11072	24-41
WED	06/23/71	BALTIMORE	L	7-5	DICK BOSMAN (5-9)	7867	24-42
THURS	06/24/71	BALTIMORE	L	6-1	JACKIE BROWN (1-1)	5765	24-43
FRI	06/25/71	AT NEW YORK	L	12-2	PETE BROBERG (0-1)	13761	24-44
SAT	06/26/71	AT NEW YORK	L	4-0	DENNY MCLAIN (4-14)	11221	24-45
SUN	06/27/71	AT NEW YORK	W	2-1	JOE GRZENDA (4-1)	41173	25-45
SUN	06/27/71	AT NEW YORK	W	8-0	DICK SHELLENBACK (2-4)	41173	26-45
MON	06/28/71	AT BOSTON	L	10-4	CASEY COX (2-4)	21000	25-46
TUES	06/29/71	AT BOSTON	L	6-2	PETE BROBERG (0-2)	25024	26-47
WED	06/30/71	NEW YORK	W	2-1	DENNY MCLAIN (5-14)	8747	27-47
THURS	07/01/71	NEW YORK	W	3-1	DICK SHELLENBACK (3-4)	3775	28-47
FRI	07/02/71	AT CLEVELAND	W	6-3	DICK BOSMAN (6-9)	12087	29-47
SAT	07/03/71	AT CLEVELAND	W	4-3	JACKIE BROWN (2-1)	4899	30-47
SUN	07/04/71	AT CLEVELAND	W	9-4	PETE BROBERG (1-2)	11264	31-47
MON	07/05/71	AT CLEVELAND	W	15-6	PAUL LINDBLAD (4-1) 13813		32-47
THURS	07/06/71	AT BALTIMORE	L	6-2	DICK SHELLENBACK (3-5)	11349	32-48
TUES	07/06/71	AT BALTIMORE	W	3-2	CASEY COX (3-4)	11349	33-48
WED	07/07/71	AT BALTIMORE	L	4-0	DICK BOSMAN (6-10)	10685	33-49
THURS	07/08/71	AT BALTIMORE	L	7-3	JACKIE BROWN (2-2)	8093	33-50
FRI	07/09/71	DETROIT	L	1-0 (11)	CASEY COX (3-5)	12800	33-51
SAT	07/10/71	DETROIT	L	4-2	DENNY MCLAIN (5-15)	11536	33-52
SUN	07/11/71	DETROIT	W	4-3 (10)	DENNY RIDDLEBERGER(3-1)	10474	34-52
WED	07/14/71	AT CINCINNATI	ALL-STAR GAME				
THURS	07/15/71	CHICAGO	W	8-3	DICK BOSMAN (7-10)	7526	35-52
FRI	07/16/71	CHICAGO	L	2-0	PETE BROBERG (1-3)	6671	35-53
SAT	07/17/71	MINNESOTA	L	5-3	DICK SHELLENBACK (3-6)	7124	35-54
SUN	07/18/71	MINNESOTA	W	3-2	CASEY COX (4-5)	9850	36-54
MON	07/19/71	MINNESOTA	W	5-2	JACKIE BROWN (3-2)	5317	37-54
TUES	07/20/71	MILWUAKEE	W	5-1	DICK BOSMAN (8-10)	3887	38-54
WED	07/21/71	MILWAUKEE	W	6-1	PETE BROBERG (2-3)	7313	39-54
THURS	07/22/71	MILWAUKEE	L	2-0	DICK SHELLENBACK (3-7)	5585	39-55
FRI	07/23/71	RAIN					
SAT	07/24/71	AT CHICAGO	L	6-5 (10)	JOE GRZENDA (4-2)	10301	39-56
SAT	07/24/71	AT CHICAGO	W	5-3	PAUL LINDBLAD (5-1)	10301	40-56
SUN	07/25/71	AT CHICAGO	L	5-1	DICK BOSMAN (8-11	24318	40-57
SUN	07/25/71	AT CHICAGO	L	9-6	JACKIE BROWN (3-3)	24318	40-58
TUES	07/27/71	AT MINNESOTA	L	4-2	PAUL LINDBLAD (1-2)	7919	40-59
WED	07/28/71	AT MINNESOTA	W	7-1	BILL GOGOLEWSKI (1-0)	10139	41-58
THURS	07/29/71	RAIN					
FRI	07/30/71	AT MILWAUKEE	W	3-2	DICK BOSMAN (9-11)	9324	42-59
SAT	07/31/71	AT MILWAUKEE	W	4-3	CASEY COX (5-5)	15166	43-59
SUN	08/01/71	AT MILWAUKEE	L	4-3	DICK SHELLENBACK (3-8)	10032	43-60
SUN	08/01/71	AT MILWAUKEE	L	3-2	BILL GOGOLEWSKI (1-1)	10032	43-61
MON	08/02/71	AT DETROIT	L	11-7	CASEY COX (5-6)	12423	43-62
TUES	08/03/71	AT DETROIT	W	4-2	DENNY MCLAIN (6-15)	22171	44-62
WED	08/04/71	AT DETROIT	L	2-1	DICK BOSMAN (9-12)	30410	44-63
THURS	08/05/71	CLEVELAND	L	7-1	MIKE THOMPSON (0-3)	4694	44-64

TWILIGHT TEAMS

DAY	DATE	OPPONENT	RESULT	SCORE	PITCHER	ATTENDANCE	RECORD
FRI	08/06/71	CLEVELAND	W	7-3	BILL GOGOLEWSKI (2-1)	8211	45-64
SAT	08/07/71	CLEVELAND	W	7-0	PETE BROBERG (3-3)	5202	46-64
SUN	08/08/71	CLEVELAND	L	6-2	DENNY MCLAIN (6-16)	13921	46-65
TUES	08/10/71	KANSAS CITY	L	3-1	MIKE THOMPSON (0-4)	6409	46-66
TUES	08/10/71	KANSAS CITY	L	9-2	DICK BOSMAN (9-13)	6409	46-67
WED	08/11/71	KANSAS CITY	L	1-0 (5)	BILL GOGOLEWSKI (2-2)	2799	46-68
THURS	08/12/71	KANSAS CITY	L	2-0	DICK SHELLENBACK (3-9)	5477	47-68
THURS	08/12/71	KANSAS CITY	W	2-1	PETE BROBERG (4-3)	5477	47-69
FRI	08/13/71	CALIFORNIA	W	4-0	DENNY MCLAIN (7-16)	4928	48-69
SAT	08/14/71	CALIFORNIA	W	2-0	MIKE THOMPSON (1-2)	4011	49-69
SUN	08/15/71	CALIFORNIA	L	4-3 (10)	PAUL LINDBLAD (5-3)	6895	49-70
TUES	08/17/71	OAKLAND	W	8-1	BILL GOGOLEWSKI (3-2)	8847	50-70
WED	08/18/71	OAKLAND	W	10-3	PETE BROBERG (5-3)	8146	51-70
FRI	08/20/71	AT KANSAS CITY	W	6-3	DENNY MCLAIN (8-16)	11523	52-70
FRI	08/20/71	AT KANSAS CITY	W	8-2	DICK BOSMAN (10-13)	11523	53-70
SAT	08/21/71	AT KANSAS CITY	L	8-5	MIKE THOMPSON (1-5)	8489	53-71
SUN	08/22/71	AT KANSAS CITY	L	4-1	JACKIE BROWN (3-4)	12502	53-72
TUES	08/24/71	AT CALIFORNIA	L	2-1	PETE BROBERG (5-4)	9004	53-73
WED	08/25/71	AT CALIFORNIA	W	5-4	DENNY MCLAIN (9-16)	7114	54-73
THURS	08/26/71	AT CALIFORNIA	W	8-3	PAUL LINDBLAD (6-3)	6221	55-73
FRI	08/27/71	AT OAKLAND	L	6-2	BILL GOGOLEWSKI (3-3)	4739	55-74
SAT	08/28/71	AT OAKLAND	L	10-6	MIKE THOMPSON (1-6)	7414	55-75
SUN	08/29/71	AT OAKLAND	L	9-0	DENNY MCLAIN (9-17)	24977	55-77
SUN	08/29/71	AT OAKLAND	L	4-3	PETE BROBERG (5-5)	24977	55-76
TUES	08/31/71	AT NEW YORK	W	6-5	PAUL LINDBLAD (7-3)	8950	56-77
WED	09/01/71	AT NEW YORK	W	2-0	BILL GOGOLEWSKI (4-3)	8467	57-77
THURS	09/02/71	AT NEW YORK	L	11-1	DICK SHELLENBACK (3-10)	7461	57-78
FRI	09/03/71	BALTIMORE	L	4-2	PETE BROBERG (5-6)	7761	57-79
SAT	09/04/71	BALTIMORE	L	6-2	DENNY MCLAIN (9-18)	7909	57-80
SUN	09/05/71	BALTIMORE	W	5-3	DICK BOSMAN (11-13)	9623	58-80
MON	09/06/71	DETROIT	L	3-0	BILL GOGOLEWSKI (4-4)	7384	58-81
TUES	09/07/71	DETROIT	L	3-2 (11)	PAUL LINDBLAD (7-4)	2369	58-82
WED	09/08/71	DETROIT	L	5-3	PETE BROBERG (5-7)	2973	58-83
THURS	09/09/71	AT BALTIMORE	L	4-2	DENNY MCLAIN (9-19)	5601	58-84
FRI	09/10/71	AT BALTIMORE	L	7-1	DICK BOSMAN (11-14)	13443	58-85
SAT	09/11/71	AT BALTIMORE	RAIN				
SUN	09/12/71	AT BALTIMORE	RAIN				
SUN	09/12/71	AT BALTIMORE	RAIN				
MON	09/13/71	AT CLEVELAND	RAIN				
TUES	09/14/71	AT CLEVELAND	L	3-1	BILL GOGOLEWSKI (4-5)	2639	58-86
TUES	09/14/71	AT CLEVELAND	SUSP	(15)		10699	
WED	09/15/71	AT DETROIT	L	4-2	DENNY MCLAIN (9-20)	8066	58-87
THURS	09/16/71	AT DETROIT	L	3-1	DICK BOSMAN (11-15)	4620	58-88
FRI	09/17/71	BOSTON	L	10-7	CASEY COX (5-7)	3856	58-89
SAT	09/18/71	BOSTON	W	6-1	BILL GOGOLEWSKI (5-5)	3671	59-89
SUN	09/19/71	BOSTON	L	4-3	PETE BROBERG (5-8)	4834	59-90
MON	09/20/71	CLEVELAND*	W	8-6 (20)	DENNY MCLAIN (10-20)	1743	60-91
MON	09/20/71	CLEVELAND	L	3-1	DENNY MCLAIN (10-21)	1743	60-90
TUES	09/21/71	CLEVELAND	W	9-1	DICK BOSMAN (12-15)	1311	61-91
WED	09/22/71	CLEVELAND	W	3-2	BILL GOGOLEWSKI (6-5)	1458	62-91
FRI	09/24/71	AT BOSTON	L	4-0	PETE BROBERG (5-9)	4351	62-92
SAT	09/25/71	AT BOSTON	L	6-3	DENNY MCLAIN (10-22)	19126	62-93
SUN	09/26/71	AT BOSTON	L	8-1	DICK BOSMAN (12-16)	15240	62-94
TUES	09/28/71	NEW YORK	W	4-2	JOE GRZENDA (5-2)	3242	63-94
WED	09/29/71	NEW YORK	L	6-3	DICK SHELLENBACK (3-11)	4003	63-95
THURS	09/30/71	NEW YORK	L	9-0	FORFEIT	14460	63-96

* Completion of September fourteenth game in Cleveland suspended after 15 innings.

EPILOGUE

Lengthening Shadows

Soon fades the spell, soon comes the night;
Say will it not then be the same,
Whether we played the black or white,
Whether we lost or won the game?

Thomas Babington
Sermon in a Churchyard

The 1971 relocation of the expansion Senators from Washington to Texas marked the end of franchise movements. Certainly the addition of five new cities between 1953 and 1958 gave more fans access to the game. By keeping the same number of teams, the owners had not watered down their product. Only Washington was left without an existing franchise. It might have made sense to move the nearby Philadelphia A's to nearby Baltimore, and the

TEAM	TEAM ATTENDANCE YEARS BEFORE DEPARTURE				
	4	3	2	1	FINAL SEASON
BRAVES	1,455,439	1,081,795	944,391	487,475	281,278
BROWNS	270,936	247,131	293,790	518,796	297,238
ATHLETICS	809,805	465,469	627,100	362,113	304,666
GIANTS	811,518	1,155,067	824,112	629,179	653,923
DODGERS	1,163,419	1,020,531	1,033,589	1,213,562	1,028,258
1960 SENATORS	431,647	457,079	475,288	615,372	743,404
1971 SENATORS	770,863	546,661	918,106	824,789	655,156

TEAM ATTENDANCE
LAST 5 YEARS IN CITY OF ORIGIN

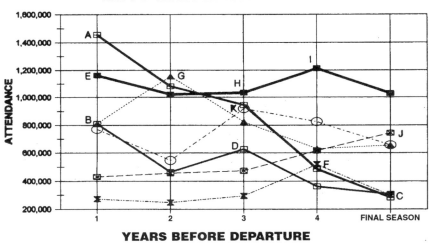

YEARS BEFORE DEPARTURE

HIGHS AND LOWS

CODE	DATE	TEAM	EVENT	CODE	DATE	TEAM	EVENT
A	1948	BRAVES	PENNANT	G	1954	GIANTS	WORLD SERIES
B	1950	ATHLETICS	MACK'S FINAL SEASON	H	1955	DODGERS	WORLD SERIES
C	1952	BRAVES	BRAVES FINAL SEASON	I	1956	DODGERS	PENNANT
D	1952	ATHLETICS	FOURTH PLACE FINISH	J	1960	SENATORS	LAST SEASON
E	1953	DODGERS	PENNANT	K	1969	SENATORS	SHORT'S FIRST SEASON
F	1953	BROWNS	VEECK'S SECOND SEASON				

Browns to stay in Missouri by moving to Kansas City, preserving a portion of the original fan base. But power struggles and personality conflicts affected the ultimate destination of these teams. Territorial rights of other teams in the area, and the availability of suitable ballparks, were also considerations.

In their final seasons, all the transferred ball clubs were playing in aging ballparks and in deteriorating urban environments. It was simply easier for owners to move or to sell than to upgrade facilities and improve their ball clubs.

Owners often abused the good will of the fans or took them for granted. They could. It was a sellers market. But despite attracting only 281,278 fans in his final season in Boston, Braves' owner Lou Perini did not want to sell. Neither did Bill Veeck of the Browns, Horace Stoneham of the Giants, Walter O'Malley of the Dodgers, Calvin Griffith of the 1960 Senators or Bob Short of the 1971 Senators. All wanted to move their teams. Forced to sell, Veeck foresaw the opportunity for success in Milwaukee, Los Angeles, and Baltimore. before others. But by the end of Perini's first season in Milwaukee, everyone was convinced.

Connie Mack of the A's preferred to sell, but sincerely wanted the team to stay in Philadelphia.

Having had baseball for so many years, city officials took the continued operation of these teams for granted, and were poorly prepared to deal with the threatened departures. They were unable or unwilling to match the enticements offered by new cities. Efforts by local businessmen to save the franchises were also poorly organized, underfinanced, and always too late. With no effective forum in which to express their views, the fans had virtually no influence. In the case of the Braves, Browns, and A's, there weren't enough of them.

Early annual attendance figures for the Braves in Milwaukee nearly doubled those for the Dodgers and tripled those for the Giants. The projected attendance figures for the considerably larger cities of San Francisco and Los Angeles enticed Major League Baseball to take a significant gamble by moving both National League teams out of the bellwether New York area. The lure of instant riches was overwhelming.

In general, the moves proved to be in the best interest of the game. The transfer of the Dodgers and Giants, two teams with an established national fan base, gave West Coast baseball instant respectability. The moves also ended New York dominance of the World Series. From 1900 to 1957, the three combined New York franchises hosted World Series games thirty times. When the Los Angeles Dodgers defeated the

Chicago White Sox in the 1959 Series, ending a string of ten straight World Series played all or part in New York ended. New York had hosted thirty-three World Series since 1903. Thirteen were entirely New York affairs involving two New York clubs.

In the forty-two years since the move of the Giants and Dodgers, the Yankees and Mets have been in a total of eighteen World Series. On the West Coast, the Dodgers, Giants, Mets and A's have been in fifteen.

ATTENDANCE—OLD AND NEW

The highest single season attendance ever for each of the transferred franchises in their city of origin was:

1947 Brooklyn Dodgers	1,807,526	First
1947 New York Giants	1,600,793	Fourth
1948 Boston Braves	1,455,439	First
1946 Washington Senators	1,027,216	Fourth
1948 Philadelphia Athletics	945,076	Fourth
1922 St. Louis Browns	712,918	Second

The attendance figures for each of the transferred teams for the first year in their new city were:

1958 Los Angeles Dodgers	1,845,566	Seventh
1953 Milwaukee Braves	1,826,937	Second
1958 San Francisco Giants	1,272,625	Third
1955 Kansas City A's	1,393,054	Sixth
1961 Minnesota Twins	1,256,723	Seventh
1954 Baltimore Orioles	1,060,910	Seventh
1972 Texas Rangers	662,974	Sixth

THE GRASS ISN'T ALWAYS GREENER

The Dodgers now consistently draw more than three million fans a year in Los Angeles. They are one of the game's strongest franchises. Not all the transplanted franchises, however, found fertile ground or lasting success in their new home.

The Braves won two pennants, and one World Series Championship, in their first six seasons in Milwaukee. The Braves drew more than 2,000,000 fans for four consecutive years. They won a World Championship in their fourth season, defeating the Yankees in the 1957 World Series after trailing three games to one. In an encore performance the Yankees defeated the Braves in the 1958 World Series after trailing three games to one. By 1965, however, the club slipped to fifth place. Attendance slipped to 555,584, resulting in another Braves move, to Atlanta, the site of their Triple-A farm team since the move to Milwaukee, in 1966. Despite Henry Aaron's successful quest to overtake Babe Ruth record of 714 home runs, attendance in Atlanta declined from peak of 1,539,801 in their first season, to just 534,672 in 1975. However, in the 1990s the Braves have become Baseball's most dominant team. Attendance figures are significantly better. All Braves games are televised on owner Ted Turner's WTBS super station cable network.

The Baltimore Orioles finished second to the then powerful Yankees in 1960, their sixth year in Baltimore. They won their first World Championship in 1966, sweeping the highly favored Dodgers in four games in the World Series. In their first twenty-five years they won four pennants, two World Championships. The Orioles won more regular season games than any other team in the major leagues. However, they seldom surpassed the 1,000,000 in attendance. However, aided by improved marketing, and the move to Orioles' Park at Camden Yards, they now consistently exceed three million in attendance, annually.

The Athletics drew over a million fans in their first two seasons in Kansas City. After attendance slipped to 528,344 in 1965, the franchise moved to Oakland, California in 1966. They were the only one of the transferred franchises that failed to ever make it to the playoffs. The club had a great deal of subsequent success in Oakland, winning eight pennants, and four World Championships.

The San Francisco Giants drew a respectable average of 1,500,000 fans their first ten seasons in San Francisco, despite playing night games in chilly Candlestick Park. They won the National League Pennant in their fourth season in 1962. Willie McCovey's line drive seared into the glove of the Yankees second baseman Bobby Richardson to end game seven of the first truly memorable World Series played on the coast.

The Senators move to Minneapolis in 1961 was a moderately successful one. The Twins won a pennant in 1965, and a World Series Championship in 1987. They drew more than 1,000,000 fans in each of the first ten years in Minnesota. But the romance has waned in recent years. Attendance is off. Local referendums to provide funding for a new ballpark have failed several times. The local independent minor league team, the Saint Paul Saints, owned by Mike Veeck, son of the master promoter Bill Veeck, and actor-comedian Bill Murray, has provided fans with an entertaining alternative to Major League Baseball.

The second offspring of the Washington American League franchise, The Texas Rangers, drew less than 700,000 fans each of their first two difficult seasons in Texas, less than in each of the final two seasons in Washington. They finally won the American League Western Division title in 1996, their twenty-fifth year, making their first post season appearance.

OWNERS VERSUS PLAYERS

If the 1971 departure of the Senators marked the end of franchise moves, it also marked the beginning of free player movements accompanied by spiraling player salaries. Curt Flood quit the expansion Senators, subsequently losing his court challenge to the reserve clause. His fight, however, opened the door. Free agency was a primary issue in all subsequent labor negotiations. Since it was first imposed in 1903, players had chaffed under the restrictive reserve clause. The owners insisted that the clause was still necessary to preserve parity among clubs, and to protect small market teams. Exempted from antitrust legislation, the owners had little incentive to bargain in good faith, maintaining a "my way or the highway" attitude.

PLAYERS ASSOCIATION FORMED

When formed in 1954, the Major League Baseball Players Association, negotiated a modest minimum salary of $6,000, and a contribution by the owners to the players' pension fund of sixty percent of the television revenue from the All-Star Game and World Series. Brought into existence for the convenience of the owners, it was hardly the independent voice of the players. When Mickey Mantle retired in 1968, he was drawing roughly the same base salary that his predecessor, Joe DiMaggio drew in his last season, 1951. Despite increased attendance and vastly improved broadcasting revenues, the owners were not ready to share their new found wealth.

MARVIN MILLER AND FREE AGENCY

In 1968, Marvin Miller, the union's first experienced labor negotiator, quickly got the minimum salary raised to 10,000. Then, to obtain a quick end to a player strike in 1972, he settled for relatively minor concessions: salary arbitration, and the establishment of a player grievance procedure. Winning a contract dispute with the Oakland A's in 1974, pitcher Catfish Hunter was declared a free agent. He immediately signed a lucrative deal with the Yankees. Dave McNally of the

Expos, and Andy Messersmith of the Dodgers, followed suit, refusing to sign new contract offers from their current clubs. They became baseball's first true free agents in 1976.

The owners were still clinging to the reserve clause. The players wanted complete free agency. Negotiations soured badly, culminating in an owner lockout in 1976. Nonetheless, the American League expanded to fourteen teams, acquiring Toronto, and giving Seattle a second chance. Thirty Major League teams were now playing in twenty-eight different cities.

FAN ALIENATION

Based on what the market would bear, player salaries were now far above those of the average worker. The average fan, the ultimate source of ticket and advertising revenues, found it hard to champion the players' cause. Owners have frequently attempted to exploit this disaffection, pitting fans against players. The tactic has been mostly counter productive. Left on the sidelines, only the semi-independent Baseball Commissioner's office gave voice to fan concerns, often arbitrating labor disputes, and pressuring owners and players to settle.

The Yankees had been able to dominate baseball prior to free agency. Nevertheless, the stockpiling of talent by several wealthier, more aggressive teams in the post free agency era represented a new threat to the competitive balance in the major leagues, threatening the very existence of small market teams.

COLLUSION

Covert agreements between club owners, designed to control salaries, were challenged by the players union. The Courts ruled collusion, assessing punitive damages. Nonetheless, the owners continued to believe that a salary cap was absolutely necessary. They insisted that the issue was non-negotiable. Though bidding wars had now escalated salaries to levels exceeding fair market value, players were just as intransigent. With the reserve clause still in existence, the players ability to win labor disputes in court was greatly diminished. The combination of the salary cap, and the reserve clause, was unacceptable.

STRIKES AND LOCKOUTS

Another costly player strike in 1981 resulted in a split season format. There was an owner lock out in 1990. After the conclusion of the 1992 season, the owners fired Commissioner Faye Vincent for involving himself in labor negotiations. Bud Selig, owner of the Milwaukee Brewers, was named acting Commissioner. In 1993 the National League added Colorado to the Western Division, and the Florida Marlins to the Eastern Division.

CANCELLATION OF THE WORLD SERIES

A strike in August 1994 resulted in cancellation of the final month of a season that promised to produce several significant records for individual achievement. This most damaging of all baseball management labor struggles resulted in cancellation of the World Series for the first time in ninety years. The owners prolonged the disagreement by locking the players out of the training camps in the spring of 1995.

REPLACEMENT PLAYERS

Most Major League teams staged spring games using minor leaguers, recently retired players, semi-pro prospects, walk-ons and scabs. Only a decision by Federal Judge Sonia Sotomayer on the day before the start of the 1995 season prevented the owners from opening the season with these so called replacement players. Sotomeyer ruled that the owners could not unilaterally impose a salary cap, allowing the operating system in place as a result of the previous collective bargaining agreement to remain in place. The players agreed to return to the field. However, the start of the 1995 season was delayed a month, and the season schedule was reduced to 140 games.

THE PEOPLES' GAME

In the 1990s professional football and professional basketball consistently generate higher TV ratings than baseball. Competition for every dollar is much greater. Professional baseball no longer holds the relatively exclusive position it held in the 1950s. However, baseball still generates enough revenue to make both the owners and players very wealthy. And it holds a unique place in the American consciousness. Perhaps because of its longer history, it is more in the public domain than the other professional sports. It is more egalitarian. There are luxury boxes in all sports. In baseball there are also bleachers. Higher ticket prices are a fact of life in all sports. Baseball is, however, still a family sport or at least we feel it ought to be. Our fathers took us to the game. The history and the mythology are passed on from father to son. It is a tradition. We should be able to take our kids at a reasonable cost. It should be as we remember it. Minor league baseball is fine. You are close to the game. The atmosphere is enjoyable. And it is a great way to introduce children, the next generation of fans, to the game. The "show", however, is the feature presentation and should be accessible to everyone.

BLACKMAIL

The reality is that if attendance, and broadcast revenues, in a city do not support the continued operation of the home team, management will look elsewhere. In April 1998 *Washington Post* staff writer Thomas Heath reported:

Since 1950 a combined total of sixty-eight franchises from the four major professional sports have relocated. In the past six years twenty cities have built stadiums to keep their sports teams from moving. The total demand by sports franchises for city and state subsidies currently totals more than seven billion dollars.

Many more teams will demand new stadiums. The name of the game is black mail and the cost to cities to retain their teams will go even higher. There are many growing metropolitan areas eagerly in search of sports franchises, offering sweetheart deals too good to pass up. There are troubled franchises in Montreal, Pittsburgh, Milwaukee, and Minnesota.

Community ownership of teams similar to that of the Green Bay Packers of the National Football League has been proposed as an alternative that would stop the use of public funding for private enterprise. This would involve local stock purchases in teams and a partnership between taxpayers and citizens in local communities. However, such efforts in the past have come too late and been poorly organized and underfinanced.

THE PAST AND FUTURE

The six original baseball franchises continue to play baseball in new locations. Their early history sinks deeper into mystery. Busch

Stadium in St. Louis, Ebbets Field in Brooklyn, the Polo Grounds in New York, and Griffith Stadium in Washington have all been torn down.

Robert F. Kennedy Stadium in Washington is still standing. Braves Field in Boston, though radically altered and renamed Nickerson Field, remains standing. It hosted Boston University football games until the university discontinued its football program in 1997.

But baseball never sheds its past. New "oldstyle" ballparks evoke images of old stadiums and the once grand teams that played in them.

Nearly fifty years later, the seemingly inconsequential move of the struggling Boston Braves franchise to Milwaukee continues to have far reaching consequences. Fans are now clearly aware that baseball is big business. There is a lost innocence, and there are no more illusions. Cities have a less tangible claim to the *home team*. The teams themselves have a less tangible claim to their players. Loyalties are strained all around.

A NEW COMMISSIONER

Baseball, in need of a stable period in owner/player relations, has its first independent commissioner since the late Bart Giamati. After holding the position of acting commissioner longer than many of his predecessors, Bud Selig was formally elected Baseball Commissioner in July of 1998. Perceived as the owners' man, he may grow into the role and gain the confidence of players and fans. Time will tell.

Meanwhile the game goes on. In 1998, new teams in Phoenix and Tampa Bay joined the show. And it is still a game, a marvelous game— great entertainment and great fun! It isn't the unchanging rock that it was once for fifty years. But there are elements of the game that remain constant. The heroes, past and present, are still there.

Perhaps the game does not deserve our complete loyalty. But it is worth forgiving. It is worth saving. It is worth caring about. Baseball's future, its continuity, is still somehow reassuring. We wait for its arrival each spring. We wait for next year. And it will come.

The lights will come on at twilight.

BIBLIOGRAPHY

Kahn, Roger. *The Era; 1947-1957, When the Yankees, the Giants and the Dodgers Ruled the World.* 1993

Bakalar, Nick. *The Baseball Fan's Companion.* New York: MacMillan, Inc, 1996

Acocella, Nicholas and Dewey, Donald. *The Ball Clubs.* New York: Harper Collins Publishers, Inc., 1996.

Ritter, Lawrence S. *Lost Ballparks.* New York: Penguin Books USA Inc., 1994

Thompson, S.C. and Turkin, Hy. *The Official Encyclopedia of Baseball.* 9th ed., New York: Doubleday & Company, 1977

Cohen, Richard M.; Deutsch, Jordan A.; Johnson, Roland T. and Neft, David S. *The Sports Encyclopedia: Baseball.* New York, Grosset and Dunlap Publishers, 1974.

Marcin, Joe; Rowe, Chris and Wigge, Larry, eds. *Official Baseball Dope Book.* The Sporting News Publishing Company, 1976.

The New York Times. 1952-1957, 1960, 1964, 1971

Bucek, Jeannine; Cothran, Traci; Deane, Bill; Kerler, Bob; Massey, Marin; Tiemann, Bob; Topp, Richard and Sammuelson, Ken, eds. *The Baseball Encyclopedia.* 10th ed, New York: Macmillan & Company, 1996

The Washington Post. 1960, 1965, 1971

The Washington Star. 1971

Veeck, Bill. *Veeck as in Wreck.* 1981

ABOUT THE AUTHOR

Jeff Stuart, shown here with his pet manx, Sark, lives in Gaithersburg, Maryland, a suburb of Washington, D.C. Formerly, a Washington Senators fan, he now follows the Baltimore Orioles.

A serious collector of all kinds of hats, his house looks like a hat museum. He also coached wrestling for ten years and now runs a recreational volleyball program for the City of Gaithersburg.

Jeff, 54, is a senior cartographer with the National Ocean Service. He graduated from Bethesda-Chevy Chase High School and the University of Maryland.